I0331994

Henry W. Clarke

The Persian Manual

a pocket companion intended to facilitate the essential attainments of conversing

Henry W. Clarke

The Persian Manual
a pocket companion intended to facilitate the essential attainments of conversing

ISBN/EAN: 9783337286958

Printed in Europe, USA, Canada, Australia, Japan

Cover: Foto ©Lupo / pixelio.de

More available books at **www.hansebooks.com**

THE PERSIAN MANUAL.

CLARKE.

THE

PERSIAN MANUAL,

A POCKET COMPANION

INTENDED TO

FACILITATE THE ESSENTIAL ATTAINMENTS OF CONVERSING WITH FLUENCY AND COMPOSING WITH ACCURACY, IN THE MOST GRACEFUL OF ALL THE LANGUAGES SPOKEN IN THE EAST.

PART I.--A CONCISE GRAMMAR OF THE LANGUAGE,

With Exercises on its more prominent peculiarities, together with a Selection of Useful Phrases, Dialogues, and Subjects for Translation into Persian.

PART II.—A VOCABULARY OF USEFUL WORDS,

ENGLISH AND PERSIAN,

SHOWING AT THE SAME TIME THE DIFFERENCE OF IDIOM BETWEEN THE TWO LANGUAGES.

BY

CAPTAIN H. WILBERFORCE CLARKE,

Royal Engineers.

LONDON:

WM. H. ALLEN & CO., 13, WATERLOO PLACE, S.W.

1878.

LONDON:
GILBERT AND RIVINGTON, PRINTERS,
52, ST. JOHN'S SQUARE, E.C.

TO

My Uncle, H. M. C.,

WHO ENCOURAGED ME IN

BOYHOOD, YOUTH, AND MANHOOD,

THIS WORK IS, WITH AFFECTION,

INSCRIBED.

PREFACE BY THE AUTHOR.

THIS work is divided into Two Parts :—

Part I. Section 1. The Grammar.
    „ 2. Progressive Lessons and Exercises.
    „ 3. Miscellaneous Dialogues and Exercises.

Part II. Vocabulary.

2. Sections 2 and 3 of Part I. and the whole of Part II. are entirely original.

The Grammar is, in part, compiled from the Persian Grammars by—

Dr. Lumsden, LL.D., 1810.
Mīrza Muḥammad Ibrāhīm Shīrāzī, 1841.
Mr. A. H. Bleeck, 1857.
Dr. D. Forbes, LL.D., 1862.

Its arrangement is entirely new; much original matter has been introduced; and the whole rendered as concisely as possible.

The Exercises and Sentences (English to be turned

into Persian) have been taken from Dr. Forbes' Manual of Hindūstānī. It was considered that these exercises and sentences were possibly as good and as well arranged as any others which could be devised, while, by adopting them for this work, the student would have the advantage of being able to compare the Hindūstānī with the Persian idiom. The great success which Dr. Forbes' Manual of Hindūstānī has obtained was a further inducement to adopt the same plan.

3. The aim throughout this work has been to gather under each sentence as many useful idioms, expressions and synonyms as possible. That portion of a sentence which may be represented by other equivalent expressions is enclosed in brackets; and the equivalent expressions—also placed within brackets and separated by semi-colons—are put at the end of the sentence. Thus, on page 126 of the Vocabulary, against the word "robbed," it is to be understood that the expressions "duzd burda;" "dast-burd-i-duzd gardīda;" "ba sirḳat rafta;" "duzdīda shuda," may each be substituted for the expression "ba duzdī rafta," in the sentence.

This plan of rendering the sentences will, it is believed, give great aid to the student in mastering the language. He will see at a glance the several ways in which a sentence may be rendered, will observe the force of words, and will be able to compare idiom with idiom.*

4. It has been customary to regard Persian as a language easy of attainment; this is far from being the case. A certain degree of proficiency may easily be reached; but to obtain a thorough knowledge of the language is exceedingly difficult, owing to—

(*a*) The vast number of words (said to be 80,000) in the language;

(*b*) The ambiguous expressions in which a Persian delights;

(*c*) The want of translations;†

(*d*) Want of properly qualified teachers.‡

That there are defects in this work is most readily allowed; yet all that care and labour could do to prevent error has been given to the task. The critic will remember that this is the first attempt ever

---

* In his Hindūstānī Manual Dr. Forbes rendered the English sentence in one way only. For Hindūstānī this may be sufficient; but a rich language, such as the Persian, requires more generous handling.

† The only Persian books translated into English are—the Gulistān, the Anwār-i-Suhaili, and the Shāh-Nāmah.

‡ This is a most serious difficulty as regards Persian and Arabic.

made by anyone to bring out a work, systematically arranged, treating of the rendering of English into Persian.

5. At the present time, the only books which *attempt* to treat of the rendering of English sentences into Persian are the following:—

(*a*) "The Persian Mūnshī," by Dosā-Biyā,ī Surābjī, a Pārsī.

This book contains 1117 sentences, rendered in Hindūstānī, Sindhī and Persian. The sentences are not arranged alphabetically, nor so as to express the rendering of a certain dominant word; they are simply grouped together under six heads,—Introductory, Mercantile, Medical, Judicial, Military and Miscellaneous.

The work is roughly lithographed on bad Indian paper. The renderings in lithographed oriental character are not easy for a beginner to decipher. But for the arrangement and the way in which it is got up it would be an excellent work. It can be obtained from Messrs. Thacker and Co., of Bombay, for 6½ rupees.

(*b*) "Modern Persian," by an Officer of the Haiderabad Contingent, revised by Mīrza Zainul 'Abadīn Shīrāzī.

This is a small book, printed in Bombay in 1871; it contains 1769 sentences, without any arrangement whatever; the vowel points in the oriental character (which is not transliterated) have all been omitted, making it very difficult for a beginner to pronounce the words. It may be obtained from Messrs. Thacker and Co., of Bombay, for 10 rs.

(*c*) "The Conversation Manual," by Captain G. Plunkett, R.E.

This is a book, printed in London, containing 670 sentences and a bare list of 1500 words, which are rendered in Hindūstānī, Pushtu and Persian. Roman character only is used. It is a small book and necessarily covers but a small extent of each of the three languages. It may be obtained from Messrs. Richardson and Co., Cornhill, London, for 6 rs.

The three books, briefly described, labour under one defect, which is, that each sentence is rendered in one way only. The student is not afforded the opportunity of contrasting idiom with idiom, word with word; nor of exercising his powers of observation.

The Persian Manual now offered to the public contains:—

In Section 2, Part I.,	555	sentences.
„ 3, Part I.,	333	„
In Vocabulary, Part II.,	1969	„
Total number of sentences,	2857	

This number 2857 represents the actual number of English sentences rendered into Persian; but almost every sentence is expressed in several ways. The actual number of Persian sentences probably amounts, *at least*, to 2857 × 3 = 8671, all *methodically* arranged.

A bald list of words is of little use; the student requires to know how to use them.* It is hoped that a study of this Manual may save the student much unnecessary drudgery with a native teacher; and that the tables of Persian weights and measures, the digest of regulations regarding examinations in Persian and Arabic, and the lists of Persian and Arabic books may prove useful.

6. I here beg to record the service which I have received, in correcting the proof-sheets of this work, and generally in bringing it out, from—

(*a*) Maulawī Allāh Bakhsh, who passed twenty-five years of his life in Persia, acted as Arabic interpreter during the Abyssinian campaign, and is now Instructor in Persian in the High School of Karachi in East India.

(*b*) Shaikh Muḥammad Ṣādik, Ḥājīu-l-ḥaramain, a native of Tahrān, who served me in the Abyssinian campaign, and followed my fortunes at divers seasons in India.†

I mention the names of these men not only because they deserve to be named, but also as a *gua-*

* This is especially the case with regard to Arabic words used in Persian.

† "Ḥājīu-l-ḥaramain" is the *title* of a Musulmān who has made a pilgrimage to Makkah and Madīna.

rantee that the Persian renderings of the sentences are *idiomatic* as well as grammatical.

7. The student's attention is drawn to the excellent manner in which the Work has been got up by the Publishers. I freely acknowledge the great obligation under which I rest for the care and trouble which they have exercised.

H. WILBERFORCE CLARKE,
CAPTAIN, R.E.

Karachi, May 1877.

The following Table gives a list of Exercises in this Manual, which will be found rendered in Persian in Forbes' "Persian Grammar." The other exercises have been taken from the "Gulistan" and "Arabian Nights' Entertainment."

No. of Exercise in this Manual.	Forbes' Persian Grammar.	
	Page.	No. of Story.
24	1	5
27	3	14
28	8	30
29	6	22
37	12	50
38	6	23
39	11	39
43	12	41
44	13	43
45	10	35
46	11	37
47	14	46
48	10	36
49	17	51
50	25	66
51	26	67
52	19	55

PERSIAN MANUAL.

PART I.

SECTION I.

ON THE LETTERS AND PARTS OF SPEECH.

1. The Persian Alphabet consists of thirty-two letters. Of these twenty are common to the Persians and Arabs, eight are peculiar to the Arabs, and four to the Persians.

These thirty-two letters are to be considered as consonants, and are written from right to left; consequently their books and manuscripts begin at what we call the end.

The letters often assume a different form according to their position in the formation of a word. Thus there will be in many cases three distinct forms; namely, the *initial*, the *medial*, the *final*.

In the following Table we have in column 1, the names of the letters in the Persian character; in column 2, the names of the letters in the Roman character; in column 3, the detached forms of the letters; and, in column 4, the corresponding English letters.

THE PERSI-ARABIC ALPHABET.

1.	2.	3.	4.	5.			6.			
NAME.		DETACHED FORM.	POWER.	COMBINED FORM.			EXEMPLIFICATIONS.			
				Final.	Medial.	Initial.	Final.		Medial	Initial.
الف	*alif*	ا	*a*, etc.	ا	ا	ا	وا	جا	بار	اب
بي	*be*	ب	*b*	ب	ـبـ	بـ	باب	شب	صَبر	بَر
پي	*pe*	پ	*p*	پ	ـپـ	پـ	آپ	چُپ	سِپَر	پُر
تي	*te*	ت	*t*	ت	ـتـ	تـ	پوت	دُست	سَتَر	تَپ
ثي	*s̤e*	ث	*s̤*	ث	ـثـ	ثـ	روث	خُبث	بَثَر	ثُور
جِيم	*jīm*	ج	*j*	ج	ـجـ	جـ	کاج	کَج	شَجَر	جَبَر
چي	*che*	چ	*ch*	چ	ـچـ	چـ	کُوچ	هيچ	بَچه	چُپ
حي	*ḥe*	ح	*ḥ*	ح	ـحـ	حـ	روح	صُبح	بَحَر	حَر
خي	*k͟he*	خ	*k͟h*	خ	ـخـ	خـ	شاخ	يَخ	تُخم	خَر
دال	*dāl*	د	*d*	ـد	ـد	د	صاد	صد	فدا	دُر
ذال	*z̤āl*	ذ	*z̤*	ـذ	ـذ	ذ	باذ	کاغَذ	نَذَر	ذِم
ري	*re*	ر	*r*	ـر	ـر	ر	مار	مَر	مَرد	رَم
زي	*ze*	ز	*z*	ـز	ـز	ز	باز	گَز	بَزم	زَر
ژي	*zhe*	ژ	*zh*	ـژ	ـژ	ژ	کاژ	پاپُژ	غَژب	ژَرف
سِين	*sīn*	س	*s*	س	ـسـ	سـ	باس	بَس	فَسق	سَر
شِين	*shīn*	ش	*sh*	ش	ـشـ	شـ	پاش	پَش	نَشُد	شُد

1. NAME.	2.	3. DETACHED FORM.	4. POWER.	5. COMBINED FORM. Final.	Medial.	Initial.	6. EXEMPLIFICATIONS. Final.		Medial.	Initial.
صاد	*ṣād*	ص	*ṣ*	ـص	ـصـ	صـ	ناص	نِص	قَصْد	صَد
ضاد	*ẓād*	ض	*ẓ*	ـض	ـضـ	ضـ	بُعُوض	بَعَض	خِضَر	ضِدّ
طوى	*ṭo,e*	ط	*ṭ*	ـط	ـطـ	طـ	خُطُوط	خَطّ	بَطَن	طَي
ظوى	*ẓo,e*	ظ	*ẓ*	ـظ	ـظـ	ظـ	حِفاظ	حِفَظ	نَظَر	ظَفَر
عَين	*'ain*	ع	*'a*, etc.	ـع	ـعـ	عـ	صِناع	صَنَع	بَعْد	عَسَل
غَين	*ghain*	غ	*gh*	ـغ	ـغـ	غـ	بَاغ	تيغ	بَغِي	غُسَل
في	*fe*	ف	*f*	ـف	ـفـ	فـ	كاف	كَف	سَفَر	فِي
قاف	*ḳāf*	ق	*ḳ*	ـق	ـقـ	قـ	باق	بَق	سَقَر	قَد
كاف	*kāf*	ك	*k*	ـك	ـكـ	كـ	خاك	يَك	بِكُن	كن
گاف	*gāf*	گ	*g*	ـگ	ـگـ	گـ	راگ	رَنگ	جِگَر	گَز
لام	*lām*	ل	*l*	ـل	ـلـ	لـ	سال	گُل	عِلْم	لَب
مِيم	*mīm*	م	*m*	ـم	ـمـ	مـ	تَمام	سِتَم	چَمَن	مَن
نُون	*nūn*	ن	*n*	ـن	ـنـ	نـ	نُون	صَحَن	چَنْد	نم
واو	*wāw*	و	*w*	ـو	ـو	و	رُو	بُو	پُور	وجد
هي	*he*	ه	*h*	ـه	ـهـ	هـ	ماه	نَه	بَها	هُنَر
يي	*ye*	ي	*y*, etc.	ـي	ـيـ	يـ	جائي	بي	حِيد	يَد

2. It will be observed that ا, د, ذ, ر, ز, ژ, و, do not alter in shape, whether *initial*, *medial*, or *final*; neither do they unite with the letter following to the left. The letters ط, ظ, do not alter; but they always unite with the letter following to the left. The eight letters peculiar to Arabic are—ث, ح, ص, ط, ظ, ع, ق. They appear only in words purely, or originally, Arabic. The four letters peculiar to Persian are پ, چ, ژ, گ.

Pronunciation of the Letters.

3. ت *t*. The sound of this letter is softer and more dental than that of the English *t*; it is identical with the Sanskrit त.

ث *ṣ* is sounded by the Arabs like *th* in the words *thick, thin*; by the Persians as *s* in the words *sick, sin*.

چ *ch* has the sound of *ch* in the word *church*.

ح *ḥ* is a strong aspirate like *h* in the word *haul*; it is uttered by compressing the lower muscles of the throat.

خ *kh* has a sound like *ch* in the word *loch*, as pronounced by a Scotchman.

د *d* is more dental than the English *d*.

ذ *z* is sounded by the Arabs like *th* in the words *thy, thine*; by the Persians as *z* in *zeal*.

ر *r* is sounded as *r* in the French word *pardon.*

ژ *zh* is pronounced like *j* in the French word *jour;* or as *z* in the word *azure.*

ش *sh* is sounded as in *shun, shine.*

ص *ṣ* has a stronger and more hissing sound than our *s.*

ض *ż* is pronounced by the Arabs as a hard *d* or *dt;* by the Persians as *z.*

ط, ظ *ṭ* and *ẓ* in Persian are sounded like ت *t*, and ز *z.*

غ *gh* is like the letter *r* as pronounced by a Scotchman.

ق *ḳ* resembles the letter *c* in *cup, calm.*

ک *k* is sounded like *k* in *king, kalendar.*

گ *g* is sounded like *g* in *go, give;* never as *g* in *gem, gentle.*

ل *l* is sounded like *l* in *law.* When *alif* is combined with it, the two take the form of لا or لا.

ن *n* at the beginning of a word, or syllable, is sounded like *n*; at the end of a word or syllable, if preceded by a long vowel, it has a soft nasal sound like that of *n* in the French word *garçon.* When followed by the labials ب *b*, پ *p*, ف *f*, it assumes the sound of *m*, as in the word گنبد, *gumbad,* not *gunbad.*

ه *h* is an aspirate like *h* in *heart, hand;* but at the end of a word, if preceded by the short vowel *a* (*fatḥa*), it has no sensible sound, as in دانَه, *dūnă*, "a grain." In this case, it is called هائي مُختَفِي *hā,e-mukhtafī*, or *obscure h*.

In a few words, where the *fatḥa* is a substitute for the long vowel *alif*, the final ه is fully sounded; as—

شه *shah* [for شاه *shāh*] "a king."

مه *mah* [for ماه *māh*] "a month."

ره *rah* [for راه *rūh*] "a road."

It is sounded in دَه *dah*, "ten," and all its compounds. It is imperceptible in the words كه *ki* and چه *chi*, with their compounds, whether conjunctions or pronouns. A Persian word ending in the obscure ه *h* will have the *h* omitted when written in Roman characters; as نامه *nāma* [not *nāmah*] "a letter," or "written communication."

4. It is difficult to distinguish between the sounds of the letters forming one of the following groups:—

ث س ص ز ض ظ ت ط ع ا ح ه

The Persians never attempt to pronounce them as the Arabs; they content themselves by sounding them according to the Persian letters, to which they most nearly assimilate.

Observation—

5. When *s* and *h*, or *z* and *h*, represent two separate letters following each other, as in اَسْهَل *as,hal*, "more or most easy," and اَزْهار *az,hār*, "plants," a comma will be inserted, as shown in the examples.

At the end of Arabic words ه *h* is often marked with two dots, thus ة, and sounded like *t*. In such words the Persians generally convert the ة into ت *t*; sometimes they leave the ة unaltered, and frequently they omit the two dots, in which case the letter becomes imperceptible in sound.

Vowels and Orthographical Signs.

6. The primitive vowels in Arabic and Persian are three in number.

The *first* is called فَتْحه *fatḥa*, and is written thus ـَ, *over* the consonant to which it belongs. It is represented by the letter *a* in *calendar*.

The *second* is called كَسْرَه *kasra*, and is written thus ـِ, *under* the consonant to which it belongs. It is represented by the letter *i* in *sip*, or *fin*. In the Roman character it is represented by *i* unaccented.

The *third* is ضَمّه *ẓamma*, which is written thus ـُ, *over* its consonant. Its sound is like that of *u* in the words *pull*, *push*; or like *oo* in *foot*, *hood*;

its sound is never that of *u* in *use, perfume.* In the Roman character it is represented by *u* unaccented.

In Persian these three short vowels are called respectively—

زَبَر *zabar,* "above."
زير *zer,* "beneath."
پيش *pesh,* "in front."

7. When a consonant is accompanied by one of the three vowels, *fatḥa, kasra,* or *ẓamma,* it is said to be مُتَحَرِّك *mutaḥarrik,* or *moveable.*

In Persian and Arabic, the *first* letter of a word is always accompanied, or *moveable,* by a vowel. When, in the middle or at the end of a word, a consonant is not accompanied by a vowel, it is said to be ساكِن *sākin, quiescent,* or inert. Thus in the word مَرْدُمْ *mardum,* the م is moveable by *fatḥa ;* the ر is inert, having no vowel; د is moveable by *ẓamma,* and, finally, the م is inert. The symbol ـْ, called جزم *jazm,* is placed over a consonant to show that it is inert, as in the example مَرْدُمْ *mardum,* "a man."

In Persian the last letter of a word is generally inert; hence *jazm* is omitted.

THE CONSONANTS ا, ع, و, AND ي.

8. At the beginning of a word or syllable ا (*alif*) depends for its sound on the accompanying vowel.

ع (*'ain*) depends for its sound on the accompanying vowel; its place of utterance is in the lower muscles of the throat, thus:—

عَب *'ab*, عِب *'ib*, عُب *'ub*,

are different in sound from

اَب *ab*, اِب *ib*, اُب *ub*.

و (*wāw*) has the sound of *w* in the words *we*, *went*.

The modern Persians pronounce the *wāw* like *v* in words such as شَوَم *shavam*, شَوِي *shavī*.

ي (*y͟ā*) is, in sound, like *y* in the words *you*, *yet*.

LONG VOWELS OR LETTERS OF PROLONGATION.

9. When ا, inert, is preceded by a letter moveable by *fatḥa*, the *fatḥa* and *alif* coalesce and give a lengthened sound, as کار *kār*, "work;" the sound is like that of *a* in *war*.

Alif, inert, is always preceded by *fatḥa*; hence

alif, not beginning a word or syllable, has always a lengthened sound.

10. When و, inert, is preceded by a consonant moveable by *ẓamma*, the *ẓamma* and و coalesce and form a sound like *u* in *rule*.

When و,* inert, is preceded by a consonant, moveable by *fatḥa*, the *fatḥa* and و coalesce, and form a sound like *ou* in *sound*.

When و, inert, is preceded by a consonant move-

---

* When و is preceded by خ, moveable by *fatḥa* and followed by *alif*, the sound of و is almost imperceptible, as in the words—

خَواب *kh̲ẉāb*, "sleep," pronounced *kh̲,āb*.

خواهم *kh̲ẉāham*, "I desire," pronounced *kh̲,āham*.

In such cases the و will *not* be sounded, and in the Roman character it will be represented by *ẉ*.

When و, preceded by خ, moveable by *fatḥa*, and sometimes by *ẓamma*, or *kasra*, is followed by any of the nine letters:— ي ه ن ش س ز ر د پ, the و occasionally loses its sound, as in the words:—

خَود pronounced *kh̲ạd*, not *kh̲aud* or *kh̲awad*.

خُود pronounced *kh̲ụd*, not *kh̲ūd*.

خِويش pronounced *kh̲ẹsh*, not *kh̲iwesh*.

This rule applies only to words purely Persian. In the Roman character, the *w* will in such words be omitted, and the vowel marked with a dot, as *kh̲ụd*.

able by *kasra*, no union takes place, and the و retains the sound of *w*, as سِوَا (*siwā*).

11. When ي (*yā*), inert, is preceded by a consonant moveable by *kasra*, the *kasra* and *yā* unite and form a long vowel, like *i* in the word *machine*.

This sound of *yā*, is called *yā,e m'arūf*, "familiar *yā*." In Persia *yā* has sometimes the sound of *ea* in the word *bear*; this sound is called *yā,e majhūl*, "unknown *yā*," or *yā,e 'ajamī*, *i. e.* "Persian *yā*."

When ي (*yā*), inert, is preceded by a consonant moveable by *fatḥa*, the *fatḥa* and *yā* unite and form a diphthong like *ai* in the German word *kaiser*, or as *i* in *wise*.

When ي (*yā*), inert, is preceded by a consonant, moveable by *zamma*, no union takes place; and the *yā* retains its sound of *y*, as in the word مُيَسَّر *muyassar*, "obtainable."

SUMMARY.

12. From what has been said we have :—

Three short vowels, بَد *bad*, بِد *bid*, بُد *bud*;

Three long vowels, بَاد *bād*, بِيد *bīd*, بُود *būd*;

Two diphthongs, بَيد *baid*, بَود *baud*;

Two long vowels peculiarly *majhūl*, "unknown," or *'ajamī*, "Persian," بيل *bel*, روز *roz*.

RULES FOR READING.

13. There are very few Persian works, manuscript or printed, in which all the vowels are marked.

The primitive short vowels ـَ, ـِ, ـُ, as well as ـْ and ـّ are almost always omitted. The following remarks may be of service :—

(*a*) The last letter of every word is inert, hence the mark ـْ (*jazm*) is omitted.

(*b*) The short vowel ـَ (*fatḥa*) is of more frequent occurrence than *kasra* or *ẓamma*; hence, in printing, it is omitted.

(*c*) The short vowel ـَ (*fatḥa*) should be supplied for every consonant in a word, except the last and those marked with ـْ, or one of the vowels.

(*d*) The letters ا, و, ي, are generally inert, when not initial; hence they are not marked with *jazm*.

(*e*) When و, ي, not initial, are moveable consonants they are marked with their proper vowels.

(*f*) When و (*wāw*) or ي (*yā*) follow a consonant unmarked by a short vowel, or by *jazm*, they have the *majhūl* or *'ajamī* sound ; as—

مور *mor*, "an ant." | شير *sher*, "a lion."

(*g*) When و is preceded by a consonant moveable by *ẓamma*, and *yā* by a consonant moveable by *kasra*, the sound is *m'arūf*, or known ; as—

سُود *sūd*, "gain." | شِير *shīr*, "milk."

(*h*) When *wāw* and *yā* follow a consonant marked with *jazm*, they are consonants, and are sounded as و (*w*) and ي (*y*).

(*i*) When *wāw* and *yā* follow a consonant, moveable by *fatḥa*, they form diphthongs ; as—

قَوم *ḳaum*, "a tribe."	سَير *sair*, "a walk."

14. Some symbols have still to be noticed. They are :—*madda, hamza, tanwīn, tashdīd*, the definite article of Arabic nouns, and *waṣla*.

(*a*) مدّه (*madda*) [~] signifies extension, and when placed over an *alif* gives it a broad and open sound, almost equivalent to that of *a* in *water*. The *madda* is used to avoid the meeting of two *alifs* at the *beginning* of a word.

Thus, instead of اا ب, the Persians write آب *āb*, "water."

(*b*) همزه (*hamza*) [ء or ءـ] is used, instead of *alif*, when one syllable of a word ends with a vowel, and [according to our ideas of orthography] the following syllable begins with a vowel ; that is, virtually with an *alif*. Thus we have :—

پائِ *pā,e*, instead of پَااِي ;

فائده *fā,ida*, instead of فَااِده .

In Persian the sound of *hamza* is that of *alif;* in Arabic the sound of *hamza* is that of *'ain*. Strictly, *hamza* ought to be used whenever a syllable, beginning with a vowel, is added to a root in the way of inflexion, as:—

دیدَئِم *dīdem*, "we saw," from root, *dīd;*

بدئِي *badī*, "badness," from root, *bad.*

This rule is seldom observed.

Practically, *hamza* in the middle of a word is equivalent to our hyphen in such words as *re-open.*

At the end of words, terminating in the imperceptible ة, *hamza* has the sound of *e.*

In the Roman character, *hamza* will be represented by a comma between the vowels, as in فائِدة *fā,ida.*

(c) تنوين (*tanwīn*) [ً, ٍ, ٌ] signifies the using of the letter ن. It is formed by doubling the vowel point of the last letter of a word. The vowel is then pronounced as though it terminated in ن *n.* In the Roman character it will be represented by *n̲.* In Arabic, *tanwīn* serves to mark the inflexion of nouns; thus the symbol:—

ٌ (*double ẓamma*) marks the nominative } sing. &
ٍ (*double kasra*) marks the genitive } plural.
ً (*double fatḥa*) marks the accusative }

In Persian only the ً (*double fatḥa*) (accusative form) is used, and that adverbially; as—

تخمينًا *takhmīnan*, "by valuation."

اتفاقًا *ittifāḳan*, "by chance."

The symbol ً (*double fatḥa*) requires *alif*, which, however, does *not* prolong the sound of the last syllable.

The ا is *not* required when the word ends with ء (*hamza*) or ة, as:—

شيءً *shai-an*, "willingly,"

حكمةً *ḥikmatan* "skilfully;"

nor when the word ends with *yā*, surmounted by *alif* [in which case *alif* only is pronounced]; as,

هوىً *hawa-an*, "lovingly."

Without *tanwīn* the *alif* is sounded like the *alif* of prolongation, as:—

تعالى *ta'ūlā* "God."

عقبى *'uḳbā*, "end," "futurity."

In the Roman character this symbol will be represented by *a* or *ā*.

(*d*) تشديد (*tashdīd*) [ّ], or "corroboration," doubles the letter over which it is placed; as—

خرّم *khurram*, "joyful;" محمّد *Muḥammad*.

(*e*) ال; this Article is used only before Arabic

Nouns. If the Noun begins with any of the fourteen letters ت ث د ذ ر ز س ش ص ض ط ظ ل ن the ل of the Article assumes the sound of the initial letter of the Noun, which is then marked by *tashdīd;* thus—

اَلنُّورُ, "the light," is pronounced *an-nūru.*

اَلشَّمس "the sun," is pronounced *ash-shams.*

اَلدِّين "the faith," is pronounced *ad-dīn.*

The ل must *always* be written, though it has lost its own sound.

When the Noun begins with ل the ل of the Article is omitted, and the initial ل of the Noun is marked by *tashdīd*, as:—

اللَّيلةُ *al-lailatu*, "the night," instead of اَللَّيلَةُ.

(*f*) وصله, (*waṣla*) [ٱ], implies conjunction, and is only inscribed over an initial *alif*, in Arabic Nouns, to mark union with the preceding vowel; as—

اميرُالمؤمنِين *amīru-l-mūminīn*, "Commander of the Faithful."

صلاحُ الدِّين *Ṣalāḥu-d-dīn*, "Saladīn, or Peace of Religion."

SUBSTANTIVES, ADJECTIVES, AND PRONOUNS.

15. The Grammarians of Arabia and Persia

reckon three parts of speech: the Noun, *ism;* the Verb, *fi'l;* and the Particle, *ḥarf.*

The Noun includes substantives, adjectives, pronouns, and participles.

The Verb agrees in its nature with ours.

The Particle includes adverbs, prepositions, conjunctions, and interjections.

Gender.

16. Males* are masculine, females are feminine, and all other words are of no gender.

---

* Animals have different names to express the male or female; thus—

مرد *mard*, "a man."	زن *zan*, "a woman."
پسر *pisar*, "a son."	دختر *du<u>kh</u>tar*, "a daughter."
خروس *<u>kh</u>urūs*, "a cock."	ماکیان *mākiyān*, "a hen."
غوچ *<u>gh</u>ūch*, "a ram."	میش *mesh*, "an ewe."

Animals have sometimes نر (*năr*), "male," and ماده (*māda*), "female," affixed or prefixed to them, as:—

شیرنر *sher-i-nar*, "a lion."	شیرماده *sher-i-māda*, "a lioness."
گاونر *gāw-i-nar*, نرگاو *nar-gāw* } a bull.	ماده‌گاو *māda gāw*, "a cow."

Arabic Nouns frequently form the feminine by adding the imperceptible ه (*h*), as:—

مَلِك *malik*, "a king."	مَلِکه *malika*, "a queen."

Formation of the Plural.

17. Nouns denoting rational beings form the plural by adding ان (*ān*) to the singular, thus:—

پدر *padar*, "a father," *plur.* پدران *padarān*.
مادر *mādar*, "a mother," *plur.* مادران *mādarān*.

Nouns denoting animals usually form the plural by adding *ān*, sometimes *hā*, as:—

اَسپ *asp*, "a horse," { *plur.* اَسپان *aspān*. / " اَسپها *asphā*.
مُرغ *murgh*, "a bird," " مُرغان *murghān*.
شُتر *shutur* / اُشتر *ushtur* } "a camel," { " شُتران *shuturān*. / " شُترها *shuturhā*.

Nouns denoting inanimate objects form the plural by adding *hā* to the singular, and *rarely ān*; as—

قَلم *ḳalam*, "a pen," *plur.* قَلمها *kalamhā*.
گل *gul*, "a flower," " گلها *gulhā*.
درخت (*dirakht*), "a tree," { *pl.* درختها *dirakhthā*. / " درختان *dirakhtān*.

Observations on the Affix *ān*.

18. If the noun ends in اَ (*ā*), or وُ (*ū*), or و (*o*), the letter ي is inserted before ان (*ān*) to prevent

the hiatus. Sometimes, though rarely, the letter ي is omitted after و; as—

دانا *dānā*, "a page," *plur.* دانایان *dānāyān.*

پریرو *parī-rū*, "fairy-faced," *plur.* پریرویان *parī-rūyān.*

بازو *bāzū*, "the arm," *plur.* بازووان *bāzūwān.*

In nouns ending in obscure ه (*h*), the ه is changed into گ, as:—

فرشته *firishta*, "an angel," *plur.* فرشتگان *firish-tagān.*

بچه *bachcha*, "a child," *plur.* بچگان *bachchagān.*

Sometimes the ه is retained; as—

مرده *murda*, "dead," *plur.* مردهگان *murdahgān.*

When ه is preceded by a long vowel the plural is formed in the usual way; as—

پادشاه *pādshāh*, "a king," *plur.* پادشاهان *pād-shāhān.*

Observations on the Affix *hā*.

19. In nouns ending in the obscure ه (*h*) the ه disappears; as—

نامه *nāma*, "a letter," *plur.* نامها *nāmahā.*

خانه *khāna*, "a house," „ خانها *khānahā.*

FORMATION OF THE PLURAL.

If the ه is preceded by a long vowel, the ه is retained; as—

راه, *rāh*, "a road," *plur.* راهها, *rāhhā*.

FINAL OBSERVATIONS.

20. Arabic words may have the Persian or the Arabic form of plural; thus—

	Sing.	Persian Pl.	Arabic Pl.
defect . .	عَيْب *'aib*	عَيبها *'aibhā*	عَوَائِب *'awā,ib* / عُيُوب *'uyūb*
viceroy .	نَائِب *nā,ib*	نائبان *nā,ibān*	نُوّاب *nūwāb*
a book .	كِتاب *kitāb*	كِتابها *kitābhā*	كُتُب *kutub*
a labourer,	عَامِل *'āmil*	عامِلان *'āmilān*	عَمَلة *'amalat*

In imitation of the feminine plural of Arabic nouns, names applicable to females, or to things without life, sometimes form the plural by the affix ات (*āt*) or یات (*iyūt*); as—

	Sing.	Plur.
a favour . .	*nawāzish*	*nawāzishāt*
an anecdote .	*naḳl*	*naḳliyāt*

When the word ends in imperceptible ه (*h*) the affix becomes جات (*jāt*), the letter ه being omitted; as—

	Sing.	*Plur.*
a letter, *or* written communication	*nāma*	*nāmajāt*
„	*nawishta*	*nawishtajāt*
a fort	*ḳ'ila*	*ḳ'ilajāt*

These terminations, *āt*, *iyāt*, and *jāt*, are considered vulgar, and are rarely used.

Formation of the Cases.

21. There is only one declension of Persian Nouns; it is extremely simple. The cases are formed as follows:—

(*a*) The Accusative, by adding را (*rā*) to the nominative (singular or plural); often the *rā* is omitted, and the accusative has then the same form as the nominative.

(*b*) The Dative, by adding *rā* to the nominative; and sometimes [omitting *rā*] by prefixing *ba*, "to" or "for." The prefix بِ (*ba*) is chiefly used when an accusative, requiring *rā*, occurs in the sentence.

(*c*) The Vocative, by *prefixing* the interjection اي (*ai*) to the nominative; and sometimes, in poetry, [omitting *ai*] by adding *alif*, as:—

اي مرد *ai mard*, "O man!"
دوستا *dostā*, "O friend!"
بلبلا *bulbulā*, "O nightingale!"

(*d*) The Ablative, by prefixing to the nominative (singular or plural) the preposition از (*az*).

(*e*) The Genitive, by the juxtaposition of two substantives; the thing possessed comes first, with its final letter sounded with *kasra*, called كسرهٔ اضافت *kasra,e iẓūfat*; thus—

پسرِ مَلِك *pisar-i-malik*, "the son of the king."

كتابِ پسرِ مَلِك *kitāb-i-pisar-i-malik*, "the book of the king's son."

If the governing word ends in ا or و the Persians use (1) ي *majhūl* with ء *hamza*; (2) or ء *hamza* alone with ـِ *kasra*, expressed or understood; as—

جاءِ پدر or جائِ پدر *jā,e padar*, "the place of the father."

پاءِ مرد or پائِ مرد *pā,e mard*, "the foot of the man."

روءِ پسر or روئِ پسر *rū,e pisar*, "the face of the son."

بوءِ گل or بوئِ گُل *bū,e gul*, "the scent of the rose."

In practice, when ي *majhūl* is used, ء *hamza* is suppressed; as پاي مرد *pā,e mard*; روي پسر *rū,e pisar*.

If the governing word ends with the obscure ه (*h*), or the long vowel ي (*ī* or *e*), the Persians use the mark ءِ *hamza* with ـِ *kasra* expressed or understood; as—

خانهٔ مرد *k͟hāna,e mard*, "the house of the man."

ماهیِ دریا *māhī,e daryā*, "the fish of the sea."

بندهٔ خدا *banda,e k͟hudā*, "the servant of God."

Observe that both ءِ and ی are pronounced as *yā,e majhūl*.

DECLENSION OF NOUNS.

22. *Kārd*, "a knife."

	Sing.	*Plur.*
Nom.	*kārd.*	*kārdhā.*
Gen.	ـِ *i-kārd.*	*i-kārdhā.*
	ی *e-kārd.*	*e-kārdhā.*
	ء *e-kārd.*	*e-kārdhā.*
Dat.	*kārd-rā.*	*kārdhā-rā.*
„	*ba kārd.*	*ba kārdhā.*
Acc.	*kārd-rā.*	*kārdhā-rā.*
„	*kārd.*	*kārdhā.*
Voc.	*ai kārd.*	*ai kārdhā.*
Abl.	*az kārd.*	*az kārdhā.*

Similarly, every substantive may be declined. The only questions to be satisfied are, whether ان (*ān*) or ها (*hā*) is to be added for the plural, and whether ِ, ي, or ۂ is to be used for the genitive. (*Vide* pars. 20 and 21.)

THE ARTICLE.

23. In Persian there is no Article.

مرد *mard*, may signify "man," or "*the* man," according to the context.

A substantive may be made definite by adding *yā,e majhūl*, or *yā,e waḥdat*, *i.e.* the *yā* of unity, thus:—

مردی *marde*, "a certain man."

زنی *zane*, "a certain woman."

کتابی *kitābe*, "a certain book."

If the noun ends in ه quiescent, the symbol ۂ (*hamza*) may be added; as—

بچه *bachcha*, "a child."

بچۂ *bachcha,e*, "a certain child."

If ه be preceded by long *alif*, ي (*yā,e majhūl*) is retained, as:—

پادشاه *pādshāh*, "a king."

پادشاهي *pādshāhe*, "a certain king."

Observation.—Since an abstract noun is formed

by adding *yā* with *kasra*, i.e. *yā,e ma'rūf*, to any adjective, or appellative noun, ambiguity may occasionally arise. Thus the difference between—

بادشاهي *bādshāhe*, "a certain king,"
بادشاهيِ *bādshāhī*, "sovereignty," or "royal,"

can be distinguished; but it often happens that the mark *kasra* is, through negligence or custom, omitted. In such a case the context alone can indicate the proper meaning.

ADJECTIVES.

24. Persian adjectives are indeclinable; in construction they *follow* * their substantives, to which they are connected by ِ (*kasra*), ي (*yā,e majhūl*), or ٔ (*hamza*), as:—

مردِ نيك *mard-i-nek*, "a good man."
روي خوب *rū,e khūb*, "a fair face."
بندهٔ خدا *banda,e khudā*, "a servant of God."

Degrees of Comparison.

25. The comparative degree is formed by adding تر (*tar*) to the positive, and the superlative by adding ترين (*tarīn*), as:—

* See p. 90.

خوب *khūb*, "fair." | خوبتر *khūbtar*, "fairer."

خوبترین *khūbtarīn*, "fairest."*

Arabic adjectives (if triliteral) form the comparative and superlative degrees by prefixing ا to the triliteral root, as:—

حَسَن *ḥasan*, "beautiful."

اِحسن *aḥsan*, "more, or most, beautiful."

عظيم *aẓīm*, "great."

اعظم *a'ẓam*, "more, or most, great."

Generally the Arabic adjectives in Persian form the degrees of comparison in the Persian manner; as—

fazl, "excellent."

afẓal-tar, or *faẓl-tar* (Pers.) } "more excellent."
afẓal (Arabic) }

faẓl-tarīn (Pers.) } "most excellent."
afẓal (Arabic) }

---

* *Tar* and *tarīn* may be written with the word or separately; *tarīn* is sometimes contracted to *īn*; as—

بهين *bihīn*, "best," for بِهتَرِين *bihtarīn*.

Tar and *tarīn* are also added to prepositions and adverbs; as—

bar, "upon," *bartar*, "higher," *bartarīn*, "highest;"
zer, "below," *zertar*, "lower," *zertarīn*, "lowest."

PRONOUNS.

26. First Person—من *man*, "I."

	Singular.	*Plural.*
Nom.	*man.*	*mā.*
Gen.	ِ *i-man.*	ِ *i-mā.*
	ي *e-man.*	ي *e-mā.*
	ٔ *e-man.*	ٔ *e-mā.*
Dat.	*marā.*	*mā-rā.*
,,	*ba man.*	*ba mā.*
Acc.	*marā.*	*mā-rā.*
Voc.	(nil.)	(nil.)
Abl.	*az man.*	*az mā.*
,,	*bā man.*	*bā mā.*
,,	*bar man.*	*bar mā.*

Second Person—تو *tū*, "thou."

	Singular.	*Plural.*
Nom.	*tū.*	*shumā.*
Gen.	ِ *i-tū.*	ِ *i-shumā.*
	ي *e-tū.*	ي *e-shumā.*
	ٔ *e-tū.*	ٔ *e-shumā.*
Dat.	*turā.*	*shumā-rā.*
,,	*ba tū.*	*ba shumā.*
Acc.	*turā.*	*shumā-rā.*
Voc.	*ai tū.*	*ai shumā.*
Abl.	*az tū.*	*az shumā.*
,,	*bā tū.*	*bā shumā.*
,,	*bar tū.*	*bar shumā.*

Third Person—او *o*, "he."

	Singular.	*Plural.*
Nom.	*o.*	*eshān.*
Gen.	ِ *i-o.*	ِ *i-eshān.*
	ي *e-o.*	ي *e-eshān.*
	ٔ *e-ȯ.*	ٔ *e-eshān.*
Dat.	*o-rā.*	*eshān-rā.*
„	*ba o.*	*ba eshān.*
Acc.	*o-rā.*	*eshān-rā.*
Voc.	(nil.)	(nil.)
Abl.	*az o.*	*az eshān.*
„	*bā o.*	*bā eshān.*
„	*bar o.*	*bar eshān.*

The third person has, in the singular, the form وي *wai*, and sometimes اوي *o,e*; and, in the plural, اوشان *oshān* and شان *shān*.

When the third person represents a lifeless thing, the demonstratives آن *an*, and این *īn*, with their plurals, آنها *ānhā* and اینها *īnhā*, are used, as will presently be seen.

27. The possessive pronoun may be rendered by the suffixes—

اَم *am*, my; اَت *at*, thy; اَش *ash*, his.
مان *mān*, our; تان *tān*, your; شان *shān*, their.

When the noun ends in ا or و long, the ا of the termination is rejected and ي inserted in its place; as—

پایم *pāyam*, my foot.

مویت *mūyat*, thy hair.

رویش *rūyash*, his face.

When the noun ends in quiescent ه, *alif* is retained; as—

خانهٔام *khāna-am*, my house.

خانهٔات *khāna-at*, thy house.

خانهٔاش *khāna-ash*, his house.

In other cases *alif* is rejected; as—

پدرم *padaram*, or پدرِ من *padar-i-man*, my father.

پدرت *padarat*, or پدرِ تو *padar-i-tū*, thy father.

پدرش *padarash*, or پدرِ او *padar-i-o*, his father.

پدرِمان *padar-i-mān*, or پدرِ ما *padar-i-mā*, our father.

پدرِتان *padar-i-tān*, or پدرِ شما *padar-i-shumā*, your father.

پدرِشان *padar-i-shān*, or پدرِ ایشان *padar-i-eshān*, their father.

Reciprocal Pronoun, خود *khụd*, "self."

28. *man khụdam* or *man khụd*, I myself.
tū khụdat or *tū khụd*, thou thyself.
o khụdash or *o khụd*, he himself.
mā khụd-i-mūn or *mā khụd*,* we ourselves.
shumā khụd-i-tūn or *shumā khụd*,* you yourselves.
eshūn khụd-i-shūn or *eshūn khụd*, they themselves.

The reciprocal pronouns are thus used:—

kitūb-i-khụdam, my own book.
ḳalam-i-khụdat, thy own pen.
asp-i-khụdash, his own horse.
jūmhū,e khụd-i-mān, our own cups.
kharān-i-khụd-i-tūn, your own asses.
ṣandūḳhū,e khụd-i-shūn, their own boxes.

Demonstrative Pronouns.

29.† این *īn*, this (for persons or things).
اینها *īnhū*, these (for persons or things).

---

* These forms are rarely used.

† When *ba* is placed in close connection with *ān* or *īn*, the *madda* of آن and the initial *alif* of این are replaced by د ; as—

بدان *badān*, to that. | بدین *badīn*, to this.

After the words *bar*, "on;" *dar*, "in;" *az*, "from;" *chūn*, "like," the initial ا of او , ایشان , این and the *madda*

اینان *īnān*, these (for persons only).
آن *ān*, that (for persons or things).
آنها *ūnhā*, those (for persons or things).
آنان *ūnān*, those (for persons only).

Examples—

این مرد	*īn mard,*	this man.
این مردان	*īn mardūn,*	these men.
آن کتاب	*ān kitūb,*	that book.
آن کتابها	*ān kitābhā,*	those books.

When این *īn* is prefixed to a noun, so as to form one word, it is sometimes changed into اِم *im*; as— *imrūz*, "this day;" *imshab*, "this night;" *imsāl*, "this year."

Interrogative Pronouns.

30. There are three in number:—

---

of آن are rejected, when they are closely connected with the preceding word; as—

دَرو *dar o*, in him.	چونو *chūn o*, like him.
بَرِیشان *bar eshān*, on them.	دَران *dar ān*, in that.
ازو *az o*, from him.	دَرین *dar īn*, in this.

ki, who? *kirā*, whom? to whom? (applicable to persons.) — Sing. or Plural.
chi, what? *chirā*, what? to what? why? (applicable to things.) — Sing. or Plural.

kudām, which? out of any number; as—
kudām shakhṣ, which person?
kudām rāh, which road?

Indefinite Pronouns.

31. These are all indeclinable.

chand, some.
yake, one, some one.
shakhṣ, a person.
kas, some one.
hech, any.
hama, all.
tane chand, sundry individuals.
har, every, all.
har ānki or *harki*, whosoever.
har kudām, whosoever, whichsover.
harchi, whatsoever.
har kujā or *harjā*, wheresoever.
harkas, everybody.
haryak, everyone.
hardū, both.
har chīz, whatsoever thing.
har shab, every night.
har rūz, every day.
har wakt, whensoever.
bahar ḥāl, however.

Relative Pronouns.

32. There are no Relative Pronouns; the particles كه *ki*, for persons, and چه *chi*, for things, are

sometimes regarded as relatives. This matter will be considered in the Syntax.

THE VERB.

33. There is only one conjugation.

All the tenses are formed from the root, or from the infinitive, as will be seen from the following example of the Verb رسیدن *rasīdan*, "to arrive;" root رس *ras*.

Tenses of the Root.

Aorist.

"I may, or can, arrive."

	Singular.	*Plural.*
1.	*rasam*	*rasem.*
2.	*rasī*	*rased.*
3.	*rasad*	*rasand.*

Present Tense.

"I arrive, or am arriving."

1.	*mī-rasam*	*mī-rasem.*
2.	*mī-rasī*	*mī-rased.*
3.	*mī-rasad*	*mī-rasand.*

Simple Future.

"I shall, will, or may arrive."

Singular.	*Plural.*
1. *bi-rasam*	*bi-rasem.*
2. *bi-rasī*	*bi-rased.*
3. *bi-rasad*	*bi-rasand.*

Imperative.

"Let me arrive."

1. *rasam*	*rasem.*
2. *ras*	*rased.*
3. *rasad*	*rasand.*

The Noun of Agency is formed by adding ـَنده (*anda*) to the root; as—

rasanda, "the arriver."

The Present Participle is formed by adding آن; as رسان *rasūn*, "arriving."

The Causal Verb is formed by adding *ūnīdan*, or *ūndan*, as:—

رَسانیدن *rasūnīdan*, "to cause to arrive."

رَساندن *rasūndan*, "to cause to arrive."

OBSERVATIONS.

34. The Simple Future differs but little from the Aorist.

Native grammarians call that tense the Aorist which is here styled the Simple Future, and they say that when the Aorist (our Simple Future) is used in the subjunctive mood, the particle *bi* is omitted, as :—

bi-bāsham, I be.	*bāsham*, I may be.

The Simple Future is most often used as follows :—

I promise that I will come,
w'ada mī-kunam ki biyāyam.

The second person (singular and plural) of the Imperative has frequently the particle *bi* prefixed; thus—

arrive thou, *bi-ras*	arrive ye, *bi-rased.*

When the first letter of the Imperative has *ẓamma* for its vowel, *bi* may become *bu ;* as—

do thou, *bu-kun.*

The third person singular of the Imperative may be rendered benedictive by lengthening the vowel *fatḥa* of its final syllable ; as—

let him arrive, *rasad.*
O that he may arrive ! *rasād.*

Similarly—
kunad, from *kardan*, "to do," makes *kunād.*
shavad, „ *shudan*, "to become," makes *shavād.*
dihad, „ *dādan*, "to give," makes *dihād.*
buvad, „ *būdan*, "to be," makes *buvād* or *bād.*
gardānad „ *gardānīdan*, "to cause to become," makes *gardānād.*

Except in poetry, and on occasions of particular formality, it is rather pedantic to use this benedictive form. The Aorist is more frequently used.

TENSES FROM THE INFINITIVE.

35. *Preterite* or *Indefinite Past.*

"I arrived."

Singular.	*Plural.*
1. *rasīdam*	*rasīdem.*
2. *rasīdī*	*rasīded.*
3. *rasīd*	*rasīdand.*

Imperfect.

"I was arriving."

1. *mī-rasīdam*	*mī-rasīdem.*
2. *mī-rasīdī*	*mī-rasīded.*
3. *mī-rasīd*	*mī-rasīdand.*

Past Potential or *Habitual.*

"I might arrive," "I used to arrive."

1. *rasīdame*	*rasīdeme.*
2. *rasīdī*	*rasīdede.*
3. *rasīde*	*rasīdande.*

Compound Future.

"I will arrive."

1. *khwāham rasīd*	*khwāhem rasīd*
2. *khwāhī rasīd*	*khwāhed rasīd.*
3. *khwāhad rasīd*	*khwāhand rasīd.*

Observations.

36. In the Imperfect همی (*hamī*) is often prefixed instead of *mī*.

The Past Potential is formed by adding *yā,e majhūl* to all the persons of the Preterite, except the 2nd person singular.

In the Compound Future, the auxiliary is the Aorist of the verb *khwāstan*, "to wish," root *khwāh*. The letter و is *not* to be sounded (see p. 10).

Preterite Participle.

37. رسیده *rasīda*, "arrived," or "having arrived."

The following three tenses are derived from the Preterite Participle.

Perfect Tense.

"I have arrived."

	Singular.	*Plural.*
1.	*rasīda am*	*rasīda em.*
2.	*rasīda ī*	*rasīda ed.*
3.	*rasīda ast*	*rasīda and.*

Pluperfect Tense.

"I had arrived."

1.	*rasīda būdam*	*rasīda būdem.*
2.	*rasīda būdī*	*rasīda būded.*
3.	*rasīda būd*	*rasīda būdand.*

Future Perfect.

"I shall have arrived."

	Singular.	*Plural.*
1.	*rasīda bāsham*	*rasīda bāshem.*
2.	*rasīda bāshī*	*rasīda bāshed.*
3.	*rasīda bāshad*	*rasīda bāshand.*

Similarly, every verb in Persian may be conjugated. In all the tenses the termination of the 2nd person singular is *yā,e m'arūf*.

In the terminations يم (*em*) يد (*ed*) (1st and 2nd persons plural), *yā,e majhūl* is sounded.*

PERSONAL TERMINATIONS.

38. These are—

Singular.	*Plural.*
اَم *am*, am.	ايم *em*, are.
ی or اِی *ī*, art.	ايد *ed*, are.
است *ast*, is.	اند *and*, are.

The personal terminations may be joined to a

* An educated native of Shīrāz informs the writer that the terminations *em, ed*—

(1) should properly be pronounced *īm, īd,*
(2) may " " *em, ed,*
(3) may never " " *aim, aid.*

The sound of *e* in the 2nd case is that of *ea* in "bear."

pronoun, adjective, or substantive. In composition—

(*a*) The initial *alif* is omitted; as—

من شاگردم *man shāgird am*, I am a scholar.
ایشان نیکند *eshān nek and*, they are good.
او سلطانست *o sultān ast*, he is Sultān.

(*b*) If the word ends in obscure ه (*h*), *alif* is retained, as:—

او بنده است *o banda ast*, he is a slave.

(*c*) If the substantive be an abstract noun, as, *hastī*, "existence," *dilīrī*, "boldness," *shādī*, "gladness," the final *yā* of the noun is omitted; as—

تو شادي *tū shād-ī*, thou art glad.
او دليرست *o dilīr ast*, he is bold.
هستيم *hastem*, we are, or exist.

(*d*) In the case of the pronouns كه "who?" چه "what?" the final ه is omitted, and the initial *alif* of the termination is changed into *yā*; as—

کیست *kīst*, who is it?
چیست *chīst*, what is it?

(*e*) If the word ends in و (*wāw*) or ا (*alif*), the

initial *alif* of the termination is changed into *yā*; as—

> داناٸم *dānāyam*, I am learned.
> داناٸیم *dānāyem*, we are learned.
> خوب رویست *khūb rūyast*, he is fair-faced.
> داناٸی *dānāyī*, thou art wise.

In the 3rd person singular and plural, *yā* need not be inserted; as—

> *khūb rūyast* or *khūb rūst*, he is fair-faced.
> *dānāyast* or *dānāst*, he is learned.
> *dānāyand* or *dānānd*, they are wise.

39. From § 38 we have:—

Singular.	*Plural.*
hastam, I am.	*hastem*, we are.
hastī, thou art.	*hasted*, you are.
hast, he is.	*hastand*, they are.

---

40. The verb *būdan*, "to be;" root, *bū* or *bāsh*.

TENSES FROM THE ROOT.

Aorist.

"I may be."

Singular.	*Plural.*
1. *bāsham**	*bāshem*.

---

* The form *buwam*, from the root *bū*, is also used. *Vide* paragraph 34, p. 35.

Singular.	*Plural.*
2. *bāshī*	*bāshed.*
3. *bāshad*	*bāshand.*

Present.

mī-bāsham, "I am," &c.

Simple Future.

bi-bāsham, "I shall, will, or may be," &c.

Imperative.

1. (no first person)	*bāshem,* let us be.
2. *bāsh,* be thou.	*bāshed,* be ye.
3. *bāshad* or *bād,* let him be	*bāshand,* let them be.

Present Participle (not in use), *bāshān,* being.
Noun of Agency (not in use), *bāshanda,* be-er.

TENSES FROM THE INFINITIVE.

Preterite, or *Indefinite Past.*

"I was."

Singular.	*Plural.*
1. *būdam*	*būdem.*
2. *būdī*	*būded.*
3. *būd*	*būdand.*

Imperfect.

mī-būdam, "I was," &c.

Past Potential or *Habitual.*

būdame, "I might be, or used to be," &c.

Compound Future.

khwāham būd, "I shall or will be," &c.

Preterite Participle, *būda*, "having been," "been."

TENSES FROM THE PRETERITE PARTICIPLE.

Perfect Tense.

būda am, "I have been," &c.

Pluperfect.

būda būdam (not in use).

Future Perfect.

būda bāsham, "I shall have been," &c.

41. The verb *shudan* (for *shūdan*) "to be" (passive), root *shaw*.

TENSES FROM THE ROOT.

Aorist.

"I may be."

Singular.	*Plural.*
1. *shavam*	*shavem.*
2. *shavī*	*shaved.*
3. *shavad*	*shavand.*

Present Tense.

mī-shavam, "I am," &c.

Simple Future.

bi-shavam, "I shall or will be," &c.

Imperative.

1. (no first person)	*shavem*, let us be.
2. *shaw*, be thou.	*shaved*, be ye.
3. *shavad*, let him be.	*shavand*, let them be.

Present Participle (not in use) *shavān*, "being."
Noun of Agency, *shavanda*, "be-er," or "become-er."

TENSES FROM THE INFINITIVE.

Preterite or *Indefinite Past.*

"I was."

1. *shudam*	*shudem.*
2. *shudī*	*shuded.*
3. *shud*	*shudand.*

Imperfect.

mī-shudam, "I was," &c.

Past Potential or *Habitual.*

mī-shudame, "I might be," &c.

Compound Future.

khwāham shud, "I will be," &c.

Preterite Participle, *shuda*, "having been."

TENSES FROM THE PRETERITE PARTICIPLE.

Perfect Tense.

shuda am, "I have been," &c.

Pluperfect Tense.

shuda būdam, I had been, &c.

Future Perfect.

shuda bāsham, I shall have been, &c.

THE PASSIVE VOICE.

42. The Passive Voice is formed by prefixing the Preterite Participle to the tenses of the verb *shudan*, "to be, become;" thus—

Present.

"I may be struck."

	Singular.	*Plural.*
1.	*zada shavam*	*zada shavem.*
2.	*zada shavī*	*zada shaved.*
3.	*zada shavad*	*zada shavand.*

and similarly for the other tenses.

CAUSAL VERBS.

43. These are formed by adding ـَانیدن *ānīdan* or ـَاندن *āndan*, to the root of the primitive verb; thus—

Jastan, "to leap," root, *jah*; *jahānīdan* or *jahāndan*, "to cause to leap," root, *jahān*: *gashtan*, "to become," root, *gard*; *gardānīdan*, "to cause to become," &c., root, *gardān*.

NEGATIVE VERBS.

44. A verb is rendered negative by *prefixing* the particle نه *na*, "not;" as—

نرسید or نه رسید *na rasīd*, he did not arrive.

With the imperative the particle مه (*ma*) is employed in like manner; as—

مه پرس or مپرس *ma purs*, ask not.
مبادا or مباد *ma būd*, let it not be! God forbid!

Observations.

When the particles به (*bi*), نه (*na*), مه (*ma*) are prefixed to a verb beginning with *alif*, not marked by *madda*, the initial *alif* is omitted, and *yā* is inserted in its place.

The *yā* takes the vowel of the rejected *alif*; thus—

اَنداخت *andā<u>kh</u>t*, he threw.
نَیَنداخت *nayandā<u>kh</u>t*, he threw not.
اُفتم *uftam*, I may fall.
بیُفتم *biyuftam*, I shall fall.
اَنگار *angār*, consider.
میَنگار *mayangār*, do not consider.

If the verb begins with آ the ا remains, but the *madda* is rejected; thus—

آرد *ūrad*, he may bring.

بیارد *biyūrad*, he will bring.

آر *ūr*, bring thou.

بیار *biyūr*, bring thou.

میار *mayūr*, do not bring.

نیارد *nayūrad*, he may not bring.

In the older poets the نه (*na*) often unites with the following آ without the intervention of *yā*; as—

نامد *nāmad*, "he came not," for نیامد *nayāmad*, "he came not."

45. The personal terminations (§ 38) are conjugated negatively, as follows:—

Singular.	*Plural.*
نِیَم *nayam*, I am not.	نئیم *nayem*, we are not.
نیِی or نهٔ *nayī*, thou art not.	نئید *nayed*, you are not.
نِیست *nīst*, he is not.	نیند *nayand*, they are not.

The substantive verb *hastam* is conjugated negatively, as follows:—

Singular.	*Plural.*
نیستم *nīstam*, I am not.	نیستیم *nīstem*, we are not.
نیستی *nīstī*, thou art not.	نیستید *nīsted*, you are not.
نیست *nīst*, he is not.	نیستند *nīstand*, they are not.

46. Interrogation is usually expressed by the tone of the voice. In writing, the word *āyā*, "whether," is prefixed to a question, or the word *yā na*, "or not," affixed.*

ROOTS OF VERBS.

47. Infinitives in دن (*dan*) are preceded by the long vowels آ (*ā*), ـَ (*a*), ی (*ī*), او (*ū*), or by the consonants ر (*r*), ن (*n*).

Infinitives in تن (*tan*) are preceded by خ (*kh*), س (*s*), ش (*sh*), ف (*f*).

Hence the following rules:—

(*a*) Infinitives in ادن (*ādan*), یدن (*īdan*), and

* Did your father go there? *pidar-i-shumā ānjā raft, yā na?* Do you know Persian? *āyā shumā fārsī mī-dāned?*

those which have *fatḥa* before the *dan*, reject these terminations for the root; as—

VERB.		ROOT.
firistādan,	to send,	*firist.*
pursīdan,	to ask,	*purs.*
āzhadan,	to sew,	*āzh.*

*Exceptions.**

to bring forth	*zādan*† *zā,īdan*	*zā,* or *zā,e.*
to create,	*āfrīdan,*	*āfrīn.*
to come,	*āmadan,*	*ā,e.*
to choose,	*guz̲īdan,*	*guz̲īn.*
to embrace,	*gādan,*	*gā* or *gā,e.*
to give,	*dādan,*	*dih.*
to hear	*shunīdan* *shunūdan* *shunuftan*	*shinau.*
to lose	*kushādan* *kushūdan*	*kushā,c.*
to see,	*dīdan,*	*bīn.*
to strike,	*zadan,*	*zan.*
to stitch,	*ak̲h̲īdan,*	*ak̲h̲īn.*
to take	*sitādan* *sitāndan*†	*sitān.*

* Verbs marked thus (†) are regular.

(*b*) Infinitives in ودن (*ūdan*) reject that termination, and substitute ا (*ū*) or اى (*ā,e*) for the root, as:—

VERB.		ROOT.
to praise,	*sitūdan,*	*sitā,e.*

Exceptions.

to be,	*būdan,*	*bū* or *bāsh.*
to become	*shudan* for *shūdan*	*shau.*
to draw,	*tanūdan,*	*tanau.*
to hear	*shunūdan* / *shunīdan* / *shunuftan*	*shunau*
to neigh,	*zinūdan,*	*zinau.*
to reap,	*durūdan,*	*durū.*
to slumber,	*ghunūdan,*	*ghunū.*

(*c*) Infinitives in دن (*dan*), preceded by *re* or *nun*, reject the termination *dan* for the root, as:—

VERB.		ROOT.
to cherish,	*parwardan,*	*parwar.*
to dig,	*kandan,*	*kan.*

Exceptions.

to bring,	*āwardan,*†	*āwar* or *ār.*
to count,	*shimurdan,*	*shimār.*

VERB.		ROOT.
to carry,	*burdan,*	*bar.*
to do,	*kardan,*	*kun.*
to die,	*murdan,*	*mīr.*
to entrust,	*sipurdan,*	*sipār.*
to offend,	*āzurdan,*	*āzār.*
to squeeze,	*afshurdan,*	*afshār.*

(*d*) Infinitives in تن (*tan*), preceded by خ (*kh*), reject the termination, and change خ into ز for the root, as:—

VERB.		ROOT.
to throw,	*andākhtan,*	*andāz.*

Exceptions.

to cook,	*pukhtan,*	*paz.*
to draw a sword,	*ākhtan,*	*ākh.*
to recognise,	*shinākhtan,*	*shinās.*
to snap	{ *gusekhtan* / *gusastan* }	*gusil.*
to weigh	{ *sukhtan* / *sanjīdan*† }	*sanj.*

(*e*) Infinitives in تن (*tan*), preceded by س, reject both *tan* and *sīn* for the root, as:—

VERB.		ROOT.
to live,	*zīstan,*	*zī.*

Exceptions.

VERB.		ROOT.
to bind,	*bastan,*	*band.*
to break,	*shikastan,*	*shikan.*
to desire,	*khẉāstan,*	*khẉāh.*
to diminish,	*kāstan,*	*kāh.*
to escape,	*rastan,*	*rih.*
to grow	*rustan* *rū,īdan*	*rū,e.*
to join,	*paiwastan,*	*paiwand.*
to know,	*dānistan,*	*dān.*
to leap,	*jastan,*	*jih.*
to place	*nishāstan* *nishāndan*†	*nishān.*
to rise,	*khāstan,*	*khez.*
to spin	*rīstan* *rishtan*	*rīs.*
to sit down,	*nishastan,*	*nishīn.*
to split,	*gusastan* *gusekhtan*	*gusil.*
to wash,	*shustan,*	*shū,e.*

(*f*) Infinitives in تن (*tan*), preceded by ش, reject *tan*, and change the *shīn* into ر, as:—

VERB.		ROOT.
to have,	*dāshtan,*	*dār.*

Exceptions.

VERB.		ROOT.
to become,	*gashtan,*	*gard.*
to embrace	*āghoshtan,*	*āghosh.*
	gādan,	*gā,e.*
to elevate,	*afrāshtan,*	*afrāz.*
to kill,	*kushtan,*	*kush.*
to let down *or* quit	*hishtan*	*hil* or *hish.*
	hilīdan	
	hishīdan	
to mix,	*sirishtan,*	*sarīsh.*
to plant,	*kāshtan,*†	*kār.*
to sow,	*kishtan,*	*kār.*
to spin	*rishtan*	*rīs.*
	rīstan	
to write,	*nawishtan,*	*nawīs.*

(*g*) Infinitives in تن (*tan*), preceded by ف, generally reject *tan*, and change ف into ب, as, "to shine,"* *tāftan*, root, *tāb*. In some verbs the ف remains unchanged, as:—

* We may add:—

VERB.		ROOT.
to deceive,	*fareftan*	*fareb.*
to obtain,	*yāftan*	*yāb.*
to beat,	*kūftan*	*kūb.*

VERB.		ROOT.
to weave,	*bāftan,*	*bāf.*
	Exceptions.	
to accept,	*pazīraftan,*	*pazīr.*
to bore,	*suftan,*	*suft* and *sumb.*
to conceal,	*nihuftan,*	*nihuft.*
to disturb,	*āshuftan,*	*āshūb.*
to dig,	*kāftan,*	*kā,o*
	kandan,†	*kan.* [*kand.*
to dig a canal,	*farkandan,*†	*farkan* and *far-*
to expand (as a flower)	*shukuftan,*	*shukuf.*
to go,	*raftan,*	*rau.*
to hear	*shinuftan* / *shunūdan* / *shunīdan*	*shinau.*
to sweep,	*ruftan,*	*rūb.*
to seize,	*giriftan,*	*gīr.*
to speak,	*guftan,*	*go* and *go,e.*
to sleep,*	*khuftan,*	*khusp.*

If the preceding rules, with their exceptions, be learned, no difficulty will be found in conjugating any Persian verb.

---

* We have also—

VERB.		ROOT.
to sleep,	*khwābīdan*	*khwāb.*
to sleep,	*khusbīdan*	*khusb.*

INDECLINABLE PARTS OF SPEECH.

48. ADVERBS.

(1) Number:—

būre } once.
yakbār }
dūbār, twice.
si bār, thrice.
kam bār, seldom.

(2) Order:—

nakhustīn }
awwalā } first.
awwal martaba }
auwalīn }

duwum }
duwumīn } secondly.
sāniyā }

siwum }
siyūm }
siyūmīn } thirdly.
siyūm martaba }
sālisā }

chahārum }
chahārumīn } fourthly.
chahārum martaba }
rūbi'an }

(3) Place:—

īnjā, here.
az īnjā, hence.
īn sū }
īn jānib } this way, this direction.
īn taraf }
ānjā, there.
az ānjā, thence.
ān sū }
ān jānib } that way, that direction.
ān taraf }

darūn }
andarūn } within.
berūn }
birūn } without.
faro }
farod } under, beneath.
bālā, over, upon, above.
har kujā ki, wheresoever.
hech jā, somewhere.
hech jā na, nowhere.

Interrogation :—

kū? where?
kujā?, *kudūm jā?*, *kudām ṭaraf?*, what place? what way? what direction?
chand? how many?
chigūna? in what way?
chūn? how?
chirā, why?
barā,e chi?, *ba chi sabab?*, why? on what account?
chi ḳadar, how much? what quantity?
kai, how? when?

Time present :—

aknūn, *kunūn*, *ḥālan*, now.
hamīndam, *īn zamān*, *hamīn zamān*, *ham aknūn*, just now, this instant, this very moment.
imrūz, to-day.
imshab, to-night.
imsāl, this year.
hanoz, yet.
shāmgāh, in the evening.
bāmdād, *saḥrgāh*, in the morning.

Time past :—

pesh az īn, *ḳabl az īn*, before this.
az pesh, *pesh*, *pesetar*, previously.
peshīn, *ḳadīm*, anciently.
dīruz, yesterday.
dīshab, yesternight.
pār sāl pārīn, last year.

Time to come:—

farda, to-morrow.

rūz-i-dīgar, *dīgar rūz*, the next day.

farda shab, to-morrow night.

shab-i-dīgar, the next night.

pas farda shab, the night after to-morrow.

pas farda, the day after to-morrow.

sāl-i-dīgar, the next year.

māh-i-dīgar, the next month.

hafta,e dīgar, the next week.

sāl-i-āyanda, the coming year.

māh - i - āyanda, the coming month.

hafta,e āyanda, the coming week.

ba'd az īn, *sipas*, *āyanda*, *pas az īn*, henceforth, in future.

'anḳarīb, *dar īn zūdī*, presently.

fi-l-faur, *fi-l-ḥāl*, *bi zūdī*, immediately, instantly, directly.

Time indefinite:—

bārhā, *bisiyār bār*, *bisiyār*, *mukarraraṇ*, often, many a time.

gāh-gāh, occasionally.

gāh waḳte, sometimes.

zūd, soon.

nādir, rarely.

hamesha, always.

paiwasta, constantly.

har rūz, *rūzāna*, daily.

har hafta, *haftagī*, every week.

Time indefinite (*continued*):—

kamtar, very seldom.
har māha, *māhiyāna*, monthly.
har sāla, *sāliyāna*, every year.
har dam, *dam ba dam*, every moment.
bar, *dīgar*, *dīgar-bār*, again.

Quantity:—

andak, a little.
bisiyār, much.
kam, little.
firāwan, *wāfir*, abundantly.
khailī, greatly, much.
kāfī, sufficiently.
bas, enough, only.
hamīn, even this, only, even.

Doubt:—

shāyad, perhaps.
bāshad, it may be.
tawānad, possibly.
būkik, peradventure.

Affirmation:—

hamāna, *har ā,īna*, certainly.
be shak, *lā shak*, *be shubha*, undoubtedly.
albatta, verily.
be hama chīz, without any doubt whatever.
be sākhta, without artifice.

Negation :—

hargiz, ever.
na, no, not.
mutlaḳan, not at all.
hech, not any.
hech waḳt, at no time.
bi hech wajh, in no wise.
hech chīz, nothing whatever.
hech kudām, none whatever.
hech kas, no person.
hech bāb, on no account.

Comparison :—

ziyādat *beshtar* *afzūn* *fuzūn*	more.
bisiyārtar	much more.
akṣ̤ar *ag͟hlab* *beshtarīn*	most.
kamtar *aḳal*	less.
kūchak *k͟hurd*	small.
kamtarīn	least.
kūchaktar *k͟hurdtar*	smaller.
miṣ̤al	alike.
musāwī	equal.
muwāzī	parallel.
rū ba rū *muḳābil* *muḥāzī*	opposite.
muwāzin *ham wazn*	of the same weight.

Arabic nouns in the *accusative* case are used adverbially, as :—

ḳaṣdan, purposely; *mukarraran*, repeatedly.

Examples.

49. I went to see him *once*,	*man yak bār ba dīdan-ash raftam.*
Once upon a time he went to see him,	*bāre ba dīdan-ash raft.*
I went to see him *once only*,	*man yak bār ba dīdan-ash raftam o bas.*
He was *only* two hours with me,	*o dū sā'at ba man būd o bas.*
God *only* knows,	*khudā mī-dānad o bas.*
You asked of me *alone*,	*shumā hamīn tanhā az man pursīded.*
I do not *exactly* recollect; it might have been mid-day,	*durust dar khāṭir-am nīst; mī-tawānist ki ẓuhr bā-shad.*
Think *well;* perhaps it may come into thy re-collection,	*khūb ta,ammul bi-kun shā-yad ba khāṭir-at biyāyad.*
Why, because just as I was returning disappoint-edly from the door of your house, I saw a number of them in the street,	*chirā ki, chūn man maḥrū-māna az dar-i-shumā bar mī-gashtam jama'e az ānhā-rā dar kūcha dī-dam.*
For I have *often* seen them eating their food at two o'clock,	*chi man bisiyār dīdaam ki eshān dar sā'at-i-dū ghizā mī-khurand.*

(*a*) The following require to be followed by the *zer-i-iẓāfat*, or sign of the genitive case.

bālā, upon, aloft.
pā,īn, down.
farāz or *zabar*, above.
zer, below, beneath.
furūd, down.
pesh, before.
pas, after *or* behind.
sū,e, towards, side of.
miyān, between.
pahlū, by the side.
nazd or *nazdīk*, near.
nazdīkī, vicinity.
berūn, out.
andarūn, in.
ḳabl, before.
ba'd, after.
jihat, toward.
jānib, side.
bahar, *barā,e*, for, on account of.
siwā,e, except.

(*b*) All the above in para. (*a*) may take *az before* them, except *ba'd*, which takes *az after* it.

(*c*) The following take *az*, before or after them, at the option of the speaker, as:—

az pas, from behind; *pas az*, after, then, afterwards.
az pesh or *pesh az*, before.
az berūn or *berūn az*, from without.
az baghair or *baghair az*, except.

When *az* is used after the preposition, *zer-i-iẓāfat* is omitted.

(*d*) The preposition *ba* may be prefixed to all the foregoing, but not to the five following:—

sipas, *barā,e*, *bahar*, *ḳabl*, *ba'd*.

Examples.

(*e*) under the ground, *zer-i-zamīn.*
above the tree, *bālā,e darakht.*
near the city, *ba nazdīk-i-shahr.*
after that, *paz az ān.*
before me, *pesh az man* (time); *pesh-i-man* (place).

CONJUNCTIONS.

53. The simple Conjunctions are:—

*wa** or *o*, and.
nīz, *ham*, also, likewise.
gar, *agar*, if.
yā, either, or.
juz, except.
magar, unless, rather.
chi, *ki*, for, as, whether.
amma, *lekin*, but.
balki, but, on the contrary.
chū, *chūn*, when.

---

* The rule for pronouncing the conjunction و, "and," is as follows:—

When it connects sentences and clauses it is pronounced *wa*, as—

he came and went, *āmad wa raft.*

When it connects words in a phrase it is sounded as *o*, sometimes as *u*; for example:—

day and night { *rūz o shab.* / *ruz u shab.* }

In transcribing it into the Roman character, و will be rendered as *o*; but the student must remember the rule given above.

Interjections and Prepositions.

50. Regret or sorrow :—

afsos / *daregh*	alas !	*āh*, a sigh !
		ḥaif, pity !

Grief, distress, want :—

amān, O quarter !	*bedād*, injustice ! tyranny!
faryād, cry !	*yārabb*, O Lord !

Admiration, real and feigned :—

afrīn, create ! (*i. e.* O Lord, let us have more.)
marḥabā, welcome !
tabārak allāh / *bārak allāh* — God is blessed !
allāh akbar, God is omnipotent !
allāh ḳādir, God is powerful !
allāh karīm, God is beneficent !
māshā allāh, God has willed !
inshā allāh, please God !

Lamentation, mourning :—

fighān / *afghān*	lament ! oh ! alas !	*wā,e* / *wā wailā*	oh, misery !

Hatred, contempt :—

uff, fie !

Call to attention:—

ainak, *hān*, *hain* } lo! behold! hark!

ai, O!

Examples.

My brother, I regret, is very seriously ill,	*afsos barādaram ki ba shiddat bīmār ast.*
How well, as God willed, yesterday did your horse run!	*asp-i-shumā dīrūz māshā allāh chi <u>kh</u>ūb dawīd!*

PREPOSITIONS.

51. Prepositions are placed before the simple, or nominative forms, both of Nouns and Pronouns.

"My father went from home to the market,"
Pidar-am az <u>kh</u>āna ba bāzār raft.

They are:—

az, from, by.	*be*, without.
bā, with (in company with).	*tā*, up to, as far as.
bar, *abar*, on, upon.	*juz*, except, besides.
ba, in, by, to.	*dar*, in.

52. The rest of the Prepositions are, properly, Substantives, or Adjectives.

(*a*) The following require to be followed by the *zer-i-iẓāfat*, or sign of the genitive case.

bālā, upon, aloft.
pā,īn, down.
farāz or *zabar*, above.
zer, below, beneath.
furūd, down.
pesh, before.
pas, after *or* behind.
sū,e, towards, side of.
miyān, between.
pahlū, by the side.
nazd or *nazdīk*, near.
nazdīkī, vicinity.
berūn, out.
andarūn, in.
ḳabl, before.
ba'd, after.
jihat, toward.
jānib, side.
bahar, *barā,e*, for, on account of.
siwā,e, except.

(*b*) All the above in para. (*a*) may take *az before* them, except *ba'd*, which takes *az after* it.

(*c*) The following take *az*, before or after them, at the option of the speaker, as:—

az pas, from behind; *pas az*, after, then, afterwards.
az pesh or *pesh az*, before.
az berūn or *berūn az*, from without.
az baghair or *baghair az*, except.

When *az* is used after the preposition, *zer-i-iẓāfat* is omitted.

(*d*) The preposition *ba* may be prefixed to all the foregoing, but not to the five following:—

sipas, *barā,e*, *bahar*, *ḳabl*, *ba'd*.

Examples.

(*e*) under the ground, *zer-i-zamīn.*
above the tree, *bālā,e darakht.*
near the city, *ba nazdīk-i-shahr.*
after that, *paz az ān.*
before me, *pesh az man* (time); *pesh-i-man* (place).

Conjunctions.

53. The simple Conjunctions are :—

*wa** or *o*, and.
nīz, *ham*, also, likewise.
gar, *agar*, if.
yā, either, or.
juz, except.
magar, unless, rather.
chi, *ki*, for, as, whether.
amma, *lekin*, but.
balki, but, on the contrary.
chū, *chūn*, when.

---

* The rule for pronouncing the conjunction و, "and," is as follows :—

When it connects sentences and clauses it is pronounced *wa*, as—

he came and went, *āmad wa raft.*

When it connects words in a phrase it is sounded as *o*, sometimes as *u*; for example :—

day and night { *rūz o shab.* / *ruz u shab.*

In transcribing it into the Roman character, و will be rendered as *o*; but the student must remember the rule given above.

101	۱۰۱	صد و یك	700	۷۰۰	هفتصد
200	۲۰۰	دوصد	800	۸۰۰	هشتصد
300	۳۰۰	سصد	900	۹۰۰	نهصد
400	۴۰۰	چهارصد	1000	۱۰۰۰	هزار
500	۵۰۰	پانصد	10,000	۱۰۰۰۰	ده‌هزار
600	۶۰۰	ششصد	100,000	۱۰۰۰۰۰	تومان لك

55. The numbers occurring between the tens are formed by adding the smaller number to the decade conjunction *o*, as :—

shast o shish, sixty and six.

To find the precise date (Christian) corresponding to any given year of the Hijra.

Let M = Mussulman date in years.
Let E = required English date in years.
Then $E = M \times 0{\cdot}970225 + 621{\cdot}54$.

This is exact to a day.

Days of the Week.

Sunday, *yak shamba.*
Monday, *dū shamba.*
Tuesday, *si shamba.*
Wednesday, *chahār shamba.*
Thursday, *panj shamba.*
Friday, *ādīna.*
Saturday, *shamba.*

DERIVATION OF WORDS.

56. SUBSTANTIVES.

(*a*) The Persian names of Agents are formed by prefixing nouns to contracted participles active, as:—

a seller of roses,	*gul-farosh.*
a cooker of broth (*i.e.* the cook),	*ash-paz.*
a shoemaker,	*kafsh-dūz.*
a hatter,	*kullah-dūz.*
a saddler,	*zīn-sāz.*

The contracted participle is sometimes corrupted, as:—

Bān, a corruption of *mān,* contracted from *mānanda,* "a remainder."

Gar and *gār* a form of *kār.*

Observe that *gar* signifies *a maker,* and that *gār* indicates *a performer.*

Examples.

a gardener,	*bāgh-bān.*
a porter (doorkeeper),	*dar-bān.*
a jailor,	*zindān-bān.*
a goldsmith,	*zargar.*
a blacksmith,	*āhangar.*
a potter,	*kūzagar.*
an attendant,	*khidmatgār.*

Nouns of Place.

(*b*) *Gāh* is added to the noun, as:—

a bed,	*khwāb-gāh*.
a resting-place,	*manzil-gāh*.
a throne-chamber capital of an empire	*takht-gāh*.
the evening,	*shām-gāh*.
halting-place,	*farūd-gāh*.
untimely,	*begāh*.

(*c*) The affixes *istān, zār, kada, dān, sār, lākh,* may be used, as:—

a rose-garden,	*gulistān*.
a salt place	*namak-zār*. *shūra-zār*.
an idol temple,	*būt kada*.
a fire temple,	*ātash kada*.
a penholder,	*ḳalam dān*.
a mountainous country,	*koh sār*.
a rough, stony place,	*sang lākh*.
a demon-haunted place,	*dew lākh*.

Diminutives.

57. A diminutive is formed by adding one of the four affixes كَ , گَ , چِه and ه to a noun.

(*a*) The affixes َك , َكه and ه only are used in the case of rational beings, as :—

a small man, *mardak.*
a small woman, *zanak.*
a small girl, *du<u>kh</u>tarak.*

In an endearing sense, as :—

My poor dear little child is sick, *t̤iflak-i-man bīmār ast.*

(*b*) In a contemptible sense َكه is used.

O thou fellow! *ai mardaka.*
Why, this woman! *ai zanaka.*

(*c*) In the case of persons not grown up it is sufficient to add ه (*h*) only, as :—

a naughty boy, *pisara,*
a good-for-nothing girl, *du<u>kh</u>tara.*

(*d*) The only affix used in the case of an irrational being is َك , as :—

a small horse, *aspak.*
a small ass, *<u>kh</u>arak.*

At the same time the adjectives *kūchak* or *<u>kh</u>urd* may be used, as :—

a small horse, *aspak-i-kūchak.*

The affix may denote pity, or compassion, as :—

the poor tired ox, *gāwak-i-khasta.*
the poor wretched ass, *kharak-i-miskīn.*

It is usual, however, to add ک (*k*) to the generic noun,* as :—

poor little creature, *ḥaiwānak.*
poor little bird, *murghak.*
poor jaded beast, *ḥaiwānak-i-khaṣta.*
the weak miserable animal, *jānwarak-i-ẓa'īf.*

(*e*) The affixes ک and چه are used with inanimate objects, as :—

a little pond, *ḥauẓak.*
a small garden, *bāghcha.*

(*f*) The affix ک is used when a noun is to be applied in an unusual way, as :—

significant wink of the eye, *chashmak.*
clapping the hands, *dastak,* from *dast,* the hand.
listening by stealth, *goshak,* „ *gosh,* the ear.
making a somersault, *pushtak,* „ *pusht,* the back.

---

* The word *murgh* applies to all birds.
„ „ *ḥaiwān* „ „ domestic animals and fish.
„ „ *jānwar* „ „ wild beasts, reptiles, and vermin.
„ „ *gardshanda* „ reptiles only.

ABSTRACT AND VERBAL NOUNS.

58. An *abstract noun* may be formed from an *adjective*, simple or compound, or from a *noun*, by the addition of *yāe ma'rūf*, as, ى.

(*a*) From an adjective :—

goodness, *nekī*, from *nek*, good.
the possessing of the world, royalty, *jahān dārī*, from *jahān dār*, world-possessing.
idleness, *bekārī*, from *bekār*, idle.

(*b*) From a noun :—

friendship, *dostī*, from *dost*, a friend.
manliness, *mardī*, from *mard*, a man.
entertainment, *mihmānī*, from *mihmān*, a guest.
sovereignty, *bādshāhī*, from *bādshāh*, a king.

If the primitive word ends in obscure ه, the ه is suppressed, and the letter گ is inserted, as :—

sadness, *āzurdagī*, from *āzurda*, sad.
infamy, *bachchagī*, „ *bachcha*, a child.
slavery, *bandagī*, „ *banda*, a slave.

59. *Verbal Nouns* are formed by changing ن of the infinitive into ار, as :—

speech, *guftār*, from *guftan*.
motion, *raftār*, „ *raftan*.
seeing, *dīdār*, „ *dīdan*

This termination occasionally gives the sense of agent, as :—

seller, *kharīdār*, from *kharīdan*.
purchaser, *farokhtār*, „ *farokhtan*.

The third person singular of the preterite may be placed (*a*) before the imperative of the same verb, (*b*) or before the third person singular of the preterite of the same or another verb, as :—

(*a*) conversation, *guft-gū,e*, or *guft-o-gū,e*.
search, *just-jū*.
buying and selling, *kharīd o farosh*.

(*b*) buying and selling, *kharīd o farokht*.
coming and going { *āmad o raft*. / *āmad o shud*. }

(*c*) To express suitableness, ي *yā,e ma'rūf*, or *yā,e liyāḳat*, is added to the infinitive, as :—

fit to be done, *kardanī*.
fit to eat, *khurdanī*.

(*d*) A noun may be formed from the root by adding ي (*ī*) or ش (*ish*) as :—

speaking, conversation, *go,ī*, from *go*, root of *guftan*.
creation, *afrīnish*, from *afrīn*, root of *afrīdan*.
burning, inflammation, *sozish*, from *soz*, root of *sokhtan*.

motion, going, path, *rawī*, from *rau*, root of *raftan*.
knowledge, *danī*, from *dān*, root of *dānistan*.

(*e*) The root itself may be used, as :—

ardour, *soz*, from *sokhtan*, to burn.
grief, *ranj*, ,, *ranjīdan*, to grieve.
know, *dān*, ,, *dānistan*, to know.

(*f*) A noun may be formed by adding اك , ان (peculiar to verbs in *ūdan*) or ه , as :—

inflammation, *sozūk*, from *sokhtan*, to burn.
an order, *farmān*, ,, *farmūdan*, to order.
trembling, *larza*, ,, *larzīdan*, to tremble.

Adjectives.

60. Adjectives denoting possession, plenty, mixture, are formed by adding to nouns the particles آ , سار , گِین , آگِین , مَند , ناك , وار , وَر and اِین , as :—

learned, *dānā*, from *dān*, know.
ashamed, *sharmsār*, ,, *sharm*, shame.
sorrowful, *ghamgīn*, ,, *gham*, sorrow.
bashful, *sharmāgīn*, ,, *sharm*, shame.
wealthy, *daulatmand*, ,, *daulat*, wealth.

frightful, *khauf-nāk*, from *khauf*, fear.

learned { *dānishwar*, or *dānishwār* } „ *dānish*, knowledge.

golden, *zarīn*, „ *zar*, gold.

(*b*) The particles آسا, دسیس, دس, سا, سار, وَش and سَان added to nouns form adjectives denoting similitude, as:—

like musk, *mushkāsā*.
like the sun, *khurdīs*.
like magic, *sihrsā*.
like dust (*i.e.* humble), *khāk-sār*.
like the moon (*i.e.* beautiful,) *māhwash*.
like the sun, *khurshīd-sān*.

(*c*) The particles *fām* (*pām*, *wām*), *gūn* and *īn* denote resemblance in respect to colour, as:—

black-coloured, *siyah-fām*.
rose-coloured, *gul-gūn*.
emerald-coloured, *zumurradīn*.
ruby-coloured, *l'al-fām*.
tulip-coloured, *lāla-gūn*.
azure-coloured, *āb-gūn*.

(*d*) Some adjectives to express fulness and completeness are repeated, the letter آ being inserted between them, as:—

brimful, *labālab*, from *lab*, lip.
entirely, *sarāsar*, from *sar*, head.
of various colours, *gūnāgūn*, from *gūn*, colour.

(*e*) Adjectives may be formed from nouns by adding ی *yā,e ma'rūf*, as:—

Persian, *īrānī* (*'ajamī*), from *īrān* (*'ajam*), Persian.
Indian, *hindī*, from *hind*, India.
of the city of Shīrāz, *shīrāzī*, from *shīrāz*, city of Shīrāz.
of the city of Baghdād, *baghdādī*, from *baghdād*, city of Baghdād.
a town, *shahrī*, from *shahr*, a city.
of the sea, *baḥrī*, from *baḥr*, sea.

(*f*) The particles وار and انه are added to denote fitness, as:—

fit for a prince, *shāhwār* or *shāhāna*.
fit for a maniac, *dewāna*.
fit for a man, *mardāna*.
fit for women, *zanāna*.

(*g*) The ordinal number is formed by adding *um* to the cardinal, as:—

the seventh, *haftum*, from *haft*, seven.
the twenty-seventh, *bīst o haftum*.

The three first ordinals are exceptions to this rule, as:—

first, *nakhustīn, awwal.*
second, *duwum* or *dūyum.*
third, *siwum* or *siyum.*
book the first, *bāb-i-awwal.*

(*h*) By adding *a* to a noun, preceded by a numeral, a compound adjective will be formed, as:—

of one day's duration, *yak rūza*, from *yak rūz*, one day.
one year old, *yak sāla*, from *yak sāl*, one year.
a man aged 30 years, *mard sī sāla*, from *mard sī sāl.*
fickle, *dū dila*, from *dū dil*, two hearts.

Verbs.

61. The principal derivative verbs are causal verbs, and are derived from Arabic roots by adding *īdan*, as:—

to seek, to send for, *talabīdan*, from *talab*, search.
to understand, *fahmīdan*, from *fahm*, understanding.

Adverbs.

62. A list of Adverbs has been already given (see p. 54).

Adjectives ending in *āna* and *wār* may be considered as adverbs, as:—

in the manner of a pedestrian, *piyāda-wār*.
wisely, *'aklāna.*
bravely, *dilīrāna.*

COMPOUND WORDS.

63. SUBSTANTIVES.

(*a*) Two nouns may be used in juxtaposition in the reverse order of the genitive, the sign of *izāfat* being rejected, as:—

the counsel-book, *pand-nāma.*
the day-book, *rūz-nāma.*
the cook-house, *bāwarchi-khāna.*
the battle-field, *razm-gāh.*
the asylum of the world, *jahān-panāh.*

(*b*) Two contracted infinitives may be used, connected by و, as:—

speaking and hearing (*i.e.* conversation), *guft o shunīd.*
coming and going, *āmad o raft, āmad o shud.*

(*c*) A contracted infinitive with the corresponding root may be used, as:—

conversation, *guft o go* or *guft-go.*
search, *just o jū,* or *just-jū.*

(*d*) Two substantives of the same, or of different significations, may be used, as:—

boundary and region (*i.e.* empire), *marz o būm.*
water and air (*i.e.* climate), *āb o hawā.*
growing and increasing (*i.e.* rearing), *nashwˀ o numāˀ.*

(e) An infinitive preceded by نا is rendered negative, as:—

the non-hearing, *nā shunīdan*.

نا corresponds with the English prefixes *un*, *in* or *non*.
نه „ „ negation *no*, *not*.

(f) A numeral and a substantive may be used, as:—

the afternoon, *si-pahar*.
a quadruped, *chahār-pā,e*.
Sunday, *yak-shamba*.

Adjectives.

64. Compound Adjectives may be formed as follows:—

(a) Of two nouns, both Arabic, both Persian, or one of each, as:—

fairy-faced, *parī rukhsār* or *parī rū,e*.
angelic disposition, *malak akhlāḳ*.
lion-hearted, *sher-dil*.
generous disposition, *karīm ṭab'*.
rose-bud mouthed, *ghuncha dahān*.
ruby-lipped, *yaḳūt lab*.
army numerous as the stars, *anjum sipāh*
kingly pomp, *sultanat dastgāh*.
justly disposed, *adālat ā,īn*.
melancholy-minded, *maḥzūn khāṭir*.

jessamine-scented, *saman bū,e.*
perspicuous in speech, *faṣīḥ kalām.*
resembling the sea, *daryā miṣāl.*
eloquent in discourse, *balīgh khitāb.*

(*b*) Of an adjective prefixed to a noun, as:—

handsome-faced, *khūb rū,e.*
pure-hearted, *ṣāf dil.*
simple-minded, *ṣalīm ḳalb.*
well-disposed, *pākīza khū,e.*
right-minded (benevolent), *nek maḥzar.*
pleasant chanting, *khūsh ilḥān.*
ugly-faced, *zisht rū,e.*
hard-hearted, *sangīn dil.*
sour-browed, *turush abrū.*
pure-minded, *ṣāf zamīr.*
pure-natured, *pāk ṭīnat.*
black-eyed, *siyāh chashm.*
sweet-tongued, *shirīn zabān.*
red-faced, *surkh rū,e.*
grey-haired, *safaid mū,e.*
ill-tempered, *kaj khulḳ.*
bitter in speech, *talkh guftār.*
sharp-witted, *tez fahm.*
swift-footed, *sabuk sair.*
ill-mannered, *bad ravish.*
pure-natured, *pāk ṭabī'at.*

of good morals, *nek akhlāḳ.*
clear in judgment, *rūshan 'aḳl.*
broken-hearted, *shikasta dil.*
distressed in heart, *tang dil.*

(*c*) Of a verbal root added to a substantive or adjective, as:—

world-conquering, *jahān-gīr.*
enemy-enslaving, *'adūw-band.*
pearl-scattering, *durr-afshān.*
amber-scented, *'ambar-āgīn.*
hero-overthrowing, *mard-afgan.*
heart-afflicting, *dil-azār.*
rose-scattering, *gul-afshān.*
assembly-adorning, *majlis-ārā.*
soul-refreshing, *rūḥ-āsā.*
fault-forgiving, *khaṭā-bakhsh.*
delight-increasing, *bahjat-afzā.*
town-disturbing, *shahr-āshūb.*
being covered with dust, *ghubār-ālūd.*
blood-shedding, *khūn-rez.*
being mixed with honey, *shahd-āmez.*
world-illuminating, *gītī-afrūz.*
fear-increasing, *waḥshat-afzā.*
dread-inspiring, *dihshat-angez.*
battle-seeking, *jang-jū.*
early rising, *saḥar-khez.*

self-indulging, *tan parwar.*
light-spreading, *ẓiyā gustar.*
stranger-cherishing, *gharīb niwār.*
heart-expanding, *dil-kushā.*
perfume-diffusing, *'iṭr-bez.*
soul-creating, *jān-afrīn.*
sweet-singer, *khūsh khwān.*
rank (of battle) breaking, *ṣaff shikan.*

(*d*) Of a past-participle added to a substantive, as:—

shame-stricken, *khajlat zada.*
stricken with darkness, *zulmat zada.*
experienced, *jahān dīda.*
" " *wāḳ'ia dīda.*
one who has been tried in battle, *jang azmūda.*
one who has laid a snare, *dām nihāda.*
one who has endured affliction, *miḥnat kashīda.*

(*e*) Of a substantive with the prefix با, as:—

possessed of wealth, *bā-māl.*
cheerful, *bā-rāmish.*

(*f*) Of a substantive with the prefix بے as:—

senseless, *be khirad.*
without discrimination, *be tamīr.*
heartless, *be dil.*

unjust, *be inṣāf.*
careless, *be bāk.*
irreligious, *be dīn.*

(*g*) Of a substantive with the prefix هم, "together," "with," as:—

being in the same house,	*ham-khāna.*
„ associates,	„ *ṣuḥbat.*
„ „	„ *rāh.*
„ „	„ *'umr.*
„ „	„ *nishīn.*
„ bed-fellows,	„ *bistar.*
„ confidants,	„ *rāz.*
„ in the same school (*i.e.* school-fellows)	„ *maktab.*
„ intimate,	„ *dam.*
sympathising,	„ *dard.*
a playfellow,	„ *bāz.*

(*h*) Of a substantive with the prefix کم, as:—

of little value,	*kam-bahā.*
thin-bearded,	„ *rīsh.*
of little resource,	„ *māya.*
with little experience,	„ *tajriba.*

(*i*) By prefixing نا to (1) an adjective; (2) a verbal root; (3) a past participle; (4) a substantive.

(1) To an adjective, as :—

impure, *nā pāk.*

of impure intention, *nā pāk-rāe.*

(2) To a verbal root :—

ignorant, *nā dān.*

(3) To a past participle :—

not commended, *nā sitūda.*

(4) To a substantive :—

worthless, *nā kār.*

not according to one's desire, *nā kām.*

unmanly, *nā mard.*

Verbs.

65. Persian Verbs may be added to Substantives, Adjectives, Participles, Prepositions and Adverbs.

(*a*) To substantives, as :—

to seek justice, *dād khwāstan.*

to mix colours, *rang amekhtan.*

an opinion, *rā,e zadan.*

(*b*) To an adjective, as :—

to do good, *nek warzīdan.*

to become sick, *bīmār shudan.*

(*c*) To a participle or noun of agency, as :—

to become a searcher, *jūyanda gardīdan.*

to sit smiling, *khandān nishistan.*

(*d*) To particles, as:—

to come in, *dar āmadan.*
„ rise up, *bar khāstan.*
„ sit down, *faro nishistan.*
„ soar upwards, *bālā parīdan.*
„ go up, *bālā raftan.*
„ come down, *pā,īn āmadan.*

(*e*) The verbs *kardan*, *sākhtan*, *farmūdan* and *namūdan* are often used with substantives and adjectives in the sense of *making*, as:—

to make an order, *ḥukm kardan.*
„ make content, *khushnūd sākhtan.*
„ pay attention, *iltifāt namūdan.*
„ peruse a letter, *muṭāla'a farmūdan.*

(*f*) The verbs *dāshtan* and *zadan* are sometimes used in the sense of making, as:—

to keep watch, *pās dāshtan.*
„ make search, *ṭalab dāshtan.*
„ express an opinion, *rā,e zadan.*
„ speak, *ḥaraf zadan.*

(*g*) The verbs *khụrdan* and *dīdan* are used in the sense of "to suffer," or "experience," as:—

to grieve, *gham khụrdan.*
„ be grieved, *ghuṣṣa khụrdan.*
„ feel regret, *ta,assuf khụrdan.*

to suffer affliction, *miḥnat dīdan.*
„ smell, *bū,e dīdan.*
„ experience kindness, *iḥsān dīdan.*

(*h*) The following verbs are chiefly used in compounds :—

to bring, *āwardan.*
„ become (passive), *shudan.*
„ „ (to turn), *gashtan.*
„ „ („), *gardīdan.*
„ bear, *burdan.*
„ be, *būdan.*
„ come, *āmadan.*
„ devour, suffer, *kh̲ụrdan.*
„ do, make, *kardan.*
„ draw, undergo, *kashīdan.*
„ find, *yāftan.*
„ have, *dāshtan.*
„ make, *sākh̲tan.*
„ order, *farmūdan.*
„ see, *dīdan.*
„ strike, *zadan.*
„ sit, *nishistan.*
„ search, *justan.*
„ show, *ṇamūdan.*
„ take, *giriftan.*
„ wish, ask, *kh̲wāstan.*

Examples.

to apologise, *'uẕr kẖẉāstan.*
„ assault, *hujūm āwardan.*
„ appear, *ṭāli' āmadan.*
„ be astonished, *muta'ajjab gardīdan.*
„ „ „ *shudan.*
„ „ *ta'ajjub kardan.*
„ „ „ *namūdan.*
„ „ „ *dāshtan.*
„ „ *'ajab āwardan.*
to be beneficent, *iḥsān farmūdan.*
„ be bereaved, *hijrān dīdan.*
„ believe, *'itiḳād dāshtan.*
„ „ „ *namūdan.*
„ „ „ *āwardan.*
„ „ „ *kardan.*
„ complete, *tamām kardan.*
„ „ „ *farmūdan.*
„ „ „ *sākẖtan.*
„ „ „ *namūdan.*
„ envy, *ḥasad burdan.*
„ expect, *intiẓār kashīdan.*
„ „ „ *kardan.*
„ „ „ *burdan.*
„ „ „ *namūdan.*
„ „ „ *dāshtan.*

to expect, *muntaẓir gardīdan.*
" " " *būdan.*
" " " *shudan.*
" " " *nishistan.*
" find (others) disappointed, *maḥrūm yāftan.*
" find fault, *'aib justan.*
" be grieved, *ghuṣṣa khurdan.*
" take profit, *nafa' giriftan.*
" return, *rujū' namūdan.*
" be sorrowful, *maghmūn būdan*

The student should observe the different ways in which the verbs "To be astonished," "To believe," "To complete," "To expect," are rendered.

Thus *intizār,* "expecting," takes the active verbs *kardan, kashīdan, namūdan,* &c., while *muntaẓir,* "one who expects," takes the neuter verbs *būdan, shudan, gardīdan, nishistan,* &c.

Similarly the other verbs may be rendered.

SYNTAX.

Arrangement of Words.

In prose compositions the nominative is put first, then the object or complement, and, lastly, the verb, as:—

the mughal purchased the parrot,	*mug͟hal ṭuṭī-rā k͟harīd.*
Timur arrived in India,	*tīmūr ba hindūstān rasīd.*

Words and phrases denoting time, manner, &c., when they apply to a whole sentence, are placed first, as:—

one day, in a certain city, a darwesh went to the shop of a certain trader,	*rūze, dar shahre, darweshe bar dukān-i-baḳḳāle raft.*

When the complement to a verb is a complete sentence it is put last, as:—

that man said, "Do you consider me a fool?"	*ān mard guft, marā aḥmaḳ mī-pindārī?*
a certain king saw in a dream that the whole of his teeth had dropped out.	*pādshāhe dar k͟hẉāb dīd ki tamām-ī-dandānhā,e-o uftāda and.*

When the object is qualified by a relative sentence the object is placed before the verb, and the qualifying phrase after it, as:—

I have heard of a king who issued the order for the executing of a certain captive.	*pādshāhe-rā shunīdam ki ba kushtanī-e-asīre ishārat kard.*
they relate of one of the kings of Persia, that he extended the hand of usurpation over the property of the people.	*yake-rā az mulūk-i-'ajam ḥikāyat kunana ki dast-i-taṭāwul ba māl-i-ra'iyat darāz kard.*

Construction of Substantives, Adjectives, and Prepositions.

Adjectives are indeclinable.

The adjective usually follows the noun which it qualifies, as:—

a good man fears God,	*mard-i-khūb az khudā mī-tarsad.*
my black horse was in the stable,	*asp-i-siyāh-i-man dar ṭawīla būd.*

When the noun is in apposition, the adjective may either precede or follow the substantive.

The word immediately before the verb has usually *yā,e ma'rūf,** as:—

thy father is a good man, *padar-i-tū mard-i-khūb īst;* or, *padar-i-tū khūb mard īst.*

---

* The full form is: *paḍar-i-tū khūb marde ast,* in which *yā,e mahjūl* is used.

London is a great city, *landan shahr īst bisiyār buzurg*; or, *landan bisiyār shahr-i-buzurgīst*; or, *landan bisiyār buzurg shahr īst*; or, *landan shahr-i-bisiyār buzurg īst.*

If the adjective express more than a simple quality, such as *good* or *bad*, or if it be of Arabic origin, it should be placed *after* the noun, whether expressed before or after the verb, as:—

thy servant is a bad man, *naukar-i-tū mard-i-sharīr** *īst*; or, *naukar-i-tū mardīst sharīr*. (It would be wrong to say, *naukar-i-tū sharīr mardīst*).

Adverbs should be placed immediately before the adjective; sometimes the second noun may intervene, as:—

England is a very good kingdom, *ingland mamlakat-ī-bisiyār khubīst*; or, *ingland bisiyār mamlakat-i-khūbīst*; or, *ingland khailī khūb mamlakate ast*; or, *ingland mamlakate ast khailī khūb*.

---

* *Sharīr* is Arabic. One might say:—
naukar-i-tū bad marde ast.

When the adjective *precedes* the substantive, it will be noticed the mark of *iẓāfat* is not used. In Persian this construction is called the inverted epithet.

The names of places and rivers are placed *after* the words city, town, &c., with the *iẓāfat* between them, as:—

the river Euphrates, *daryā,e farāt.*

The *iẓāfat* sometimes supplies the place of the conjunction و, as:—

a mistress with rosy cheeks *and* honied speech, *yār-i-gul 'iẕār-i-shīrīn sukhan.*

Two nouns, in common use, *sometimes* omit the *iẓāfat;* they are:—

a companion, master
a possessor of, endowed with } *ṣāḥib.*
head, top, extremity, *sar,*

as:—

a possessor of wealth,	*ṣāḥib māl.*
possessed of skill,	*ṣāḥib hunar.*
fountain-head,	*sar chashma.*
head of the way,	*sar-rāh.*
source of wealth, capital,	*sar-māya.*

The following noun is used with the Arabic *al,* "the":—

a lord, master, endowed with, *ẕū.*

as :—

possessed of dignity, *z̲ū-l-jalāl.*
possessed of motion, *z̲ū-l-ḥarakat.*
possessed of life, *z̲ū-l-ḥayāt.*
Alexander the Great, *z̲ū-l-ḳarnain.*
(two-horned or powerful).

The following noun, similar to those just mentioned, takes the *iẓāfat*, as :—

people belonging to any profession, an inhabitant, lord, master, worthy, fit, endowed with } *ahl.*

as :—

veiled, *ahl-i-ḥijāb.*
an artificer, *ahl-i-san'at.*
a councillor of state, *ahl-i-dewān.*
a traveller, *ahl-i-siyāḥat.*

COMPOUND ADJECTIVES.

Any noun with a particle prefixed to it may become an epithet, as :—

a man possessed of wealth, *mard-i-bāmāl.*

Some epithets consist of several words, as :—

a country taken in war, *mulk-i-bajang girifta.*
a slave with a ring in his ear, *banda,e ḥalḳa bagosh.*
the All-wise, who endows the tongue with speech, *ḥakīm-i-sukhan bar zabān āfrīn.*

NUMERAL ADJECTIVES.

Numeral adjectives precede the substantives to which they belong. The noun must always be in the *singular* number, as :—

a thousand men, *hazār mard* (not) *hazār mardān.*
twenty brave men, *bīst mard-i-dilāwar* (not) *bīst mardān-i-dilāwar.*

The greatest number should be expressed first; the rest following in the same order, as :—

two hundred and fifty-four thousand seven hundred and eighty-three sheep,	*dū ṣad o panjāh o chahār hazār o haft ṣad o hashtād dū si gūsfand.*

From eleven to nineteen, however, the smaller number is expressed first. (See p. 65.)

A *definite* noun may be used in the plural number to answer the cardinal number, as :—

the men were two thousand,	*mardān dū hazār būdand.*

Sometimes a phrase from the Arabic is introduced as an epithet to a Persian substantive, as :—

a darwesh whose prayers are answered,	*darwesh-i-mustajābu-d-da'wāt.*
a man sincere of speech, generous of soul,	*mard-i-ṣādiḳu-l-ḳaul karīmu-n-nafs.*

The adjective pronouns *ān, īn,* precede their substantives.

Some adjectives of a pronominal nature, as *hama,* "all," *dīgar,* "other," *chand,* "some," or "several," precede or follow their substantives; for example:—

all the people,	*hama mardumān;* or, *mardumān-i-hama.*
the other woman,	*dīgar zan;* or, *zan-i-dīgar.*
some, or several days,	*chand rūz;* or, *rūz-i-chand.*

COMPARISON.

The word *than* after the comparative degree is expressed in Persian by *az,* as:—

more splendid than the sun,	*roshantar az āftāb.*
women are more delicate than men,	*zanān nāzuk-tar az mardān and.*

Sometimes *bih,* "good," in the positive form, is used, when denoting comparison, for "better," as:—

silence is better than evil-speaking; but speaking well is better than silence,	*k͟hāmoshī bih az suk͟han-i-bad ast; wa suk͟han-i-nek bih az k͟hāmoshī.*

The superlative degree governs the genitive as:—

the best of men,	*nektarīn-i-mardumān.*
they say that the meanest of animals is the ass,	*goyand ki kamtarīn-i-jānwarān <u>kh</u>ar ast.*

The same rule applies to superlative forms from the Arabic, as:—

the most illustrious of the Prophets,	*ashraf-i-ambiyā.*

The particles called prepositions are few in number. The most common are:—

Az, " from," *bā,* " with," *bar,* " on," *ba,* " in, into," *be,* " without," *tā,* " till," " as far as," *juz,* " except," " besides," and *dar,* " in."

Prepositions take the simple or nominative form of a noun or pronoun after them, as:—

from Ba<u>gh</u>dad to Shiraz I will go with thee,	*az ba<u>gh</u>dād tā shīrāz bā tū <u>kh</u>wāham raft.*

Such other words as are used like prepositions require *zer-i-iẓāfat*, as:—

near the minister,	*nazd-i-wazīr;* or, *ba nazd-i-wazīr.*
above his head,	*bālā,e sarash.*
before me,	*pesh-i-man;* or, *dar pesh-i-man.*
under the earth,	*zer-i-zamīn.*

PRONOUNS.

The affixes are :—

Pers.	*Sing.*		*Plur.*	
1. my	اَم	*am,*	our	مان *mān.*
2. thy	اَت	*at,*	your	تان *tān.*
3. his	اَش	*ash,*	their	شان *shān.*

Mention has already been made (see page 28 Gr.) of the use of these affixes when attached to nouns. It will be sufficient in this place to add that the plural terminations are rarely used; and that when the noun to which the affix belongs is in construction with an adjective, the affix is usually added to the *adjective,* as :—

thy dear life, *'umr-i-azízat.*

The affixes ام , ات , اش may be employed to denote the dative and accusative cases *to me, to thee,* or *me, thee,* &c., as well as the possessives *my, thy, his.*

The affixes may be joined to the verb which governs them, or to any word* in the sentence, as :—

* Except the simple prepositions and a few of the conjunctions, as *wa* and *yā.*

the porter did not admit me,	*darbā-nam rahū na kard.*
the earth has so much consumed it,	*khāk-ash chunān bukhurd.*

Sometimes there is ambiguity; thus, in the first sentence, *darbā-nam*, by itself, might mean *my porter*. In a case of this kind the context must be considered.

The reciprocal pronoun خود corresponds to our pronoun *self*, as:—

I myself,	*man khud.*
thou thyself,	*tū khud.*

It may be the nominative to *any person* of the verb, the termination of the verb showing sufficiently the sense, as:—

I myself went,	*khud raftam.*
they themselves went,	*khud raftand.*

It is used as a substitute for a possessive pronoun, as:—

the goldsmith went to *his* house,	*zargar ba khāna,e khud raft.*
I was coming from *my* garden,	*man az bāgh-i-khud āmadam.*
Zaid beat his (*own*) slave,	*Zaid ghulām-i-khud-rā zad.*
Zaid beat his (*another's*) slave,	*Zaid ghulām-i-o-rā zad.*

The affix *khudash* is used in the third person singular, as:—

I saw Zaid in his (*own*) house,	*Zaid-rā dar khāna-e khud-ash dīdam.*

Demonstrative Pronouns, *īn* and *ān*.

When the name of an irrational being, or of an inanimate object has been mentioned, and reference is afterwards made to it by a pronoun (as *it* or *they*), *īn* and *ān*, with their plurals are used, as:—

the lion said the painter of it was a man,	*sher guft muṣawwir-i-īn insān ast.*
the wise men were at a loss in the explanation of it,	*ḥukamā az tāwīl-i-ān 'ājiz mandand.*

The phrases *ān-i-man, ān-i-tū, az ān-i-man, az ān-i-tū*, &c., are equivalent to the English words, *mine, thine*, &c., as:—

the throne of Egypt is thine,	*maṣnad-i-miṣr ān-i-tūst.*
whose house was this originally?	*īn khāna awwal az ān-i-ki būd?*
he said, that of my grandfather's,	*guft az ān-i-jaddam.*
when he died, whose did it become?	*chūn o bi-guzasht az ān-i-ki shud?*

he said, that of my father's,	*guft az ān-i-padar-am.*

كه and چه are simply connectives, not relatives, as :—

I saw a prince who possessed wisdom,	*malik-zāda-rā dīdam ki 'aḳl dāsht.*

After *ki*, *o* is understood, "that he."

the fool who sets up a camphor candle in a clear day.	*abla,e ki o* (usually written *ko*) *rūz-i-rūshan shama'-i-kāfūrī nihad.*

Example in the genitive :—

many a renowned personage have they deposited beneath the dust, of whose existence (*lit.*, that of his existence) no trace remains on the face of the earth,	*bas nāmwar ki zer-i-zamīn dafn karda and ki az* (usually written *kaz*) *hastiyash ba rū,e zamīn yak nishān na mānad.*

Again :—

I am not he whose back you will see in the day of battle (*lit.*, that you should see my back),	*ān na man bāsham ki rūz-i-jang bīnī pusht-i-man.*

Example in the dative:—

O (thou) to whom my person appeared contemptible (*lit.*, that my person appeared to thee),	*ai ki shakhṣ-i-manat ḥaḳīr namūd.*

Example in the accusative:—

he whom I beheld all fat, like the pistachio nut (*lit.*, he that I saw him),	*ān ki chūn pista dīdam ash hama maghz.*

Example in the ablative:—

that (proceeding) in which there is suspicion of danger,	*ān ki dar wai mazzina,e khaṭr ast.*

The terms *harki, harchi* correspond respectively to "whosoever," "whatsoever." *Harki* refers to rational beings; *harchi* to inferior animals or inanimate objects.

For example:—

whosoever shall wash his hands of life, the same will utter whatever he has on his mind,	*harki dast az jān bishūyad, harchi dar dil dārad bigoyad.*

When a substantive is expressed after *har*, the particle *ki* may follow, as:—

everything which,	*har chīz ki.*

When *yā,e majhūl* is added to a noun, followed by *ki* or *chi*, the substantive is rendered more definite, as :—

envy is such a torment that it is impossible to escape from its pangs except by death,	*ḥasad ranje ast ki az mashakkat-i-ān juz ba marg na tawān rast.*

The particles *ki* and *chi*, when used interrogatively, are to be considered as substantives, as :—

whose horse may that be?	*ān asp-i-ki bāshad?*
to whom are they speaking?	*kirā mī-goyand?*
who are they?	*eshan kiyand?*
on account of what are you come?	*az bahar-i-chi āmadaī?*
for what did you go?	*chirā raftī?*

The particle *tā* is frequently added to numerals; it implies individuality, as :—

I have two or three letters to write (*lit.*, two or three individual letters),	*man ham dū si tā kāghaz dāram binawīsam.*

When two nouns come together, so as to form one compound word, the genitive is formed by adding *az* to the first noun, which should be made definite by affixing *yā,e waḥdat*, or by prefixing a numeral, as :—

a sword of steel, *shamshīre az fūlād,* or *shamshīr-i-fūlādī.*

two swords of steel, *dū shamshīr az fūlād.*

Concord of Verbs.

If the nominative to a verb be expressive of rational beings, the verb will agree with its nominative, as:

the brothers were vexed, *barādarān ranjīdand.*

Two or more nouns, in the singular, require a plural verb, as:—

the goldsmith and carpenter seized the images, *zargar wa najjār butān-rā giriftand.*

If the nominative to a verb be expressive of irrational beings, the verb is *usually* in concord with its nominative; but sometimes it is in the singular, as:—

four horses were killed, *chahār asp kushta shudand;* or, *chahār asp kushta shud.*

the animals of the forest made a noise, *jānwarān-i-besha āwāz namūdand.*

When two or more nouns (expressive of distinct genera) have a common verb, the verb will be in the plural, as:—

the horse and the ass are not of the same genus,	asp wa k͟har az yak jins nīstand.
a horse, an ass, and an ox were killed,	aspe, wa k͟hare, wa gāwe kushta shudand.

In respect to nouns representing inanimate objects, the verb is sometimes made to agree with its nominative, sometimes put in the singular.

It is not absolutely necessary to use a verb in the singular when the nominative is in the plural; at the same time the verb is often so used, *especially in the passive voice*, by eminent writers and correct speakers. In the Active Voice the verb should usually agree with its nominative. For example :—

the houses of the people were destroyed,	k͟hānahā,e mardum k͟harāb shudand ; or, k͟hānahā,e mardum k͟harāb shud.
the houses of this city are very small,	k͟hānahā,e īn shahr bisiyār kūchak and ; rarely, k͟hānahā,e īn shahr bisiyār kūchak ast.

If several nouns representing *distinct* classes of objects have a common verb, the verb will be in the plural, as :—

water, fire and earth are of opposite nature,	āb, ātash wa k͟hāk az azdād-i-yak dīgar and.

If, however, tney be of the same *quality* or *class*, the verb may be in the plural, but is usually in the singular, as :—

in our garden grapes, figs, and apples are not to be found,	*dar bāgh-i-mā angūr wa anjīr wa seb yāft na mī-shavad;* or, rarely, *na mī-shavand.*
at this season snow, rain, hail, thunder, and lightning frequently come together,	*dar īn mausim baraf wa bārān wa tagarg wa ra'd wa barḳ mukarrar bāham mī-āyad;* or, rarely, *mī-āyand.*

If the nouns be expressive of things which have no material existence; *e.g.*, time, day, night, joy, grief, &c., the verb is usually put in the singular, as :—

grief, joy, death, life, all come from God,	*gham wa shādī wa marg wa zindagī hama az khudā mī-āyad.*
manliness and generosity make this demand,	*jawān-mardī wa muruwat chunīn iḳtizā mī-kunad.*

When a numeral precedes a noun the latter does not require the plural termination; yet if the noun express a rational being, the verb will be in the plural, as :—

ten darweshes will sleep on one carpet,	*dah darwesh dar gīlīme bi-khuspand.*

Irrational beings and inanimate objects take the verb in the singular, as:—

a hundred thousand horses were ready,	*ṣad hazār asp ḥāẓir shud.*
there were two thousand rooms and a thousand vestibules,	*dū hazār ghurfa wa hazār aiwān būd.*

Nouns of multitude, denoting rational beings, are followed by verbs in the singular or plural, according to the unity or plurality of the idea conceived in the mind of the speaker, thus:—

to the just monarch the people is an army,	*shāhinshāh-i-'ādil-rā ra'īyat lashkar ast.*
a gang of Arab thieves had settled on the summit of a certain mountain,	*ṭā,ifa,e duzdān-i-'arab bar sar-i-kohe nishista būdand.*
the whole nation through partiality flocked to him,	*khalke ba ta'aṣṣab bar o gird āmadand.*

The rule for addressing persons is as follows:—

Among persons in the same sphere of life *you* is used.

Between intimate friends, either *you* or *thou*. From a superior to an inferior, *thou*; but if the inferior be an independent person, it is better to use *you*.

Kings are addressed in the third person singular, sometimes third person plural. The phrase "His Majesty" is used, *not* "Your Majesty." Sovereigns, when speaking of themselves, say, "His Majesty," never "I" or "We." In writing they use "We."

Great personages address each other in the third person singular. Inferiors speak of their superiors in the third person singular.

It will have been noticed that where several nouns have a common verb, the conjunction *wa*, "and," is required.

Har and *hama* take the noun in the singular; *har* takes the verb also in the singular; *hama* in the plural, as:—

all the people came, *hama kas āmadand.*

In speaking of exalted personages the plural verb is used, as:—

if the king wishes, *agar pādshāh ḳabūl farmāyand.*

The verb is used in the singular, when speaking of God.

Government of Verbs.

An active verb does not, as a rule, require that its complement should have the sign of the accusative case. For example:—

O, cup-bearer, bring a goblet of wine! *sāḳiyā saghir-i-sharāb biyār.*

the darwesh preserved *the* stone in his possession,	*darwesh sang-rā ba <u>kh</u>ud nigāh dāsht.*
a certain villager had *an* ass,	*dih<u>k</u>āne <u>kh</u>are dāsht.*
the people of the garden used to beat *the* ass,	*mardumān-i-bā<u>gh</u> <u>kh</u>ar-rā mī-zadand.*

When the accusative case is used indefinitely, *rā* is omitted. When any ambiguity would arise from its omission, *rā* should be inserted, as :—

| the goldsmith struck the carpenter, | *zargar najjar-rā zad.* |
| the man slew the lion, | *mard sher-rā kusht.* |

In these cases *rā* is obviously necessary. In the case of compound verbs, *rā* is never added to the substantive (see page 86).

When *rā* is used to denote the *dative* case, its insertion is absolutely necessary, as :—

| I gave a book to that man, | *ān mard-rā kitābe dādam.* |

In this case *kitābe*, the accusative, is indefinite, and the dative case is expressed by *rā*.

When a verb governs an accusative and a dative case, *rā* cannot be used for both cases. If the *accusative* requires *rā* the *dative* will be expressed by *ba*. For example :—

| let them give *the* ruby to that woman, | *la'l-rā ba ān zan dihand.* |
| give me the book, | *kitāb-rā ba man bi-dih.* |

When the object is in a state of construction with another noun or with an adjective, and from its nature requires *rā*, that termination is added to the latter noun or adjective. Moreover, however complex the sentence may be, *rā* should be placed at the end, as:—

I saw Zaid the son of the minister,	*Zaid pisar-i-wazīr-rā dīdam.*
one of the kings of Khurāsān saw in a dream Sultān Mahmud, the son of Sabaktagīn,	*yake az mulūk-i-khurāsān Sulṭān Mahmūd-i-Sabaktagīn-rā bakhwāb dīd.*
they sent forward several individuals from among men who had seen service and had experienced war,	*tane chand az mardān-i-wāḳi'a dīda wa jang azmūda-rā bi-firistādand.*

The termination *rā* is often used in the sense, "in respect of," as:—

they relate a story with regard to a certain tyrant,	*ẓālime-rā ḥikāyat kunand.*
I have heard of a darwesh,	*darweshe-rā shunīda am.*

After a generic noun, used generically, *rā* is omitted,* as:—

---

* Generic nouns may be used in three ways: definitely, indefinitely, and generically. Thus we may say either *the* man, *the* bird; *a* man, *a* bird; or *man*, *bird*, with reference to the entire species.

Greediness brings both bird and fish into the net,	*dar ārad ṭama' murgh wa māhī ba band.*

The *rā* is equivalent to the definite article "the" used *definitely*, and is, therefore, omitted after generic nouns.

If, however, the noun is in construction with *ki*, the noun is considered definite, and *rā* must be added, as:—

bring, O Sūfī, the cup which is pure as a mirror,	*Ṣūfī biyār ki ā,ina ṣāf ast jām-rā.*

In the old Persian writers the accusative is formed by prefixing the particle *mar* to the noun, as:—

I saw the man,	*mar mard-rā dīdam.*

The particle *rā* is sometimes used in the sense of of the genitive, as:—

Zaid's head,	*Zaid-rā sar.*
a certain person had lost his heart,	*yake-rā dil az dast rafta būd.*

When an *indefinite* noun occurs at the commencement of a sentence *rā* is required, as:—

I saw a holy man,	*pārsā,e-rā dīdam.*

Sometimes *rā* is omitted, as:—

I had a companion,	*rafīḳe dāshtam.*

The pronouns and the Arabic word *fulān*, "such a one," always take *rā*, as:—

I saw thee,	*tū-rā dīdam.*
I saw such an one,	*fulān-rā dīdam.*
such a person has concealed himself,	*fulān shakhṣ khụd-rā pinhān karda ast.*

The *rā* is always used in the case of specific nouns, as:—

Zaid struck Omar,	*Zaid 'Umr-rā zad.*

The pronominal suffixes reject *rā*, as:—

I said to him,	*guftam-ash.*

Sometimes *rā* is used, as "Gulistān," book iii. tale 8:—

(one of the sages) prohibited his son from eating too much,	*pisar-ash-rā nahī kard az bisiyār khụrdan.*

Again, Firdūsī's "Shah-nāma":—

he gave arms and money to his army,	*silāḥ wa dirham dād lashkar-ash-rā.*

When an entire phrase is used in apposition to a noun, *rā* is placed at the end of the phrase, as:—

I saw 'Alī (may Allah be pleased with him!) in a dream,	*'Alī (raẓiyu-l-lāh 'anhū) rā ba khwāb dīdam.*

When an *adjective* is placed in apposition to a noun, *rā* is added to the *noun*, as:—

I saw a tyrant asleep,	*ẓālime-rā khufta dīdam.*

The verbs *bāyistan*, to be necessary; *shāyistan*, to be fit; *tawānistan*, to be able; are used impersonally, as:—

it is necessary to do,	*bāyad kard.*
it is proper to say,	*shāyad guft.*
one may do,	*tawānad kard*

The root of *tawānistan* is more frequently used, as:—

one may do,	*tawān kard.*

Some impersonal verbs take a nominative of cognate meaning, as:—

it rains,	*bārān mī-bārad.*
it thunders,	*r'ad ṣadā mī-ẓanad;* or, *r'ad mī-ghurad.* *tundar mī-tundad.*
it lightens,	*barḳ mī-darakhshad.*

Two tenses of the Potential Mood, present and past, can be formed by adding the contracted infinitive to the aorist and preterite of the verb *tawānistan*, "to be able":—

I am able to go,	*tawānam raft.*
I was able to go,	*tawānistam raft.*

The verb *khwāstan*, "to desire," is similarly used, as:—

I will go,	*khwāham raft.*

If the infinitive precede the governing verb, it takes the full form, as:—

I cannot do this deed,	*īn kār kardan na mī-tawānam.*

When the infinitive and its governing verb are separated by an intervening clause, the full form is used, as:—

it does not become persons of our sort, in the presence of kings, to speak other than the truth,	*abnā,e jins-i-mārā na shāyad dar ḥuzrat-i-pādshāhān juz ba rāstī sukhan guftan.*

Often after *khwāstan*, *shāyistan*, *bāyistan*, and *tawānistan*, the present subjunctive with the particle *ki* is used, instead of the infinitive, as:—

I wish to go,	*mī-khwāham ki bi-ravam.*
it is proper that I should read,	*shāyad ki bi-khwānam.*

This construction is sometimes necessary, for the sentence *turā bāyad zad* might stand for—"I must strike you," or "you must strike."

The infinitive is often used as a verbal noun, in

which case the noun which follows is put in the genitive, as:—

from the arrival of spring and the departure of winter the leaves of our lives are folded.	*az āmadan-i-bahār, az raftan-i-dai, aurāḳ-i-ḥayāt-i-mā mī-gardad ṭai.**

The Tenses.

After verbs signifying "to command," "to order," the perfect tense is used to imply that the order given was *immediately* carried out, as:—

the king gave orders to put him into prison,	*pādshāh farmūd tā o-rā dar zindān nihādand.*
the sage commanded that they should throw the boy into the sea.	*ḥakīm farmūd tā ghulām-rā ba daryā andākhtand.*

If the fulfilment of the order was not *immediate*, the present subjunctive is used, as:—

(the king) commanded them to wrestle,	*bi-farmūd ki muṣāra'at kunand.*
he gave orders so that they bestowed a robe of honour and a reward on the master,	*farmūd tā ustād-rā khil'at o ni'mat dādand.*

* To become rolled up; to close, *ṭai gardīdan.*

In narration, when a second verb occurs after a verb in the preterite, the present, or aorist, is used, as :—

the young tiger saw that he *has* not the power of resisting.	*palang bachcha dīd ki ṭāḳat-i-muḳāwamat na dārad.*

In recounting a conversation the very words of the speaker are used, as :—

Ḥātim told her that he would not eat,	*Ḥātim o-rā guft ki na khẉāham khụrd.*

SECTION II.

COMPOSITION OF SENTENCES.

Lesson 1.

Substantives.

man,	*mard; ādam; mardum; insān.*
father,	*padar; wālid; ab; abū;* (parents) *wālidain.*
husband,	*shauhar; zauj;* k͟haṣm.
brother,	*barādar; a*k͟h.
son, or child,	*pisar; walad;* (child) *ṭifl; ibn.*
boy,	*kodak; ṭifl,* (plur.) *aṭfāl; bachcha.*
animal,	*jānwār; jānwar; ḥaiwān-i-g͟hair nāṭiḳ;* (beast of prey) *na*k͟h*chīr;* (wild beast) *waḥsh,* (plur.) *wuḥūsh.*
horse,	*asp; markab; faras.*
house,	k͟h*āna; kad; buḳ'a; maḳām; makān; bait; maskin; ma,wā;* (hut) *kulba;* (building) *'imārat;* (palace) *maḥall.*
pen,	*ḳalam.*
dog,	*sag; kalb.*
elephant,	*fīl; pīl.*
woman,	*zan;* (married lady) k͟h*ātūn;* (lady of rank) *begam.*
mother,	*mādar; wālida.*
wife,	*zan; zauja.*
sister,	{ *k͟hwāhar* (elder). { *hamshīra* (younger).
daughter,	*du*k͟h*tar; ṣabīya.*
girl,	*du*k͟h*tarak; zan-i-shabāb.*
thing,	*chīz; shai* (plur.) *ashiyā.*
mare,	*mādiyān.*
table,	*mez.*

book,	*kitāb ; daftar ; jarīdat.*
fox,	*rūbāh.*
cow,	*mādah gāw;* (cattle) *baḳar* or *mawāshī.*

Adjectives.

good,	*khūb ; nek ; bih ; ṯaiyab ; nafīs.*
bad, wicked,	*bad ; kharāb ; khabīṣ ; fāhish ; fāsid.*
great, large,	*kalān ; buẕurg ; 'aẕīm ; a'ẕam ; kabīr.*
little, small,	*khụrd ; khwār ; kotah ḳad,* or *kāṣir ḳad* (stature).
lazy,	*sust ; tamhal.*
wise,	*dānā ; 'aḳlmand ; dānishmand ; ẕakī ; khiradmand.*
ignorant,	*nādān ; nā fahm ; jāhil ; nā khwānda.*
swift,	*tez ; chust ; chālāk ; tezrau ; chābuk.*
high, lofty,	*buland ; 'ālī.*
handsome,	*khūb-ṣūrat ; ḥasīn ; zebā ; marghūb ; khūsh shakl ; khūsh haikal ; ḳabūl-ṣūrat ; jamīl ; wajīh.*
ugly,	*bad-ṣūrat ; bad haikal ; zisht ; karīhu-l-manẕar ; ṯal'at-i-nā-mauzūn ; shaklu-l-mal'ūn ; ḳabīh-ṣūrat ; nā khūsh ṯal'at.*

EXAMPLES.

this is my brother,	*īn barādar-i-man ast.*
that is your son,	*ān pisarat ast.*
these are their houses,	*īn khānahā,e eshān and.*
this is my father's house,	*īn khāna,e padaram ast.*
that is your brother's horse,	*ān asp-i-barādar-i-*[*tū ast*] or [*tūst*].
this is that man's mother,	*īn mādar-i-ān mard ast.*
that is your sister,	*ān khwāharat ast.*
thy sister's horse is swift,	*asp-i-khwāharat tezrau ast.*
this pen is very good,	*īn ḳalam bisiyār khūb ast.*
that is a very good book,	*ān kitāb bisiyār khūb ast.*
she is a little woman,	{ *o zan-i-kotah-ḳad ast.* / *o zanak ast.*
his father was a great man,	*padar-i-o buẕurg būd.*

your sister was very handsome, — *khwāhar-i-tū mah-wash būd.* / *khwāhar-i-tū mah-ṭal'at būd.* / *khwāharat bisiyār marghūb būd.*

my brother's horses were extremely swift, — *aspān-i-barādaram nihāyat tez-raftār būdand.*

their children's books were very good, — *kitābhā,e bachchagān-i-eshān bisiyār khūb būdand.*

Exercise.—I am that man's brother. This woman is my brother's daughter. That boy is my brother's son. This is my sister's book. That man is this boy's father. These houses are very lofty. That girl's mother was very wise. Your father's horse was very swift. My brother's children are handsome. My sister's daughters are very good girls. That man's brother's wife was a very ignorant woman. That was a very handsome woman. This boy is very lazy. These girls are very lazy. These women were excessively ugly. The man's horses were very small. They are very bad husbands. She is a bad wife. They are very bad wives.

Lesson 2.

EXAMPLES.

the elephant is larger than the horse, — *fīl az asp kalān-tar ast.*

the fox is smaller than the dog, — *rūbāh az sag khurd-tar ast.*

the horses are swifter than the elephants, — *aspān az fīlān tezrau-tar and.*

the elephant is the largest animal of all, — *fīl az hama jānwārān buzurg ast.* / *fīl buzurgtarīn-i-hama ḥaiwānāt ast.*

the elephant, the horse, and the dog, are wiser than all other animals,	*fīl, asp, o sag az ama jā n-warān-i-dīgar dānā-tar and.* / *fīl, asp, o kalb az hama ḥaiwānāt-i-dīgar zakā-wat-tar dārand.*

Exercise.—The cow is more lazy than the horse. These men are more wicked than dogs. The boys are more ignorant than the girls. The horses and the dogs are handsomer than the elephants. My pen is better than your pen. This boy is wiser than that boy. My father's horse is swifter than your brother's mare. Our dogs are swifter than your horses. The men are worse than the women. The fox is wiser than the dog. This pen is the worst of all (worse than all). This woman is the handsomest of all (more handsome than all). That girl was much wiser than her mother. She was the wisest of all the girls (wiser than all the girls).

Lesson 3.

EXAMPLES.

who is that man?	*ān ādam kīst?*
who is this woman?	*īn khātūn kīst?*
who are these boys?	*īn kodakān kīstand?* / *īn aṭfāl kīstand?*
who are those girls?	*ān dukhtarān kīstand?*
whose house is this?	*īn khāna,e kīst?*
whose children are these?	*īn bachchagān-i-kīstand?*
whose books are these?	*īn kitābhā,e kīstand?*
whose daughter is she?	*o dukhtar-i-kīst?*
where is my father?	*padaram kujā ast?*
where is his brother?	*barādarash kujā ast?*
where are your father's horses?	*aspān-i-padar-i-shumā kujā and?*

where are my brother's children's books?	*kitābhā,e bachchagān-i-barādar-i-man kujā and?*
where may be that man's mother's mare?	*mādiyān-i-mādar-i-ān ādam kujā bāshad?*
is this your house?	*āyā, īn khāna,e shumā ast?*
was that my father's horse?	*āyā, ān asp-i-padar-i-man būd?*
may this be my sister's table?	*āyā, mez-i-khwāhar-i-man bāshad?*
how many pens will there be?	*chand ḳalamhā khwāhand būd?*
what-like books will they be?	*kitābhā,e chi ḳism khwāhand būd?*

Exercise.—Where is your brother? Where is this man's mother? Whose son are you? Whose horses are these? How many houses are there? What sort of book is this? Is that your sister's table? Is this pen yours? Where had you been yesterday? Where will these children be to-morrow? When will you be at home (in the house)? Was your father at home yesterday? Will your brother be at home to-morrow? Were my two books on the table yesterday? Where are his four sons? Have his three daughters been at home? Were there seven horses there yesterday? Will there be eight men in the house three days hence? Were there five or six dogs there two days ago? What is this thing? What animals are these? Is that animal a horse or a cow?

LESSON 4.

day,	*roz; yaum.*
city,	*shahr; balad* (plur. *bilād*).
river,	*daryā; rūd-khāna.* (canal) *nahr.*
forest,	*besha; bādiya;* (desert) *dasht; ṣaḥrā; biyābān ḳā'-i-basīṭ.*
a plain,	*maidān.*

water, *āb*; (drinking) *āb-i-zulāl*; (dirty) *āb-i-mukaddar*, or *manjal āb*; (iced) *āb-i-yakh*; (pure) *salsabīl*; (impurity of) *kadūrat*; (purity of) *'uzūbat*; (boiling) *āb-i-ḍāgh*; (warm) *āb-i-malūl*; (still) *āb-i-khufta*; (running) *āb-i-rawān*.
fish, *māhī*; *samak*.
street, *kūcha*.
night, *shab*; *lail*.
a boat, *māshūya*; *zauraḳ*; *safīna*; *kishtī,e khurd*.
a tree, *darakht*; *shajar*; (young) *nihāl*; (branch) *shākh*.
a road, *rāh*; *răh*; (high) *shāh-rāh*; *shāri'*; *jāda*.
fruit, *mewā*; *bar*; *ṣamar* (plur.) *aṣmār*.
bird, *paranda*; *murgh*; *ṭair* (plur.) *ṭuyūr*.
name, *nām*; *ism*.
people, *ahl*; *ins*; *insān*; *ḥaiwān-i-nātiḳ*.

Intransitive Verbs.

to stay, dwell, { *māndan*. / *manzil dāshtan*; *sākin būdam*. }
to come, *āmadan*.
to go, *raftan*.
to run, *dawīdan*; *pūyidan*.
to sleep, { *khwābīdan*. / *khuftan*. / *khushīdan*. }
to arrive, *rasīdan*; *wārid* or *wurūd shudan*.
to flow, { *jārī shudan*. / *rawān shudan*. / *sail-i-āb shudan*. }
to proceed, advance, *pesh raftan*; *muḳaddam shudan*.
to retreat, fall back, { *pas pā shudan*. / *'aḳab āmadan*. / *muta'āḳib shudan*. }
to sit, *nishastan*.
to return, *bāz* or *pas gashtan*.

to die,	*murdan.* *wafāt yāftan.* *ba jahān-i-bāḳī raftan.* *intiḳāl kardan.* (ready) *ba jān āmadan.*

EXAMPLES.

I am staying in the city,	*man dar shahr mī-mānam.* *man dar shahr manzil mī-dāram.* *man dar shahr sukūnat [pazīram]. [mī-dāram.]*
my father dwells in that house,	*padaram dar ān [khāna] tashrīf mī - dārand. [manzil.]*
we came from the forest yesterday,	*dī rūz az besha mā āmadem.*
we will go to the city to-morrow,	*mā farda ba shahr khwāhem raft.*
the bird was sitting on the tree,	*murgh bālā,e shākh-i-darakht mī-nishast.*
where are you going ?	*kujā mī-raved ?*
whence does this river flow?	*az kujā īn [daryā rawān ast]? [rūd - khāna mī - ravad.]*
do these men sleep in the city ?	*īn mardumān dar shahr mī-khwāband ?*
where does this road lead to (go to) ?	*īn rāh ba-kudām jā sar mī-kashad ?* *īn rāh ba-kujā mī-rasad ?*
is the fish in that river very large ?	*dar ān daryā māhīyān bisiyār buzurg and ?*
who were those that were sitting underneath the tree ?	*ānān kīstand ki zer-i-darakht nishasta būdand ?*

Exercise.—The forest near the city is very large. How many men are sleeping beneath the tree ? The road towards the forest is not very good. The horses were running from the plain. The water flows from the river into the city. In that forest there were many large trees. The boats on the river are coming towards the city. How many boats are there? There will be 250 horses on the plain to-morrow. There were 2500 men on the large plain near the city yesterday. A hundred and fifty men have retreated from the river towards the forest. The horses are dying on the plain, and a hundred men died yesterday within the city. That man stayed nine days in my house. I slept one night in the forest, but I will not sleep there a second night. The water is flowing from the river into the streets of the city. The men are advancing towards the city. The fruit on these trees is very good. Where do all these people come from? What is the name of that city? What is the name of that river which flows from the forest? What is the name of the street in which you dwelt? The people were sitting beneath the trees. When did you arrive in this city? When will you return home?

Lesson 5.

Substantives.

bread,	*nān.*
butter,	*maska; kara; zubdat.*
wine,	*sharāb; mai; bāda; ṣahbā;* (fermented liquor) *khamr.*
tea,	*chā* or *chā,e;* (urn) *samāwar.*
breakfast,	(very early) *nāshta;* (between 11 and 12) *nahār;* (about noon) *chāsht.*
dinner,	*shām; ṭa'ām-i-shām;* (food) *khurish; khorāk; ghizā; āshām; ma'īshat.*
knife,	*kārd;* (penknife) *chākū.*
fork,	*changāl.*
meat,	*gosht;* (cold meat) *gosht i-shabīna* or *gosht-i-sard; gosht-i-shabmānda.*
milk,	*shīr;* (cream) *sar-i-shīr; zabd.*
rice (boiled),	(raw) *birinj;* (cooked) *chalāw.*

plate,	*bushkāb; rikāb; ṭabak;* (large) *ḳāb;* (cover) *sar posh-i-ḳāb.*
spoon,	*ḳāshugh.*
sugar,	*shakar, ḳand, nabāt;* (sugar-cane) *naishakar;* (loaf) *kulla,e ḳand;* (refined) *ḳand-i-mukarrar.*
a letter,	*khaṭṭ; ruḳa'a; risālat;* (royal) *nāma;* (official) *khaṭṭ-i-sarkār;* (private) *khaṭṭ-i-khānagī.*
news,	*khabar; akhbār; i'lām.*

Adjectives.

cold, *sard;* (intense) *zamharī*	clean, *sāf; pāk; pākīza; naẓīf*
hot, *garm; ḥārr*	pure, *khāliṣ; maḥẓ; khulūṣ*
sweet, *shirīn*	ready, *taiyār; muḥaiyā*

Verbs.

to swim,	{ *shināwidan.* { *shināw kardan.*
to bring,	*āwardan.*
to make (prepare),	{ *sakhtan.* { *taiyār* or *muḥaiyā kardan.*
to eat,	*khurdan.*
to drink,	{ *khurdan.* { *naushīdan.*
to eat and drink,	*akl wa sharb farmūdan.*
to make, do,	*kardan.*
to place, put,	*nihādan.*
to take away,	{ *burdan.* { *bar dāshtan.* { *bar giriftan.*
to call,	*ṭalabīdan.*
to learn,	*āmokhtan.*
to give,	{ *dādan.* { *bakhshīdan.* { *'ināyat kardan.* { *'aṭa kardan; arzānī dāshtan.*

to say, tell,	*guftan.* *ḥarf zadan.* *sukhan guftan.*
to see, look,	*dīdan.* *mushāhida kardan.* *mu'aiyana kardan.* *mulāḥaẓa kardan.*
to hear,	*shunīdan; iṣghā kardan.* *shunūdan; gosh kardan.* *shinuftan.* *istimā' namūdan.*
to strike,	*zadan.* *ẓarb zadan.*
to read,	*khwāndan.*
to write,	*nawishtan; raḳam* or *taḥrīr kardan.*
to take,	*giriftan;* (seize) *dast dar girebān zadan.*

EXAMPLES.

he is bringing bread,	*o nān mī-ārad.*
we drink water,	*mā āb-i-zulāl mī-khurem.* *mā āb-i-zulāl mī-naushem.*
they drink wine,	*eshān sharāb mī-naushand.*
my brother will drink cold pure water,	*barādaram āb-i-sard o ṣāf khwāhad khurd.*
make tea,	*chā taiyār bi-kun.* *chā bi-sāz.*
bring a spoon,	*kāshughe biyār.*
give me some meat,	*ḳadre gosht marā bi-dih.*
bring a knife and fork,	*kārde o changāle biyār.*
make breakfast ready,	*nahār taiyār bi-kun.*
bring a clean plate,	*bushḳāb-i-ṣāf biyār.*
when will you get dinner ready?	*kai shām-rā khwāhed āward?*
will you drink wine?	*sharāb khwāhed khurd?*
what will you eat?	*chi khwāhed khurd?*

Exercise.—Do you eat any fruit? Bring me some tea, sugar, and milk. Put a knife and fork on the table for my father. Cool (make cold) some wine for us. Prepare dinner for six people. You will bring us some rice and milk. Will you give me some wine and some cold water, that I may drink? Do you drink tea? Will your brother drink wine? Bring us three knives, three forks, three spoons, and three clean plates. He reads very good books. He writes a letter to me every day. She was writing letters when I came to her house. He hears good news of him. We were reading their letters when they arrived. Tell us all the news of the city. I will tell you the news of the city when I return. Give us some bread and butter.

Lesson 6.

EXAMPLES.

put the water on the table,	*āb-rā bar mez* [*bi-nih*]. [*bi-guzār.*]
take away the sugar,	*shakar-rā* [*bar dār*]. [*bar gīr.*] / *ḳand-rā bi-bar.*
give me the wine,	*sharāb-rā ba-man bi-dih.*
clean (make clean) the plate,	*bushḳāb-rā ṣāf bi-kun.*
cool the water,	*āb-rā sard bi-kun.*

Exercise.—The dog is drinking the milk. They were putting the water on the table. Who has taken away the sugar? He is cleaning the plate. They are cooling the water. Take away the meat and put the wine on the table. Put the water near me on this table. The dogs will drink the water. Beat (or strike) that idle boy. He was eating the sugar and drinking the wine. I shall see him to-morrow. We shall see them to-day in the city. If they see us here, they will beat us very much. We shall not see that man, if we remain in this house.

Lesson 7.

EXAMPLES.

he has placed good food upon the table,	{ *o bar mez ṭa'ām-i-khūb nihāda ast.* / *o bar mez khụrish-i-nafīs guz̲āshta ast.*
she has made tea,	*ān zan chā taiyār karda ast.*
my father has drunk all the wine,	*padaram tamām sharūb-rā khụrda ast.*
we drank cold water,	*mā āb-i-sard khụrdem.*
who has eaten the rice?	*birinj-rā ki khụrda ast?*
he called all the servants into the house,	*o hama naukarān-rā andarūn-i-khāna talabīd.*
we had given very good bread to the men,	*mā mardumān-rā bisiyār khūb nān dāda būdem.*
the women ate bread and drank milk,	*zanān nān o shīr khụrdand.*

Exercise.—Have you learned the Persian language? I have read a few pages. Have you seen the city of Teherān? You have made the voyage of the sea, what wonders did you see there? I may say what one of the sages said, "The wonder that I saw on the sea was this,—that I came safe to land." How much money have your friends given you? My father gave me an order for one thousand rupees. How much did you give to the man? How many rupees did he demand of you? He demanded ten rupees, and I gave him three rupees and a half. Have you prepared breakfast? Have you prepared a good dinner for two people? Have you put the bread on the table?

Lesson 8.

to be able, *tawānistan;* root *tawān.*

EXAMPLES.

he can (or is able to) speak our language,	{ *o zabān-i-mā mī-tawānad guft.* / *o zabān-i-mā guftān mī-tawānad.*

are you able to read my writing?	*shumā nawishta,e marā khwāndan mī-tawāned?* *dast-i-khaṭṭ-i-man khwāndan mī-tawāned?*
no one will be able to read this but yourself,	*siwā,e shumā kase īn-rā khwāndan na khwāhad tawānist.*
he can speak a little English,	*ḳadre dar zabān-i-inglīsī mī-tawānad ḥarf zad.*
they have done eating,	*eshān az khurdan fārigh shuda and.* *eshān az tanāwul-i-ṭa'ām pardākhta and.* *eshān-rā az tanāwul-i-ta'ām farāghat ḥāṣil shud.*
have you done writing?	*shumā az nawishtan fārigh shuda ed?*
they had done reading when I arrived there,	[1] *dar ḥīn-i-rasīdan-i-man, eshān az khwāndan fārigh shuda būdand.* *waḳte ki man rasīdam eshān, &c.* *ba-mujarrad-i-rasīdan-ī-man, eshān, &c.*

Exercise.—When he had done writing the letter, then I came away from the house. When you come (*i.e.* shall come) here to-morrow, I shall have done reading the book. Can you swim across this river? I cannot swim at all, but my brother is an excellent swimmer. So great was the darkness that I could not see anything. The ruler of this village cannot speak English, but he can speak Persian well. I hope I shall be able to learn the language of this country in the space of six months.

[1] "Come punctually," *waḳt-i-[mau'ūda] biyā.* [*ma'hūd; mu'aiyan.*]

Lesson 9.

to rise,	*khāstan.*	root *khez.*
to begin,	*giriftan.*	„ *gīr.*
to allow,	*dūdan.*	„ *dih.*
	guzāshtan.	„ *guzār.*

EXAMPLES.

he arose and began to say,	*o bar khāst wa guftan girift.*
they began to read,	*eshān khwāndan giriftand.*
you began to eat,	*shumā khurdan girifted.*
he allows them to come into the house,	*dar khāna eshān-rā ijāzat-i-āmadan dihad.*
let him go,	*o-rā raftan bi-dih.* *o-rā bi-guzār ki bi-ravad.*
he is allowed to come,	*o mī-tawānad āmad.* *o rukhsat-i-āmadan yāfta ast.*
he will allow us to do what we like,	*harchi mā mī-khwāhem, o rāwā dārad ki mā bi-kunem.*

Exercise.—He sat down, and began to tell this story. One man began to say, I shall not be able to eat this bread. Another began to say, I will not allow the children to read these books. He will give you leave to walk in this beautiful garden every day. My father is allowed to go to Shīrāz on account of transacting (making) business. Go to my brother's house, present to him my compliments, and bring home my saddle. Strip off your clothes, swim across this river, and bring the boat to this side.

Lesson 10.

EXAMPLES.

he is in the habit of reading every morning,	*o har sabāh 'ādat-i-khwāndan dārad.* *o har sabāh mī-khwānad.*

he is in the habit of writing something every day,	o har rūz chīze mashḳ-i-nawishtan dārad. / o har rūz chīze 'ādat-i-nawishtan dārad.
he used always to give (make) this injunction to the scholar,	o hamesha shagird-rā 'ādat-i-tākīd mī-kard.
I wish to learn the Persian language,	man zabān-i-fārsī āmokhtan mī-khwāham. / marā arzū,e āmokhtan-i-zabān-i-fārsī ast.
what do you wish to say?	kudām sukhan guftan mī-khwāhed?
I wish to write a letter,	khaṭṭ nawishtan mī-khwāham.

Exercise.—I am accustomed every day to rise at the dawn. He is in the habit of dining every day at two o'clock. We make it a practice to read three hours in the morning. I wish very much to learn the language of this country. Do you wish to read this book? It is necessary to learn the Arabic language in order to speak and understand well the Persian. It is desirable to know the language of the country in which you are dwelling.

Lesson 11.

EXAMPLES.

who killed that man?	ān ādam-rā ki kusht? / kudām kas ḳatl-i-ān ādam karda ast?
he has placed all the things on the table,	o hama chīzhā bar mez [nihāda] ast. [guẕāshta.]
lay my watch on the shelf,	ṣā'at-i-man bar ṭāḳ [biguẕār]. [bi-nih.]

they have eaten up all the dinner,	*eshān tamām shām-rā bi-l-kull k͟hurda and.* *eshān shām tamām tanāwul karda and.*
write a letter for me,	*az barā,e man k͟haṭṭe bi-nawīs.*
he has cut down all the trees in the garden,	*tamām darak͟ht ki dar bāg͟h ast, burīda ast.* *o hama darak͟hthā,e bāg͟h-rā munḳaṭi' karda ast.*

Exercise.—Put all the things on the table. That man has killed my companion. Has he written out the two letters, as I told him? The king said to the soldier, Cut off this man's head in my presence. Throw out the water from this basin. They all spoke out, saying, We will not sit down in your house unless you make an apology for this conduct. His father, mother, brothers, and sisters have all died. The goat has smashed the looking-glass with his horns. He has lost a great sum of money (very many rupees) in gambling. You will sit down in this room until I return from the king's audience (*darbār*). The dog has eaten up the whole of the butter. Who has cut down that fine tree?

Lesson 12.

EXAMPLES.

I read my book,	*man kitāb-i-k͟hud-rā mī-k͟hwānam.*
thou readest thy book,	*tū kitāb-i-k͟hudat mī-k͟hwānī.* *tū kitāb-i-k͟hud mī-k͟hwānī.*
he reads his (own) book,	*o kitāb-i-k͟hudash mī-k͟hwānad.*

she reads her (own) book,	ān zan kitāb-i-<u>kh</u>ud-rā mī-<u>kh</u>wānad.
we have seen our father,	mā pidar-i-[<u>kh</u>ud] dīda em. [<u>kh</u>ud-i-mān.]
have you written your letter?	shumā <u>kh</u>a<u>tt</u>-i-<u>kh</u>ud-rā na-wishta ed?
the goldsmith and carpenter went to their (own) city,	zargar o [najjār] ba shahr-i-<u>kh</u>ud-i-shān raftand. [darrūdgar.]
the women feed their (own) children,	zanān bachchagūn-i-<u>kh</u>ud-i-shān mī-parwarand.

Exercise.—Did you see your father yesterday? Bring your dogs here to-morrow, that we may go a-hunting. Wait in this room till I shall have done writing my letter to your master. Give my compliments to your master and say that Mr. F. is not at home. Why do you beat your servants in that manner? In my country every man considers his own house as his castle. My friend is gone to his native country for the benefit of his health. The judge said to the plaintiff, Go and take your money from the woman. The plaintiff came back and said, Sir, I cannot get my money from this woman.

Lesson 13.

EXAMPLES.

where did you find this dog-like, unclean animal?	īn jānwar ki najis mi<u>s</u>al-i-sag ast kujā yāfted?
a wise man like you,	{ mi<u>s</u>al-i-shumā dānā. { hamchū shumā dānā.
what-like animals are these?	{ īn <u>h</u>aiwānāt chi sān and? { īn jānwarān mi<u>s</u>al-i-ki and?
he took up a very large stone,	o sange bisiyār kalān bar dāsht.
a fine-looking stag came in sight,	āhū,e <u>kh</u>ūsh man<u>z</u>ar ba na<u>z</u>ar āmad.

a black woman like an ogress,	*zan-i-siyāh misal-i-dew.* *zan-i-siyāh misal-i-ghūl.* *zan-i-siyāh misal-i-'ifrīt.* *zan-i-siyāh misal-i-jinn.*

Exercise.—Her face was fair as the moon, her eyebrows were like a bow, and her hair (*lit.* hairs) black as night. Her form was straight as the cypress, her lips red as the *kandūrī* (a beautiful red flower), and her feet delicate as the flower of the lotus. She was beautiful as *Zulaikhā*, and faithful as *Lailī*. The young prince was handsome as *Yūsuf*. The king was wise as *Sulaimān*, just as *Naushīrwān*, liberal as *Ḥātim*, and brave as *Rustam*.

Lesson 14.

to drink,	*naush-i-jān farmūdan.*
to come,	*tashrīf āwardan.*
to have an inclination for,	*khwāstan mail kardan*, or *mail dāshtan; mā,il shudan.*
I have an inclination for water,	*man mail-i-āb mī-kunam.* *man āb-rā mail mī-kunam.* *man āb mī-khwāham.* *man ba āb [maile dāram].* *[mā,il mī-shavam.]*

EXAMPLES.

I shall see him myself,	*man khud o-rā khwāham dīd.* *man khudam o-rā khwāham dīd.*[1]
will she herself come?	*ān zan khud khwāhad āmad?* *ān zan khudash khwāhad āmad?*[1]

[1] These forms are rarely used.

will you come yourself to-morrow?	*shumā khud farda khwāhed āmad?* *shumā khud-i-tān farda khwāhed āmad?* [1]
will you, sir, come to-morrow?	*shumā khud tashrīf khwāhed āward?*
how is the health of your honour?	*mizāj-i-sharīf chigūna ast?* *mizāj-i-janāb chi* [*sān*] *ast?* [*ṭaur.*]
will you, sir, drink any wine?	*shumā khud ḳadre sharāb naush-i-jān khwāhed farmūd.* *janāb khud mail-i-sharāb khwāhand farmūd.*
may it please monsieur to sit down,	*janāb-i-'ālī ba kursī tashrīf bi-dāred?* *bismi-l-lāh bi-farmāyed* (at the time of eating).
how is the health of your highness?	*mizāj-i-janāb-i-'ālī ba khairiyat ast?* *mizāj-i-janāb-i-'alā ba 'āfiyat ast?*

Exercise.—I am going there myself this very day. Will you come yourself to-morrow? If he himself cannot give the money, perhaps his brother will be able to advance it for him. We do not wish to appear ourselves in this business. I am your worship's faithful slave. I have sought for the child in your honour's garden. Your worship's (master's) dinner is ready. Master's pālkī (*vulg.* palanquin) is now at the door. You, sir, are my father and mother; there is no one in the world, except your honour, who will assist your poor miserable slave. Where is the native country of your highness? Will your majesty ride on the white elephant to-day?

---

[1] This form is rarely used.

Lesson 15.
EXAMPLES.

you must go home,	tū-rā ba kh̲īna,e kh̲ud raftan bāyad. bāyad ki tū ba kh̲āna,e kh̲ud bi-ravī.
I must buy a good horse,	az barā,e kh̲ud asp-i-kh̲ūb marā bāyad kh̲arīd.
do not commit such folly,	chunīn ḥimākat ma kun. dar chunīn bādiya,e zalālat ma rau.
do not go to that country,	badān mulk ma rau.
I do not now intend to go to Persia,	ilḥāl ba īrān irāda,e raftan na mī-dāram. ḥālan marā irāda ba raftan-i-īrān nīst. aknūn man irāda,e raftan-i-'ajam na dāram. ilḥāl az barā,e raftan-i-fārs irāda na dāram.

Exercise.—We must not do evil to the end that good may result. That wounded soldier must not eat so much fruit. You must read three pages of this book every day. Do not speak more nonsense. Never strike your horse on the head. Do not strike your dog in that manner. Do not drink any of the foul water of that river. When do you intend going to Europe? He is about to travel in Persia (*Fārs*), Arabia ('*Arab*), and Turkey (*Rūm*). She does not mean to remain in this country after the cold season. The officers do not intend to go to the tiger-hunt.

Lesson 16.
Use of the Relative.
EXAMPLES.

that which you say is all true,	ānchi shumā mī-goyed, hama rāst ast.

speak plainly whatever comes into your mind,	*ānchi dar dil-i-tū bi-āyad, ṣāf bi-go.*
the man whom you saw in the city yesterday died this morning,	*ān mard ki shumā o-rā dar shahr dī rūz dīded imrūz ṣubḥ murd.* *marde ki o-rā dī rūz dar shahr dīded, imrūz dam-i-ṣubḥ [wafāt yāft]. [ba jahān-i-bāḳī raft.]*
the letter which you wrote to me has not arrived,	*khaṭṭe ki ba-man nawishted, na rasīda ast.*
where there is a rose there is also a thorn,	*ba-jāe ki gul ast, khār ast.*
as you act, so will you experience,	*ānchi mī-kārī, bi-duravī.* *ānchi mī-kunī, biyābī.* *harki shākh-i-maẓarrate kārad, mewā,e manfa'at kujā chīnad.*
wherever you go, thither will I also go,	*har jā,e ki tū ravī hamrāh-i-tū khwāham būd.* *har jā,e ki tū ravī ['aḳab-i-tū] khwāham āmad. [muta'āḳib-i-tū; dar pai,e tū.]*
as the master, so will be the scholars,	*ānchi ustād bāshad, shāgirdānash bāshand.* *ānchi mu'allim[1] bāshad, talāmīẕash bāshand.* *hamchū zāgh, hamchū bachcha.* *hamchū rīsh, hamchū shāna.*

Exercise.—That very foolish young man has lost in play all the money that his father had given him when he left home. They broke to pieces all the furniture

---

[1] master, *mudarris; mu,addib:* pupil, *talmīẕ,* (plur.) *talāmīẕ; muta'allim.*

which they found in the people's houses. The king highly approved of the horses which you sent to him last year from Arabia. Why have you not done what I told you? The officer rewarded the soldier who saved his life. Have you made a copy of the petition which the villagers brought to me yesterday? At the root of the very tree under which you are now standing there is buried a potful of *ashrafīs.* The servant whom you recommended to me is a great rascal.

Lesson 17.

On Oriental Phraseology.

chess,	*shatranj*	game of hazard,	*ḳimār*
checkmate,	*māt ; shāh*	gambler,	*ḳimār bāz*
check,	*kisht*	knight (at chess),	*faras ; asp*
card,	*ganjīfa*	opponent (in a game),	*ḥarīf*
card-maker,	*ganjīfa sāz*	pawn (at chess),	*piyāda*
cheating,	*dagha bāzī*	king "	*shāh*
a cheat,	*dagha bāz ; ghaddār*	queen "	*farzīn ; wazīr*
dice,	*k'abat ; ḳimār* *k'abatain*	bishop "	*pīl ; fīl*
		castle "	*rukh*

to bet,	*sharṭ kardan.*
to checkmate,	*māt kardan.*
to be checkmated,	*māt shudan.*
to gamble,	*ḳimār bākhtan.* *bāzī bākhtan.*
to lose a game,	*bāzī bākhtan.* *bāzī na yāftan.*
to win a game,	*bāzī yāftan.*
to play at cards,	*ganjīfa bākhtan.*
to play at dice,	*ḳimār bākhtan.*

EXAMPLES.

my brother said to me that he was going to the desert of Persia next day,	*barādaram ba-man guft, ki pas farda ba dasht-i-be-daulat khwāham raft.*

he told me to go home,	*o marā guft ki ba khāna,e khud bi-rau.*
did he not tell you that he had lost all his money at play?	*āyā, o ba shumā na guft ki man hama pūl-i-khud-rā dar bāzī būkhtam?*
he says that his parents have died,	*o mī-goyad ki wālidain-i-man wafāt yāfta ast.*
ask him whether that horse be his own or not,	[1] *az o bi-purs ki ān asp az ān-i-o ast yā na?*
he says it is assuredly his own,	*o mī-goyad ki albatta az ān-i-man ast.*

Exercise.—My master sends you his compliments, and desires me to say that he cannot come to see you to-day, as he is busy writing. I told him, that if he would prove to me that he did not charge me more than the market price (or price current) for the grain, then I would give him the sum he asked. I wrote to my friend this morning, and told him that I would send him the book in a day or two, if he did not require it sooner. He told me that he had suffered great hardships on the journey; that he had been robbed of part of his property, and obliged to sell the rest in order to pay his expenses during his way home. He wished to come here this morning to see you, but he told me that his horse was dead, and therefore he could not come.

Lesson 18.

bring breakfast,	*nahār biyār.*
bring dinner,	*shām biyār.*
bring bread,	*nān biyār.*
bring milk,	*shīr biyār.*
give sugar,	[*shakar*] *bi-dih.* [*kand* or *nabāt.*]

[1] "Whose will it be?" *kirā bāshad?*

eat your dinner,	*shām-i-khụd bi-khụr.*
drink milk,	*shīr bi-[naush]. [khụr.]*
light the lamp,	*chirāgh-rā roshan [bi-kun]. [biyāfroz.]*
light the candle,	*shama'-rā roshan bi-kun.*
bring the shade,	*fānūs biyār.*
put out the candle,	*shama'-rā khāmosh bi-kun.*
raise the shade,	*fānūs [bar dār]. [bar gīr.]*
don't forget,	*ān-rā farāmosh ma kun.* / *az yād-i-ān zamāne ghāfil ma shau.*
come here,	*īn jā biyā.*
come near,	*nazdīk biyā.*
where do you come from?	*shumā az kujā [mī-āyed]? [tashrīf mī-āred?]*
where are you going?	*shumā ba kujā [mī-raved]? [tashrīf mī-bared; ḳadam ranga mī-farmāyed.]*
make ready the tea,	*chā,e [taiyār bi-kun]. [bi-sāz.]*
turn to the right,	*ba rāst [bar gard]. [rū,e bi-kun.]*
turn to the left,	*ba chap [bar gard]. [rū,e biyār; rū,e bi-nih.]*
go home quickly,	*ba khāna,e khụd zūd bi-rau.*

Exercise.—Who is bringing the breakfast? Sir, I have brought the breakfast. What is there to-day for dinner? They eat good bread and drink fresh milk. Have you lighted the candles? Bring us some tea, sugar, bread, and milk very quickly. Where have all the servants gone to? Sir, they have all gone home. When will they come back? When you go there, you will first turn to the left and then to the right. Ask these soldiers of what regiment they are. What is the name of the officer? At what hour to-morrow morning will they march for Ispahān?

Lesson 19.

move straight on,	*rāst bi-rau.* *rāst bar bīnī bi-rau.*
call the porters,	*mazdūrān-rā bi-ṭalab.*
take away the table,	*mez-rā [bar dār]. [bi-bar.]*
take away the things,	*asbāb-rā bi-bar.*
raise the table,	*mez-rā [bar dār]. [bi-gīr.]*
be careful,	*khabar-dār bāsh.* *hoshiyār bāsh.* *nigāh dār.*
what is your command?	*ḥukmat chīst?*
get ready the carriage,	*kāliska [taiyār] bi-kun. [āmāda.]*
it is of no consequence,	*muẓāyaḳa nīst.*
are you at leisure?	*āyā, ba shumā farāghat ast?*
be pleased to forgive me,	*marā mu'āf bi-farmāyed.* *luṭf karda marā [mu'āf bi-farmāyed]. [ma'ẕūr bi-dāred.]* *az rū,e 'ināyat marā ma'ẕūr bi-dāred.* *marḥamat karda marā mu'āf bi-farmāyed.* *az rū,e talaṭṭuf 'uẕr-i-marā ḳabūl kuned.*
bring a little bread,	*ḳadre nān biyār.*
have you made the bed?	*shumā [bistar]-rā gustarda ed?* [1] *[rakht-i-khwāb.]*
fasten the door,	*dar bi-band.* *dar muḳaffal bi-kun.*
they are old,	*eshān [ḳadīm] and. [derīna; kuhna.]* *shakhṣān-i-ḳadīm and.*

---

[1] court dress, *rakht-i-salāmī.*
to set off on a journey, *rakht bar bastan.*

this is a misfortune,	[1]*īn* [*bad*] *bakhtī ast.* [*kam.*]
they are ignorant,	*eshān jāhilān and.*
bring my book,	*kitāb-i-man biyār.*
bring my shoes,	[*kafsh*]*-i-man biyār.* [*pā posh, pā afzār,* or *pā,e zār,* or *pā,e dān,* or *mūza.*]
go to the market,	*ba būzār bi-rau.*
bring a little meat,	*ḳadre gosht biyār.*

Exercise.—Sir, all the porters have come. Tell them to put the things in the carriage. Have you fastened the door of the house? When I shall be at leisure I shall see him. Has the servant brought the meat from the market? Have you put my books on the table? Sir, pray forgive me, I had forgotten. Well, do not forget again. What a great misfortune this is! Sir, I have brought your shoes. I am not at leisure to see him to-day, tell him to come early to-morrow. Who is that old man who is standing near the door?

Lesson 20.

who are you?	*shumā kīsted?*
why are you come?	*chirā āmaded?*
you will say something to me,	*shumā chīze khwāhed guft.* *shumā mī-khwāhed ki marā chīze bi-goyed.*
don't be troublesome,	*marā ma ranjūn.* *dast az man dār.* *takhlīfam ma dih.* *marā mutakhallif ma shau.* *marā dar mashaḳḳat mayandāz.*
call my house steward,	[*darogha,e*] *pesh khidmatgārān-i-marā bi-ṭalab.* [*nāẓir-i.*]

[1] misfortune, *āfat; balā; sakhtī; muṣībat; shiddat; tīrā-bakhtī; āshūb; nakbat; āsīb; ṣammā.*

order dinner,	*shām biyār.* *shām ba mez nigăh dār.* *shām ba mez nig h dār.* *shām ba mez bi-guzār.* *ḥukm-i-āwardan-i-shām bi dih.*
I will go out,	*man, ba kāre, berūn khwāham raft.*
bring my clothes,	[1] *rakhūt-i-poshīdan-i-marā biyār.*
please come quickly,	*zūd tashrīf biyāred.*
repair the warehouse,	*marammat-i-khāna,e tijārat bi-kuned.*
bring the newspaper,	*akhbār biyār.* *akh b art biyār.*
is this the very thing?	*īn chīz bi-'ainihi hamān ast.*
they are all there,	*eshān hama ānjā and.*
who is he?	*o kīst?*
is any one there?	*āyā, ān jā kase ast?*
say that again,	*bāz bi-go.*
how are you?	*chigūna ī?* or *chi ṭaur ī? aḥwālat chi ṭaur ast?*
we shall go to-morrow,	*farda man khwāham raft.*
move this way,	*īn [rāh] bi-rau.* [*ṭaraf.*]
move that way,	*ān [rāh] bi-rau.* [*jānib.*]
has the gun fired?	[2] *top sar shuda ast?* *top zada ast?*

Exercise.—Who is that man, and why has he come here? Is the newspaper come to-day? Where have you put my clothes? Has the *khānsāmān* yet returned from the market? Tell me when he comes back. Sir, the *khānsāmān* says there is no good meat in the market

[1] *rakhūt* is the plur. of *rakht*, apparatus, apparel.

[2] to fire, *top-rā sar dādan; tufang-rā sar dādan.* / *top-rā sar kardan.* / *top-rā zadan.*

to-day. Carry the books and newspapers to the warehouse. What will he say to you to-morrow? How is he to-day? He says that he is now much better. The gun in the fort is fired every morning at dawn, and also at the end of evening twilight. Such is the custom of this country.

LESSON 21.

send for the palanquin quickly,	[1] *az barā,e 'amārī,e rawān zūd bi-firist.*
has the master risen?	*āyā, ṣāḥibat az khwāb [bar khāsta ast]. [bedār shuda ast.]*
this is a very fine fruit,	*īn mewa [lazīz] ast. [nafīs; laṭīf.]*
this is wonderful news,	*īn akhbār-i-'ajīb ast.*
we are hungry and thirsty,	*mā gursina o tushna em.*
he is a careful man,	*o shakhṣe [dūr andesh] ast. [hoshiyār; bā khabar; ṣāḥib-i-intibāh.]*
they are great rogues,	[2] *eshān kalān [bad ma'āsh] and. [aubāsh; dūnān o khasīs himmatān; fāsiḳān; ishrār; nā-kasān.]*
the whole land is level,	*hama zamīn [barābar] ast. [hamwār; musaṭṭah.]*
his heart is grieved,	*dil-i-o [maghmūm] ast. [ranjīda; mukaddar; malūl; majrūḥ.]*
is your business now completed?	*ilḥāl kār-i-shumā [tamām shuda ast]? [ba itmām rasīda āst.]*

---

[1] Litter for an elephant, *'amārī.*
Litter for a camel, *haudaj,* or *kajāwa* (for women).
A palanquin, *'amārī,e rawān.*

[2] Victuals, *kifāf-i-ma'āsh.*

is the proof of it strong?	*ṣabūt-i-ān amr maẓbūṭ ast?* *dalīl-i-ān kār kāmil ast?*
she is very impudent,	*o bisiyār gustākh ast.* *o bisiyār be adab ast.*
the sky is quite clear,	*āsmān khūb muṣaffa ast.*
these are mischievous children,	*īn bachchagān [shokh] and. [muẓirr.]*
he received great punishment,	*o [sazā] bisiyār yāft. [siyāsat; ta'zīb; 'akūbat; 'ikāb.]*
they all remained hidden,	*eshān hama [nihufta] māndand. [poshīda; dar pinhān.]*
his heart is restless,	*khāṭir-i-o [muẓṭarib ast]. [jam' nīst.]* *dil-i-o bekarār ast.* *dil-i-o dar iẓṭirāb mī-āyad.*
he is a fool,	*o [aḥmak] ast. [abla; nā-dān; nā-fahm.]*
this paper is moist,	*īn kāghaz [tar] ast. [namnāk.]*
who is making a noise?	*ki [shor] mī-kunad? [ṣaut; ṣadā; ghaughā.]*
what are you saying?	*shumā chi mī-goyed?* *shumā chi ḥarf mī-zaned?*

Exercise.—Sir, the pālkī is ready. Bring me some paper, that I may write. Ask that man if his master has yet risen. What is the name of this fruit? Is there much fruit on that tree? I shall come home when I have completed my business. Do not make so much noise there. You said that these men were great liars. You say that you are very careful. The fool says everything that comes into his heart; but whatever comes into the heart of the wise, the same remains hidden. The news from the army this week is by no means favourable. The man who brings the news is a very great rogue, and those who believe him are fools.

Lesson 22.

speak easy Persian,	fārsī,e [salīs] bi-go. [āsān.]
whence are you come?	az kujā āmada ed?
go away, you have leave,	{ bi - rau [murakhkhaṣ ed]. [shumā-rā rukhṣat ast; shumā rukhṣat ed.]
go not there again,	ān jā bāz ma rau.
put us on shore,	{ mā-rā ba sāḥil pā,īn bi-kun. mā-rā ba kināra,e daryā bi-guẕār.
who lives there?	{ ān jā ki manzil dārad? ān jā ki mī-mānad? ān jā kudām kas manzil dārad?
go on straightforward,	rāst bi-rau.
bring some wine and water,	ḳadre sharāb o āb biyār.
cool the water well,	āb-rā bisiyār sard bi-kun.
the dinner is on the table,	shām [bar mez] ast. [muḥaiyā.]
what is your name?	nām-i-shumā chīst?
he is very clever,	{ o bisiyār hoshiyār ast. o bisiyār 'aḳlmand ast. o ẕī shu'ūr ast.
wake me very early,	mārā [waḳt-i-ṣubḥ] bedār bi-kun. ['alā-s-ṣabāḥ; bāmdād.]
it is fair to-day,	imrūz rūz-i-[bahārī] ast. [muṣaffa.]
he has made confession,	o iḳrār karda ast.
make a signal to the porter for coming here,	ba ḥammālishārat-i-āmadan-i-[īn-jā] bi-kun. [in ṭaraf.]
have patience a little,	ẕarra ṣabr bi-kun.
send them to my house,	eshān-rā ba khāna,e man bifirist.
sprinkle a little water,	ḳadre āb biyafshān.
turn back that leaf,	ān waraḳ-rā būz bi-gardān.
tie their hands and feet,	dast o pā,e oshān bi-band.

Exercise.—You say that the Persian language is very easy. He put them all ashore there yesterday. Have you well cooled the wine and the water? Tell me when the dinner is on the table. Why did you not wake me very early, as I told you? If you forget another time, then you will get great punishment. Have they seen our signal for their coming here? Send the wine and water to my house. We do not live there. These boys are very clever. He has made no confession as yet. Who has torn the leaf from my book? The magistrate caused the prisoners to be bound hand and foot.

LESSON 23.

put those rupees in the bag,	[1] *dar* [*kīsa*] *ān rūpiyahā bi-guẕār.* [*jīb.*]
there is a fakir at the door,	*bar dar darweshe istāda ast.*
he is very intelligent,	*o bisiyār ẕakī ast.*
this is very good bread,	*īn nān bisiyār kh͟ūb ast.*
come back this way,	*ba īn rāh bāz ā.*
move a little slower,	*andake āhista bi-rau.*
come, take off my boots,	*biyā kafsh-i-man pāyīn bi-kun.*
come out of the house,	*az kh͟āna berūn biyā.*
wash your hands and face,	*dast o rū,e kh͟ud bi-*[*shūe*]. [*shū.*]
he has many friends,	*o bisiyār dostān dārad.*
what benefit will there be in that?	*dar ān amr chi fā,ida kh͟wāhad būd?*
they have suffered much sorrow,	*eshān bisiyār gh͟am kh͟urda and.* / *ba eshān bisiyār gh͟am rasīda ast.*

[1] a bag for money or letters, *kīsa*.
a cut-purse, *kīsa bur;* (thief) *duẕd;* (highwayman) *rāh-zan; ṭarrār.*
a purse-bearer or letter-carrier, *kīsadār; ḳāṣid.*
a purse, *ṣurra.*
a letter-bag, a letter, *kh͟arīṭa.*

he has got a long beard,	*o rīsh-i-darāz dārad.*
what bird is this?	*īn kudām murgh ast?* *īn murgh chīst?*
he is a great drunkard,	*o bisiyār sharābī ast.* *o bisiyār [sharāb khwār] ast. [sharāb khur; khammār.]* [1]
they are decidedly guilty,	*yaḳīnan eshān [mujrim] and. [muḳaṣṣar.]*
whose field is this?	*īn kisht az kīst?*
there are many flies here,	*īn jā bisiyār magasān and.*
they have great prudence,	*eshān bisiyār [ʼāḳibat andeshī] dārand. [ḥaẕar; ḥazm; iḥtirāz.]* *eshān bisiyār iḥtiyāṭ bajā mīārand.*
how many people were present?	*chand mardumān ḥāẓir būdand?*

Exercise.—How many rupees are there in the bag? Bring water, that I may wash my hands and face. I have suffered much sorrow on your account. What is the name of this fine bird? These flies give me much trouble. That *faḳīr* has a very long beard. Give him a rupee and tell him to go away. Tell him that if he makes such a noise another day, I will punish him severely. Where do your friends live? Are all the people present to-day? His friends afford him one hundred rupees a month. That man is quite innocent. There are many very fine trees in that field. These men never speak the truth; I cannot place any reliance upon what they tell me.

---

[1] eating, or consuming, *khur.*
devouring men, *mardūm khur.*
inheriting, *mīrāṣ khur.*

Lesson 24.

there is no oil in the lamp,	hech rūghan dar chirāgh nīst.
pray give me a sample,	marā namūna,e ['ināyat] bi-farmāyed. [luṭf.]
this is a mere stratagem,	īn fakat [ḥīla] ast. [dām; fareb; makr; zark.]
where is his shop?	dūkān-i-o kujā ast?
have you got a rope,	[1] āyā, shumā rassane dāred?
the king sat upon the throne,	[2] bādshāh bar takht julūs farmūd. bādshāh bar takht nishast. bādshāh jālis-i-takht gardīd.
his voice is good,	āwāz-i-o khūsh ast. īn shakhs khūsh alḥān ast.
what sort of animal is this?	īn ḥaiwān kudām kism ast?
what is your advice?	ṣalāḥ-i-shumā chīst?
what is your age?	'umr-i-shumā chīst?
send the palki near me,	nazd-i-man 'amārī,e rawān bi-firist.
give me the whip and hat,	[tāziyāna] o kulā,e marā bi-dih. [chābuk.]
bring water for washing the hands,	āb-i-dast shū,e biyār. [3] āb-i-dast shorī biyār. āb az barā,e shustan-i-dast-i-man biyār.

---

[1] string, rishta; a dependent, rishta dār.
 rope, rassan; thick rope, rassan-i-kuluft; thin rope, rassan-i-bārīk or rishtak.
[2] to sit, to sit down, to ascend the throne, julūs kardan.
[3] to wash, { shustan, root shū,e or shū.
        { shorīdan, root shor.

how is your health?	*mizāj-i-sharīf chigūna ast?* *aḥwāl-i-janāb chi ṭaur ast?* *mizāj-i-muḳaddas chigūna ast?* *ṭabī'at-i-a'lā chigūna ast?* *mizāj-i-shumā chigūna ast?*
give me the tooth-brush and powder,	*miswāk o sūda,e dandān shorī bi-dih.* *miswāk o safūf-i-dandān shū,e bi-dih.*
bring a suit of clothes,	[1] *yak dast-rakht-i-poshīdan biyār.*
bring ink, pen, and paper,	[2] *murakkab, ḳalam, kāghaz biyār.*
whose horse is that?	*ān asp az ān-i-kīst?* *ān asp az kīst?* *ān asp māl-i-kīst?*
who is that European?	*ān farangī kīst?*

Exercise.—One day, in the summer season, a king and his son went a-hunting. When the air became very hot, then they placed each his cloak on the back of a certain jester. The king, having laughed, said, "Now, O jester, there is an ass's burden on thy back." The jester gave answer, "Verily, your majesty, I bear the burdens of two asses."

Lesson 25.

whose house is this?	*īn khāna māl-i-kīst?* *īn khāna az ān-i-kīst?*

---

[1] best suit of clothes, *yak dasṭ-rakht-i-*[*a'lā*]. [*bihtar* or *kashang.*]

[2] blotting paper, { *kāghaz-i-murakkab kash.* / *kāghaz-i-murakkab khushk kun.* }

this soil is barren,	*īn zamīn [wairān] ast. [shora-būm.]*
they are very avaricious,	*eshān bisiyār [ṭām'i] and. [ḥariṣ.]*
this rupee is adulterated,	*īn rūpiya kāsid ast.*
its shape is bad,	*ṣūrat-i-ān bad [haikal] ast. [shakl; ḥaiyar.]*
the English language is difficult,	*zabān-i-inglīsī [mushkil] ast. [mughlaḳ.]*
brush off the spider's web,	*khāna,e 'ankabūt pāk bi-kun.* *tār-i-'ankabūt pāk bi-kun.* *lu'āb-i-'ankabūt pāk bi-kun.*
what crime has he committed?	*[1] o chi [taḳṣīr] karda ast? [khaṭā.]* *az o chi taḳṣīr ṣādir shuda ast?*
there is much dew on the grass,	*bar sabz-zār bisiyār shabnam ast.* *bar kāh bisiyār shabnam uftāda ast.* *bar giyāh bisiyār shabnam bārīda ast.*
now they are very helpless,	*ilḥāl bisiyār [be 'ilāj] and. [lā 'ilāj; lā chār.]*
what business are you doing?	*īn jā chi kār mī-kuned?*
there is no end of his chattering,	*behūda goī,e o ākhir na dārad.* *[ākhirat]-i-yāwa goī,e o nīst. [ikhtitām.]* *maḳālāt-i-muhāl amez wa maḳaula,e mustaḥīlāt-i-o ikhtitām na dārad.*

---

[1] right and wrong, *ṣawāb o khaṭā.*

they made much apology,	*eshān bisiyār 'uẕr kardand.* / *eshān dar maḳām-i-i'tiẕār āmadand.*
my parents have gone to their house (other people's house),	*wālidain-i-man ba khāna,e oshān rafta and.*
there are many fruits in that garden,	*dar ān bāgh bisiyār mewahā and.*
I have a headache,	*sar-i-man dard mī-kunad.* / *man ṣudā' dāram.*
where did you hear this news?	*shumā kujā īn khabar-rā shunīded?*
it is late, let us depart,	*der shuda ast, biyā ki mā bi-ravem.*

Exercise.—They thus say, that in a certain house a tiger and a man saw a picture, in which the man was drawn as victorious, and the beast subdued. The man said to the tiger, "Dost thou see the bravery of the man, how he has overcome the tiger?" The tiger gave answer, "The painter was a man: if a tiger had been the painter, then the drawing would not have been in this manner."

Lesson 26.

he has a liver complaint,	*o bīmārī,e jigar dārad.*
this is a fine season,	*īn mausim khūb ast.*
sow that seed in the garden,	[1] *dar bāgh ān tukhm-rā bi-kār.*
he has a toothache,	*o [dard]-ī-dandān dārad. [waja'.]* / *dandān-i-o dard mī-kunad.*
there are many playthings in the bazar,	*dar bāzār bisiyār chīzhā,e bāzīcha and.*

---

[1] a field, *mazra'*; *zara'*; *zirā'at*; to sow a field, *kishtan*, root *kār*.

what is your occupation?	[*kār*]*-i-shumā chīst?* [*pesha; kasb; ishtighāl.*]
this translation is very good,	*īn tarjuma bisiyār khūb ast.*
his case will come on to-day,	*muḳaddama,e o imrūz khwāhad shud.* [*ḳaziya,*]*e o imrūz rujū' khwāhad shud.* [*murāfa'a.*]
your watch goes well,	*sā'at-i-shumā khūb mī-ravad.*
this is a wax candle,	*īn shama',e momī ast.*
how much is the fare of the boat?	[*kirāya,e*] *māshūya chi ḳadar ast?* [*ujrat-i-.*]
what o'clock is it?	*chand sā'at ast? chi waḳt ast?*
brush my hat and coat,	*kulā o ḳabā,e marā ṣāf kun.*
what is the fare for a day?	*az barā,e yak rūz kirāya chi ḳadar ast?*
lift up the blinds, take away the dishes,	*pardahā bar dār, bushḳābhā bi-bar.*
place my watch on the table,	*sā'at-i-marā bar mez bi-guzār.*
this fruit is very acid,	*īn mewa bisiyār talkh ast.*
why are you angry?	*chirā* [*khafa ed*]? [*baham bar āyed; rū,e darham mī-kashed; dar khashm mī-āyed; chīn ba jabīn shuda ed.*]

Exercise.—One day, a stag, from fear of the hunters, having fled, entered within a certain cave. There a large tiger having gone, seized and began to eat the stag. At the time of dying, that helpless animal said, in his own heart, "Alas, what a great misfortune is mine! I fled hither from fear of man, and now I have fallen into the claws of an animal whose cruelty is even greater than man's."

Lesson 27.

this is a very difficult business,	*īn kūr bisiyūr* [*mushkil*] *ast.* [*dushwār; muta'azzir; muta'assir.*]
they are very artful,	*eshūn bisiyār farebī and.* *eshān ḳadam dar būdiya,e ghadar wa kufrūn nihūda and.*
that is a very beautiful garden,	*ān bāgh bisiyūr* [*zībā*] *ast.* [*khūb ārāsta.*]
this cloth is very coarse,	*īn pārcha bisiyār* [*durusht*] *ast.* [*kuluft.*]
are you fit for the business?	*āyā, shumā ḳūbil-i-kūr ed?* *āyā, shumā sazūwār-i-kūr ed?*
it is colder to-day than yesterday,	*az dī rūz, imrūz sard-tar ast.*
this line is better,	*īn saṭar bihtar ast.*
his heart is very sorrowful,	*dil-i-o ghamgīn ast.* *gham bar o* [*ghālib ast*]. [*mustaulī ast.*] *o pareshān khāṭir o parāganda dil ast.*
she is dumb and deaf,	*ān zan gung o kar ast.*
this story is all a lie,	*īn ḳiṣṣa hama darogh ast.*
these are fine raisins,	*īn keshmish bisiyār* [*khūb*] *and.* [*nafīs.*]
he has a large house,	*o khāna,e kalān dārad.*
this room is well lighted,	*īn ḥujra khūb roshan karda shuda ast.* *īn ūṭāk khūb roshan ast.*
this room is very lofty,	*īn ḥujra bisiyār buland ast.*
how long is this cloth?	*īn pārcha chi ḳadar* [*darāz*] *ast?* ['*arīẓ.*] *īn pārcha chi ḳadar ṭūl dārad?*

these are very wicked children,	īn bachchagān bisiyār sharīr and.
his disposition is cruel,	{ <u>kh</u>ulk-i-o be raḥm ast. ṭabī'at-i-o be raḥm ast.
they are lazy and negligent,	eshān sust o <u>gh</u>āfil and.
they are of a very stern disposition,	eshān bisiyār [sa<u>kh</u>t ṭabī'at] and. [durusht <u>kh</u>ulḳ; tund <u>kh</u>ū; bad <u>kh</u>ū.]

Exercise.—In a dark night a blind man, having taken a lamp in his hand, and a jar on his shoulder, was going along in the market. Somebody said to him, "O fool! in thy eyes day and night are alike; of what use is a lamp to thee?" The blind man, having laughed, said, "O you great blockhead! do you imagine that the lamp is for my benefit? No, it is entirely on thy account, that thou mayest not break my jar amidst the darkness."

Lesson 28.

this pen is too soft,	īn ḳalam bisiyār narm ast.
this paper is very coarse,	¹ īn kā<u>gh</u>az bisiyār [kuluft] ast. [zibbir.]
this letter is ill-shaped,	īn ḥaraf [bad ṣūrat] ast. [bad <u>kh</u>att.]
you speak very slowly,	{ shumā bisiyār āhista mī-goyed. shumā ba bisiyār āhistagī mī-goyed.
can you speak English?	zabān-i-inglīsī ḥaraf zadan mī-tawāned?
descend, otherwise you will fall,	[pāyīn] biyā, warna shumā <u>kh</u>wāhed uftād. [farod.]

¹ thin, fine, *bārīk*; *nāzuk*.

you must go with me,	*bāyad ki bā man bi-raved.*
take away this bundle,	*īn basta bi-bar.*
it is cloudy, yea, it rains a little,	*imrūz saḥābī ast, balki ḳadre mī-bārad.* / *imrūz saḥābī ast, balki tarashshuḥ dārad.*
see, has it cleared up a little?	*bi-bīn ki ḳadre ṣāf shuda ast, yā na?*
we know it all,	*mā hama mī-dānem.*
they know a great deal,	*eshān bisiyār mī-dānand.*
he gave me much trouble,	*ȯ marā bisiyār [takhlīf] dād. [zuḥmat.]*
why do you laugh without cause?	*shumā be sabab chirā mī-khanded?*
they have annoyed us very much,	*eshān mārā bisiyār tashwīsh dāda and.* / *az kirdār-i-eshān munaghghiṣ shuda em.*
this is not my house,	*īn khāna az ān-i-man nīst.* / *īn khāna az māl-i-man nīst.* / *īn khāna az milk-i-man nīst.*
allow me to smell that flower,	*luṭf bi-farmāyed ki [bū,e āngul-rā bi-bīnam]. [gul-rā bū bi-bīnam; gul-rā bū bi-shinavam.]* / *az rū,e luṭf bū,e ān gul bar giriftan marā bi-dihed.*
apply oil to that chair,	*ān kursī-rā rūghan bi-māl.*
open the lock of that door,	*ḳufl-i-ān dar-rā wā kun.*

Exercise.—A very poor man went to a very rich man and said, "We two are sons of Adam and Eve (*Adam o Ḥawā*), therefore we are brothers; you are very rich and I am very poor; give me a brother's share." The rich man, on hearing this, gave to the poor man one *kauṛī*. The poor man said, "Oh, sir! why do you not bestow upon me a brother's share?" He replied, "Be content, my good friend; if I give all my poor brothers one *kauṛī* each, I shall not have any remaining."

Lesson 29.

some of our soldiers have been wounded,	*b'aẓe sar-bāzān-i-mā majruḥ shuda and.*
beat that lazy boy,	*ān kodak-i-sust-rā bi-zan.*
dig up that underwood,	*ān darakhthā,e khụrd-rā bar kan.*
having said this, he departed,	*īn guft o [rukhṣat girift]. [rawāna shud.]*
wring the moisture from the clothes,	*az jāmahā [nam] bar gīr. [tar; namnāk.]* / *az jāmahā [nam] biyafshār.*
they sleep carelessly (soundly),	*eshān ghāfilāna mī-khuspand.* / *eshān ghāfilāna mī-khwāband.*
what is the amount of your bill?	*jam',e ḥisāb-i-shumā chīst?*
a wasp has stung me,	[1] *zambūr marā [gazīda] ast. [nesh-zada.]*
what is the tonnage of this ship?	*īn jahāz chi ḳadr bār bar mī-dārad?*
what need is there of so much care?	*iḥtiyāj-i-īn ḳadr-i-khabar-dārī chīst?* / *iḥtiyāj-i-īn ḳadr-i-ḥifāẓat chīst?* / *īn ḳadar iḥtiyāṭ chi maṣlaḥat dārad?*
what is the price of these things?	*ḳīmat-i-īn chīzhā chīst?*

[1] a bee { *magas-i-'asal.* / *magas-i-shahd.* / *magas-i-ambagīn.* }
purified honey, *'asal i-muṣaffā.*

what is the depth of this tank ?	*'umuḳ-i-īn ḥauẓ chi ḳadr ast?* *īn yambūgh chi ḳadr 'amīḳ ast?*
what is the difference between these two ?	*mā bain-i-īn har dū faraḳ chīst?* *dar miyān-i-īn har dū tā tafrīḳ chīst?* *miyān-i-īn har dū tufāwat chīst?* *chi faraḳ az īn badān ast?*

Exercise.—A person went to a scribe, and said unto him, "Write a letter for me." He said, "There is a pain in my foot." The man said, "I do not wish to send you anywhere, why are you making this unreasonable excuse?" The scribe replied, "You are speaking the truth; but when I write a letter for any person, then I am always sent for to read it; for nobody else is able to read my handwriting."

Lesson 30.

this army does not know its exercise,	*īn lashkar ḳawā'id-i-khud na mī-dānad.*
between you two what fighting is there ?	*mā bain-i-shumā har dū [ḳaẓiya] chīst? [d'awā; taḳrā,e; ma'raka; mujādilat o munāza'at; jang o jadal o ḥarb; munākisha o muḳābila; mukhāṭiba o mu'ātibā.]*
in this book how many chapters are there ?	*dar īn kitāb chand [bābhā] and? [faṣlhā.]*
on these goods is there any discount ?	*bar īn asbāb hech [ḳaṣr] ast? [kaṣr; kasr.]* *īn asbāb-rā chand pūl tanzīl mī-kunand?*

the drum beats every day in the fort,	*dar ḥiṣār har rūz* [*kos kofta mī-shavad*]. [*ṭibl mī-zanand.*] *dar ḳila' har yaum duhul mī-nawāzand.*
this boy is much loved by us,	*īn kodak bisiyār 'azīz-i-mā ast.*
in this tank are there any fish?	*dar īn* [*ḥauẓ*] *hech māhī ast?* [*āb-gīr ; birka.*]
make a hole here in the earth,	*īn jā dar zamīn* [*maghāke*] *bi-kan.* [*gaude.*]
I caught a fish with a rod,	*bā dām māhī,e girijtam.*
this cow has no horns,	*īn mādah-gāw-rā shākhhā nayand.* *īn mādah-gāw shākhhā na dārad.*
of what kind is this cloth?	*īn* [*pārcha*] *chi kism ast?* [*ṭāḳa.*]
do you intend going to Europe?	*āyā,irāda,e raftan-i-farang-istān mī-kuned?*
hang up this lamp in the hall,	[1] *dar dālān īn fānus-rā* [*mu-'allaḳ bi-kun.*] [*biyāwez.*]
do you go by land or by water?	*ba khūshkī yā ba tarī khwāhed raft?*

Exercise.—A certain hare having gone to the presence of the tigress, said to her, "O tigress, of me every year there are many young ones, but of you, during the whole of your life, there are no more than two or three." The tigress, having smiled, replied, "What you say is very true: of me, indeed, there may be only one young one in all my life, but that one is a tiger."

---

[1] hall, *dālān ; aiwān.*

Lesson 31.

there is no lock to your box,	*ṣandūḳ-i-shumā-rā ḳufl nīst.* *ṣandūḳ-i-shumā ḳufl na dārad.*
there is much mud on the river side,	*bar lab-i-daryā bisiyār [khilāb] ast. [gil; shor; waḥal.]*
how many passengers were in that vessel?	*dar ān jahāz chand 'ābirān būdand?*
the whole room was scented,	*tamām-i-ḥujra khūsh bū karda shuda ast.* *tamām-i-ḥujra mu'aṭṭar karda shuda ast.*
are you the owner of this house?	*āyā, mālik-i-īn khāna ed?*
from idleness is loss,	*az [sustī] nuḳṣān ast. [ihmāl; taghāful.]* *natīja,e kāhilī nuḳṣān ast.*
such as you will do, so will you find,	*harchi shumā khwāhed kard, khwāhed yāft.*
resignation is the best companion,	*taslīm khūbtarīn-i-muṣāḥib ast.* *taslīm a'lātarīn-i-muṣāḥib ast.* *taslīm yake az khūbtarīn-i-muṣāḥibān ast.*
the world is the house of deceit,	*[dunyā] khāna,e fareb ast. [kurra,e arẓ.]*
the fruit of rashness is repentance,	*natīja,e [ta'jīl] tauba ast. [be tadbīrī; tahawwar].*
patience is au excellent quality,	*ṣabr kamāl khulḳ ast.* *ṣabr 'ālī khaṣlat ast.*
temperance is excellent physic,	*parhez khūb dawā ast.*
hearing is better than speaking,	*shunīdan az guftan bihtar ast.*
from labour results greatness,	*natīja,e miḥnat buzurgī ast.*

Exercise.—A certain old woman had a goose which every day used to lay an egg of gold. One day the old woman thought in her own mind, thus: "If I increase the food of this goose, then she will every day give two golden eggs." Having thus determined, the old woman began to give the goose every day as much food as she could eat. Now, after some days, the goose having become very fat, gave no more eggs.

Lesson 32.

such as you speak so will you hear,	*ānchi tū goyī, bi-shinavī.*
this world is the harvest for the next,	*īn dunyā kisht-i-'ālam-i ['akabat] ast. ['ālam-i-ākhir; sarā,e jāwadānī; dāru-l-baḳā; 'uḳbā.]* *jahān-i-fānī khirmān-i-jahān-i-bāḳī ast.*
contentment is the key of repose,	*ḳinā'at [kalīd-i-ārām] ast. [musabbib-i-rāḥat; wajh-i-'aish.]*
to be ignorant is death to the living,	*jāhil shudan maut-i-zindagī ast.*
moderation in everything is best,	*[ausaṭ-i-aḥwāl] bihtar ast. [i'tidāl.]*
to the wise a hint is enough,	*'āḳil-rā ishāra,e bas ast.*
death laughs at expectations,	*bar ummed [maut] mī-khandad. [ajl.]*
assist your brother in distress,	*barādar-i-khud-rā [dar ḥālat-i-sakhtī] madad bidih. [dar ḥālat-i-iḥtiyāj; dar muḥtājī.]*
very frequently medicine is sickness,	*aksar auḳāt dawā bīmārī ast.*
God is upright and holy,	*allāh ta'ālā [ḥaḳḳ o pāk] ast. [rāst-bāz o muḳaddar.]*

man becomes known from his conduct,	*ādam az mu'āmala,e khụd mashhūr mī-shavad.* *ādam az 'amalhā,e khụd [mashhūr mī-shavad]. [shuhrat mī-yābad.]*
from prohibition desire increases,	*az mana' kardan khwāhish ziyāda mī-shavad.* *az muzāḥamat khwahish taraḳḳī mī-pazīrad.*
fortune does not increase with wisdom,	*az 'aḳl [nafaḳa] ziyāda na mī-shavad. [rozīna; kifāf.]*

Exercise.—One day a large bull was grazing in a field, when a conceited fly came and sat on one of his horns. The fly began to say in her own mind, "I am very heavy, and if I remain here, assuredly the bull will not be able to lift his head from the ground." Then tho fly said aloud, "O bull, I am afraid I am giving you great inconvenience; if so it be, then speak out, and I will immediately depart." The bull answered, "O fly, be not uneasy on my account, for I was not in the least aware of your being there till you spoke to me."

Lesson 33.

during this month much rain fell,	*dar īn māh bisiyār bārān uftād.*
send a servant there,	*ān jā [naukare] bi-firist. [mulāzim; khādime; chākar.]*
sit under this tree,	*zer-i-īn darakht bi-nishīn.*
what is the price of these pearls?	*ḳīmat-i-īn dānāhā,e durr chīst?* *ḳīmat-i-īn dānāhā,e marwārīd chīst?*
how heavy will this stone be?	*wazn-i-īn sang chi ḳadr mī-shavad?*

what is the name of this village?	[1] *nām-i-īn [dih] chīst?* *[mauẓa'; ḳarya.]*
bring the riding-horse,	*asp-i-sawārī-rā biyār.*
brush the curtains well, so that no mosquito may remain,	*parda-rā k͟hūb biyafshān tā ki pasha,e na mānad.*
clean the shoes well,	*kafshhā-rā k͟hūb [ṣāf] bi-kun. [pāk.]* *kafshhā-rā siyāh rang bi-dih.*
we ought to be benevolent,	*bāyad ki [karīm] bāshem. [mushfiḳ.]* *sharṭ-i-ādmiyatān ast, ki karīm bāshem.*
we have fallen into great difficulties,	*dar mushkilāt-i-kalān uftāda em.*
many ships have been damaged by the storm,	*az ṭufān bisiyār jahāzhā nuḳṣān k͟hurda and.* *az ṭufān ba bisiyār jahāzhā nuḳṣān rasīda ast.*
he every day drinks new milk,	*o har rūz shīr-i-tāza mī-naushad.*
to sit still is better than quarrelling,	*ba k͟hamoshī nishastan az bar khāstan ba ḳaẓiya bihtar ast.*
grind this wheat in the mill,	[2] *dar āsiyā īn g͟halla biyās.* *dar āsiyā īn g͟halla bi-sāb.*
do you know who is his agent?	*shumā mī-dāned ki [waḳīl]-i-o kīst? [gumāshta; nā,ib.]*

Exercise.—A man went, for the purpose of seeing a certain person, to his house, at the time of midday. That person, from his own house, saw the man coming,

[1] village, *dih, or dīh*; plur. *dīhāt.*
[2] to grind, *sābīdan* or *āsīdan.*

and said to his servants, "When he asks where the master of the house is, you will say that he is now gone to dine with some one." In the meanwhile, the man having arrived, asked, "Where is the master of the house?" They said, "Our master is gone out." The man said, "A great fool he is to have gone out of his house in the midst of such heat." The master of the house, having put his head out of the window, said, "You are a very great fool to wander about at this time: for I have been all day in my own house."

Lesson 34.

buy two candlesticks for me,	[1] *az barā,e man dū 'adad-i-shama'dān bi-khar.* (with glass shades) *ba jihat-i-man yak juft-i-pāya,e lāla bi-kharīd.*
this cat has large claws,	*īn gurba kalān [panja] dārad.* [*nākhun; khanj.*]
take away this counterpane into the other room,	*dar ḥujra,e dīgar īn liḥāf bi-bar.*
is this place in the district of Shīrāz?	*āyā, dar 'alāḳa,e Shīrāz īn mauẓa ast.*
I will show you a beautiful picture,	*man shumā-rā taṣwīre [ḥasīn] khwāham namūd.* [*maḳhul; marghūb; nādir; ma'ḳūl.*]
your signature is necessary to this bond,	*ba īn tamassuk dastkhaṭṭ-i-shumā [ẓarūr] ast.* [*lāzim; malzūm.*]

---

[1] one pair of candlesticks, *yak juft-i-shama'dān*; i.e., two articles.
one pair of scissors, *'adad-i-miḳrāẓ*; i.e., one article.

to-day there is a guest in their house,	*imrūz dar khāna,e eshān mihmāne ast.*
who is this boy's governor?	*[aṭālīḳ]-i-īn ḳodak kīst? [murabbī.]*
it is very late, permit us to go home,	*bisiyār der shuda ast mā-rā ba khāna,e khud raftan bi-dih.* *bisiyār der shuda ast [biyā] ki ba khāna bi-ravem. [ijāzat bi-dih.]*
in this affair there is much cruelty,	*dar īn mu'āmala [ẓulm] ast. [bisiyār beraḥmī; bisiyār be murūwatī.]*
they commit oppression of every sort,	*eshān [ẓulm]-i-har ḳism mī-kunand. [jaur; sitam; be dād.]*
we have at present a long journey,	*īn waḳt mā safr-i-darāz dar pesh dārem.*

Exercise.—A certain feeble old man having gathered a load of wood (*literally* sticks) in a forest, was carrying it to his own house. After having gone some distance, the old man became very tired, and having thrown down the burden from his shoulder on the ground, he began to cry out, "O Angel of Death, deliver me from this misery!" At that very instant the Angel of Death stood before him, and said, "Why have you called me, and what do you want with me?" On seeing this frightful figure, the old man, trembling, replied, "O friend, be pleased to assist me, that I may lift once more this burden upon my shoulder: for this purpose only have I called you."

Lesson 35.

have you a glass for holding the medicine?	[1] *āyā shumā barā,e giriftan-i-dawā finjān-i-shīsha dāred?*

[1] a glass-blower, *shīsha-gar.*

man has reason, a brute none,	insān 'aḳl dārad, ḥaiwān na.
please give me a letter of introduction,	{ az rū,e luṭf marā sifārish nāma bi-dihed. az sar-i-luṭf marā sifārish nāma marḥamat bi-kuned.
why do you write with a bad pen?	ba ḳalam-i-bad chirā shumā mī-nawīsed?
of these two which is the best?	az īn har dū tū kudām bihtar ast?
I will take the business from you and give it to him,	man az tū 'amal khwāham girift o bado khwāham dād.
your going there is not necessary,	ān jā raftan-i-shumā ẓarūr nīst.
he is well versed in science,	{ [1] o dar 'ilm khūb wāḳif ast. o az 'ilm khūb mahārat yāfta ast. o dar 'ilm khūb mahārat dārad.
he is very learned and intelligent,	o bisiyār 'ālim ast o tez-fahm.
this will be best of all,	{ īn [bihtarīn-i-hama] khwāhad būd. [az hama bihtar.]
tell me what he is saying,	bi-go ki o chi mī-goyad.
tell the groom to get the horse ready,	mihtar-rā bi-go ki asp taiyār bi-kunad.

Exercise.—In a country of Kashmir a certain merchant had an Abyssinian slave whose skin was as black as charcoal. One day in the winter season the slave took off his clothes, and having taken up some snow, he began, with great labour, to rub it on his body. During this, his master came that way, and having seen this curious circumstance, said, "What are you doing here?" The

---

[1] experience, *wāḳif kārī; tajriba kārī.*

slave answered, "I am rubbing my body with snow, so that I may become white like the people of this country." His master, laughing, said, "O fool, do not labour in vain; your body may, indeed, dissolve the snow, but your skin will not thereby become white."

Lesson 36.

I also wish to go out,	*man mī-khwāham ki berūn bi-ravam.* *man nīz berūn raftan mī-khwāham.* *marā nīz irāda,e berūn raftan ast.* *man khwāhish-i-berūn raftan dāram.*
why do you climb the tree?	*chirā ba dirakht bar mī-āyed.*
when will you be able to depart?[1]	*kai judā shudan khwāhed tawānist.*
is the saddle on the horse or not?	*bar asp zīn [basta] ast yā na?* [*karda shuda.*]
we will return in a few minutes,	*mā dar chand [daḳīḳa] bāz khwāhem āmad.* [*laḥẓa.*]
if dinner be ready, bring it,	*agar [shām] taiyār ast biyār.* [*khurish, khurāk.*]
give my compliments to your master,	[*salām*]*-i-man ba ṣāḥib-i-khud bi-dih.* [*taslīm.*]
do you know this man?	*shumā īn mard-rā mī-dāned?*
he has acquired much science,	*o bisiyār 'ilm ḥāṣil karda ast.*
he has amassed much wealth,	*o bisiyār daulat jama' karda ast.*

[1] To leave a person, *az kase* [*judā*] *shudan.* [*rukhṣat.*] To leave a town, *az shahre rukhṣat shudan.*

come, let us two have some talk,	*biyū, ki mū har dū būham guft-gū bi-kunem.*
will one horse be able to draw so great a weight?	*āyā īn ḳadr bār-i-girān yak asp mī-tawānad kashīd?*
you go on, we are coming,	*shumā pesh bi-raved, ki mā [ham] mīyāyem. [dar-pai.]*
these things are come from Europe,	*az walāyat-i-farang īn chīz-hā rasīda and?*
where shall we pass the night?	*mā kujā shab ba sar bi-[kunem]? [guzārem; guzrānem.]*
we have no time to play at present,	*ilḥālmā-rā furṣat-i-bāzī nīst.* *ilḥāl mā furṣat-i-bāzī na dārem.*

Exercise.—One day an ox was grazing in a field in which several young frogs were playing. By chance one of the young frogs was crushed under the foot of the ox, and died. The other frogs having seen this, went home, and having told their mother what had occurred, they then said, "O mother, we never before saw so large an animal." On hearing this, the old frog, having distended her belly very much, said, "Is he as large as this?" The young ones replied, "Assuredly, he is much larger than that." She then, having distended herself twice as much, said, "Is he so large?" They answered, "O mother, he is a thousand times larger." The old frog, however, through pride, continued to distend her body more and more, till at last her skin burst, and she died.

Lesson 37.

he has scalded his foot,	*o pā,e khud-rā ba āb-i-[garm] sozānīda ast. [dāgh; josh.]*

all these knives are rusty,	*hama īn kārd zang* [*ālūda*] *and.* [*girifta.*]
these children are screaming all day,	*īn bachchagān hama rūz* [*shor o ghul*] *mī-kunand.* [*ghaughā.*]
we were seeking for this all day,	*mā tamām rūz barā,e īn just o jū dāshtem.*
have you sealed your letter?	*āyā khatt-i-khud-rā muhr* [*karda ed*] ? [*zada ed.*]
our house is shaded with trees,	*khāna,e mā dar zer-i-sāya,e dirakht-hā ast.*
it is raining, give us shelter,	*aknūn bārān mī-bārad, mārā panāhe bi-dih.*
go forward there, and stand still,	*ān jā pesh bi-rau o ba khāmoshī biyist.*
bring out these things from the pālkī,	*az 'amārī,e rawān īn chīz-hā biyār.*
speak loud, then I shall hear you,	*ba āwāz-i-buland bi-go ki bi-shinavam.*
what do you call that in Persian?	*ān chīz-rā dar zabān-i-fārsī chi mī-goyed ?*

Exercise.—From the house of a certain person, a bag of rupees was stolen. The owner of the money gave information to the judge of that city. The judge immediately called before him all the people of the house; but after much investigation he was unable to detect the thief. At last he said to them, "This night I will give each of you a stick one cubit in length, and it will so happen that the stick of him who is the thief will become one inch longer than those of the rest." Having thus spoken, the judge gave each a stick, and dismissed them. During the night, the thief being afraid, said to himself, "If I cut off one inch from my stick, in the morning it will be of the same length with the rest." Thus, having considered, he cut off an inch from his stick, and next day attended, along with the others. The judge, having looked at the sticks, thus discovered the thief.

Lesson 38.

set up something as a shelter from the sunshine,	*barā,e tābish-i-āftāb panāhe bar ār.*
he agreed with me this time,	*o īn waḳt ba-man muwāfiḳ āmad.* *o īn waḳt ba rā,e man* [*muwāfiḳ*] *shud.* [*muttafiḳ.*]
you exercise yourself in writing and reading,	*dar nawishtan o khwāndan khud-rā mashāk bi-sāz.*
on hearing this news they were much frightened,	*az shunīdan - i - īn-khabar eshān tarsīdand.* [1] *az shunīdan-i-īn-khabar* [*dar ḥālat-i-pareshānī āmadand*]. [*dar ḥālat-i-iẓṭirāb āmadand; dahshat wa pareshānī bar oshān mustaulī shud,* or *istīlā yāft.*]
how much indigo will this chest contain?	*dar īn ṣandūḳ chi ḳadr nīl khwāhad ganjīd?* *dar īn ṣandūḳ chi ḳadr nīl khwāhad āmad?* *īn ṣandūḳ chi ḳadr nīl khwāhad girift.*
they are all offended with one another,	*hama az yak dīgar* [*khafa*] *shuda and.* [*shakar ranj.*]

---

[1] to vex, *pareshān kardan.*

tell the coachman not to drive so quick,	*kāliskabān-rā bi-go ki chandān* [*zūd*] *na rānad.* [*tez* or *tund.*]
we have escaped from the hands of the enemy,	*mā ba makr o fareb az dast-i-dushmăn* [*rihā shuda em*]. [*rihā,ī yāfta em ; jān ba salāmat burda em.*] *mā az dast-i-dushman ba ḥīla khalāṣ shuda em.*
the whole city has been flooded,	*tamām shahr* [*gharḳ*] *shuda ast.* [*gharīḳ ; daryā burd.*]
put these two trays together,	*īn har dū ḳāb-rā ba ham bi-guẕār.*
with this our joy will be increased,	[1] *badīn khūshī,e mā ziyāda khwāhad shud.*

Exercise.—A certain person having a pain in the stomach went to a physician, and said, "For God's sake, doctor, give me some physic, otherwise I die from a pain in the stomach." The doctor asked him what he had eaten that day. The man said, "Merely a piece of burnt bread." On hearing this, the doctor said, "Let me look at your eyes." Then, having called one of his servants, he said, "Bring me the medicine for the eyes." The sick man, on hearing this, screamed out, "O doctor, is this a time for your joking? I am dying from a pain in the stomach, and you talk of medicine for the eyes. What connexion is there between medicine for the eyes and a pain in the stomach?" The doctor replied, "I wish, in the first place, to make your eyes sound, for it is evident that you are unable to distinguish between black and white, otherwise you would never have eaten burnt bread."

---

[1] joy, *shādmānī ; faraḥ ; khurramī ; ṭarab ; mubāsaṭat ; imbisāṭ ; nishāṭ.*

Lesson 39.

we have much reduced our expenditure,	*mā kharch-i-khud-rā bisiyār takhfīf karda em.*
this money must be sent back to him,	*īn pūl ba o ẓarūr wāpas bāyad kard.*
the commander-in-chief has pardoned a soldier,	*sipăh-sālār az taḳṣīr-i-sipāhī,e dar guẕăshta ast.* *sipăh-sālār sipāhī,e-rā mu'āf karda ast.*
rule your paper, then write,	*kāghaz-i-khud-rā awwal [mistar bi-kun] pas bi-nawīs. [khaṭṭ bi-kash.]*
all the people have died with hunger,	*hama mardumān az [gursinagī murda] and. [jū' ba jān āmada.]*
they have fallen one upon another,	*eshān [dar-ham] uftāda and. [bar yak dīgar.]*
splice these two ropes together,	*īn har dū rassan-rā bā-ham dīgar bi-paiwand.*
they live in great affliction, or through much toil,	*ba miḥnat-o-mashaḳḳat-i-bisiyār eshān guzrān mī-kunand.*
he has built a house on the bank of the Euphrates,	*ba lab-i-daryā,e farāt, 'imārate ta'mīr karda ast.*
he drove the chariot two parsang, when one of the wheels broke,	*b'ad az rāndan-i-dū parsang, yake az pāyahā,e kāliska [shikast]. [bar āmad.]*

Exercise.—Two women were quarrelling with one another about a child, and neither of them had any witness. Having gone before the judge, the one continued saying, "The child is mine;" and the other also was saying, "The child is mine, O your worship, give me justice." The judge, being helpless, sent for the executioner, and said to him, "Of this child make two pieces, and give one to each of these women." On hearing the order of the judge, the executioner drew the sword, and was about to cut the child in two. During this, one of the women stood still, and said nothing, but the other woman, weeping aloud, said, "O sir, do not kill my child; if such is justice, I give up my claim. For God's sake give her the child." On hearing this, the judge became convinced that this indeed is the real mother. To her he gave up the child; and to the other woman having given punishment, he ordered his people to expel her from the country.

Lesson 40.

why should we run away, there is no danger there?	*ān jā khaṭra hech nīst, pas chirā mā bi-gurezem?*
he has abandoned his late friends,	*o dostān-i-ḳadīm-i-khud-rā guẕāshta ast.* *muṣāḥibat-i-dostān-i-sābiḳa-rā ba dil-i-khud inkār karda ast.* *az yārān-i-sābiḳa ṣuḥbat ḳaṭa' karda ast.*
they went to Europe six months ago,	*pesh az īn shish māh eshān ba mulk-i-farang raftand.*
on hearing a statement of this sort, they began to laugh,	*az shunīdan-i-īn sukhanhā, [bunyād]-i-khanda nihādand. [binā.]* *b'ad az shunīdan-i-īn chunīn sukhanhā eshān khandīdan [giriftand]. [aghāz kardand; aghāz nihādand; shurū' kardand.]*
gardener, sow the seed of this flower in the garden,	*ai bāghbān dar bāgh [tukhm]-i-īn gulb i-kr. [bazr; baẕr.]*

he has taught us with great labour,	*o mū-rū ba miḥnat-i-bisiyūr [āmokhta] ast. [dars dāda.]*
by the grace of God we have found repose,	*mū az fazl-i-khudā ārām yāfta em.*
it is very cloudy, perhaps it will rain much,	*imrūz bisiyār [ṣaḥābī] ast, shāyad bisiyār bārān khwāhad bārīd. [abr muḥīṭ,* or *abr muḥīṭ-i-āsmān.]*
he has amassed much wealth and property,	*o bisiyār daulat o māl jama' karda ast.*
in this house there is a hall and three rooms,	*dar īn khāna yak dālān o si ḥujra and.*
how long is it since you received this news?	*chand wakt ast ki īn akhbūr ba shumā rasīda ast? b'ad az ān ki īn akhbār girifted, chand wakt guzashta ast?*

Exercise.—A fox having seen a crow sitting on the branch of a tree, with a fine piece of cheese in his mouth, began to think in her own heart, "How shall I get this delicious morsel into my own possession?" She then said aloud, "O Master Crow, I am quite delighted to see you this morning: your elegant figure and black feathers have entirely fascinated my heart. Will you sing to me one of your charming songs, so that the pleasure of my ears may be like that of my eyes?" On hearing this flattery, that foolish crow opened his mouth that he might show his skill in music. As soon as he opened his mouth to sing, the piece of cheese fell upon the ground. The fox immediately seized it, and walked away, saying, "My dear friend, your voice is a little out of tune to-day: pray remain silent till I have gone some distance. In the mean time, receive this advice of mine—Never pay any attention to the words of those who flatter you."

LESSON 41.

they live with their parents,	*eshān bā wālidain-i-khud mī-mānand.*
we have taken a walk on the bank of the river,	*ba lab-i-daryā mā [gashta] em. [gardīda.]* [1] *ba sāḥil-i-daryā mā [sair] karda em. [tamāsha.]*
for how much will you sell (this) to my master?	*ba [ṣāḥib]-i-man ba chand ḳīmat īn rā khwāhed farokht?* [2] *[walī n'imat; murabbi; khudāwand-i-n'imat.]*
is there anything to be had there for eating and drinking?	*yā hech chīz barā,e khurdan o naushīdan ḥāṣil mī-āyad?* *āyā hech chīz barā,e khurdan o naushīdan [muyassar mī-shavad]? [ba-ham mī-rasīd; dast yāb mī-shavad.]*
are you at all aware where they are gone?	*hech m'alūmat ast ki hama kujā rafta and?*
remain here until we return,	*hamīn jā [bi-mān] tā ki mā bāz bi-gardem. [bāsh.]*
the knife fell from my hand into the river,	*kārd az dast-i-man [dar] daryā uftād. [ba.]*

---

[1] to walk to see anything, *barā,e sair raftan.*
to walk, or travel, for amusement, *sair kardan.*

[2] heir apparent, *walī,e 'ahd.*

in speaking Persian, our general fault is in not pronouncing each individual letter fully,	*dar sukhan guftan-i-zabān-i-fārsī ḳuṣūr-i-mā īn ast ki mā ḥasbu-l-ma'mūl har lafẓ ba tafrīḳ talaffuẓ na mī-kunem.*
a man who cannot speak the language of the people among whom he sojourns may sometimes be in danger of starving,	[1] *shakhṣe ki dar diyāre sukūnat paẕīr shuda bāshad wa zabān-i-ahliyān-i-ān mulk na dānad, pas tarsast ki shāyad az [gursinagī] khwāhad murd. [be āzūḳa.]*
he tells you to speak to him in his own language,	*o mī-goyad ki dar zabān-i-man bi-go.*

Exercise.—A certain washerman had an ass, which he used to let go in a garden for the purpose of grazing. The people of the garden used to beat the ass, and drive him away from thence. One day, the washerman fastened around him a tiger's skin, and said, "At the time of night go you into the garden to graze, and do not make any noise." Even so, every night the ass in the tiger's skin used to go into the garden. Whenever the people saw him by night, they used to think for certain that this was a tiger. One night the gardener himself saw him, and from fear he went up into a tree. In the mean time, another ass which was in that neighbourhood

[1] do you live there? *shumā ān jā sukūnat paẕīr hasted?*

he lives there,
- *ān jā o sukūnat paẕīr ast.*
- *ān jā o maskan dārad.*
- *ān jā maskan-i-o ast.*

I like this book,
- *īn kitāb marā paẕīr ast.*
- *īn kitāb marā maṭlūb ast.*
- *īn kitāb marā marghūb ast.*
- *īn kitāb-rā pasand dāram.*

made a noise, and the ass of the washerman, on hearing that, also raised his voice, and began to bray in the manner of all asses. The gardener, on hearing his noise, discovered what he was. He came down from the tree, and having thoroughly beaten the ass, he drove him out of the garden. Hence, on this subject the wise men have said, "For asses silence is best."

A LIST OF USEFUL WORDS.

an axe,	*tabar.*
baker,	*k͟habbāz ; nān paz ; nān bā.*
button,	*tukma ; dukma ; gīra.*
bald,	*kal ; dāg͟h sar ; dăg͟h-sar.*
bath,	*ḥammām.*
basin,	(metallic) *ṭasht ; lagan aftāba ;* (baked clay) *kāsa.*
"	(holder) *ṭasht dār.*
bed furniture,	*rak͟ht-i-k͟hẉāb.*
bedstead,	*k͟hẉāb-gāh ; chahār pā,e.*
bed,	*bistar.*
blanket,	*chādar-i-pashmīna.*
basket,	(wicker) *sapad ;* (grass) *gīra.*
bracelet,	*dastīna ; dastwāna ; 'alankū dast ; mi'ẓad.*
bottle,	(glass) *shīsha ;* (jug) *kūza ;* (earthenware) *ṣurāḥī.*
broom,	*miknasat ; jārūb ; jā-rū ; ruftan-rūb.*
bellows,	*minfāk͟h ; tannūr-tab.*
butcher,	*ḳaṣṣāb.*
bundle,	*basta ; dasta.*
bag (leathern),	*ambān* or *ambāna ;* (carpet) *k͟hurjīn.*
canvas,	*palās.*
coat,	*ḳabā ; durrā'at.*
coat (great),	*farg͟hūl ; labāda.*
china-ware,	*kāsa-chīnī.*
cup,	*finjān ; piyāla ; ṭas ; jām ;* (goblet) *ḳadaḥ.*
chair,	*kursī.*
chair bench,	*sandalī ;* (bench) *sandal.*
counterpane,	*liḥāf.*
cork,	*disām ; sadād-i-ag͟hār.*
cork (screw),	*pech.*
carpet,	*farsh ; gilīm ; bisāṭ ;* (prayer) *sijjāda ;* (decapitation) *naṭ'.*

clothes,	*pārcha; libās; poshāk; jāma; kiswat;* (patched) *khirḳa; dalḳ; jāma,e zhanda; dalḳ-i-muraḳḳa;* (honour) *khil'at;* (religious) *iḥrām.*
cord,	*rīsmān.*
candle,	*shama'; ḳandīl.*
"	(wax) *shama',e mūmī.*
chandler,	*shama' sāz.*
candlestick,	*shama' dān.*
cloth,	*pārcha; ṭāka;* (broad) *māhūt;* (striped) *burd;* (brocade) *dībak;* (damask) *dībā;* (dimity) *damiyāṭ;* (thick) *jāma,e hanguft.*
cooking-pot,	*deg; ẕarf-i-pukhtan* (sing.) *ẕurūf-i-pukhtan* (plur.)
cook,	*ashpaz; ṭabbākh.*
crumb,	*reza,e nān.*
chapter (of a book),	*bāb; faṣl.*
corn,	*ghalla.*
cotton,	*pumba.*
compliments,	*salām; du'ā o salām.*
cupboard,	*paimāna-gāh; ganjīna; ṭāḳ-i-paimāna.*
door,	*dar; darwāza; bāb.*
ewer,	*ibrīḳ.*
engraver,	*ḳalam-kār; hakkāk.*
envelope,	*lifāfa.*
furniture,	*sāmān-i-khānagī; khānumān; khānmān; rakht-i-khāna.*
fan,	*bād-zan; bād-kash; mirwaḥa.*
fire-works,	*naft-andāzī; ātash bāzī.*
fire-wood,	*hezum; hīma.*
fire,	*ātash; nā,irat;* (flame) *zabāna;* (spark) *akhgar; sharār; ātash-pāra; ghuncha,e arghawan.*
gutter,	*badar-rau; nāv-dān.*
glass-ware,	*āb-gūn.*

grocer,	*baḳḳāl.*
gum,	*samagh; samagh-i-'arabī.*
glove,	*dast tāba; dast afrāz; dastāna; dastposh.*
house,	(master of) *kat-khudā; kad-khudā; ṣāḥib-i-buḳa'.*
,,	(hold) *khāndān;* (establishment) *lawāḥiḳ-i-khāna.*
host,	*mezbān; ṣāḥib-i-da'wat.*
hospitality,	*mihmānī.*
hat,	*kulāh.*
hammer,	*chākūj; chakush; mitraḳat.*
hand-saw,	*dast-ar.*
hand-mill,	*dast ās.*
hotel, inn,	*sarā,e; khān; wurūd-gāh; farod-gāh; ribāṭ.*
kitchen,	*maṭbakh.*
knife,	(clasp) *chākū;* (table) *kārd.*
,,	(pen) *ḳalam tarāsh.*
key,	*kalīd; miftāḥ.*
light,	*roshanī; nūr.*
leaf,	(of a book) *waraḳ.*
,,	(of a tree) *barg.*
letter (of condolence),	*ta'ziyat nāma.*
lock,	*ḳufl.*
,,	(pad) *ḳufl-i-rūmī.*
,,	(intricate) *ḳufl-i-waswās.*
match,	*kibrīt.*
mat,	*boriyā; ḥaṣīr.*
mirror,	*ā,īna; āb-gīna; sajanjal.*
nail,	*mekh; mismār.*
needle,	*sūzan.*
naphtha,	*naft.*
napkin,	*dastmālcha; dast-khwān.*
oven,	*tannūr;* (stove) *tūn; manḳal; ātash-tāb.*

pocket,	*jīb*; within the pocket, *tū,e jīb*.
potsherd,	*khazaf-reza*.
pot (flower), earthen vessel,	*khazaf; sifālīn*.
potter,	*khazafī; sifāl-gar; gil-gar*.
pincers,	*minkāsh*.
pitcher,	*sabū; khum*.
portico,	*dihlīz-i-khāna*. *pesh-gāh*.
pipe,	(water) *āb-rah; mīzāb; mirzāb;* (tube) *lūla*.
pantry,	*rikāb-khāna; tasht-dār khāna*.
pin,	*sanjāḳ*.
a porter,	*ḥāmil; ḥămmāl*.
paste,	*sirīsh*.
pencil,	*ḳalam-i-surb; siyāhī-dār ḳalam; ḳalam-i-siyāhī-dār*.
papa,	*pāpā*.
pope,	*rīm pāpā*.
razor,	*ustura*.
stick (walking),	*chūb-i-dastī*.
staff,	*'aṣā*.
scissors,	*miḳrāẓ*.
saucer,	*nalbakī; ṭabaḳcha; tishtarī*.
shirt,	*pairāhan; ḳamīṣ*.
scale,	*mīzān; tarāzū;* (beam) *shāhīn;* (pan) *kafa*.
sheet,	*chādar*.
screen,	*parda*.
shade,	*fānūs*.
sash,	*kamar-band; miyān-band*.
shawl,	*shāl*.
skirt (of dress),	*dāman*.
satin,	*aṭlas*.
silk,	*āb-resham; āb-reshīm; harīr; khazz;* (painted) *parniyān;* (stuff) *nasīkh*.
sock,	*jurāb; pā-tāba*.

signature,	*dast-khaṭṭ ; ṣaḥīḥ.*
sack,	*juwāl ; juwālif.*
a scribe,	*kātib ; nawīsanda ; muḥarrir.*
seal,	*muhr.*
slate,	*lauḥ.*
spring (of water),	*āb-khez ; chashma.*
screw (turn),	*pech-kash.*
towel,	*dast-māl ; badan-i-khushk kun.*
turban,	*dastar ; 'amāma.*
trousers,	*shalwār ; pā,e jāma ; zer-jāma.*
title (of a book),	*ism-i-kitāb.*
tape,	*nakh ; fīt.*
tavern,	*mai-kada ; khum-khāna ; kharābat.*
table (cloth),	*sufra.*
tray,	*khwān ; khwāncha.*
„	(cover) *khwān-posh.*
threshold,	*āstāna.*
thread,	*rishta.*
tumbler,	*istīkān.*
tools,	*auzār ; dast afrāz.*
tongs,	*dast-pănāh ; ambūr.*
tailor,	*khayāṭ.*
velvet,	*makhmal.*
vessel,	*ẓarf,* (plur.) *ẓurūf.*
window,	*ghurfa ; darīcha.*
wool,	*pashm.*
ward-robe,	*pesh-pā.*
wheat,	*gandum ;* (stalks), *darakht-i-gandum.*
washerman,	*gāzur.*
to arrange,	*bar chīdan.*
to bathe,	*ghusl kardan.*
„	(another) *ghusl dādan.*
to knock at the door,	*dar zadan ; ḥalḳa,e dar zadan.*
to light a candle,	*shama'-rā āfrokhtan ; shama'-rā roshan dādan.*
to make the bed,	*bistār gustardan.*

to put on one's clothes,	*poshāk poshīdan; libās dar bar kardan; libās zadan; jāma dar sarw bar kardan.*
to sew,	*do<u>kh</u>tan,* (root) *doz;* (to hem) *sajāf kardan.*
to stitch,	*ā<u>kh</u>īdan,* (root) *a<u>kh</u>īn;* (to pipe) *sahīj kardan.*
to spread the table-cloth,	*sufra gu<u>z</u>āshtan;* or, *sufra gustardan.*
to spin,	*rishtan,* (root) *rīs.*
to thread a needle,	*rishta ba sūzan andā<u>kh</u>tan; sūzan-rā na<u>kh</u> kardan.*
to thread pearls,	{ *durr suftan.* { *durr munsalik kardan.*
to thread rubies,	*lāl munsalik kardan.*
to extinguish a fire,	*ātash nishāndan.*
to take fire,	*ātash giriftan.*
to set fire (to a house),	*<u>kh</u>āna-rā ātash zadan.*

CONVERSATIONAL TERMS.

Good night!	*masā,u-l-khair!*
Peace be on you!	*salām 'alaikum!*
Good morning!	*ṣabāḥu-l-khair!*
Praised be God!	*al ḥamdu-li-llāh!*
And on you be peace and the blessing of God!	*o 'alaikumu-s-salām o raḥmatu-l-lāh!*
God bless you!	*khudā ḥāfiẓ-i-shumā!*
God be with you!	*khudā hamrāh-i-shumā!*
On whom be the peace of God!	*raḥmatu-l-lāhi 'alaihi!*
Blessing on him!	*'alaihi-s-salām!*
May it be well!	*khair bāshad!*
No, by God!	*lā wa-l-lāh!*
With heart and soul,	*ba jān o dil.* *ba sar o chashm.* *ba chashm.* *ba jān o minnat.*
The great and glorious God,	*khudā,e 'azza wa jalla.*
[1] In the name of God the merciful and compassionate!	*bismi-l-lāhi-r-raḥmani-r-raḥīm!*
[1] To God be praise and glory!	*li-l-lāhi-l-ḥamdu wa-l-minnatu!*
[1] There is no power, nor virtue, but in God,	*lā ḥaula wa lā ḳūwata illā bi-l-lāhi.*

---

[1] These expressions are in common use. As they are at once common and peculiar they are given in character.

بِسۡمِ ٱللَّهِ ٱلرَّحۡمٰنِ ٱلرَّحِيمِ

لِلَّهِ ٱلۡحَمۡدُ وَ ٱلۡمِنَّةُ

لَا حَوۡلَ وَ لَا قُوَّةَ إِلَّا بِٱللَّهِ

The student should note :—

(*a*) The use of *waṣla*.

(*b*) The use of *fatḥa*, as a final termination, in the words *azza*, *jalla*, *ḥaula*, *ḳūwata*.

(*c*) The use of *ẓamma*, as a final termination, in the words, *ḥamdu*, *minnatu*.

(*d*) That الله is pronounced as *allāh*; that لله *li-l-lāhi* is contracted from لالله, in respect to which the following remark is important :—

"When the particle ل is prefixed to a noun beginning with ل, which, when definite, ought to have the article: the initial *alif* of the noun disappears, and (in order to avoid the meeting of three ل's) the *lām* of the article is dispensed with, or represented by *tashdīd*."

SECTION III.

Lesson 43.—On Breakfast.

sabaḳ chihil o siwum dar nāshtā.

get the breakfast equipage ready,	*lawāzima,e chāsht taiyār bi-kun.* / *sāmān wa asbāb-i-chāsht bi-sāz.*
toast some bread, and butter it properly,	*ḳadre nān ba āt̤ash garm bi-kun o ba khūb t̤araḥ maska-ash bi-māl.*
does the water boil?	*āyā āb ba josh mī-āyad?* / *āyā āb mī-joshad?*
give me a clean cup and saucer,	*finjān o nalbake ṣāf marā bi-dih.*
give that gentleman another cup of tea,	*ān ṣāḥib-rā finjān-i-dīgar az chā bi-dih. barā,e ān ṣāḥib yak finjān-i-chā biyār.*
make it strong enough; and by putting in it plenty of milk and sugar you will always make it good, provided the water be actually boiling,	*chā-rā barābar durust bi-kun, o az andākhtan-i-shīr-i-bisiyār o shakar hamesha khūb laẕīẕ mī-shavad, ba sharṭe ki āb joshīda bāshad.*
bring the cold meat, fowl, ham, tongue, salt fish, rice, and split pease in the twinkling of an eye,	*gosht-i-shabīna, murgh, rān-i-khūk-i-namak-zada, zabān, māhī,e namkīn, khushka o dāl-i-mun-sharik ba chashm zadan biyār.*
give me a cup of coffee and a little more sugar,	*finjān-i-ḳahwa o ḳadre (andake) shakar-i-ziyāda marā bi-dih.*

boil some eggs, but do not let them get hard,	*chand dānā,e tukhm-i-murgh-rā josh bi-dih, magar ān-rā sakht shudan ma dih.* *chand dānā,e baiza bi-joshān* [*amma nīm pukhta bāshand*] or [*amma ma guzār ki sakht shavand*].
set the egg-cups and salt-cellar on that side, and the tea-pot and coffee-pot here,	*tukhm-i-murgh-dānhā o namak-dān ba ān taraf biguzār o chā-dān o kahwa-dān ba īn taraf.*
what a blockhead you are to require repeated orders for such things!	*chi kadar ahmak ed! ki barā,e īn chunīn chīzhā bār bār hukm mī-khwāhed.* *chi sān abla ed! ki barā,e īn chunīn chīzhā shumā-rā* [*bār bār hukm dādan bāyad*]. [*zarūrat-i-hukm-i-mukarrar bāshad.*]
bring bread, biscuit, sweet-meats, cake, &c.,	*nān, kulīcha, lauziyāt, nān-i-khūsh, waghaira, biyār.*
you know I cannot drink tea without cream,	*shumā mī-dāned ki chā be īmāgh na mī-tawānam naushīd.*
the bread is very bad, and full of sand,	*nān bisiyār bad ast, o pur az reg.*
discharge the baker if he ever dare to send such bread here,	*agar nān-paz bār-i-dīgar jur,at-i-firistādan-i-chunīn nān bi-kunad, o-rā ma'zul kun.*[1]

[1] Or, *murakhkhas bi-kun; maukūf bi-kun.*

the water with which this tea is made has not been boiling; it has no taste at all,	*ābe ki az ān īn chā sākhta shuda ast barābar na joshīda* [*maza na mī-dihad*]. [*bi-l-kull maza na dārad; bad ṭ'am ast; ṭ'am na dāraḍ.*]
these eggs are not fresh; from whom have you brought them? Never bring any to the table but those that are laid at home,	*īn dānāhā,e tukhm-i-murgh tāza nīstand, az ki* [or *kujā*] *āwarda ed, siwā,e baiẓa,e -khānagī hargiz bar sufra mayār.*

Exercise.—One night a *ḳāẓī* found in a book that whoever has a small head and a long beard is a fool. The *ḳāẓī*, having a small head and a long beard, said to himself, "I cannot increase the size of the head, but I will shorten the beard." He sought for scissars, but could not find them. Having no other course, he took half his beard in his hand, and carried the other half towards the lamp: when the hair took fire, the flames reached his hand; upon which, letting go his hold, the beard was entirely consumed, and the *ḳāẓī* overwhelmed with shame, as it verified what was written in the book.

---

almond,	*bādām.*
apple,	*seb.*
apricot,	*zardālū.*
beet-root,	*chu ghundur; pāzhū.*
burrage,	*pudīna.*
capers,	*turushī,e kabar.*
cherry,	*ālū-bālū.*
citron,	*turunj.*
cocoa-nut,	*nārjīl.* / *jauz-i-hindī.*
cress (water),	*tara,e tezak.*

curry,	*ḳaurma.*
date,	*khurma*; (green, ripe) *ruṭab*, pl. *arṭāb.*
fig,	*anjīr.*
fruit,	*mewa*; *ṣamr.*
garlic,	*sīr.*
grape,	*angūr*; (bunch of) *khūsha,e angūr*; (small bunch) *tilinga,e angūr.*
herb (odoriferous)	*rīḥān*, (plur.) *riyāḥīn.*
kernel,	*maghz.*
leek,	*gandāna.*
lemon,	*līmū*; (lime) *līmū,e kāghazī.*
mango,	*amba.*
melon,	(musk) *kharbūza*; (water) *hinduwāna.*
mushroom,	*ḳārch.*
nectarine,	*hulū.*
onion,	*piyāz.*
orange,	*turunj.*
pea,	*bāḳilā,e mūsh.*
peach,	*shaft ālū.*
pear,	*nāshpatī.*
pepper,	(white) *filfil-i-abiaẓ*; (red) *filfil-i-surkh*; (black) *filfil-i-aswad.*
pickles,	*turush.*
plum,	*ālū*; (mogul) *bālụ-zard.*
pomegranate,	*anār*; *rumān.*
quince,	*bih.*
shell,	*post-i-jauz.*
thyme,	*ipār*; *tar khūn.*
walnuts,	*girdū*; (peeled) *maghz-i-jauz girdū.*
an omelette,	*khāgīna.*
flour,	*ārd.*
to lay an egg,	*tukhm dādan*; *tukhm nihādan.*
to roast,	*ba sīkh kardan*; *kabāb kardan.* *gūsht kofta ba sīkh nihādan.*
to fry,	*biriyān sākhtan.*

to poach an egg,	*baiẕa gawāza kardan.*
to fry an egg,	*baiẕa nīmru kardan.*
raw,	*khām.*
cooked,	*pukhta.*

Lesson 44.—On Dinner.

sabaḳ chihil o chahārum dar ṯa'ām.

tell the cook to have the dinner ready at three o'clock,	[*ash paz*]-*rā ḥukm bi-dih ki khurāk-i-shām ba waḳt-i-sā'at-i-si taiyār bi-kunad.* [*ṯabbākh ; muṯabbikh.*]
sir, dinner is ready,	*ṣāḥibā, shām taiyār ast.*
where is the soup and the soup-spoon ?	*shorba o ḳāshugh-i-shorba kujā ast ?*
bring a hot-water plate, some bread, potatoes, greens, asparagus, cabbage, cauliflowers, turnips, carrots, cucumbers,	*bushḳāb-i-āb-i-garm, ḳadre nān, ālū, sabza, asfarāj, karam-kalla, karam-kalla,e shugufta, shalgham, gazar, khiyār, biyār.*
let me have a clean plate, knife, fork, spoon, salt, mustard, vinegar, pepper, horse-radish, olive-oil, sauce, and everything of this sort,	*az barā,e man bushḳāb-i-ṣāf, kārd, changal, ḳāshugh, namak, khardil, sirka, filfil, turb-i-tez, raughan-i-zait, turshī o waghaira az īn ḳism biyār.*
let me have of every sort of vegetable on the table daily, and tell me the name of each,	*har rūz az barā,e man bar sufra sabza,e har ḳism bi-guẕār, o az nām-i-har chīz nishān bi-dih.*
what do you call that vegetable ?	*ān baḳlat-rā chi mī-goyed ?*

get one dressed for me every day, and tell me the name of each as I eat it, till you see I can call for everything of this sort by its proper name,	*har rūz barā,e man yake bi-paz, o ba waḳt-i-khurdan-i-o az nāmash nishān bi-dih tā ki ba shumā m'alūm shavad ki man nām-i-īn gūna chīz barābar giriftan mī-tawānam.*
do so with everything else, as this will be a capital plan for learning and digesting this useful tongue, being at once a meal and a lesson,	*ba har chīz ham badīn ṭaur bi-kun, zīrā ki barā,e āmokhtan o yād dāshtan-i-zabān-i-mufīd bisiyār khūb tajwīze khwāhad būd, ki ham sabaḳ o ham tabaḳ ast.*
bring some beef, mutton, veal, fish, fowl, and venison,	*ḳadre gūsht-i-gāw, gūsht-i-gūsfand, gūsht-i-gūsāla, gūsht-ī-māhī, gūsht-i-murgh, wa gūsht-i-āhū biyār.*
can you dress Persian dishes well?	*shumā ṭa'ām chū ahl-i-fārs ba ṭaraḥ-i-khūb mī-tawāned pukht?*
what fruits are in season now? bring me some of each sort,	*[mausim-i-kudām mewā ast?] ḳadre az har ḳism biyār. [īn waḳt mewā,e kudām ḳism rasīda bāshad?]*
to-morrow we shall dine in the country, send everything in time,	*fardā berūn-i-shahr shām khwāhem khurd, har chīz [bar waḳt] bi-firist. [ba waḳt.]*
will this meat keep so long in this weather?	*āyā dar īn mausim īn gosht tā ba īn ḳadar der tāza khwāhad mānd?*
now you may all depart, you have leave,	*ilḥāl shumā bi-raved, rukhṣat ast. īn waḳt shumā tashrīf bi-bared, murakhkhaṣed.*

Exercise.—A person said to his servant, "If you see two crows together early in the morning, apprize me of it, that I may also behold them, as it will be a good omen, whereby I shall pass the whole day pleasantly." In short, the servant saw two crows in one place: he informed his master; but when the latter came, he saw only one, the other having flown away. He was very angry, and began to beat the servant; at which time a friend sent him some victuals. The servant said, "O my lord! you saw only one crow, and have obtained victuals; had you seen two, you would have got a beating."

LESSON 45.—ON NAMING, TELLING, SPEAKING, &c.

sabaḳ chihil o panj dar nūmīdan o guftān.

what is the name of this?	*nām-i-īn chīz chīst?*
what do you call this thing?	*shumā īn chīz-rā chi [mī-goyed?] [mī-nāmed.]*
what do they call that in Persian?	*ān-rā dar zabān-i-fārsī chi mī-goyand?*
can you tell me where Mr. —— lives?	*marā mī-tawāned guft ki ṣāḥib-i-fulān kujā manzil dārad?*
tell me the name of this in your own language,	*dar zabān-i-khud marā az nām-i-īn chīz nishān bi-dih.*
do not tell any one what I said to you about that book,	*az bābat-i-ān kitāb ānchi ba tū guftam ba kase ma go.*
he would not tell me which of the two was yesterday's or to-morrow's lesson,	*marzī,e o na būd ki bi-goyad az īn har dū sabaḳ kudām sabaḳ-i-dīrūza būd, yā kudām sabaḳ-i-fardā khwāhad būd.* *o ba man guftan na mī-khwāhad, ki az īn har dū kudām sabaḳ-i-dīrūza, o kudām az fardā khwāhad būd.*

your servant does not mind what you say to him,	*ba ānchi shumā mī-goyed naukar-i-shumā mutawajjih nīst.* *naukar-i-shumā bar ḥukm-i-shumā [mutawajjih na mī-shavad]. [khayāl na mī-dihad; gosh na mī-dihad.]*
tell him he is a great rogue, and that he is always telling his master no end of lies.	*o-rā bu-go ki tū bisiyr aubāshī wa hamesha a ṣāḥib-i-khud [darogh az ḥadd ziyāda mī-goyī]. [daftar-i-darogh mī-kushā,ī.]*
well, I will not speak to him, as I may get angry and beat him; but give him his wages aud dismiss him,	*bisiyār khūb, man ba o sukhan na khwāham kard az īn sabab ki shāyad khashmnāk shavam, o o-rā bi-zanam; ammā shumā o-rā muwājib-ash bi-dihed, o rukhṣat kuned.*
what did he say when you told him to remain till I returned?	*o chi guft, wakte ki shumā ḥukm dāded ki tā bāz gashtan-i-man [īnjā bāsh]* or *[bi-mān].*
he said he had business, and could not possibly remain,	*o guft ki marā [kār] ast, o man na mī-tawānam mānd. [shughle.]*
did you ask him of what nature the business was?	*az o pursīded ki kār-at chi būd?*
yes, I did ask; but he said it was an affair of secrecy which he could not divulge,	*bale, man az o pursīdam, lekin guft ki [kār-i-makhfī] ast, o ān-rā ẓāhir na mī-tawānam kard. [sukhan-i-parda.]*

they speak English among themselves and Persian with us,	*[darmiyān-i-khud-i-shān] zabān-i-inglisī mī-goyand, o bā mā fārsī. [bāham.]*
they will know him to be a foreigner, though he speaks the Persian very grammatically,	*eshān khwāhand dānist ki o [ghair mulkī,e] ast agarchi zabān-i-fārsī ba ḳā,ida mī-goyad. [gharību-l-waṭne.]*
could I speak the Persian I would with pleasure; but, alas, I cannot join two sentences together in that tongue,	*agar zabān-i-fārsī mī-tawānistam guft ba khūshī mī-guftam, ammā afsos! ki dar-ān zabān dū jumla bāham na mī-tawānam sākht.*
you will be able to speak it in a few months, and you ought to practise speaking it with every one who is able to tell you how to speak it well,	*dar 'arṣa,e chand māh shumā barābar khwāhed tawānist guft, ammā bāyad ki bā har shakhṣ,e ki az ṣiḥḥat-i-kalām agāh tawānad namūd mukālima bi-kuned o ist'imāl-i-mashḳ-i-ḥaraf zadan karda bashed.*
how much I regret not to be able to understand what they say,	*bisiyār maghmūm am! ki ānchi eshān mī-farmāyand, ba fahm-i-man na mī-āyad.*
I take the liberty to inform you that nothing but practice will enable you to speak with fluency,	*agdrchi gustākhī ast, ba shumā iẓhār mī-kunam ki ba juz mashḳ dīgar chīz tawānāī,e guft-gū ba ṭarrārī na mī-bakhshad.*

Exercise.—A poet went to a rich man, and bestowed great praises on him; at which the latter, being pleased, said, "I have not any money at command, but a large quantity of grain: if you come again to-morrow I will give you some." The poet went home, and early the next morning went again to the rich man, who asked him why he was come. He answered, "Yesterday you promised to give me some grain, and I am now come for it." The other replied, "You are an egregious fool; you delighted me with words, and I have also pleased you; why, therefore, should I give you any corn?" The poet went away ashamed.

Lesson 46.—On Visiting, Shopping, &c.

sabaḳ chihil o shishum dar mulāḳāt kardan o khₕarīdārī.

bring the pālkī near me,	*nazd-i-man [pālkī] biyār. [takht-i-rawān.]*
take me to Mr. ——'s,	*marā ba khāna,e ṣāḥib-i-fulān bi-bar.*
send the footman on before to see if the gentleman be at home or not,	*piyāda,e-rā pesh bi-firist, ki āyā janāb-i-mirzā ba khāna tashrīf dārand yā na.*
bring the pālkī close to the door,	*nazd-i-darwāza pālkī biyār.*
go as fast as you can,	*ba harchi tamāmtar ba [ta'jīl] bi-rau. ['ujlat.]*
ask if the gentleman has gone out, and when he will return,	*bi-purs, āyā ṣāḥib berūn rafta, o agar rafta and kai bāz [khwāhand āmad]. [tashrīf khwāhand āward.]*
give my compliments to your master, and give this note to him when he returns,	*salām-i-man ba ṣāḥib-i-khudat bi-rasān, wa waḳte ki o bāz bi-āyand, īn khaṭṭ ba oshān bi-dih.*
you have lost the road to Mr. ——'s house; this is not it.	*rāh-i-khāna,e ṣāḥib-i-fulān gum karda ed; [īn nīst ki mī-raved]. [īn rāh khaṭā ast.]*
ask the people in that house to show you the way,	*az mardumān-i-ān khāna rāh bi-purs.*
go to the China bazar,	*ba bāzār-i-chīnī bi-rau.*

13

keep on this side or on that side,	*īn ṭaraf yā ān ṭaraf bi-gīr.*
take care you do not go near that bull,	*khabar-dūr ki nazd-i-ān nār gaw na ravī.*
keep clear of that dust on the road,	*az [khāk]-i-rūh ba kinār bāsh. [yard.]*
let that chair go on before,	*bi-guzār ki ān kursī-rā pesh bi-barand.*
keep behind my brother's chair,	*dar pai [or 'aḳab]-i-kursī,e barādar-am bāsh.*
why do you pass any gentleman's chair in that way?	*chirā ba ān ṭaraḥ az pahlū,e kursī,e kudām ṣāḥib mī-guzarī.*
bring the umbrella to this side,	*ba īn ṭaraf chatr biyār.*
do not go near the carriage,	*nazd-i-kāliska ma rau.*
put down the pālkī,	*pālkī pā,īn bi-guzār.*
stop, I am going to this shop,	*istāda bāsh, ba īn dūkān mī-ravam.*
what is the price of this book?	*ḳīmat-i-īn kitāb chīst?*
I will not give so much,	*ān ḳadar [chandīn] ḳīmat na khwāham dād.*
I won't give half the price you ask,	*ūnchi ḳīmat ki shumā mī-khwāhed nisf-i-ān nīz man na khwāham dād.*
I do not want the book, but if you sell it very cheap I may purchase it,	*marā ẓarūrat-i-kitāb nīst, ammā agar arzān khwhed farokht, shāyad ki bi-kharam.*
I have no cash about me, but if you will follow me you will receive your money at my house,	*[nazd-i-khud-am pūl nīst,] agar shumā 'aḳab-i-man khwāhed āmad, ba khāna,e man khwāhed yāft. [ba khud pūl na dāram.]*

bring the book with you, and then receive its price,	*kitāb ham rāh-i-khud biyār, o pas ķīmat-ash bi-gīr.*

Exercise.—One day a tyrannic king having gone out of the city unattended, saw a person sitting under a tree, of whom he inquired, "What is the character of the king of this country? Is he oppressive or just?" He answered, "He is a great tyrant." The king said, "Do you know me?" He answered, "No." The king rejoined, "I am the monarch of this place." The man was terrified, and asked, "Do you know who I am?" The king said he did not. He rejoined, "I am the son of such a merchant; three days in every month I lose my senses, and this is one of those three days." The king laughed, and ended the conversation.

COLOURS—*ranghā.*

ashy,	*khākistarī.*	green,	*sabz; akhzar.*
azure,	*āb-gūn; lūjaward.*	red,	*surkh.*
colour,	*rang.*	rusty,	*zangārī.*
black,	*siyāh; aswad; shūm.*	violet,	*binafsh.*
blue,	*kabūd.*	white,	*safaid; abyaẓ.*
blue, indigo,	*nīl.*	yellow.	*zard.*
brown,	*gandum-gūn.*		

Lesson 47.—On Walking, Riding, &c.

[1] *sabaķ chihil o haftum dar sair o sawārī.*

he is gone out somewhere to walk,	*az barū,e [gashtan] ba jā,e rafta ast. [sair; tamāsha.]*

---

[1] *sabaķ chihil o haftum dar gashtan bar rāh o sawār shudan.*

I shall go out also, and walk round the fort,	*man nīz berūn khwāham raft o gird-i-ḳila' khwāham gasht.*
in my country people walk a great deal,	*dar mulk-i-man mardumān bisiyār mī-gardand.*
can you walk much ?	*shumā pā-piyāda bisiyār mī-tawāned gasht ?*
I like walking on foot very much, and, were I not lame, I would walk out with you,	*pā-piyāda raftan bisiyār pasand dāram [mī-khwāham], o agar lang na būdam man ba ham rāh-i-shumā mī-gashtam.*
walking in the open field when it is cool is highly beneficial to health,	[1] *waḳte ki mausim sard ast dar maidān gashtan barā,e ṭabī'at bisiyār mufīd ast.*
do not walk among that grass, lest you tread on a snake,	*darmiyān ān 'alaf-zār ma gard [ki pāyat bar māre nayuftad].* *[ki pāyat bar māre na khurad.]* *[ki pā,e tūrā māre na zanad.]*
is the horse ready ?	*asp taiyar ast ?*
put the saddle wel on,	*bar asp zīn ba khūbī bi-band ; asp-rā zīn ba khūbī kun.*
hold the bridle till I be fairly mounted,	*tā man bar zīn barābar bar āyam, lagām girifta bāsh.* *ligām-rā barābar bi-gīr tā man muḥkam sawār shavam.*
take up the stirrup one hole,	*ba ḳadar-i-yak sūrākh-i-dīgar [rikāb bālā bi-gīr]. [sūḳaṭ-rā kotāh bi-kun.]*

[1] winter, *zamistān.*

see that the reins are strong and kept in constant repair,	*bi-bīn ki zamāmhā ḳawī and yā na, o hamesha ānhā-rā marammat karda bāsh.*
here, you groom, hold the horse, I must dismount for a little,	*ai sā,is! asp-rā bi-gīr ki marā, barā,e andak furṣate pā,īn shudan bāyad.*
take care, he will get out of your hands,	*khabar dār ki asp az dast-i-shumā na gurezad.*
see, is that ground proper for the horse to go over,	*bi-bīn ki ān zamīn munāsib-i-raftan-i-asp ast yā na.*
coax him that he may not be restive,	*o-rā nawāzish bi-kun, ki khīra na shavad.*
put a cloth over the horse's eyes,	*bar chashmhā,e asp parda bi-guzār* [or *bi-band*].
where is the saddle-cloth, crupper, the bit, belly-band, housings, &c.?	*zīn-posh, dumchi, dahana,e lagām, tang, ajlāl, waghaira kujā and?*
examine the place carefully, and see how far the water comes up,	*ān jā,e-rā ba khabardārī mulāḥaza bi-kun o [m'alūm bi-namā] ki āb tā kujā mī-rasad. [muṭṭali' shau.]*
you must not give the horse water now whilst he is so very warm,	*asp-rā āb na bāyad dād tā ki īn chunīn garm bāshad.*
is this a quiet horse for the road?	*barā,e rāh raftan īn asp ṣalīm ast, yā na?*
does he stand fire?	*az āwāz-i-top o tufang [ram na mī-kunad]? [na mī-ramad.]*
walk him about, rub him well down, and take care, at your peril, that he does not catch cold,	*o-rā bi-gardān, ba khūbī mālish-i-o, bi-kun o [khabardār bāsh ki īn kār, ba zimma,e tūst] ki sard na gīrad. [khabar dār.]*

Exercise.—A learned man used to attend a mosque,

and preach to the people. One of the congregation wept constantly. One day the preacher said, "My words make a great impression on this man's heart, which is the reason of his crying so much." Others observed thus to the man who wept: "The learned man does not make any impression on our minds; what kind of a heart must you have to be always in tears?" He answered, "I do not weep at his discourse, but I had a favourite goat, of which I was exceedingly fond. When the goat grew old he died: now, whenever the learned man speaks and wags his chin, the goat comes to my remembrance, for he had just such a long beard."

STABLE TERMS—*dar bāb-i-[iṣṭabal].* [*ṭawīla.*]

bay,	*kahar; surkh.*	grey,	*khing.*
black,	*adḥam; shabdez.*	piebald,	*ablaḳ.*
chesnut,	*kumait.*	white,	*nuḳra.*
dun,	*kuran; samand.*		

FORAGE—*'alaf.*

barley,	*jau.*		*sabza; giyāh; giyāh-i-akhẓar.*
bran,	*ḳaẓīm.*	grass,	*kāh; giyāh.*
corn,	*ghalla.*	hay, straw,	*kāh.*
gram,	*nakhud.*	purslain,	*giyāh-i-namnāk.*
grain,	*dāna.*		
green grass (barley)	*khawīd;*		

PARTS OF THE HORSE.

back,	*pusht.*	hoof,	*sum.*
chest,	*sīna.*	leg,	*sāḳ.*
ear,	*gosh.*	mane,	*ayāl.*
eye,	*chashm.*	neck,	*gardan.*
forehead,	*peshānī.*	shoulder,	*shāna.*
foot,	*pā,e.*	thigh,	*shalwār.*
head,	*sar.*		

---

a broker,	(horse) *dallāl-i-asp; saudāgar-i-asp.*
farrier,	*n'al-band.*
rider (good)	*shāh sawār ; chābuk sawār.*
bucket,	*taghār ; dalw.*
cart,	*'arāba ;* (carriage) *kāliska.*
a colt,	*khung ; kurra.*
dung,	(horse) *sargīn-i-asp ;* (cow) *sargīn-i-gāw.*
halter,	*nukhta ; pālāhang ; pālhang.*
horse,	(trappings) *sāz-o-yarāḳ-i-asp ;* (harness) *rakht-i-kāliska ;* (cloth) *gardanī.*
leather,	*postīn ; charm.*
peg (to which to fasten the heel ropes),	*gur mekh.*
stirrup,	*rikāb ;* (leather) *rikāb-duwāl ; sāḳat.*
shoe,	*n'al ;* (shoeing) *n'al-bandī.*
saddle cloth,	*namad zīn ; namda.*
tether,	*ṭawīla ; ṭūla ; tasma.*
whip,	*tāziyāna ;* to whip, *tāziyāna zadan.*

---

broad,	*'arīẓ.*
beautiful,	*maḳbūl.*
clean and straight,	*pāk o rāst.*
cheap,	*arzān.*
dear,	*girān.*
expansive,	*pahan.*
elegant form,	*khūsh-shakl ; khūsh andām.*
graceful action,	*khūsh ḥarakat.*
hand,	*wajab ;* (half) *nīm-wajab.*
open,	*wasī'.*
quiet,	*salīm ; gharīb ; ḥalīm.*
quick,	*chālāk.*
slender,	*bārīk.*
tall,	*buland.*
taper,	*ḳalāmī.*

vicious,	*sharīr.*
wide,	*kushāda.*
horse,	(pleasant-paced) *asp-i-shāh gūm;* (slow-paced) *asp-i-kam raw; kam-rāh;* (fleet-paced) *asp-i-bād pā,e rawān.*
to curry (a horse),	*asp tīmār kardan.*
to dismount,	*az asp pā,īn āmŭdan.* *az asp pā farūd āmădan.*
to drive,	*dar kāliska nishasta asp rāndan.*
to graze,	*charīdan.*
to gallop,	*tā<u>kh</u>tan.*
to goad a horse,	*bar asp mahmez zadan.*
to leap,	*jastan.*
to be lame,	*langīdan.*
to mount,	*bar asp sawār shudan.* *bar asp ba zīn bar āmadan.* *bar asp ba zīn bar nishastan.*
to neigh,	*zinūdan.*
to ride,	*sawār-i-asp būdan; sawār shudan; sawār raftan.*
to stumble,	*la<u>gh</u>zīdan;* (a slip) *la<u>gh</u>zish.*
to understand horses,	*asp shinā<u>kh</u>tan.*
a thorough bred Arab horse,	*asp-i-'arabī,e <u>kh</u>āliṣ* [or *<u>kh</u>āṣṣ*]*; asp-i-tāzī.*
blood,	(good) *<u>kh</u>ūsh rag; aṣīl;* (bad) *bad rag;* (mixed) *dū rag.*
good marks,	*<u>kh</u>ūsh nishān.*

Lesson 48.—On Sporting.

sabaḳ chihil o hashtum dar bāb-i-shikār [or *na<u>kh</u>chīr*].

is there much game in this neighbourhood?	*dar īn* [*nawāḥī*] *bisiyār shikār ast?* [*aṭrāf; aknāf.*]

there are wild buffaloes in abundance, a few tigers, and all kinds of smaller game.	*bisiyār gāmesh - i - dashtī, chand sher o ṣaid az har ḳism and.*
in every field there are partridges, and that swamp is full of water-fowl,	*dar har kisht kabakān and o ān tālāb az murghābīyān pur ast.*
clean all the fowling-pieces well, and put up a few bullets also for the large guns,	*hama tufanghā ba khūbī ṣāf bi-kun o nīz barā,e tufang hā,e-kalān chand gulūlahā bi-guẕār.*
call some of the villagers to show the usual haunts of the game,	*chand [dihḳānān]-rā bi-ṭalab nishān dihand ki kujā shikār mī-mānand. [ahl-i-dih; nafrān.]*
behind that copse there are two wild buffaloes; do you fire at the one towards the left, I shall take the other,	*pas-i-ān besha dū gāmesh-i-dashtī and, shumā ba ān gāmesh ki ba chap ast tufang bi-zaned, man bū rāst.*
you have hit the mark, but I have missed,	*shumā nishān zada ed, o man khaṭā karda am.*
how many birds have you killed?	*chi ḳadar murghān [kushta] ed? [zada.]*
do you think there is any game here, or any beast of prey?	*ayā, shumā mī-dāned ki īnjā ṣaide ast, yā nakhchīre.*
when it gets cool, towards the evening, we shall go to that wood; perhaps we may see something or other,	*chūn ḳarīb-i-waḳt-i-shām sard khwāhad shud, ba ān besha mā khwāhem raft; bāshad ki chīze dīgar bi-bīnem.*
if you can swim, bring out that duck and those two geese: the duck has dived, but will soon appear again,	*agar shumā shinā mī-tawāned kard, ān baṭ wa ān har dū ḳāz bar āred; baṭ ghoṭa khurda ast zūd ba naẓar khwāhad āmād.*

give me some small shot and a turnscrew ; this powder is damp,—dry it a little in the sun,	*marā ḳadre sāchima bi-dih o pech-gard ; īn bārūt* [*nam-nāk ast*] ; *o-rā dar āftāb bi-guẓār ki khushk bi-shavad.* [*nam girifta ast*] or [*nam kashīda ast*] or [*tar shuda ast*].
take the people with you, and beat all the bushes well,	*mardumān-rā ham rāh-i-khud bi-gīr o besha-rā ba khūbī bi-zan.*
keep close there, I see a tiger near that bush,	*ān jā* [*poshīda bāsh*] *ki nazd-i-ān dirakht shere mī-bīnam.* [*pinhān shau ; sākit bāsh.*]
why do you fire in that careless manner ? you will wound the country people,	*chirā ba ān chunān be kha-barī tufang mī-zaned ? dihḳānān - rā zakhmī khwāhed kard.*
take a good aim, do not be confused, but lodge the ball in the tiger's head, otherwise we are all dead men,	*shist-rā khūb bi-gīr, pareshān ma bāsh, ammā dar sar-i-sher gulūla bi-zan ; warna bi-dān ki hama* [*murdagān khwāhem būd*]. [*khwāhem murd*, or *mī-mīrem.*]
have you brought the fishing apparatus with you ? there are some good fishing stations here,	*lawāzima,e māhī-gīr ba ham rāh - i - khud - i - tān āwarda ed ; īn jā barā,e giriftan - i - māhī bisiyār jāhā,e khūb and.*

Exercise.—A woman was walking, and a man looked at her, and followed her. The woman said, "Why do you follow me ?" He answered, "Because I have fallen in love with you." The woman said, "Why are you in love with me ? my sister is much handsomer than I am ; she is coming after me ; go and make love to her." The man turned back, and saw a woman with an ugly face.

Being greatly displeased, he went again to the other woman, and said, "Why did you tell a falsehood?" The woman answered, "Neither did you speak truth; for if you are in love with me, why did you go after another woman?" The man was confounded, and went away in silence.

NAMES OF ANIMALS.

animal,	*jānwar; jānwār; ḥaiwān.*
„ flesh-eating,	*daranda; sabā'* (sing. *sabu'*).
„ grazing,	*charanda;* (creeping) *girdshanda.*
„ flying,	*paranda; murghan; ṭair* (plur. *ṭuyūr*).
„ stinging,	*gazanda.*
„ four-footed,	*chār pā;* (stall-fed) *'alaf-khur.*

Quadrupeds.

ass,	*darāz-gosh; ḥimār; khar; ulāgh;* (wild) *gor; gor khar.*
antelope,	*āhū;* (deer) *hiran;* (stag) *gawazn.*
beast,	(wild or tame) *bahīmat* (sing.); (wild) *bahā,im* (plur.); *waḥsh,* (plur. *waḥūsh*); (of prey) *nakh-chīr.*
buffalo,	*gāmūs; gāo mesh.*
camel,	*shutur; ushtur;* (riding) *bukhtī;* (hump of) *kahūn.*
calf,	*gūs āla.*
cattle,	*ḥaiwānāt; mawāshī* (plur. of *mā-shīya*).
cat,	*gurba.*
dog,	*sag; kalb;* (pup) *tūla.*
dragon,	*azhdahā.*
elephant,	*fīl; pīl;* (trunk of) *khurṭūm;* (elephant body) *pīl tan.*
fox,	*rūbāh.*

goat,	*buz*; *khaṣī*; *kurk*; (kid) *ghala*.
jackal,	*shaghūl*; *shaghād*.
hare,	*khar-gosh*.
hog,	*khinzīr*; *khūk*; *gurāz*; (hedge) *khār-pusht*.
leopard,	*palang*.
lion,	*sher*; *ẓaigham*; *asad*; *ẓarghām*; *hizbar*; *sabu'*; (fierce) *sher-i-zhiyān*; *sher-i-sharza*.
mule,	*ḳāṭir*; *astar*.
mouse,	*mūsh*.
mongoose, weazel,	*rāsū*.
mole,	*mūsh-i-kūr*; *mushak*; (squirrel) *mūshak-i-parrān*.
monkey,	*būzīna*; *būzna*; *maimūn*.
panther,	*palang*; (small) *yūz*; (tiger) *sher*.
rhinoceros,	*karkaddan*.
sheep,	*gūsfand*.
wolf,	*gurg*.

[1] BIRDS—*paranda*.

bird,	(fabulous) *simurgh*; *'anḳā*; *rukhkh*.
bat,	*shab-pāra*; *shabpara*; *shab pūr*.
bustard,	*bālwād*.
crow,	*zāgh*; (raven) *ghurāb*.
cock (dunghill),	*khurūs*.
fowl,	*murgh*; (water) *ṭiṭū*; *murghābī*; (young) *chūza*.
hawk,	*bāz*; (sparrow) *mush-gīr*; *bāsha*.

[1] wing, *bāl*; (feather) *par*.
strong of wing, *ḳawī bāl*; *tez-bāl*; *janāh-i-isti'jāl*.
beak of a bird, *minḳār*.
to peck at (a thing), *bar chīze minḳār zadan*.
to expand the wings, *bāl afshāndan*.
to moult, *par rekhtan*.
to build a nest, *bālūdan*; *āshiyāna kardan*.

nest (bird's), *āshiyāna ; āshiyān.*
nightingale, *bulbul ; 'andalīb ; shab-khwān.*
owl, *būm ; chughd ; kokan ; kokah ; kokanak.*
parrot, *ṭūṭī.*
pelican, *rakham ;* (heron) *māhī-khwār ;* (crane) *kalang.*
peacock, *ṭā,ūs.*
partridge, *kabk ;* (note of) *ḳahḳaha ;* (mountain) *kabk-i-darī.*
pheasant, *tazarv ; tadarv ;* (quail) *tīhū.*
pigeon, *kabūtar ; kūkū ;* (green) *kabūtar-i-sabz rang ;* (ring-dove) *fākhta ; fākhta,e mutawwaḳ ; mutawwaḳa ;* (tumbler) *kabūtar-i-mu'allaḳī.*
sparrow, *kunjashk ; 'usfūr.*
swallow, *bālwāh ; abābīn.*
vulture, *kargas; nasr;* (eagle) *'uḳāb;* (falcon) *shāhīn ; shāh-bāz ;* (kite) *zaghan.*

[1] INSECTS.

ant, *mor.*
bee, *zambūr-i-'asal.*
beetle, *kushtak.*
cricket, *shab-gīr.*
fly, *magas ;* (butter-) *parwāna ; farāsh ; shāh-para.*
flea, *kaik ; shab gaz ;* (tick) *kāna ;* (louse) *shubsh.*
hornet, *zambūr-surkh.*
locust, *malakh ;* (grasshopper) *malakh-i-piyāda.*
mosquito, *pasha,e kurak ;* (gnat) *rumd.*

---

[1] sting, *nesh.*
stinger, *nesh-zan.*
striking with a sting, *nesh-zanī.*

moth,	*parwāna.*
spider,	*'ankabūt ; sher-i-magas.*
spider's web,	*khāna,e 'ankabūt ; tār-i-'ankabūt.*
wasp,	*zambūr-i-zard ; zambūr-i-kāfir ; zambūra.*

Reptiles and Fishes.

alligator, crocodile,	*nahang ; sher-i-ābī.*
chameleon,	*būḳ alamūn ; ăbū-ḳurrat.*
frog,	*ghūk ; ẓafda'.*
lizard,	*karfash.*
leech,	*zalū.*
millipede,	*jānwār-i-hazār pā,e.*
snake,	*mār* ; (large) *af'a* ; (python) *awb.*
scorpion,	*kazh dum ; 'aḳrab.*
tortoise,	*kashtūk ; kashaf.*
turtle,	*sang-pusht ; sipar-posh.*
worm,	(silk-) *kirim-i-bādūma* ; (glow-) *kirim-i-shab tāb* ; (earth) *kharāṭīn.*
fish,	*māhī* ; (torpedo) *ra'ād* ; (oyster) *ṣadaf* ; (scales of) *pulak* ; (crab) *kalankhār* ; *kharchang* ; (whale) *ḥūt* ; (porpoise) *khūk-i-daryā.*

Lesson 49.—On Travelling.

sabaḳ chihil o nuhum dar siyāḥat [or *saiyāḥī*].

how many stages is Shirāz from this town?	*shīrāz az īn shahr chand manzil [ast]? [dārad.]*
is your boat ready?	*āyā māshūh,e shumā taiyār ast?*
are all your people ready to go a voyage to Mecca?	[1] *āyā hama mardumān-i-shumā ba safr kardan-i-k'aba taiyār and?*
what is the hire of this boat for two months?	*az barā,e dū māh kirāya,e īn kishtī chīst?*

[1] the aim of one's life, *k'aba,e jān.*

at which hour does the tide serve to go up the river to-day?	*imrūz ba chi sā'at āb bālā mī-ravad ki mā ba daryā raftan mī-tawānem?*
as soon as the tide serves, let the boat be taken above the shipping to such a *ghāṭ*, where we will embark in the evening,	*ba mujarrad-i-munāsib shudan-i-madd māshūh bālā,e jahāzhā ba fulān 'ubūr-gāh bi-gīr, ki imshab sawār shavem.*
we must not commence such a journey without being provided with every necessary and comfort, few of which are procurable on the way,	*bidūn-i-maujūd shudan-i-sāmān-i-safr o waghaira ẓarūriyāt īn chunīn safr kardan na bāyad, zīrā ki dar rāh bisiyār chīzhā kam [dastyāb] mī-shavad. [muyassar.]*
both to avoid expense and inconvenience, we must reduce our baggage to as small a quantity as possible,	*az barā,e kam kharch wa parhez-i-takhlīf munāsib ast, ki dar sāmān ba har ḳadar ki tawānem takhfīf namāyem.*
I am not going by water, I prefer going by land,	*az daryā na mī-ravam, balki rāh-i-khushkī pasand dāram.*
we must have everything well packed, to guard against all accidents, which occur frequently by the carelessness of servants, independent of those common to all travellers,	*bar hama wāḳi'āt nigāh dāshta bāshem ki az ghafilat-i-naukarān wāḳi' mī-shavad [siwā,e har] wāridāte ki bar musāfirān mī-uftad mā-rā bāyad ki hama asbāb-rā ba ṭaraḥ-i-khūb bi-bandem. ['ilāwa,e ān hama.]*
come, chairman, in whose service are you, and when did you arrive in Balkh?	*ai ḥammāl! shumā naukar-i-kīsted, o kai ba balkh rasīded?*

how many other chairmen are with you?	ḥammālān-i-dīgar hamrāh-i-shumā chand nafarand?
desire the people always to pitch the tents near water, and, if possible, under trees,	mardumān-rā bi-go ki hamesha nazd-i-āb, o agar mumkin ast zer-i-dira<u>kh</u>thā, <u>kh</u>aimahā istāda bi-kunand [or bar pā bi-kunand].
are they all your countrymen only, or your relations?	eshān hama ham-waṭanān-i-shumā and, yā <u>kh</u>weshān-i-shumā?
what tribe of chairmen is there here who make more money than the rest?	kudām ṭā,ifa,e ḥammālān ast ki az dīgarān ziyāda pūl ḥāṣil mī-kunand?
what district is this village in, and who is the magistrate of it?	īn dih dar kudām ta'alluḳa ast, o ḥākim-i-ān kīst?
how very highly cultivated the country is, through which we passed to-day!	mulke ki mā az ān imrūz guzāshta em [chi ābād ast]? [chi bisiyār mazāri'; mazrū' ast.]
tell the proprietor of that village to send some of his people in the evening to beat up the game for us,	zamīndār-i-ān dih-rā bi-go, ki chand mardumān-i-<u>kh</u>ud-ash-rā ba waḳt-i-shām bi-firistad ki eshān barā,e maṣaid-rā gird biyāwarand.
take care that everything is paid for, and that no violence be used against the villagers,	<u>kh</u>abardār ki ḳīmat-i-har chīz dāda shavad, o ba dihḳānān [zabar dastī] karda na shavad. [ẓulm; taẓallum.]

Exercise.—A miser said to a friend, "I have now a thousand rupīs, which I will bury out of the city, and I will not tell this secret to any one besides yourself." In short, they went out of the city together, and buried the money under a tree. Some days after, the miser went alone to that tree, but found no signs of his money. He said to himself, "Excepting that friend, no other has taken it away; but if I question him, he will never confess." He therefore went to his house, and said, " A great deal of money is come to my hands, which I want to put in the same place ; if you will come to-morrow, we will go together." The friend, by coveting this large sum, replaced the former money, and the miser the next day went there alone, and found his money. He was delighted with his own contrivance, and never again placed any confidence in friends.

COUNTRIES AND TOWNS.

Aleppo,	ḥalb.
Bassora,	baṣra.
Bushir,	būshahr ; ābūshahr.
Bokhara,	buk͟hārā.
Bagdad,	bag͟hdād.
Balkh,	balk͟h.
Baalbec,	ba'albak.
Canaan,	kan'ān.
Constantinople,	istambūl ; kusṭunṭuniya.
Damascus,	dimishḳ.
Greece,	yunān, rūm.
Ispahan,	isfahān ; ispahān. sipahān.
Jerusalem,	yarūsalam. ḳuds ; arshalīm. maḳdis. baitu-l-muḳaddas.
Khiva,	k͟haiva.
Kashgar,	kūshg͟har.
Khorassan,	k͟hurāsān.

Mecca,	*maka, ḳibla.* *k'aba.*
Shirāz,	*shīrāz.*
Turkey,	*rūmiya ; mulk-i-rūm.*
Yemen,	*yaman.*

SEAS AND RIVERS.

Aral,	*baḥru-l-āral.*
Azov,	*baḥru-l-abyaẓ.*
Black Sea,	*baḥru-l-aswad.*
Caspian,	*gaug ; baḥru-l-khazar.*
Euphrates,	*farāt.*
Indus,	*daryā,e sind.* *abāsīn ; āb-i-hind.*
Nile,	*rūd-i-nīl.*
Persian Gulf,	*baḥru-l-fāris.* *khalīj-i-fārs.*
Red Sea,	*baḥru-l-aḥmar.*
Tigris,	*dajla.* *nahru-s-salam.*

anchor,	*langar.*
admiral,	*amīru-l-baḥr.*
abyss,	*lajjat ; 'āḳūl.*
a boat,	*māshūh ; safīna ; zauraḳ ;* (skiff) *būṣī.*
a blow,	*luṭma ;* (of waves) *talāṭum.*
compass,	*ḳuṭb numā.*
chart,	*naḳsha,e baḥr.*
cable,	*zanjīr-i-langar ; ḳaṭāj.*
captain,	*nā khudā ; kishtī-bān.*
cabin (of a ship),	*dabūs.* *dabūsa.*
capstan,	*āhanjad.*
dock,	*gūdī ; sinār.*

drowned,	*maghruḳ.*
a drowning person,	*gharīḳ.*
depth,	*'umuḳ.*
ferry,	*ma'abar.* *āb-guẕār.*
ferry-boat,	*kishtī,e guẕāra.*
horizon,	*ufḳ* (plur. *āfāḳ*).
light-house,	*manār; fānūs; fanūr; manāra.*
leadsman,	*raimānachi,e āb.*
loadstone,	*sang-i-maḳnāṭīs; āhan-rŭbā.*
mast of a ship,	*tīr-i-jahāz; sitūn-i-jahāz.*
maritime,	*baḥrī.*
navigation,	*mallāḥat.*
oar,	*halīsa;* (blade of) *pala.*
port (sea),	*kishtī gāh; bandar.*
pilot,	*rāh numā,e jahāz.*
rudder,	*sukkān; dumbāl-i-kishtī khalla.*
rock (in the sea),	*koh.*
rigging,	*auzār-i-jahāz.*
rower,	*halīsa-zan.*
sail,	*bād bān.*
sea,	*baḥr; ḳalzan;* (saore) *sāḥil;* (gulf) *khalīj;* (stormy) *baḥr-i-mashauwash; makhshūsh; tamawwuj.*
salt,	*milḥ; namak;* (being) *malāḥat.*
sailor,	*mallāḥ.*
storm,	*ṭūfān.*
steamer,	*jahāz-i-dukhānī.* *markāb-i-ātashī.* *kishtī,e dūdī.*
ship,	*jahāz; kishtī;* (deck) *paṭh-i-jahāz;* (sides) *aẓlā'-i-jahāz.*

a swimmer,	*shināwar ; shinār.* *shināb.*
swimming,	*shinā.*
wharf,	*furza ; farūd-gāh-i-jahāz.*
water,	*āb.*
„ shallow,	*āb-i-tunak.*
„ deep,	*āb-i-'amīḳ.*
„ running,	*āb-i-rawān.*
„ still,	*āb-i-ghair mutaḥarrik.*
wave,	*mauj* (pl. *amwāj*).
wind,	*bād;* (cold, boisterous) *bād-i-ṣarṣar.*
„ stormy,	*bād-i-tund.*
„ fair,	*bād-i-shurṭa.*
„ adverse,	*bād-i-mukhālif.*
„ hot,	*bād-i-samūm.*
„ -vane,	*bād-numā.*
whirlpool,	*gird-āb; warṭa; āb-i-gardish.*
north,	*shamāl.*
south,	*janūb.*
east,	*mashriḳ.*
west,	*maghrib.*
north-east,	*mā bain-i-shamāl o mashriḳ.*
south-east,	*mā bain-i-janūb o mashriḳ.*
to blow (like the wind),	*wazīdan.*
to coil a rope,	*rassan pechīdan.*
to embark,	*bar kishtī sawār shudan.*
to founder,	*gharḳ shudan.*
to let go the sail,	*bād-bān pā,īn kardan.*
to let go the anchor,	*langar kardan.*
to row,	*halīsa zadan.*
to swim,	*shinā kardan.*
to steer the ship,	*jahāz-rā gardānīdan.*
to set sail,	*bād-bān bar dāshtan.*
to strike (ground),	*ba zamīn chaspīdan.* *ba zamīn nishastan.* *ba koh khurdan.*

to fall to pieces,	*pāra pūra shudan.*
admission ticket,	*madkhal nāma ; sanad-i-madkhal.*
[1] railway ticket,	*kāghaz-i-rasīd-i-kirāya,e fī. nafar [az rāh-i-āhanī]. sanad-i-kirāya,e 'arāba,e dukhānī.*
theatre ticket,	*madkhal nāma,e [tamāsha gāh]. [mazhar.]*
free pass by rail,	*sanad-i-mu'āfī,e kirāya,e 'arāba,e dukhānī.*
bank note,	*barāt.*

Lesson 50.—With a Munshī.

sabak panjāhum dar guft-o-gū,e mā bain shakhse az farang o mu'allim-i-fārsī.

munshī sāhib, I am very glad to see you ; why have you been absent so long ?	*munshī sāhib man az dīdan-i-shumā bisiyār khūsham ; chirā īn kadar muddat ghair hāzir mānda ed ?*
have you brought me the works of Sa'dī ?	*az barā,e man kulliyāt* [or *ash'ār*]*-i-sa'dī āwarda ed ?*

---

[1] For the part within brackets we may use—
az 'arāba,e [ātashī]. [dukhānī ; dūdī.]

Similarly we may say for the steamer ticket—

az jahāz-i-ātashī.
az markāb-i-dukhānī.
az kishtī,e dūdī.

can you teach me both the Persian and Arabic languages?	*marā har dū zabān fārsī o 'arabī mī-tawāned āmokht?* *marā [ta'līm-i-har dū zabān] mī-tawāned dād. [dar har dū zabān ta'līm.]*
what are the best books?	*āyā bihtarīn-i-kitābhā kudām and?* *kudām az kitābhā bihtar ast?*
do not allow me to pronounce badly,	*marā bad talaffuz kardan ma dih.* *ma guzār ki man bad talaffuz bi-kunam.*
do not use so many hard words,	*chandīn lafzhā,e mushkil ba kār nayār* (or *mayār*).
tell me a short history, or the news of the day; for, unless we converse much together, how can I learn to speak?	*marā kissa,e khurd yā akhbār-i-īnrūzhā bi-go: zīrāki agar bisiyār guft-o-gū baham na khwāhem kard, [chigūna] guftan khwāham tawānist. [chi taur.]*
your business is to teach me the real pronunciation and practice of the language,	*kār-i-shumā īn ast, ki marā barābar talaffuz o ist'imāl-i-zabān biyāmozed.*
is this correct or not?	*īn barābar ast, yā na?*
pray, sir, in your opinion, is the Arabic or Persian language the more difficult?	*sāhibā dar rā,e shumā kudām mushkil-tar ast 'arabī yā fārsī? jawāb-i-īn sū,āl bi-farmāyed.*
as to the difficulty of the Arabic there can be no doubt, but it is more necessary than the Persian; we therefore are striving to learn it. Can you teach us?	*ba nisbat-i-mushkilāt-i-zabān-i-'arab shakk nīst, magar az zabān-i-fārs zarūr-tar ast; az īn sabab īn-rā koshish-i-āmokhtan mī-kunem. āyā marā dars dādan mī-tawāned?*

do say, in your idea, for the person who has transactions of all sorts with both the low and the high throughout Persia, of these two languages, viz. Arabic and Persian, which is the most requisite?	*shumā ba khayāl-i-khud chi mī-goyed, barā,e shakhṣe ki mu'āmala,e har ḳism, ba adnā o a'lā har dū dar tamām-i-fārs, dārad kudām zabān* [*ẓarūr*] *ast, āyā 'arabī yā fārsī?* [*lāzim.*]
in regard to the mere Arabic words which occur in the language, they are not so very difficult, but the masculine and feminine, with the discrimination of pronunciation in the pure Arabic, to learn them is so arduous a task, that no one as yet hath properly acquired it, nay, never will; for perfection in science is like an enchanted bird, which, the more one tries to catch, the farther that imp flies from him,	*ba nisbat-i-alfāẓ-i-'arabī ki darmiyān-i-zabān wāḳi' mī-shavand, chandān mushkil nīst; ammā, az tashkhīṣ-i-muẓakkar o mu,annaṣ, bā ma'-i tamīz-i-talaffuẓ-i-khāliṣ 'arabī chandān sakht kār ast, ki hech kas tā īn waḳt ba khūbī ḥāṣil na karda ast; balki, kase na khwāhad kard, az īn sabab ki kamāl-i-'ilm miṣal-i-paranda,e* [*afsūn sāz*] *ast, ki har chand kase koshish-i-akhẕ-i-o mī-kunad ān ḳadar ān kāfir az dast dūrtar mī-shavad.* [*musaḥḥar.*]
in acquiring the Persian tongue, what is your advice? Speak candidly, that I may learn the language accordingly, and remain eternally obliged to you on that account,	*ba nisbat-i-āmokhtan-i-zabān-i-fārsī chi farmāish mī-dihed? ba ṣadāḳat bigoyed tāki man ba muwāfiḳ-i-ān zabān bi-āmozam; o az ān sabab, az shumā* [*mamnūn*] *tā rūz-i-ḳiyāmat bāsham.* [*iḥsānmand; mashkūr.*]

if you obtain an acquaintance with the inflections of words, which is to be attained from the grammar only, your progress will then soon be complete,

agar az gardān-i-alfāẓ o muḥāwara shumā muṭṭali' [or *wāḳif*] *khwāhed shud ki faḳat az ṣarf o naḥw ḥāṣil mī-shavad* [*'ilmiyat-i-shumā zūd kamāl khwāhad girift.*] [*'ilmiyat-i-shumā kāmil khwāhad shud.*]

it is true; for we can neither apply the words properly, nor do we know the reason of their application, without the grammar,

rāst ast, zīrā ki mā alfāẓ-rā ba khūbī isti'māl kardan na mī-tawānem, o be ṣarf o naḥw [*ṭarīḳ*]*-i-isti'māl-i-ānhā na mī-dānem.* [*wajh.*]

sir, your remark is just; and I am surprised that other English gentlemen do not think the same way,

ṣāḥibā, ḳaul-i-shumā rāst ast, o man ta'ajjub mī-kunam ki ṣāḥibān-i-dīgar chunīn [*na mī-andeshand*]. [*khayāl na mī-kunand; ba ghaur na mī-pardāzand.*]

in European languages we reckon eight or nine parts of speech; in Persian you reckon only three, viz. the noun, the verb, and the particle,

dar zabānhā,e farang mā haft yā nuh ḳism-i-kalimāt mī-shumārem, ammā dar zabān-i-fārsī ṣirf si ḳism, y'anī ism, o fi'l, o ḥarf.

Exercise.—A horseman went to a city, and hearing there were many thieves in the place, said to his groom at night, "Do you sleep, and I will keep watch, for I cannot rely on you." The groom answered, "Alas! my lord, what words are these? I cannot consent to be asleep and my master awake." In short, the master went to sleep, and three hours afterwards awoke, when he called out to the groom, "What are you doing?"

He answered, "I am meditating how God has spread the earth upon the water." The master said, "I am afraid lest the thieves come and you know nothing of it." He replied, "O, my lord! rest satisfied, I am on the watch." The horseman went to sleep again, and awaking at midnight, he called out, "Holloa, groom! what are you doing?" He answered, "I am considering how God has supported the sky without pillars." He replied, "I am afraid that amidst your meditations the thieves will carry away the horse." He replied, "O, my lord! I am awake; how can the thieves come?" The cavalier again went to sleep, and an hour of night remaining, he awoke, and asked the groom what he was doing. He replied, "I am considering, since the thieves have stolen the horse, whether I shall carry the saddle upon my head to-morrow, or you, sir."

Lesson 51.—With a Persian Officer.

sabaḳ panjāh o yakum dar guft-o-gū,e ba sarhange fārsī.

the recruits will go to ball practice every evening,	*sipāhīyān-i-nau-rā* [*har shām barā,e mashḳ-i-nishān zadan bāyad raft*]. [*bāyad ki ba ḳawā'id-i-gulūla andāzī bi-ravand.*]
there will be an inspection of arms to-morrow morning; see that they are all very clean,	[1] *farda 'alạ-s-ṣabāḥ* [*mu'āyana,e asliḥa*] *khwāhad būd; bi-bīn ki ānhā hama durust ṣāf bāshand.* [*numā,esh-i-asliḥa;* or *mulāḥaẓa,e asliḥā.*]

[1] *asliḥa*, plur. of *silāḥ*, military arms.

take care that the supernumerary arms are cleaned every day,	*khabardār ki* [*asliḥa,e afzūd*] *har rūz ṣāf karda shavand.* [*asliḥa,e ziyād; asliḥa,e zā,id.*]
bring me a written report of the company daily,	[*rūz marra iṭṭilā' nāma,*]*e dasta,e sipāhīyān biyār.* [*har rūz iṭṭilā'-i-nawishta.*]
when was this man enlisted?	*kudām waḳt īn sipāhī mulāzim shuda būd?* *nām-i-īn 'askarī kai dākhil-i-daftar-i-lashkar shud?* *chand muddat īn sipāhī muḳarrar shuda būd?*
press the butt well to the shoulder,	*ba shāna maẓbūṭ ḳundāḳ-i-tufang bi-guẕār.*
pull the trigger strong with the middle finger,	[1] *ba angusht-i-miyāna kamān-rā maẓbūṭ bi-kash.*
tell off the company into three sections,	*dasta,e sipāhīyān-rā dar si farīḳ bi-kun.* *munḳasim-i-dasta,e sipāhīyān-rā ba si ḳism bi-kun.*
the company will wheel in echelon of sections,	*dasta kajī* [*ba ṣūrat-i-nard bān*] *khwāhad shud.* [*ba mānind-i-zīna;* or *ba miṡal-i-zīna.*]
at what time does the battalion march to-morrow morning?	*kudām waḳt fauj-i-piyādagān farda ṣubḥ kūch khwāhad kard?*
how many men are for piquet to-night?	*chand sipāhīyān imshab ba ṭilāya and?*
pray, sir, to what regiment do you belong?	*ṣāḥibā, shumā ba kudām fauj* [*ta'alluḳ*] *dāred?* [*ilāḳa; nisbat.*] *ṣāḥibā, shumā dar kudām fauj* [*manṣab dāred*]? [*muḳarrar ed.*]

[1] *angusht-i-shahādat*, fore-finger.

is your whole regiment at present on duty here, or elsewhere?	*dar īn rūzhā īn jā tamām fauj muta'aiyin ast, yā dar jā,e dīgar?*
do you know where it was first raised?	*shumā mī-dāned, kujā dar awwal īn fauj [mukarrar] shuda būd? [bār pā; jama'.]*
what rank do you hold, and how long have you been an officer?	*kudām 'uhda dāred, o [az chand rūz] 'uhdadār būda ed? [az kai.]*
what is your pay, and do you receive the whole monthly or not?	*muwājib-i-shumā chīst, o māhāna tamām mī-gīred, yā na?*
under such officers as you in our army, how many men are generally placed?	*zer dast-i-'uhdadārān mi-sal-i-janāb, dar fauj-i-mā chand sipāhīyān hasb-u-l-m'amūl guzāshta mī-shavand?*
when you are stationed anywhere in the country, does the magistrate of the place where you are on duty ever make you a present of anything, or not?	*wakte ki dar mulk ba jā,e [mukarrar] mī-shaved hākīm-i-mauza' chīze in'ām gāhe mī-dihad, yā na? [muta'aiyin; ta'aiyin karda.]*
pray tell me, when any of your soldiers are guilty of oppression on the country people, what steps do you take to prevent such an offence again?	*mihrbānī karda bi-farmāyed ki chūn kase az sipāhīyān-i-shumā bar dihkānān zulm bi-kunad o mujrim sha-vad, dar rafa' kardan-i-ān jurm chi [fikr] mī-kuned? [tadbīr.]* *wakte ki kase az sipāhīyān-i-shumā ba zulm kardan bar dihkānān mujrim mī-sha-vad, dar daf'a kardan-i-ān jurm chi mī-andeshed?*

does a soldier's continuance on guard last from sunrise till nine o'clock, or till twelve o'clock ?	*az ṭulū',e āftāb tā sā'at-i-nuh-i-ṣubḥ sipāhī [pāsbānī] mī-kunad, yā tā ẓuhr ? [bar maḳām-i-pāsbānī tawaḳḳuf.]*
have you clearly understood all that I have said, or not?	*hama sukhanān ki man gufta am, shumā ba khūbī fahmīda ed, yā na ?*
be not in the least apprehensive in answering me ; speak whatever you please without reserve, I will not take it in the least amiss,	*dar jawāb dādan ba man hech andesha ma kuned, harchi mī-khwāhed be lait o la'all bi-goyed ; hargiz bad na khwāham burd.*

Exercise.—A certain man went to a darwesh, and proposed three questions: First : Why do they say that God is omnipresent ? I do not see Him in any place ; show me where He is." Second : "Why is man punished for crimes, since whatever he does proceeds from God ? Man has no free will, for he cannot do anything contrary to the will of God : and if he had power, he would do everything for his own good." Third : "How can God punish Satan in hell-fire, since he is formed of that element ; and what impression can fire make on itself ?" The darwesh took up a large clod of earth, and struck him on the head with it. The man went to the *ḳāẓī* and said, "I proposed three questions to such a darwesh, who flung a clod of earth at me." The *ḳāẓī* having sent for the darwesh, asked, "Why did you throw a clod of earth at his head, instead of answering his questions ?" The darwesh replied, "The clod of earth was an answer to his speech : he says he has a pain in his head ; let him show the pain, then I will make God visible to him: and why does he make a complaint to you against me ; whatever I did was the act of God,—I did not strike him without the will of God,—what power do I possess ?

and as he is formed of earth, how can he suffer pain from that element?" The man was confounded, and the *ḳāẓī* highly pleased with the darwesh's answer.

Lesson 52.—Military Affairs—*Aḥwāl-i-jang.*

accoutrements,	*sāz o yarāḳ-i-sarbāz;* (halberd) *ḥarba.*
ally,	*madad gār.*
ambassador,	*rasūl; elchī; safīr; mursal.*
ambush,	*kamīn;* (ambuscade) *kamīngāh.*
arms,	*silāḥ; silāḥ-i-jang.*
"	(to take off) *az badan silāḥ kushādan.*
"	(to put on) *bar badan silāḥ* [*poshīdan*]. [*ārāstan; bastan.*]
armed,	*musallaḥ;* (to be) *asliḥa bar badan dāshtan.*
armourer,	*āhangar; silāḥ-sāz;* (armoury) *silāḥ-khāna.*
army,	*lashkar; 'askar; jaish.*
arrow,	*tīr; paikān.*
artillery,	*top-khāna;* (battery) *ta'bi,at; morcha.*
attack,	*ḥamla; yūrish.*
battalion,	*fauj.*
battle,	*jang; kār-zār.*
"	(axe) *tabar zīn.*
bayonet,	*sar nīza,e tufang.*
a blow,	*sīla; laṭma; sīlī.*
a bow,	*kamān; ḳaus.*
brave,	*bahādur; dilāwar; shujā'; ẕū-sh-shujā'at.*
bravery,	*shujā'at; dilīrī.*
camp,	*khīma-gāh-i-lashkar; mu'askar.*

cannon, *top.*
captain, *sardār-i-jamā'at ; ṣad-bāshī.*
captive, *asīr ; giriftār-i-jang.*
cartouche, *toshdān ; kīf ;* (cartridge) *fīshang.*
clean, *ṣāf ; be zang ; mujallī.*
coat of mail, *jaushan.*
commandant, *ḳila' dār ; mu'askir.*
company, *jamā'at-i-ṣad laskarī.*
comrade, *mushārik ; sharīk ; rafīḳ.*
conquered, *maghlūb ; maḳhūr ; maftūḥ ; musakhkhar ;* (conquering) *taskhīr ;* (conqueror) *kishwar-kushā ; manṣūr.*
council of war, *mashwarat-i-jang.*
court martial, *'adālat.*
coward, *nā mard ; buzdil ; kam-jurat ; jabān.*
cowardice, *nā mardī ; buzdilī.*
crime, *khaṭā ; taḳṣīr.*
defeat, *shikast.*
deserter, *gurezānda ; mafrūr ; manjūz.*
detachment, *dasta,e lashkar.*
dirty, *zang ālūda ; ghair mujallī ; palīd ; ghalīẓ.*
discipline, *niẓām ; ẓabṭ o rabṭ-i-lashkar ; intiẓām.*
ditch, *tarak ; khandaḳ ; maghāra.*
drum, *kos ; ṭabl.*
enemy, *dushman.*
executioner, *jallād.*
fine, *jurmāna ; jarīma ; muṣādira.*
flag, *nishān ; bairaḳ ;* (standard) *rāyat.*
flank, (right) *maimana ;* (left), *maisara ;* (centre) *ḳalb ;* (wing) *janāḥ.*
ford, *ubūr-gāh ; pā-yāb ; āb-guẕār.*
fort, *ḳila' ; ḥiṣn-i-ḥaṣīn ; ḥiṣn-i-matīn ;* (citadel) *ḥiṣār ;* (impregnable) *ḥiṣn-i-ghair madkhal ; ḥiṣn-i-mumtani'u-l-wuṣūl ; ḥiṣn-i-mumtani'u-d-du-*

	khūl; (a small turret) *burj*, (plur. *burūj*); (trenches) *morchāl*; *muḥāsir*; (a refuge) *malāẕ*; *maljā*; *ma'ḳil*.
general,	*pesh-āhang*; *pesh-rau*.
gladiator,	*silāḥ-shor*; *shamshīr-bāz*; *shamshīr zan*.
gun,	*tufang*; *madfa'*; (rifle) *tufang-i-nāb-dār*; (barrel) *lūla*; (hammer) *ḳāshlūḳ*; (equipment) *sāz o yarāḳ-i-top*; (carriage) *'arāba,e top*; (foresight) *pesh bīn*; (back sight) *pas bīn*; (sight) *bīn-i-tufang*; (shot large) *gūla,e top*; (cock) *chaḳmāḳ*; (bullet) *ghulūla*; (powder) *bārūt*.
helmet (iron),	*tark*; *khūd*; *maghfar*.
horse and foot,	*sawār o piyāda*.
hostage,	*yarghamāl*; *girau*; *kafīl*.
hurler (quoit),	*charkh andāz*.
inspection,	*mulāḥaẓa*; *mu'aiyana*; (inspector) *nāẓir*.
interpreter,	*mutarajjim*; *tarjumān*.
irregular,	*be zabṭ*; *be nasḳ*; *be naẓm*.
kit,	*chū yarāḳ*; *asbāb-i-sipāhiyāna*.
magazine,	*makhzan*; (powder) *bārūt-khāna*.
march,	*kūch*.
a mediator,	*miyānjī*; *myāndār*; *wāsiṭ*; *wasīṭ*.
mediation,	*myānagī*; *tawassuṭ*; *wasāṭat*.
military profession,	*sipāh garī*.
military tactics,	*naẓm o nasḳ-i-'askar*.
mud,	*khilāb*; *lā,e*; *gil*.
a muster,	*iḥẓār*; (to) *iḥẓār-i-fauj giriftan*.
mustered,	*ṣaff-zada*.
mutineer,	*bāghī*; *munharif*; *ṭughiyān-afroz*.
mutinous,	*bāghī*; *fasādī*.
mutiny,	*baghāwat*; *fasād*; *inhirāf*.

news,	*khabar*; (doubtful) *afwāh.*
neutral,	*ghair-i-muta'allaḳ; musāwī; bejānib-dārī.*
neutrality,	*tasāwī; 'adm-i-jānib-dārī.*
officer (military),	(commanding) *'uhdadār-i-mukhtār*; (commander-in-chief) *amīru-n-niẓām*; (general) *sipāh-sālār*; (lieut.-gen.) *amīr-i-tomān*; (major-gen.) *amīr-i-panj*; (colonel) *sartīp*; (lieut.-col.) *sarhang*; (major) *yahvar*; (captain) *ṣad-bāshī*; (lieut.) *nā,ib*; (serjeant) *'uhdadār-i-khurd.*
omen,	*shugūn; fāl.*
parade,	*sān; ḳawā'id.*
pass (mountain),	*darra; guẕar-gāh-i-koh; shi'b-i-jabal; ma'bar-i-koh.*
passport, safe conduct,	*kāghaẕ-i-amān; khaṭṭ-i-rāhdārī; barāt-i-salamī.*
pay,	*tankhwāh; muwājib; mushāhira; māhiyāna*; (arrears) *baḳiya,e muwājib*; (advance of) *peshgī,e tankhwāh*; (pension) *idrār.*
peace,	*ṣulḥ.*
piquet,	*ṭilāya*; (vanguard) *ṭālī'at; muḳaddama.*
pistol,	*tamāncha*; (revolver) *mudaḥrij; ṭamāncha,e shish khānadār.*
plunder,	*ghanīmat; ghārat; yaghmā; tārāj.*
punishment,	*siyāsat; sazā.*
pursuit,	*ta'āḳub.*
quarter,	*al amān; amn; amān.*
recruit,	*tāza-'askarī.*
regulations,	*ā,īn.*
retreat,	(to) *hazīmat namūdan; pas pā shudan; pusht dādan; pas nishastan; firār kardan; rū,e ba gurez nihādan.*
review,	*mulāḥaẓa,e ḳawā'id.*

a rocket,	*gulūla,e ḳīz ; tīr-charkh.*
a runaway,	*hazīmatī.*
safety, security, respite,	*amn ; amān.*
sentence of court-martial,	*fatwā.*
sentinel,	*pās-bān ;* (the guard) *kashīk.*
shield,	*sipar.*
siege,	*muḥāṣara.*
soldier,	*sarbāz ; sipāhī ; 'askarī ;* (horse) *sawār ;* (experienced) *kār-dīda ; kār āzmūda; wāḳi'a-dīda;* (service) *jang-āzmūda.*
spear,	*naiza ; nīza.*
spur,	*mahmez.*
spy,	*jāsūs ;* (scout) *ṭalāba ;* (spying) *tajassus.*
store,	*ambār.*
surrender,	*ṭaslīm ;* (to) *chīze-rā ṭaslīm kardan.*
surrendering,	*sipar andāzī.*
a sword,	*shamshīr ;* (scabbard) *miyān ; ghilāf.*
,,	(belt) *kamarband-i-shamshīr.*
a tactician,	*nasaḳchi ;* (tactics) *'ilm-i-ārā,ish-i-lashkar mansūb.*
tax,	*khirāj ; maḥṣūl ; waẓī'at ; ḳaṭī'at.*
terms of peace,	*sharā,iṭ-i-ṣulḥ.*
treaty,	*'ahd-nāma ; 'ahd o paimān nāma.*
,,	(of peace) *'uhd o paimān nāma,e ṣulḥ.*
treasure,	*ganj ; khizāna.*
tribute,	*khirāj.*
truce,	*muhlat ; tawaḳḳuf-i-jang.*
trumpet,	*būḳ ; ḳarnā.*
victory,	*fatḥ ; naṣr ; ẓafr ;* (victorious) *muẓaffar.*
war,	*jang ḥarb ; muḥārabat ; razm.*
,,	(articles of) [*ḳawā'id*]*-i-jang.* [*ā,īn.*]
warrior,	*jang jū ; zor āwar ; jang āwar ;*

	maṣāff āzmūda; (for religion) *mujāhid.*
wound,	*zakhm; resh; jarāḥat.*
the wounded,	*zakhmīyān; majruḥān.*
wrestler,	*kushtī-bāz.*
to raise the standard,	[*naṣb-i-rāyat*] *kardan.* [*rāyat bar pā.*]
to hit the mark,	[*nishāna-rā*] *zadan.* [*ba ḥadaf; ba āmāj.*]
to collect an army,	*lashkare jama' kardan.*
to punish (a person),	[*kase-rā*] *siyāsat kardan; siyāsat namūdan; 'uḳūbat kardan.*
to pursue the enemy,	*ta'āḳub-i-dushman kardan.* *darpai,e dushman* [*būdan*]. [*uftādan.*] *'aḳab-i-dushman giriftan.* *dar 'aḳab-i-dushman raftan.*
to pitch a tent,	*khīma istāda kardan.* *khīma zadan.*
to strike a tent,	*khīma bar andākhtan.* *khīma bar kandan.*
to stick in the mud,	*ba waḥal giriftār shudan.* *dar kaṣa'at māndan.*
to proclaim (by beat of drum),	*manādī* [*kardan*]. [*zadan; dādan.*]
to proclaim,	[*mashhūr*] *kardan.* [*tashhīr.*]
to consult,	*ba kase* [*mashwarat*] *kardan.* [*maṣlaḥat; tadbīr.*]
to draw a sword,	*ākhtan* (root *ākh*).
to plunder,	*māl-rā ghārat kardan; māl-rā ba yaghma* [*burdan*]. [*āwardan.*]
to ravage,	*mulk-rā* [*pā māl kardan*]. [*wairān sākhtan.*]
to besiege,	*jā,e-rā muḥāṣara kardan.*
to march,	*kūch kardan;* (advance) *pesh raftan; ḳadam peshtar guzāshtan.*
to attack,	*bar kase ḥamla kardan.*

to fortify,	*jā,e-rā* [*ḥiṣār*] *kardan*, [*muḥāṣir*]; (form square) *burj bastan*.
to fire a gun,	*bar kase tufang-rā khālī kardan*.
to wound (a person),	(*kase-rā*) *majrūḥ kardan; zakhmī kardan*.
to cross over a river,	*az daryā guzashtan*. *az daryā 'ubūr kardan*.
to advance,	(obliquely) *maḥrif o ghair-i-niẓām pesh raftan*.
to arrange,	(a battery) *mūrcha,e top-khāna ārāstan*; (intrenchments) [*morchāl*] *sākhtan*. [*kandak* or *khandaḳ*.]
to blow up,	*ba bārūt kase-rā ba hawā* [*burdan*]. [*afgandan; dādan*.]
to cock a gun,	*chaḳmāḳ-rā sar pāya āwardan*; (half cock) *chaḳmāḳ-rā bar nīm pāya kashīdan*.
to escalade,	*nird-bān bar dīwār guzāshtan*.
to flash in the pan.	[*tufang o chaḳmāḳ*] *gul kardan*.
to hold out to the last,	*tā nihāyat ḥālat-i-lāchārī dar muḥāfiẓat koshish namūdan*.
to impress,	*kase-rā ba sukhra giriftan*.
to stockade,	*jā,e dar sangur kardan*.
to storm,	*bar ḳila' yurish āwarda* [*musakhkhar*] *namūdan* [*taskhīr*]; *ḳila' az ḥamla fatḥ kardan*; (storming party) *kasāne ki yurish burda az rakhna ḳaṣd-i-dākhil-i-jā,e kunand*.
to stand a charge,	*tāb-i-ḥamla,e dushman dāshtan*.

Exercise.—Certain Arab merchants went to a king of Persia, and exhibited some fine horses for sale. The king liked them very much, and bought them. He gave the merchants two lakhs of rūpīs over and above the purchase, and told them to bring more horses from their own country as soon as possible. The merchants upon this agreement, took their leave. One day afterwards, the king being exhilarated with wine, said to the wazir, "Make out a list of all the fools in my dominions." The wazir represented that he had already done so, and had put his majesty's name at the very head of the list. The king asked why so. He replied, "Because you gave two lakhs of rūpīs for horses to be brought by merchants, for whom no person is security, neither does any one know what part of Arabia they belong to; and this is a sign of the greatest folly." The king said, "But if the merchants should bring the horses, what is then to be done?" The wazir answered, "Sire, if they should be such fools as to bring the horses, I will insert the names of the merchants at the head of the list, and your majesty's name will in that case occupy only the second place."

Lesson 53.—With a Head Servant.

sabaḳ pànjāh o siwum dar guft-o-gū,e mā bain shakhṣe farang o darogha,e khuddām.

do you speak our language?	*āyā ba zabān-i-mā sukhan mī-goyed?*
yes, sir, I can speak a little English,	*bale, ṣāḥib, man ḳadre zabān-i-inglisī mī-tawānam guft.*
I have not yet learned to speak Persian,	*tā [ḥāl] zabān-i-fārsī guftan nayāmokhta am. [hanoz.]*
where do you now live?	{ *aknūn kujā manzil dāred?* *ilḥāl būd o bāsh kujā [mī-kuned]? [dāred.]*
pray what is your name? let me know also your master's name,	*nām-i-shumā chīst, o nām-i-[mālik]-i-khud ba man bi-go. [arbāb.]*

how long have you been in that gentleman's service?	*az chand waḳt* [*dar naukarī,e ān ṣāḥib mulāzim būda ed*]? [*dar* (or *ba*) *naukarī,e ān ṣāḥib mashghūl ed.*]
where is your native country, and how far may it be hence?	[*waṭan*]-*i-shumā kujā ast, o az īn jā chi ḳadar dūr bāshad?* [*zād-būm; maulid.*]
do people in general go there by land or water?	*az rāh-i-khushkī yā tarī, hama mardumān akṣar ān jā mī-ravand?*
what is the most important article of trade in that country, and what things are produced in greatest abundance there?	*dar ān mulk kudām jins lā,iḳtar-i-tijārat ast, o kudām chīz ba* [*afzūnī*] *dar ān jā paida mī-shavad?* [*kasrat; firāwānī; afzā,ish.*]
are your parents alive or not, and do you ever go to see your relations and friends?	[1] *wālidain-i-shumā zinda and, yā na, o ba mulāḳāt kardan-i-khweshān o ḳarībān o dostān gāhe mī-raved, yā na?*
do you know at what rate copper sells in the market here?	*āyā mī-dāned īn jā ba kudām nirkh dar bāzār mis farokhta mī-shavad?*

---

[1] visiting the sick, *'ayādat kardan.*
visiting one's spiritual guide, *ziyārat kardan-i-murshid.*
visiting one's parents, { *ḳadam bos shudan-i-wālidain.* / *ḳadam bosa dādan-i-wālidain.* / *ziyārat kardan-i-wālidain.* }

what, cannot you even say that one penny's worth of copper will be the weight or size of a penny or not?	*mut'ajjibam, ki shumā na mī-tawāned guft, ki āyā mis, ba ḳadar-i-yak fils, barābar-i-wazn o andāz-i-yak fils khwāhad būd, yā na?*
do you know nowadays at what rate a quart of milk sells in the city, and in the country for how much?	*dar īn rūzhā ba chi nirkh yak aṣār-i-shīr dar shahr farokhta mī-shavad, o dar dihāt ba chand?*
you may now depart,	*shumā-rā rukhṣat ast?* *shumā murakhkhaṣ ed.* *shumā rukhṣat [bi-gīred]. [shaved.]*

Exercise.—A certain king had a wise wazir, who resigned his office, and employed himself in worshipping God. The king asked the nobles what was become of the wazir; they answered, that having quitted his exalted station, he employed himself in serving the Deity. The king went to the wazir, and asked, "O wazir, what offence have I committed that you quitted my service?" He answered, "Sire, for five reasons have I done this: firstly, because you used to sit and I remained standing in your presence; now, I serve God, who has commanded me to sit at the time of prayer: secondly, you ate whilst I was looking on; now, I have found a Providence who eateth not himself, but sustains me: thirdly, you slept, whilst I watched; now, I have a master who knows not slumber, but protects me whilst I rest: fourthly, I was always afraid, that if you should die I might experience some misfortune from enemies; now I serve a God who is immortal, neither can enemies do me any injury: fifthly, with you I was afraid, that if I should have committed a fault, you would not have forgiven me; but He whom I now serve is so merciful, that if I commit a hundred sins every day he pardons me."

Lesson 54.—Between a European Doctor and a Persian Patient.

sabaḳ panjāh o chihārum dar guft-o-gū,e mā bain ṭabīb,e az farang wa bīmār-i-fārsī.

tell me what is the matter with you,	*shumā-rā [chi] shud? [chi 'āriẓ.]* *marā bi-go, [ḥālat-i-shumā chīst]? [chi dard dāred.]*
how long have you been ill?	*az chand bīmār būda ed?*
how did the fever attack you at first?	*ba awwal, ba chi ṣūrat tab girifted?* *ba awwal, ba chi ṣūrat tab shumā-rā girift?* *ba awwal, chigūna tab 'āriẓ shud?*
with great coldness, shivering, pains in all my limbs, headache, and a sensation in my back as if one were pouring cold water down my backbone,	*ba bisiyār sardī, wa [larza], wa dard-i-andām, wa dard-i-sar wa iḥsās-i-pusht chunān ki kase āb-i-sard bar ṣulb-i-man faro mī-rezad. [ra'sha; irti'-āsh; ḳusha'rīrat.]*
after some time a perspiration broke out, which relieved me much, and I fell asleep,	*b'ad az chande 'araḳ az a'ẓā bar āmad, har ā,ina marā bisiyār ifaḳa [or shifā] bakhshīd, o dar khwāb raftam.*
what medicine have you taken?	*[dawā] chi ḳism khurda ed? [ṭabb.]*
none with any regularity,	*hech [pai dar pai] na khurda am. [mutawātīr; ba iḥtiyāṭ.]*
you must take some active medicine,	*bāyad ki shumā dawā,e [ḳawī] bi-khured. [muḳawwī; pur zor; mus,hil; is,hāl.]*

I suppose you have no appetite,	*gumān dāram ki shumā-[rā ishtihā nīst]. [ishtihā na dāred.]* *taṣauwar dāram ki shumā-rā khwāhish-i-ṭa'ām nīst.*
let me feel your pulse,	*nabẓ-i-khud-i-tān-rā iḥsās kardan marā bi-dihed.* *dast-i-khud-i-tān biyār ki nabẓ-i-shumā bi-bīnam.*
put out your tongue,	*ẓabān-i-khud berūn bi-kash.* *zabān-i-khud-rā badar bi-[namā]. [āwar.]* *zabān-i-khud nishān bi-dih.*
I suspect there is something wrong with your liver,	*rā,e man ast ki dar jigar-i-shumā chīze bīmārī ast.* *gumān kunam ki [dar jigar-i-shumā chīze 'aib ast]. [shumā-rā marẓ-i-jigar ('āriẓ shuda ast) (ast).]*
let me well examine it; does that pain you?	*ba khūbī ān-rā dīdanam bi-dih; az īn [darde iḥsās mī-kuned]? [fishurdan dar badan-i-shumā darde ast,* or *mī-gīrad.]* *bi-guẕār ki tashkhīṣ-i-jigar ba khūbī bi-kunam; fishurdan badan-i-shumā dard mī-kunad?* *jigar-i-shumā-rā ba khūbī mushakhkhaṣ kardan bi-dihed; az mālīdan-i-dast-i-man darde maḥsūs,* or *ma'lūm mī-shavad?*
yes, that is the very spot where the pain is most acute,	*bale dar ham īn jā [dard ziyād] ast. ['ain-i-dard; ranj ba shiddat.]*

have you any heartburn ?	*shumā-rā sozish-i-dil ast ?* *sozish-i-dil* [*dāred*] ? [*karda ed.*] *shumā-rā bīmārī,e sozish-i-dil 'āriẓ shuda ast ?* *dil-i-shumā sozish dārad ?*
you must use mercury both inwardly and by friction, until a salivation is produced,	[1] *bāyad ki shumā* [*zībaḳ ba kār biyāwared*] [or *dawā,e jīwa bi-khured*] *ba har dū ṣūrat darūn o ba mālish berūn tā* [*ki lu'āb nayāyad*]. [*dahan-i-shumā na joshad.*]
do whatsoever you please with me, for I have great confidence in your prescriptions,	*harchi mī-khwāhed bi-kuned, zīrā ki man bar ḥikmat-i-shumā bisiyār i'timād mī-dāram* [or *mī-kunam*].
I shall send you some medicines; and you are to take them in the evening according to my instructions,	*barā,e shumā chīze dawāhā khwāham firistād; bāyad ki ba waḳt-i-shām muwāfiḳ-i-farmā,ish-i-man* [*ba kār āwared*]. [*ba 'amal āwared; isti'māl kuned.*]
do not be persuaded by native doctors to take their medicines,	*az targhīb-i-ṭabībān-i-mulk-i-fārs dawāhā,e eshān na khured.*
I am well convinced they will do you no good, and they may do you much injury,	*marā bi-l-kull yaḳīn ast ki eshān shumā-rā hech fā,ida na khwāhand dād, o shāyad shumā-rā bisiyār ranj bi-dihand.*

[1] inwardly and outwardly, *bāṭinan o ẓāhiran.*

Persian doctors frequently administer our medicines, but they are utterly unacquainted with them,	*ṭabībān-i-fārsī 'umūman mu'alijahā,e mā istiʼmāl mī-kunand, magar az ānhā bi-l-kull na wāḳif and.*

Exercise.—One of the kings of Persia sent a skilful physician to the prophet Muhammad (upon whom be peace!). He had been some years in Arabia without any one having come to make trial of his skill, neither had they applied to him for any medicine. One day he came to the prince of prophets, and complained, saying, "They sent me to dispense medicines to your companions, but to this day no one hath taken notice of me, that I might have an opportunity of performing the service to which I had been appointed." Muhammad replied, "It is a rule with these people never to eat until they are hard pressed by hunger, and to leave off eating whilst they have a good appetite." The physician said, "This is the way to enjoy health." He then made his obeisance and departed. The physician begins to speak when evil would result from his silence; either when there is eating to excess, or when death might ensue from too much abstinence. Then, doubtless, his speech is wisdom, and such a meal will be productive of health. (*Gulistān*, chap. iii., tale 4.)

NAMES OF PARTS OF THE BODY.

arm,	*bāzū;* (-pit) *baghl.*
back,	*pusht;* (bone) *ṣulb.*
beard,	*rīsh;* *khaṭṭ;* (whisker) *ẓamma.*

[1] belly,	*baṭn* (plur. *baṭnān*); *shikam.*
bladder,	*zihār*; *shāsha dān*; *maṣāna.*
blood,	*khūn.*
body,	*paikar*; *badan*; *jism*; *tan*; *wujūd.*
bone,	*ustukhwān*; *aẓam*; (collar) *tarḳū-wat.*
bowels,	*rūdah*; *buṭnān*; (navel) *nāf.*
brain,	*dimāgh*; *maghz.*
cheek,	*'iẕār*; *'āriẓ*; *rukhsār.*
[2] chin,	*zanakh dān*; *zanakh*; (dimple of) *chāh-i-zanakh.*
countenance,	*ṭala'at.*
down,	*khaṭṭ-i-sabz*; *nabāt-i-'āriẓ.*
ear,	*gosh*; (lobe) *banā gosh.*
elbow,	*ārzan*; *mīrfaḳ*; (joint) *mafṣil-i-bāzū.*
eye,	*chashm*; (blue) *azraḳ chashm*; (-brow) *abrū*; (-lash) *mizhgān*; (-lid) *parda,e chashm.*
face,	*rū,e*; *paikar*; *bashra*; *sīmā.*
finger,	*angusht-i-dasht*; (thumb) *ibhām*; *shust.*
fist,	*musht.*
foot,	*pā,e*; *pā*; (heel) *'aḳīb.*
gall-bladder,	*zahra.*
gums,	*liṣa* (plur. *liṣā*).
hair,	*mū,e*; (moustache) *fatha*; *sabīl*; (ringlet) *zulf.*
hand,	*past*; *yadd.*

---

[1] to creep as an insect, *ba shikam raftan.*
wind in the bowels, *būd-i-shikam.*
sensualist, *shikam parwar*; *shikam banda*; *baṭīn.*

[2] to wag the chin, to talk, *zanakh zadan.*

head, *sar*; (fore-) *jabīn*; *jabhā*; *nāṣiya*; *peshānī*; *sīmā*.
heart, *dil*; *ḳalb*; *ẓamīr*; *k͟hāṭir*.
heart, lungs, liver, spleen, intestines, *aḥshā*, plur.; *ḥasha*, sing.
joint, *mafsil*; *'izw*.
knee, *zānū*.
leg, *sāḳ*; *pā,e*; (ankle) *shitālang*.
limbs, *andām*; *a'ẓā* (sing. *'iẓw*).
lip, *nabāt*; *lab*; (upper) *lab-i-zabarīn*; (lower) *lab-i-zerīn*.
liver, *jigar*.
lungs, *shush*.
mouth, *dahan*.
neck, *gardan*.
nerve, *'aṣab* (plur. *a'ṣāb*).
palate, *kām*.
palm of the hand, *kaf*.
shoulder, *shāna*; *dosh*; (joint) *a'ṣab-i-shāna*; *mafsil-i-dosh*; (blade) *katif*, or *kitf*.
side, *pahlū*; (rib) *danda*.
[1] skin, *post*.
stomach, *ḥauṣila*; *mi'da*.
thigh, *rān*.
throat, *ḥalk*; *gulū*; (windpipe) *ḥanjar*.
tongue, *zabān*; *lisān*.
tooth, *dand*.
vein, *'irḳ* (plur. *'urūḳ*).
wrist, *sā'id*; *ma'ṣim*.

---

[1] skin, raw hide, *post*, or *pūst*.
the shell of a nut, *post-i-jauz*.
to flay, *post kandan*.
a snake's slough, *post-i-mār*.
leather, *postīn*.
a furrier, *postīn doz*.

aloes,	*ṣibr.*
cancer,	*khwarą; saraṭān.*
cholera,	*haiza; wabā; ṣadma,e wabā.*
a cold,	*zukām; chāhish;* (to have) *zukām dāshtan;* (to catch) *chāhīdan.*
colocinth,	*ḥanẓal.*
convalescence,	*shifā.*
a cough,	*surfa;* (whooping) *siyāh-surfa;* (to cough) *surfa' kardan; surfīdan.*
cramp,	*tamaddud.*
delirium,	*hazī; haẕīān-i-maḥrūr;* (delirious) *haẕiyān; mad-hosh.*
diarrhœa,	*shikam-jārī; jiriyān-i-shikam; iṭlāḳ.*
a doctor,	*ṭabīb* (plur. *aṭibbā*); *ḥakīm;* (horse) *baiṭār.*
dropsy,	*istisḳā;* (cupping glass) *shākh-i-ḥajāmat.*
fever,	*tap; tab;* (heat of) *ḥarārat.*
giddiness,	*daurān; daurān dar sar.*
gout,	*niḳris.*
gripe,	*pechish.*
lancet,	*neshtar.*
leper,	*pīs; juẕām; mabrūṣ; ahl-i-baraṣ;* (leprosy) *baraṣ; pīsī.*
medical art,	*ṭibābat.*
medicine,	*dawā; dārū;* (pill) *ḥabb,* plur. *ḥubūb;* (powder) *ṣafūf;* (alum) *āb-i-zāj-i-safaid;* (castor oil) *kinatū; raughan-i-bedanjir;* (opium) *afyūn; tiryāḳ;* (quinine) *gina;* (antidote) *tiryāḳ.*
ophthalmia,	*ramad.*
a patient,	*bīmār; marīẓ;* (disease) *marẓ; bīmārī; ranjūrī.*
plague,	*ṭā'ūn; wabā.*

plaster,	*marham ; ẓamad.*
a purge,	*jallāb ; muṣhil ; shikam-rāṇ.*
rheumatism,	*waja'-i-mufāṣil.*
slime,	*balg͟ham ;* (clamminess) *luzūjat.*
to feel weak,	*dar badan naḳāhat ma'lūm shudan.* *ẓa'f maḥsūs kardan.*
to feel stronger,	*dar badan ḳuwat ziyāda shudan.*
to feel better,	*az awwal ḳadre [bihtar būdan].* *[ifāḳa ma'lūm shudan.]*
to feel quite well,	*sālim shudan.*
to have jaundice,	*yarḳān berūn āwardan.*
to have small-pox,	*abla,e chīchak berūn āwardan.*
to have chicken-pox,	*zabrak berūn āwardan.*
to have fever spots,	*tabk͟hāl berūn āwardan.*
to be teething,	*dandān berūn āwardan.*
to be prevalent,	*g͟hālib būdan ; jārī shudan ; ḳuwat dāshtan ; istīlā yāftan.*
to purge,	*jallāb dādan ;* (to take a purge) *jallāb giriftan.*
to swell,	*waram kardan.*
to try a remedy,	*'ilāj-i-marẓe kardan.*
to vomit ; or to wish to vomit,	*kai kardan.* *kase-rā [kai] shudan. [tahauwu'.]* *dil-i-kase [barham k͟hurdan]. [tahauwu' shudan.]*
he is getting worse,	*bīmārī,e o ['urūj] dārad. [ziyādatī ; rū ba taraḳḳī.]*
he is getting better,	*bīmārī,e o rū ba [tanazzul] dārad. [nuzūl.]* *bīmārī,e o kam mī-shavad.*

LESSON 55.—BETWEEN A CIVILIAN AND A SARISHTA-DAR, OR NATIVE OFFICIAL.

sabaḳ panjāh o panjum dar guft-o-gū,e mā bain 'āmile az farang o ṣāḥib-i-dīwān.

pray, my friend, are you somewhat versed in the revenue department?	*dostā! marā bi-farmāyed ki az kār-i-[taḥṣīldārī] khūb wāḳif ed yā na? [maḥṣūl.]*
what do they call a lease, and what its counterpart?	*[ḳabāla,]e zamīn chi chīz-rā mī-goyand, o ḳabūliyăt chīst? [ijāra nāma.]*
have you any other names for the rate or rent adjustment of lands?	*barā,e band o bast wa [khirāj] nām-i-dīgar dāred? [māl-guzārī; madkhūl; madākhil; maḥṣūl.]*
should you not recollect another word for the rate, then explain the nature of it in detail,	*agar lafẓ-i-dīgar barā,e khirāj ba yād-i-shumā na mī-āyad, ḥaḳīḳat-i-ān [tafṣīlwār bayān bi-kuned]. [mufaṣṣal taḳrīr bi-kuned.]*
do the farmers pay the revenue to government by instalments, or in the gross?	*āyā kisht-i-kārān ba sarkār khirāj-rā [ba aḳsāṭ ya ba yak jumla] mī-dihand. [az ḳarār-i-ḳisthā yā mujmil.]*
does this species of revenue come in before, or during, or after the crop?	*īn ḳism-i-pūl-i-khirāj pesh yā darmiyān, yā ba'd az faṣl ba khizāna [mī-rasad]? [mī-razānand.]*

does free land, or that not assessed, pay anything at all to government, or not, by way of acknowledgement?	az zamīn-i-lā-_khi_rāj, yā mu'āfī, chīze _khi_rāj ba sarkār ba ṭaur-i-tuḥfa mīdihand, yā na? az zamīn-i lā-_khi_rāj kudām māl-guzārī ṭaur-i-peshkash ba sarkār adā mīnamāyand, yā na? az zamīn-i-lā-_khi_rāj kudām rusū_khī_yat, ba ṭaur-i-hidāya, sarkār ḥāṣil mī-namāyad, yā na?
who used to settle formerly the assessment of the several districts?	ḳabl az īn band o bast-i-_khi_rāj-i-zamīn kudām sha_khṣ_ muḳarrar karde?
in what respects does the county registrar differ from the town or village clerk?	darmiyān-i-ḳānūngo o paimā,ish kunanda chi faraḳ ast?
pray tell me the true state of what are called _shikamī_ portions of a village or farm,	aṣl ḥaḳīḳat-i-ān ḳaṭ'a,e mauẓ'a, yā mazr'a ki ānrā shikamī mī-goyand bifarmāyed.
is any paper called a deed of abdication or rejection, and what does it imply?	hech ḳabāla,e tark kardan yā lā-d'awā ast yā na, o m'anī,e ān chīst?
in these days, when constables are put over any landholder, is dunage exacted, or not, and to what amount?	dar īn zamān, waḳte ki bar kudāmīn zamīndārān muḥaṣṣilān (or ahl-i-iḥtisāb) mu'aiyan (or muḳarrar) karda mī-shavand ṭalabāna ṭalab mī-shavad yā na, o ba chi ḳadr.

[1] in the country does the contracting farmer or the landholder receive the sustenance money ?	*āyā dar ta'alluḳa nafaḳa ba* [*mustājir*] *mī-shavad, yā ba zamīndār ?* [*multazim.*]
what is the name of the paper which contains an account of the tanks, orchards, boundaries, &c. of any village ?	*nām-i-ān kāg͟haẕ ki dar ān tafṣīl-i-tālābhā 'alafzār, ḥaddhā,e mauẓ'a and, chi bāshad ?*
they call it *muwāzina*, or boundary sketch,	*muwāzina ya'nī naḳsha,e zamīn yā kāg͟haẕ-i-*[*ḥadd*] *bandī mī-goyand.*[*raḳba.*]
why does a servant call himself *sarkār, k͟halīfa, mihtar*, &c.	*chirā naukare k͟hud-rā k͟hitābhā,e 'izzat, ya'nī sarkār, k͟halīfa, mihtar o wa-g͟haira, mī-dihand ?*
that he may appear a great man in the eyes of his master and of the other servants,	*zīrā ki dar naẓar-i-mālik-i-k͟hud, wa nazd-i-sā,ir-i-naukarān* [*mu'aẓẓam bi-bāshad*]. [*buzurg m'alūm bi-shavad ; buzurg bi-namāyad ; mu'azzaz bi-bāshad.*]

Exercise.—A certain lawyer had a very ugly daughter who was arrived at a marriageable age ; but although he

[1] a farmer, *ḥarrāṣ; kishtkār; kāshtkār; dihḳān, muzār'ī ; fallāḥ ;* (of taxes) *ijāradār.*

harvest, *ḥaṣād ;* (time of) *ḥaṣādat ;* (a reaper) *ḥaṣṣād* or *ḥāṣid* (pl. *ḥuṣṣād*) ; (autumnal—of rice) *faṣl-i-k͟harīf ;* (spring—peas, barley, wheat) *faṣl-i-rabī' ;* (wheat) *faṣl-i-gandum.*

to sow, *kishtan* or *kāshtan ; zirā'at kardan.*

a green field, *ḳisht zār ;* (sown) *mazra' ; mazra'a.*

a meadow, *'alaf zār ; murg͟hzār.*

a plough, *ḳulba ;* a ploughman, *ḳulba rān.*

offered a considerable dower and other valuables, no one was inclined to wed her. Brocade and damask, and pearls and jewels, will appear disgusting on a bride who is ugly. At last, through necessity, he married her to a blind man. It is said that, in the same year, there arrived from the island of Sarandip (Ceylon) a famous physician who could restore sight to the blind. They asked the father, "Why do you not have your son-in-law cured?" He said, "Because I am afraid that, if he should recover his sight, he will divorce my daughter, who is now his wedded wife. It is best that the husband of an ugly woman should be blind." (*Gulistān*, chap. ii. tale 47.)

Lesson 56.—On General Business.

sabaḳ panjāh o shishum dar guft-o-gū,e mu'āmala,e 'ām.

Here (speaking to a servant), take the draft, and bring the money: be quick,	*ai mulāzim barāt bi-gīr o pūl biyār : zūd shav.*
what must be done? it is now eleven o'clock,	*chi bāyad kard? aknūn sā'at-i-yāzdah ast.*
be quick, that I may have the money in time,	*zūd kun ki bar waḳt pūl ba dast-i-man bi-rasad* (or *biyāyad*).
let me have it by one o'clock,	*ba sā'at-i-yak ān-rā ba man bi-rasān.*
go to the counting-house, and speak to the head accountant,	*ba muḥāsib khāna bi-rau, o ba muḥāsib-i-a'ẓam bi-go.*
tell the accountant to take bank notes, and pay the amount of the draft,	*ba muḥāsib bi-go ki dast āwez-i-ṣarrāfa* (or *ṣarrāf-khāna*) *bi-gīr o pūl-i-ān adā kun* (or *bi-dih*).
the money must now be sent to Mr. ——	*ḥālan bāyad ki shumā pūl ba ṣāḥib-i-fulān bāyad firistād.*

request Mr. —— to order what remains to be paid in before three o'clock,	*ba fulān ṣāḥib 'arẓ bi-kun ki ḥukm bi-kunad ki ānchi bāḳī ast pesh az si sā'at* [*dāda shavad*]. ['*aṭā karda shavad; marḥamat karda shavad.*]
have you ever been to Mr. ——'s garden?	*gāhe az barā,e tafarruj-i-bāgh-i-fulān ṣāḥib rafta ī?* / *gāhe* [*multafit*]*-i-bāgh-i-fulān ṣāḥib shuda ī?* [*mutawajjih.*]
sir, I go that way every day,	*ṣāḥibā! har rūz az ān rāh* [*guẕar*] *mī-kunam.* ['*ubūr; murūr.*]
you must go there immediately, else nothing will be done,	*fi-l-faur ān jā shumā-rā bāyad raft warna hech chīz shudan na mī-tawānad.*
send some one to hire a boat,	*az barā,e kirāya kardan-i-māshūh nafare bi-firist.*
I will go to Karāchī to-day,	*man imrūz ba karāchī khwāham* [*raft*]. [*shud.*]
go to the bazar, and buy a pair of globe lanterns,	*ba bāzār bi-rau, o dū tā fānūs-i-mudawwir bi-khar.*
who will collect the bills?	*kudām kas pūl-i-ḥisāb jama' khwāhad* [*kard*]? [*namūd.*]

Exercise.—There was a king, who had no son; he tried many remedies and expedients, but derived no advantage whatever from them; he was, therefore, greatly dejected, but would not discover the cause of this to any one. By chance a strolling mendicant arrived; he then disclosed this his affliction to him, on which the holy man wrote out a charm, and thus prescribed: "After dissolving this in rose-water, you must drink it along with your queen; and on your having a son, you must call him *Mihr Munīr*, bestowing on him every science, and all sorts of accomplishments; but beware of marrying him against his consent." Having thus directed, he wandered away. This divine prescription being dissolved in rose-water, the king and queen drank it off, and by its blessed influence they had at last a fine healthy boy. Whatever the pilgrim had enjoined respecting him was all put in practice.

Lesson 57.—*In continuation.*

[1] ***sabaḳ panjāh o haftum dar muttaṣil-i-mazbūr.***

Hārūnu-r-rashīd is clever in collecting bills,	*hārūnu-r-rashīd dar* [*taḥṣīl-i-ḳarẓ hoshiyār ast*]. [*ḥuṣūl-i-ḳarẓ fiṭnat dārad;* or *wuṣūl-i-wām khūb mahārat dārad.*]

---

[1] in continuation.
- *dar maṭlab-i-mā sabaḳ.*
- *dar maṭlab-i-bālā,e.*
- *dar maṭlab-i-peshīn.*
- *dar maṭlab-i-mazkūr.*
- *dar maṭlab-i-mazbūr.*
- *dar maṭlab-i-mūḳabl.*
- *dar maṭlab-i-mauṣūf.*

In place of *maṭlab*, the following words may be used:—

maḳūla, from *ḳaul.*	*tafṣīr.*
mabūḥṣ or *baḥṣ.*	*tafṣīl.*
baiyūn.	*ẕikr.*
taḳrir.	*guft o gū.*

it is very difficult to get money of such a one,	*az chunīn shakhṣ pūl yāftan mushkil ast.*
I have been to the bazar: sugar is now 3½ ounces a rupee,	*man dar bāzār būda am; nirkh-i-shakar fī rūpiyă si o nīm ūḳīya ast.*
it will be better to wait a few days, and then buy the cloth,	*tā chand rūz ṣabr kardan, o b'ad az ān pārcha-rā kharīdan bihtar ast.*
of what use are such people? they know nothing of business,	[*īn mardumān ba chi kār mī-āyand?*] *hech kār na mī-dānand.* [*īn mardumān be kār and.*]
I understand business—I am not easily imposed upon,	*man kār mī-dānam ba āsān fareb na mī-khẉuram.*
raisins are six lbs. for a rupee, buy about one thousand rupees' worth,	*kishmish shish raṭl fī yak rūpiya farokhta mī-shavad, ba ḳadar-i-yak hazār rūpiya* [*kharīd bi-kun*]. [*bi-khar; kharīd bi-namā.*]
there is no understanding the bazar prices,	*nirkh-i-bāzār yaksān nīst.* *nirkh-i-bāzār muḳarrar nīst.* *tabdīl-i-nirkh-i-bāzār ma'lūm na mī-shavad.*
in Shiraz the bazar rate is scarcely for two hours alike,	*dar shīrāz nirkh-i-bāzār tā dū sā'at ba mushkil yaksān mī-mānad.*
I made a deposit; to-morrow I shall see them weighed,	*īn chīzhā ba amānat guzāshtam,* [*farda wazn khẉāham kard*]. [*pesh rū,e khẉud farda waznash khẉāham kard; rū ba rū,e khẉud farda waznash khẉāham dīd.*]

see that you are not imposed upon,	*khabardār ki shumā fareb na khured.*
have you compared them with the sample? do they agree?	*ba namūna ānhā-rā mukābil karda ed?* [*muwāfik and?*] [*īn misal-i-ān mī-mānad.*]
two or three packages are superior,	*dū si basta az kism-i-a'lā ast.*
go and procure a pass for the things that are ready,	*bi-rau o az barā,e chīzhā ki taiyār and khatt-i-rāhdārī hāsil kun.*

Exercise.—When the prince became a man, he one day took leave of his father and went away to enjoy the chase, where a beautiful deer came in sight, grazing on a plain, with a golden collar round its neck. He then gave these orders to the people who were with him:—"You must manage to catch this fawn alive,—surround it on all sides; if we thus get it, so much the better; otherwise, the person over whose head she bounding escapes, must put his horse to full speed after it." Just as they had completely encircled it, the deer all at once made a spring over the prince's own head; the rest checked their horses' reins, while he spurred his horse hard at its heels. She bounded away at such a rate as to leave the attendants many miles behind, and at last outrunning him, vanished from his sight. He then stopped in amazement, himself he knew not where, and his followers far away; neither had he a place to lodge in, nor enough of the day left to return.

Lesson 58.—*In continuation.*

sabak panjāh o hashtum dar zikr-i-mazkūr.

get a boat, and send them on board the ship,	*māshūh bi-gīr o chīzhā-rā bar jahāz bār kun.*
sir, the captain's agent said the goods cannot be shipped to-day,	*ṣāḥibā, kār-guzār-i-nākhu-dā guft ki imrūz asbāb bar jahāz bār shudan na mī-tawānad.*
don't mind what the agent says, but mind what I say,	*ānchi kār-kun mī-goyed bar ān [ma shinau] [khayāl ma kun,* or *gosh ma kun]; magar ānchi man mī-goyam ba [gosh-i-jān bi-shinau]. [gosh o dil bi-shinau.]*
sir, as you bade me, I am going,	*ṣāḥibā, [chunānchi farmūda ed ba muṭābiḳ-i-ān] mī-ravam. [ba mūjib-i-farmān.]*
go and ask the head accountant when the ship sails, and bring me word,	*bi-rau o az muḥāsib-i-a'ẓam bi-purs ki jahāz kai [langar khwāhad bar dāsht], o jawāb biyār. [rawāna khwāhad shud.]*
servant, call the cashier,	*ai nafar, khizānchī-rā bi-ṭalab.*
how much was collected yesterday?	*dī rūz chi ḳadar pūl jama' shuda būd?*
keep the money by you, don't pay away any,	[1] *pūl-rā nazd-i-khud nigāh bi-dār, ba kase hech ma dih.*

[1] make this money your charge, *īn pūl-rā ḥawāla,e khud bi-dār; pūl-rā nazd-i-khud amānat dār.*

what is the discount on the Company's paper ?	[1] *ṣad rūpiya,e kāghaẕ-i-dīwān-rā chi kasr mī-gīrand?* *fī ṣad rūpiya,e barāt-i-Kampanī bahādur chi ḳadar tanzīl mī-kunand?*
if you purchase the Company's paper of six per cent. interest, the discount is two tumans six ḳirān; if you sell, it is two and a half tumans.	*dar kāghaẕ-i-dīwān fī ṣad shish tūmān sūd mī-gardad, agar bi-khared dū tūmān o shish ḳirān kasr ast; yā bi-faroshed dū tūmān o nīm.* *agar kāghaẕ-i-barāt-i-dīwān, ki fī ṣade shish tūmān sūd mī-dihand, bi-khared dū tūmān o shish ḳirān kasr mī-gīrand; agar bi-faroshed, fī ṣad dū o nīm tūmān waẓī'at ast.*
take these four thousand tumans, with what money has been received for bills, and buy Company's paper,	[2] *īn chahār hazār tūmān bā m'a ān pūl ki az ḳarẓhā wuṣūl karda shuda ast bi-gīr o barāt-i-dīwān bi-khar.*
send these letters as directed,	*ba muwāfiḳ-i-sar nāmahā,e īn khuṭūṭ [rawāna] bi-kun. [rawān.]*

Exercise.—While in this perplexity, the eyes of the prince lighted on a dwelling, and thinks he, "Well, let me at least learn to whom this house belongs." He then beheld a venerable aged darwesh seated there, to whom, after salutation, he observed, "With your leave may I

---

[1] Sindh and Punjab Railway Company.
jamā'at-i-rūh-i-āhanī,e Sindh o Panjāb.

[2] a debt, *ḳarẓ* (plur. *ḳurūẓāt*); debtor, *ḳarẓdār*.

remain all night here?" "By all means, my child," replied the venerable man, "the house is at your service." Having quickly given the necessary directions for his guest's repast, as well as the horse's grain and fodder, when done also with entertaining him, he asked, "Pray who are you, young gentleman, and why have you come here?" He then related the whole of his late adventure. In the mean time, what does he see? Lo! on a splendid throne, four fairy queens, exquisitely beautiful, clad in rich brocade, and covered from head to foot with jewels and precious stones, suddenly descended, who, having alighted, made their obeisance to the reverend sage, and seated themselves respectfully in his presence.

Lesson 59.—*In continuation.*

sabaḳ panjāh o nuhum dar mubāḥaṣa,e mazbūr.

bring those goods in bullock carts from the custom-house,	*az gumruk khāna ān asbāb-rā dar 'arāba,e gāw [guzāshta] biyār. [karda; nihāda; bar dāshta.]*
you must attend to everything,	*shumā-rā ba har chīz mutawajjih shudan bāyad.* / *bāyad ki shumā ba har chīz [multafit bi-shaved]. [tawajjuh bi-kuned.]*
put the store No. 2 into order, and see that there is no damage,	[1] *asbāb khāna,e duwum durust bi-kun, wa khabar-dār ki nuḳṣān na shavad.*

[1] an armoury, *salāḥ-khāna.*
a counting-house, [*muḥāsib*]-*khāna.* [*ḥisāb.*]
a bank, *ṣarrāf-khāna*; *ṣarrāfa.*
a factory, *kār-*[*khāna*]. [*gāh.*]
an office, *daftar-khāna.*
a post-house, *manzil-khāna.*

if you don't look to everything, who else will?	*agar shumā [ba] har chīz naẓar na khẉāhed kard ki khẉāhad kard? [dar.]*
I am going out, let me see everything ready when I come back,	*man berūn mī-ravam b'ad az āmadan-i-khụdam hama chīzhā barābar [mu'aiyana] bi-kunam. [mushāhida; mulāḥaẓa.]* *man ḥālan berūn mī-ravam, khabardār ki pesh az āmadan-i-man hama chīzhā taiyār bāshand.*
door-keeper, are the counting-house accountants come?	*ai darbān! muḥāsibān-i-muḥāsib-khāna āmada and?*
who is at work in the iron-factory?	*dar kār-khāna,e āhan kudām kas kār mī-kunad?*
sir, nobody is yet come,	*ṣāḥibā, kase ila ḥāl nayāmada ast.*
how is this, not yet come?—what time of day do they mean to come?	*chigūna [ast] ki kase nayāmada ast, ba kudām sā'at-i-rūz eshān irāda,e āmadan mī-dārand. [ittifāḳ mī-uftad.]*
this is the case every day, and therefore Mr. ——'s work is not yet done,	*har rūz chunīn [ast], o az īn sabab kār-i-fulān ṣāḥib tā hanoz tamām na shuda ast. [ittifāḳ mī-shavad.]*
when they come to-day, we will settle this business,	*ẉaḳte ki imrūz āyand mā īn kār-rā [faiṣal] khẉāhem kard. [faiṣala; taṣfiya.]*
Saladīn is speaking to me daily about this work,	*ṣalāḥu-d-dīn har rūz az barā,e īn kār ba man guft o gū mī-kunad.*
when they come send them to me,	*dar waḳt-i-āmadan eshān-rā ba man bi-firist.*

Exercise.—The sage remarked, " Well, this was not your visiting-day here, pray tell me on what account you have come." They replied, " Worshipful saint, there is a princess named *Badar Munīr ;* we intended to pay her a visit, this is the road, and we could not find it in our hearts to pass by without first paying our respects to you." He then said, " Good, do take this prince also along with you ; he will at all events see whether *Badar Munīr* is more lovely than the ladies of his palace, or they fairer than she." To this the fairies agreed, and having handed him to their throne, flew away, and in the twinkling of an eye reached the palace of *Badar Munīr.* The instant that *Mihr Munīr* discovered that angel's face, bright as the moon, he became enamoured with her, while she also admiring his radiant countenance, and flushed by love's magic bloom, shone resplendent with the charms of a damask rose.

Lesson 60.—*In continuation.*

sabaḳ shastum dar maḳāla,e mā ḳabl.

how long are those Europe goods to lie at the custom-house ?	*tā chand dar [gumruk] ān asbābhā,e farang khwāhad mānd. [jaziyat-khāna.]*
sir, without an invoice to know what they are, how can I bring them ?	*ṣāḥibā, baghair-i-fihrist-i-chīzhā, chigūna sāmān āwardan mī-tawānam, ki m'alūm am nīst ?* *ṣāḥibā, baghair-i-fard-i-irsāl az barā,e shinākhtan chigūna asbāb mustakhliṣ mī-tawānam kard ?*
different sorts of goods pay different rates of duty,	*ba asbāb-i-ḳism-i-mukhtalif maḥṣūl farḳ dārad.* *ba har ḳism-i-asbāb maḥṣūl-i-dīgar ast.* *maḥṣūl-i-har matā' judā judā ast.*

by opening the boxes and seeing their value, you will be able to understand,	*az kushādan-i-ṣandūḳhā wa az mulāḥaẓa,e ḳīmat-i-asbāb ba shumā [inkishāf] khwāhad shud. [munkashif.]* *az kushādan-i-ṣandūḳhā wa takhmīna kardan-i-ḳīmat-i-asbāb shumā-rā m'alūm khwāhad shud.*
sir, I cannot myself open the packages,	*ṣāḥibā, tanhā ṣandūḳhā na mī-tawānam kushād.*
in opening the packages, the goods may be injured,	*az kushādan-i-bastahā shāyad [nuḳṣān-i-asbāb shavad]. [ba asbāb nuḳṣān rasad.]*
Here, take the invoice and go directly,	*ai nafar! fihrist-i-asbāb bigīr o fi-l-faur bi-rau.* *ai nafar! fard-i-asbāb bigīr o ba zūdī bi-rau.*
sir, I am going; please to give me the invoice,	*ṣāḥibā, ilḥāl mī-ravam, mihrbānī karda fard-i-irsāl ['ināyat] bi-farmāyed. [marḥamat; 'aṭā.]*
at two o'clock the custom-house officer came and opened the boxes,	*ba sā'at-i-dū ['uhdadār]-i-maḳāṭ' āmad o ṣandūḳhā kushād. ['āmil.]*
when I have signed each invoice, I will give them to the accountant to be copied, and then send them to you,	*waḳte ki ba har fard dast khaṭṭ khwāham kard ān-rā ba muḥāsib, az barā,e naḳl kardan khwāham dād, wa pas az ān ba tū khwāham firistād.*
clerk, copy these, and give them to the sergeant,	*[kātibā!] īn-rā naḳl bi-kun o ba ḥawāladār bi-dih. [ai muḥarrir.]*

call a blacksmith, and open the boxes ; compare the value and quantity of the goods with the invoice, then make them tight again,	*āhangar-rā bi-ṭalab o ṣandūḳhā-rā bi-kushā ; ḳīmat o wazn-i-asbāb bā bījak muḳābil bi-kun, ba'd az ān bāz* [*bi-band*]. [*band kun.*]

Exercise.—Three watches of the night glided away in such pleasure, harmony, and delight, as human tongue cannot express. When these four fairy damsels were about taking leave, they addressed the prince thus: "Come along." He being pierced to the heart with the arrow of love, replied, "I will not go ; if you must set off, by all means depart." On representing this to *Badar Munīr*, that she might persuade him to take leave, they perceived that she also had no desire to let him away. In this perplexity they observed, "Now what is to be done ? if we leave him, how shall we show our faces to the holy man ? and if we convey him hence in the present posture of affairs, she will be offended ; the best advice is to wait a little longer, till both begin to slumber." After this, with the fatigue of sitting up, both got a-nodding ; they then gently and artfully raised him on the throne, and with some philter lulling him asleep, flew off with him.

LESSON 61.—*In continuation.*

sabaḳ shaṣt o yakum dar maṭlab-i-peshīn.

sergeant, when you have signed your name, give them to the cashier,	*ai ḥawāladār wakte ki dast ḳhaṭṭ karda bāshed ānhā-rā ba taḥwīl-dār bi-dihed.*
the officer having entered the particulars of every case in his book, and the duty on each article, wrote the amount,	*ṣāḥib-kār-i-a'lā dar kitāb-i-ḳhud mutafarriḳāt wa maḥṣūl-i-har jins ṣabt karda mablaghāt-rā* [*darj*] *namūd.* [*taḥrīr ; masṭūr ; tasṭīr ; irḳām ; indirāj ; mundaraj.*]

taking the invoice, I had to go again, and show it to the head officer,	*i'lām-nāma girifta marā ba ḥuẓūr-i-'āmil-i-* [*buzurg*] *bāz raftan wa namūdan ẓarūr uftād.* [*a'ẓam; a'ṭā.*]
having done all this, it had struck four o'clock, and the custom-house was shut,	*ba'd az tamām kardan-i-īnhā sā'at-i-chahār shud o gumruk-khāna band gardīd.*
the next day I delivered the invoice to the officer,	*rūz-i-dīgar fihrist-rā* [*ba āmil-i-muḳāṭa'at ḥawāla kardam*]. [*ba ḥawāla,e 'āmil-i-gumruk-khāna kardam.*]
having examined the value of the articles, and their duty, he signed it,	*ba'd az mulāḥaẓa kardan-i-ḳīmat-i-asbāb o maḥṣūl-i-ānhā dast khaṭṭ bar* [*fihrist*] *kard.* [*ta'līḳa; fard.*]
afterwards, paying the duty to the cashier, having got an order for a pass and cleared the cases, I hired coolies, and brought them away,	*ba'd az adā namūdan-i-maḥṣūl ba ṣarrāf ḥukm-i-ijāzat-nāma yāftam; ṣandūḳhā mustakhliṣ kardam wa ḥāmilān-rā* (or *ḥammālān-rā*) *ba muzd girifta ba khāna ān asbāb-rā burdam.*
accountant, I will not give a farthing to the custom-house people or the policeman at the wharf,	*ai muḥāsib, ba ahl-i-gumruk-khāna yā ba yake az ahl-i-iḥtisāb-i-furẓa* [*dirame*] *na khwāham dād.* [*pashīze.*]
accountant, why did you not go to the police-office and get a pass?	*ai muḥāsib, chirā ba daftar khāna,e ẓabṭ o rabṭ-i-shahr barā,e yāftan-i-* [*ijāzat*]*-nāma na raftī?* [*khalāṣī.*]

Exercise.—On their arrival, they delivered him to the good father, and with his permission returned to their own mansions. By dawn of day, when he (the prince) awoke, neither the sparkling dome nor its refulgent orb was there ; he heaved a deep sigh, and calling, " Alas, *Badar Munīr !*" again fell into a doze, from the effects of the potion upon him. Soon after, when a watch and a half of the day had elapsed, on the appearance of a crowd, the darwesh from circumstances guessed that these must be his attendants, and having called them, he consigned him to their charge. His companions were of course gratified by finding him ; but noticing his condition, they got alarmed about what reply they should give the king, and thus interrogated the good anchorite : " Please your reverence, why is our prince thus distracted ?" " Ask himself," said he. On hearing this, they accosted the prince in the following words : " Son of our sovereign, why are you thus beside yourself ? "

Lesson 62.—*In continuation.*

sabaḳ shaṣt o duwum dar baḥṣ-i-mazbūr.

sir, what can I do ? for two or three days I have not had a moment's leisure, one can't get a thing done at once at the court,	*ṣāḥibā ! chi kunam, az dū si rūz marā furṣat-i-chashmak zadan na būda ast o fauraṉ ba 'adālat* [*chīze na tawān kard*]. [*kase hech na mī-tawānad kard.*]
if I don't go myself, nothing is done,	*baghair raftan-i-khudam* [*hech karda na mī-shavad*]. [*hech na mī-shavad ; hech kār bar na mī-āyad.*]

sir, I know, five days ago, you wrote to Shiraz that the things would be forwarded to-morrow or next day, and no pass is obtained,	*ṣāḥibā! man mī-dānam ki panj rūz pesh az īn ba shīrāz nawishta ed ki farda yā pas farda chīzhā firistāda <u>kh</u>wāhad shud, wa ḥāl ānki hech ijāzat-nāma ḥāṣil na shuda ast.*
how can they go? they can't be sent without a pass,	*pas chigūna ba<u>gh</u>air-i-ijāzat nāma tawānand raft?*
is the order for screws gone to Shiraz factory?	*āyā ḥukm barā,e sā<u>kh</u>tan-i-pechhā ba kār-<u>kh</u>āna,e āhanī,e shīrāz rafta ast, yā na?*
they promised to send them to-day,	*eshān wa'da kardand ki imrūz [bi-firistem]. [ān chīzhā-rā <u>kh</u>wāhem firistād.]*
if they don't come this evening, you go there before gun-fire,	*agar ānhā imrūz shām na rasand pesh az waḳt-i-top zadan ān jā birau.*
for want of these screws the bales of cotton are lying loose,	*ba sabab-i-[na būdan-i-][1] pechhā bastahā,e pumba [wā][2] uftāda and. [1]['adm-i-maujūdī,e.] [2][be band.]*
no one knows when the vessel will sail,	*kase na mī-dānad ki jahāz kai [langar bar <u>kh</u>wāhad dāsht]. [rawān <u>kh</u>wāhad shud.]*
have you collected the bills I gave you yesterday?	*fihrist-i-muṭālabāt ki dīrūz shumā-rā dādam ānhā-rā [mujtami'] karda ed? [jam'; firāham; baham.]*

sir, I have given in the money for all you gave me,	*ai khudāwand, ān ḳadr-i-muṭālibāt ki badīn banda az ḥuẓūr [dāda] shuda būd majmū'a,e pūl-i-ān dākhil-i-khizāna,e 'āmira karda am. [sapurda; ḥawāla karda; taḥwīl karda]*

Exercise.—The prince neither distinctly articulated with his mouth, nor opened his eyes, all that he raved being, "Alas, *Badar Munīr!*" In short, they placed him in the palki, and conveyed him with fear and trembling to the king, to whom they stated the matter so: "May it please your majesty, yesterday afternoon a lovely fawn came in sight, and the prince, after forbidding us, set his horse after it himself at full gallop; we nevertheless followed at a respectful distance. She took shelter in so wild a wood, that the prince escaped our sight entirely, though we were all following him with our eyes; besides which, darkness overtook us, and we being helpless, passed the whole night in that place; but rising by daybreak we continued our inquiries; at last we found him in this distracted condition, at the lodge of a hermit there. When we inquired of him, he also gave us no information whatever, though we naturally conjecture that the person's name which is mentioned must be one with whom the prince is in love."

Lesson 63.—*In continuation.*

sabaḳ shaṣt o siwum dar guft-o-gū,e mauṣūf.

do you know where Najamudīn is?	*najmu-d-dīn kujā ast, shumā mī-daned?*
sir, I heard he is not coming to-day; his brother says he has a fever,	*ṣāḥibā! man shunīda am ki o imrūz na mī-āyad; barādar-ash guft ki o tap karda ast.*

how does he mean to do his work? he has a fever daily,	*chigūna kār-i-khud-rā mī-kunad, ki o har rūz tap dārad.*
was the cloth examined yesterday, and placed to Muhammad Ali's account?	*nirkh-i-pārcha-rā dīrūz dar-yāft karda, shumā dākh-il-i-ḥisāb-i-muḥammad 'alī karda ed, yā na?*
sir, it is entered in the waste-book, not in the ledger,	*ṣāḥibā! dākhil-i-khasra shuda ast, magar dākhil-t-tafrīḳ-nāma na shuda.*
why so, if he objects to the brokerage, how is it to be settled?	*chirā agar i'tirāẓ-i-dalālat kunad, chigūna [band o bast] khwāhad shud? [muḳarrar; munfaṣil.]*
sir, I will thank you to settle it with him; he does not mind us in the least,	*ai ṣāḥib! man [az shumā iḥsānmand][1] khwāham shud agar bā o faiṣala,e ān mu'āmala khwāhed kard; [o ba sukhan-i-man hech wazn na mī-nihad].[2]* [1][*mamnūn-i-iḥsān-i-shumā.*] [2][*ki kalām-i-man nazd-i-o wazn na mī-gīrad.*] [2][*o sukhan-i-marā hech ba khayāl-i-khud na mī-ārad.*] [2][*o ba sukhan-i-man hech i'tinā na mī-kunad.*]
make out the account of what cloth he has purchased up to this time,	*ḥisāb-i-ān pārcha ki o tā īn zamān kharīda ast bi-kun.*
balance the account, leaving out the cloth bought yesterday,	*pārcha,e dīrūza [dar ḥisāb nayāwarda] tamṣīl ḥisāb pārcha,e peshīna bi-kun. [wā guẕāshta; dar guẕāshta.]*

the account ought not to remain unbalanced,	[1] *ḥisāb-i-o baghair-i-tamṣīl dādan na bāyad guẕāsht.* *dar ḥisāb-i-o jam' wa kharch waẕa' namūda baghair-i-nawishtan-i-baḳāyā ān-rā na bāyad guẕāsht.*

Exercise.—The king then tenderly began: "My child, if you will discover your affliction, we shall then consider of a remedy for it." After much entreaty, he returned, "O my dear father, the only specific I want is *Badar Munīr;* possessed of her I would recover." They next interrogated about her address and residence. The prince sorrowfully said, "I know not, indeed." He rejected all food, continued day and night heaving deep sighs, and weeping bitterly. Witnessing this distress, his parents also were sorely afflicted, and kept beating their breasts in such anguish for their son, that the affairs of the state were running fast into disorder and confusion. The minister was a prudent man, and thus remonstrated to his majesty: "Let not your highness be so woe-begone, but attend as usual to the interests of your kingdom; your slave is despatching messengers in every direction; should a princess of the name be found anywhere, we may then get the prince married to her; if the parents agree with a good grace, all is well; if not, why, let us force them."

[1] outstanding balances, *baḳāyā,e ḥisāb.*
a remainder, residue, *baḳīyat* (plur. *baḳāyā*).

Lesson 64.—*In continuation.*

sabaḳ shaṣt o chahārum dar ẕikr-i-maẕkūr.

the account of shawls, handkerchiefs, baftas, &c., which have been agreed for, is all settled,	*ḥisāb-i-shālhā, dast mālhā, bāfta o waghaira [ki ḳīmat-i-ānhā faiṣal shuda būd ba sar-anjām rasīda ast]. [ki dar ḳīmat faiṣal shuda būd ba anjām rasīda ast.]*
there is nothing else due to him; if you please to compare Dr. and Cr. you will see,	[1] *az mā o-rā hech dādanī nīst; agar az rāh-i-mihrbānī jam'a o wāṣil-rā [muḳābil] khwāhed kard, khwāhed fahmīd. [tanẓīr; tamṡīl; taṭbīḳ.]*
Kāsim accountant, what are you doing? see that the accounts are correct,	[2] *ai ḳāsim muḥāsib! chi mī-kuned? bi-bīn ki ḥisābhā [durust] and, yā na. [ṣaḥīḥ.]*
I am afraid there are errors in Saladdin's last year's account,	*man mī-tarsam ki dar ḥisāb-i-par sāla,e ṣalāḥu-d-dīn [ghalaṭhā] wāḳi' shuda and. [aghlāṭ.]*

[1] compare this with that.
īn chīz-rā ba ān chīz muḳābil bi-kun.
muḳābila,e īn chīzhā bi-kun.
īn chīz wa ān chīz-rā muḳābil bi-kun.

[2] to correct, amend, *ṣaḥīḥ kardan.*
authentic news, *ṣaḥīḥ khabar.*
excellent proof, *ṣaḥīḥu-l-'aiyār.*

I can't make out what sugar, coffee, sugar-candy, and raisins have been purchased,	khabar na dāram, ki chi kadar shakar, kahwa, na-bāt o kishmish kharīda shuda ast.
sir, here is nothing without a written order; the accounts agree with what is written,	ṣāḥibā ! baghair-i-ḥukm-nā-ma,e ḥuẓūr hech dākhil-i-ḥisāb na shuda ast; ḥisābhā ba ānchi nawishta shuda ast [muwāfiḳ] and. [mutābiḳ; barābar.]
that's not what I mean. I say it's not clear what belongs to each account,	ān maṭlab-i-man nīst, balki mī-goyam ki ānchi ba har ḥisāb ta'alluḳ dārad, ān ṣāf m'alūm nīst. man īn na mī-goyam, balki maṭlab-i-man ān ast ki ta'alluḳa,e har chīz ba har ḥisāb-i-['alā ḥaddah] ṣāf m'alūm nīst. [muta-farriḳa.]
sir, there is no fear about that—I have by me the accounts of sales and pur-chases,	ṣāḥibā ! ba nisbat-i-ān hech khauf nīst, man ḥisābhā,e kharīd o farokht dāram.
tell me what is the amount of Saladdin's account— what quantity and kind of articles,	marā jam'-i-ḥisāb-i-ṣalā-ḥu-d-dīn bi-go, wa kadar o ḳism-i-asbāb-ash nishān bi-dih.

Exercise.—This plan was applauded by the sovereign, and scouts were accordingly sent to all quarters, with a requisition in due form. One of these emissaries found his way to *Badar Munīr's* country, and on making the requisite inquiries there, he learned that her situation was still more deplorable, by pining at the absence of her lover. On this the fleet envoy, quite overjoyed, entered the presence of her illustrious father, and presented the formal request to him; who, though drooping with sorrow for his daughter, on reading the contents of the paper, became much exhilarated. He instantly, without loss of time, preparing an answer, delivered it to the messenger, with this injunction, "Do you quickly proceed by night and by day till you deliver this from me." The purport of it was thus: "The friendly epistle hath reached us, in which you solicit my daughter *Badar Munīr's* hand for your son *Mihr Munīr*, to which I have consented: it is now incumbent on you to reflect, that the sooner you arrive for the nuptials, so much the better: you will therefore be pleased to make no delay, nor take any trouble about the bridal preparations."

LESSON 65.—*In continuation.*

sabaḳ shaṣt o panjum dar maḳūla,e mā ḳabl.

sir, wait a moment, the articles had on the 4th instant are not entered,	[1] *ṣāḥibā! ḳadre ṣabr bi-farmāyed; asbāb-i-tārīkh-i-chahārum-i-māh-i-ḥāl [dar kitāb nawishta] na shuda ast. [dākhil-i-ḥisāb; madkhūl-i-daftar; dākhil-i-daftar; dar daftar ḳaid; dar ḥisāb mundarij; dar daftar indirāj; darj-i-ḥisāb.]*
Mr. —— will sail to-morrow; is his account ready?	*fulān ṣāḥib farda [sawār-i-jahāz] khwāhad shud; āyā hisāb-i-o taiyār ast? [dar jahāz rawāna.]*

[1] current month, *māh-i-ḥāl.*
current year, *sāl-i-rawān.*

it is here, sir; the amount due from him is 56,411 rupees,	*ṣāḥibā! ḥisāb hamīn ast mablagh ki az o* [*rasīdanī*] *ast panjāh o shish hazār chahār ṣad o yāzdah rūpiya mī-bāshad.* [*muṭāliba.*]
give me the account; I will go on board the ship, settle it, and get the money,	*ba man ḥisāb-i-o bi-dih, man bar jahāz rafta, faiṣal khwāham kard, wa mablagh-rā khwāham girift.*
you come with me, then I shall have no trouble in explaining,	*hamrāh-i-man biyā ki marā* [*hech zuḥmat-i-fahmāish-i-ān na khwāhad shud.*] [*hech zuḥmat dar tafṣīl-i-ān na bāshad; ki man dar takrīr-i-tafṣīl-i-ān ḥisāb hech zuḥmat na baram.*]
Kudrat-Ullā, bring the waste-book, journal, and ledger with the book of sales with you,	[1] *ḳudrat allāh!* *kitāb-i-yād dāsht,* waste-book. *kitāb-i-mutafarriḳa,* / *kitāb-i-tafrīḳ,* / *kitāb-i-rūz-nāma,* } journal. *kitāb-i-madkhal o makhraj,* / *ḳitāb-i-āmadanī o kharch,* } ledger. *kitāb-i-farosh,* sales-book. *hamrāh-i-khud biyār.*

[1] To be written thus:—*ḳudratu-l-lāh.*

show me the amount of what is due to and from each of the shopkeepers,	pūl-i-madkhal o ḳarẓ-i-har dukāndār ba man nishūn bi-dih. ba man bi-namā mablaghāt-i-dād o sitad-i-har dukāndār.
it appears to me all the accounts are in confusion,	marā [mī-namāyad] ki hama ḥisāb darham barham ast. [ma'lūm mī-shavad.]
hark you! are all my things ready?	ai nafar! hama chīzhū,e men taiyār and, yā na?
sir, some one has taken money for them; no doubt they will be here by two o'clock,	ai ṣāḥib! fulān nafare barū,e ān kār mablagh girifta ast. yaḳīn dāram ki ḳarīb-i-sā'at-i dū in jā khwāhand [būd]. [rasīd.]
when they come, send them immediately to the new landing-stage,	[1] waḳte ki bi-rasand fi-l-faur ba ma'abar-i-nau bi-firist.
it is now high water, I can't wait longer,	aknūn madd bālā ast, ziyāda az īn [tākhīr] na mī-tawānam kard. [der; tawaḳḳuf.]

Exercise.—When the bearer of such cheering intelligence delivered the letter into the minister's hands, he forthwith conveyed it to the emperor's court; and when his majesty cast his eyes over the lines, he felt his heart glow with renovated vigour. In short, he was supremely happy, and accordingly ordered a reward for the bringer of these glad tidings. That day, in every house over the whole city, there were great rejoicings, and the king thus instructed the minister: "I will set out on such a

---

[1] it is high-tide, *madd bālā ast.*
it is low tide, *jazr pā,īn ast.*

day to celebrate the auspicious marriage of *Mihr Munīr*; in the mean time, get all the equipage immediately ready for the royal nuptials, as well as the necessaries for our journey." In that period every requisite was prepared, and the king set forth in great pomp and splendour, along with his army, with a retinue and procession so numerous and resplendent, that a detail here would prove too tedious. In a few weeks he entered the other's territories with becoming grandeur and dignity, with flying colours and bands of music, and thence, having accomplished the object of his journey, he returned to his own capital in a very splendid manner, bringing with him his son and daughter, attended with melody, pleasure, and delight.

PERSIAN MANUAL.

PART II.

VOCABULARY.

ENGLISH AND PERSIAN.

The following selection of phrases will be found to answer two distinct purposes: 1st, To exercise the student in readily turning into Persian every possible variety of English expressions; 2nd, To serve as a vocabulary of useful words, each sentence containing a leading word, arranged according to the order of the alphabet.

A.

abandoned—able.

Abandoned—The crew having abandoned the ship, had run away.—*mallāḥān jahāz-rā guẕāshta* (*mafrūr gashta*) *būdand.* (*firār karda; rū ba firār nihāda.*) Or, *mallāḥān tark-i-jahāz girifta gurekhta būdand.*

Abate—He does not abate me one diram.—*o* (*yak diram kam*) *ba man na mī-kunad.* (*takhfīf-i-yak diram.*) Or, *o az ān ḳīmat yak diram az man kam na mī-gīrad.*

Abide—Abide with me a few days.—*bā man chand roz* (*bi-māned.*) (*tashrīf bi-dāred.*) Or, *chand roz īn* (*banda*)-*rā az ṣuḥbat-i-khud mamnūn bi-farmāyed.* (*khāksār; fidwī.*)

Ability—He possesses great ability.—*o bisiyār* (*ḳābilīyat dārad*). (*ḳābil ast.*) Or, *o dar 'ilm kāmil ast.* Or, *o ba kamāl-i-'ilmīyat rasīda ast.* Or, *o ṣāḥib-i-*(*balāgh*) *ast.* (*isti'adād.*)

Able—He is an able man.—*o* (*ṣāḥib-i-aswād*) *ast.* (*musta'idd; māhir; ahl-i-isti'adād.*)

ABLE—Are you able to do this?—*īn kār mī-tawāned kard?* Or, *shumā mī-tawāned ki īn kār bi-kuned?* Or. *shumā ḳābilīyat-i-īn kār kardan dāred?*

ABSENT—I have been absent ten days.—*dah roz* (*ghair-ḥāẓir*) *būda am.* (*ḥāẓir na.*) Or, *ghaibat-i-man tā dah roz ṭūl kashīda ast.*

ABSTAIN—We ought to abstain from committing evil.—*mā-rā bāyad ki az bad-kārī* (*parhez bi-kunem*). (*bāz biyāyem; dast bi-dārem*) Or, *mā-rā az kār-i-shanī'* (*dast kotāh*) *bāyad kard.* (*tajannub.*)

ABSURD—It is absurd to speak thus.—*chunīn guftan* (*behūda*) *ast.* (*lā-ya'nī; 'abaṣ.*)

ABUNDANCE—Take as much as you please; I have abundance.—*har ḳadar ki khwāhed, bi-gīred; man* (*ba kaṣrat*) *dāram.* (*ba ifrāṭ; ba wafūr; ba wafrat; ba firāwānī; ba farṭ.*)

ABYSSINIAN—That is an Abyssinian slave.—*o* (*ghulām*)-*i-ḥabshī ast.* (*banda; zar-i-kharīd; mamlūk; 'abd.*)

ACADEMY—He goes to an academy daily.—*o rozmarra ba madrassa mī-ravad.*

ACCEDE—Do you accede to what I propose, or not?—*ānchi mī-goyam ḳabūl mī-kuned, yā na?*

ACCENT—I still retain my Persian accent.—*tā ḥāl lahja,e zabān-i-fārsī dāram.*

ACCEPTABLE—The book you sent me was acceptable.—*kitābe ki shumā ba man firistāded* (*pasandīda*) *būd.* (*pasand; maṭbū'; maḳbūl.*)

ACCEPTED—He immediately accepted my offer.—*o fi-l-faur sukhan-i-marā* (*ḳabūl kard*). (*pazīraft; ijābat kard.*) Or, *hamān sā'at bar sukhan-i-man rāẓī shud.*

ACCOMPANY—Except you accompany me, I will not go.—*man baghair* (*ham-rāhī,e*) *shumā na khwāham raft.* (*rafāḳat-i-; ṣuḥbat-i-.*) Or, *man na mī-ravam tā ānki shumā hamrāh-i-man nayāyed.*

ACCOMPLISH—I was not able to accomplish my wishes.—*man* (*ba murād-i-khud rasīdan*) *na tawānistam.* (*ārzū,e khud bar sar āwardan; ummed-i-khud ba anjām rasānīdan; gul-i-murād-i-khud-rā chīdan.*) Or, *mudda'āyam az dastam bar nayāmad.* Or, *maksūdam hāsil* (*nayāmad*). (*na shud.*)

ACCOUNT—Have you an account with him?—*shumā bā o hisābe dāred?*

ACCUSED—He is accused of robbing his master.—*bar o tuhmat-i-duzdī kardan-i-āghā,e khud-ash āmada ast.* Or, *tuhmat bar ān shakhs nihāda and ki o māl-i-mālik-i-khud-rā duzdīda ast.* Or, *ān kas ba tuhmat-i-duzdī kardan-i-āghā,e khud* (*giriftār āmada*) *ast.* (*mat'ūn gardīda; muttahim gardīda; mansūb gashta.*)

ACCUSED—I am accused of breach of my word, personal levity, and weakness of judgment.—*man ba tanākis-i-kaul wa khiffat-i-zāt wa rakākat-i-rā,e mansūb gardīda am.*

ACCUSTOM—Accustom yourself to read and write.—*dar khwāndan wa nawishtan khud-rā mashāk bi-kun.* Or, (*istī'māl*)-*i-khwāndan wa nawishtan bi-kun.* (*rabt; sawād.*)

ACID—This fruit is very acid.—*īn mewa khailī* (*turush ast*). (*talkhī dārad.*)

ACQUAINTANCES—He has many acquaintances.—*o bisiyār* (*āshnāyān*) *dārad.* (*musāhibān; rufakā; mūnisān.*) Or, *o ba mardumān-i-bisiyār ma'rifat dārad.*

ACQUAINTED—I am acquainted with all.—*man hama-rā mī-shināsam.* Or, *man bā hama* (*wākif am*). (*ma'rifatī dāram; rū shinās hastam.*)

ACQUIRED—He has acquired great knowledge.—*o 'ilm-i-wāfir* (*hāsil*) *karda ast.* (*paida; andokhta.*) Or, *o tahsīl-i-'ilm ba darja,e kamāl karda ast.*

ACQUITTED—He has been tried and acquitted.—*murāfa'a,e o tamām shud wa chīze bar o sābit nayāmad.* Or, *tahkīkāt-i-o kardand wa lekin az* ('*adm-i-sabūtī rihā,ī yāft*). ('*uhda,e ān jurm berūn āmad.*)

ACTION—A good action deserves our praise.—*fi'l-i-nek* (*lā,ik-i-afrīn wa tahsīn*) *ast.* (*wājibu-l-ta'rīf.*)

ACTIVE—He is exceedingly active in that business.—*o dar ān kār bisiyār* (*chālāk*) *ast.* (*shāṯir; kār-rān; tez-kār; chust; tez-dast.*)

ADJACENT—This is adjacent to that.—*īn badān muttaṣil ast.*

ADAM—The angel of God expelled Adam and Eve from paradise.—*firishta,e khudā az bihisht ādam wa ḥawwā-rā ikhrāj kard.* Or, *malaku-l-ḥakk az jannat ādam wa ḥawwā-rā* (*badar kard*). (*jilā kard; berūn kashīd.*)

ANGEL—The angel of death seizes upon all men.—*malaku-l-maut* (*jān-i-har insān mī-gīrad.*) (*kābiẓu-l-arwāḥ ast.*) Or, *azrā,il ākhir jān-i-hama-rā mī-gīrad.* Or, *ajal ākhir ba hama kas mī-rasad.* Or, *hama kas-rā ajal firār mī-rasad.* Or, *mā hama 'alūfa,e marg hastem.*

ADDITION—He has received an addition to his salary.—*o iẓāfa,e mushāhira,e khud yāfta ast.* Or, *bado iẓāfa,e muwājib rasīda ast.* Or, *dar tankhwāh-i-o* (*tarakkī*) *gardīda ast.* (*afzūnī; ziyādatī.*)

ADDRESS—Pray can you tell me his address?—*ṣāḥibā, nishān-i-khiṭāb wa nām wa makām-ash farmūdan mītawāned?*

ADJOURNED—To-day's meeting is adjourned till Monday next.—*majlis-i-imroz tā dū shamba,e āyanda maukūf ast.* Or, *maḥfil-i-imroz tā dū shamba,e āyanda mu'aṯṯal karda and.*

ADJUST—Let us first adjust this matter.—(*biyā tā awwal mukarrar*)-*i-īn kār-rā bi-kunem.* (*bi-guẕār ki awwal rafa' wa rujū'.*)

ADMIRABLE—This is admirable writing.—*īn khaṯṯ bisiyār* (*nafīs*) *ast.* (*khūsh-khaṯṯ.*)

ADMIRE—I greatly admire him for his great learning.—*man az kamāl-i-'ilm-ash bisiyār ta'ajjub dāram.*

ADMIT—I do not admit what you say.—*man ānchi shumā mī-goyed,* (*kabūl na dāram*). (*manẓūr na mī-kunam.*) Or, *man kā,il-i-kaul-i-shumā nīstam.* Or, *bar ānchi shumā mī-goyed man kā,il nīstam.*

ADMITTED—May a stranger be admitted?—*begāna-rā dar*

*īn jā ijāzat-i-(dā**kh**il shudan) ast?* (*madkhal kardan; dakhl kardan; dukhūl kardan; tadakhkhul sākhtan.*) Or, *gharībe-rā rukhṣat ast ki dar īn jā bār yābad?*

ADULT—A school has been opened for adult persons.—*maktabe az barā,e shakhṣān-i-bāligh bar pā shuda ast.* Or, *ta'līm-khāna,e-rā ba jihat-i-nau jawānān binā nihāda and.*

ADVANCE—Can you advance me this sum?—*īn pūl ba taur-i-peshgī marā mī-tawāned dād.*

ADVANCED—The enemy had advanced as far as Shīrāz.—*dushman tā ba shahr-i-shīrāz pesh rafta būd.*

ADVANTAGE—Of what advantage will that be to me?—*az ān chi fā,ida ba man khwāhad rasīd?* Or, *ān chīz chi manfa'at-am khwāhad bakhshīd?* Or, *az ān kār chi zarafī khwāham bast?* Or, *īn kār ba jihat-i-man chi manāfi' dārad?* Or, *ān ba dard-i-man chi dawā dārad?* Or, *az ān chīz chi tamattu' ba man khwāhad rasīd?* Or, *ān chīz chi manfa'at ba man rū khwāhad namūd?*

ADVERSITY—She has long been in adversity.—*ān zan tā muddat-i-madīd dar muṣībat uftāda ast.* Or, *ān za'ifa tā wakt-i-darāz ba balā giriftār būda ast.*

ADVERTISE—You had better advertise the sale.—*bihtar ast ki ishtihār-i-(farokht) ba bāzār-i-'āmm bi-kuned.* (*ḥarrāj; mazād.*)

ADVICE—What is your advice in this affair?—*dar īn mu'āmala ṣalāḥ-i-shumā chīst?* Or, *dar īn amr chi maṣlaḥat mī-(dāned)?* (*dihed; kuned.*) Or, *dar īn kār chi (mau'iẓat) mī-bīned?* (*ṣawāb.*)

ADVISABLE—Do you think it advisable to do so?—*āyā shumā īn chunīn kār kardan (munāsib mī-bīned)?* (*maṣlaḥat mī-dāned.*) Or, *īn chunīn kār kardan nazd-i-shumā maṣlaḥat dārad?*

AFFECTED—He affected a great show of kindness.—*ān shakhṣ ẓāhiran khāṭir-dārī,e firāwan wā namūd.*

AFFECTING—This history is affecting.—*īn ḥikāyat (dard-āmez) ast.* (*gham-angez.*) Or, *īn miṣal dar kase (aṣar mī-kunad).* (*dar mī-gīrad.*)

AFFECTION—He shows great affection for the people.—*o bar mardumān-i-khud bisiyār muḥabbat mī-kunad.* Or, *o ba 'awāmu-n-nās uns-i-tamām dārad.* Or, *o-rā* (*ulfat*)-*i-balīgh ba ahl-i-mulk ast.* (*hawādārī.*)

AFFIRMED—He affirmed this to be a certain fact.—*o ba yaḳīn guft ki īn sukhan* (*ṣaḥīḥ*) *ast.* (*ḥaḳīḳī ; rāst.*) Or, *o bar ṣadāḳat-i-īn* (*ṣābit mānd*). (*ḳā,im nishast ; istiḳlāl girift.*)

AFFLICTED—He on hearing the news became greatly afflicted.—*o az shunīdan-i-īn khabar bisiyār* (*pareshān*) *shud.* (*mutaraddid ; parāganda-dil ; muẓṭaribb ; mushawwash ; sar gardān.*) Or, *ba istimā'-i-īn wāḳi'a khailī ḥairān gasht.* Or, *ba'd az isghā kardan-i-īn kaifiyat* (*dil-ash sokht*). (*bīkh-i-gulbun-i-shādī,e o burīda gasht.*)

AFFLICTION—They have suffered great affliction.—*eshān* (*ranj*)-*i-firāwan kashīda and.* (*miḥnat ; 'aẓāb ; gham.*)

AFRAID—I am afraid to go there.—*az raftan-i-ān jā* (*marā khauf ast*). (*khauf mī-gīram ; khauf dāram ; mukhawwaf-am ; mī-tarsam.*) Or, *man mī-tarsam ki ān jā bi-ravam.*

AFFORD—I cannot afford to give so much monthly wages.—*chandān mushāhira ba shumā na mī-tawānam dād.* Or, *man na mī-tawānam ki īn ḳadr-i-muwājib māhāhana ba shumā bi-diham.*

AFFORD—Pray afford me your assistance.—*marā madad bi-farmāyed.* Or, *mihrbānī karda, marā dastgīrī bi-kuned.* Or, *luṭf farmūda, marā pushtī bi-farmāyed.* Or, *az rū,e iltifāt ba man ḥimāyat bi-kuned.*

AFFRONT—I do not wish to affront him.—*o-rā* (*khafgī dādan*) *na mī-khwāham.* (*ba khashm āwardan.*) Or, *man na mī-khwāham ki o az man ranja-khāṭir gardad.*

AGE—Her age is not more than ten years.—*'umr-i-ān dukhtar az dah sāl* (*ziyāda*) *nīst.* (*beshtar ; mutajāwiz.*)

AGENT—Do you know who is his agent?—*āyā shumā mī-dāned ki* (*gumāshtā*),*e o kīst?* (*wakīl ; kār-guzār ; fā'il* ; 'āmil.*)

---

* *fā'il* is only used in grammar.

AGITATED —Standing before the court, he began to bo much agitated.—*wakte ki o dar 'adālat istūd (o-ra bisiyār larzish girift). (bisiyār larza bar andāmash uftūd; dil-ash tapīdan girift; khauf wa hirās bar o mastaulī shud.)*

AGREE—I agree to what you say.—*ānchi shumā mī-goyed (kabūl mī-kunam). (manzūr mī-dāram; bar ān rizā mī-diham.)* Or, *bā muwāfikat-i-kaul-i-shumā dar āmada am.* Or, *ba shumā dam-i-muwāfikat mī-zanam.*

AGREEABLE—His company is very agreeable.—*rafūkat-ash pasandīda ast.* Or, *mu,ānasat-i-o pasand-khātir ast.* Or, *unsiyat-i-o marghūb ast.* Or, *az mukhālitat-i-o haz-i-bisiyār paidā mī-shavad.*

AGREEMENT—What agreement had you with him?—*bado chi 'uhda wa paimān basta ed?* Or, *bado chi (wa'da) karded? (ta'ahhud; i'tirāf-nāma.)* Or, *bado chi karār-dād ba 'amal āwarded?*

AGREED—They agreed to a rendezvous at that place.—*eshān ba yak dīgar mī'āde nihādand.*

AIR—The air of this country is very unfavourable.—*āb o hawā,e īn mulk bisiyār nā (sāz-kār) ast. (muwāfik.)*

ALAS—Alas! it is all true.—*afsos! īn hama rāst ast.*

ALIKE—The two are perfectly alike.—*īn har dū tā ba yak dīgar bi-l-kull mushabbah and.* Or, *dar mushābahat-i-īn har dū tā sar-i-mū,e farak nīst.* Or, *īn har dū 'alā kull-i-hāl misal-i-yak-dīgar and.*

ALLIGATOR—I saw an alligator in the Euphrates.—*dar rūd-khāna,e farāt yak (nihange)-rā dīdam. (timsāhe.)*

ALLOW—Allow me to go with you.—*bi-guzāred ki ham-rāh-i-shumā bi-ravam.* Or, *lutf farmūda, marā ham-rāh-i-khud bi-bared.*

ALLOW—Do not allow delay.—*ta,akhīr (rawā) ma dār. (jā,iz.)*

ALLOWANCE—He made me an allowance of ten rupees.—*o dah rūpiya ba man dastūrī dād.* Or, *(wajh-i-kifāf)-i-man ba kadar-i-dah rūpiya dād. (ma'ishat; idrār; wazīfa.)*

ALMANAC—Have you got this year's almanac?—*(takwīm-i-imsāl) dāred? (tanjīm-i-imsāla.)*

ALPHABET—I have not yet learned the alphabet.—*tā hanoz (ḥurūf-i-tahajjī nayāmokhta am). (dar abjad ta'līm na yāfta am; alif,bā,pā na dānam.)*

ALOUD—Speak aloud, that I may hear you.—*ba āwāz-i-buland bi-go tā turā bi-shinavam.*

ALTERATION—What alteration shall I make?—*ba chi ṭaur īn-rū (tabdīl) bi-kunam. (tabaddul; taghaiyur; taḥwīl; ḥaraf; inḥirāf.)*

ALTERED—It is now done, and can't be altered.—*ilḥāl tamām shud, hech tabaddul shudan na mī-tawānad.* Or, *aknūn ba itmām rasīda ast, ba hech wajh (taghaiyur shudan) na mī-tawānad. (mubaddal gashtan; muta-ghaiyir shudan; munḥaraf gardīdan.)*

AMASSED—He has amassed great wealth.—*ān kas bisiyār daulat jam' karda ast.*

AMOUNT—The bill will amount to 500 rupees.—*jam'-i-ḥisāb panj ṣad rupiya būda bāshad.*

AMOUNT—What is the amount of your bill?—*jam'-i-ḥisāb-at chīst?*

AMAZED—I was amazed at the amount.—*az jam'-i-ḥisāb bisiyār (ta'ajjub kardam). (muta'ajjib shudam; muta-ḥaiyir shudam; ḥairān shudam.)*

AMUSE—Amuse yourself awhile in the garden.—*ḳadre der ba bāgh mashghūl bi-shau.* Or, *chande (tafarruj-i-rauẓa bi-namā). (khud-rā ba bostān dar ishtighāl bi-dār.)*

ANCIENT—Shīrāz is an ancient city.—*shīrāz shahr-i-ḳadīm ast.* Or, *shīrāz shahrīst ḳadīm.*

ANGRY—Does this make you angry?—*īn sukhan shumā-rā (khashm-nāk mī-kunad)? (ghaiẓ mī-dihad.)* Or, *az īn sukhan shumā-rā khashm mī-āyad?* Or, *az īn sukhan shumā (ghaiẓ mī-āred)? (khashm mī-kuned; dar ghuṣṣa mī-shaved; mutaghaiyur mī-shaved; mutaghaiyiẓ mī-shaved; ḳahr mī-gīred: baham bar mī-āyed.)* Or, *az īn sukhan 'aish-i-shumā talkh mī-shavad?* Or, *bar īn sukhan khashm mī-gīred?*

ANSWER—Can you give an answer to this question?—*jawāb-*

i-īn su,āl mī-tawāned dād? Or, *az jawāb-i-īn su,āl kase-rā mustafīz farmūdan mī-tawāned?*

Answer—This will answer my purpose.—*īn ba kār-i-man khwāhad khurd.* Or, *īn ba ḥasb-i-muddā'-i-man khwāhad būd.* Or, *az īn ijrā,e kār-i-man khwāhad shud.*

Anxious—I am very anxious to get there.—*man bisiyār (mushtāḳ-am ki ān jā bi-ravam). (ishtiyāḳ dāram ki ān jā bi-rasam.)*

Anywhere—I have not seen him anywhere.—*man o-rā hech jā na dīda am.* Or, *bā o hech jā (mulāḳāt na karda) am. (mulāḳī na shuda.)*

Apology—He made no apology for his misconduct.—*o az barā,e bad raftārī,e khud hech ('uzr na kard). ('uzr nayāward; mu'āfī na khwāst; ma'zrat na kard; i'tizār na kard.)* Or, *o bar bad raftārī,e khud istighfār na guft.*

Appeal—He made an appeal to Government.—*o ba sarkār rujū'-i-murāfa'a,e khud kard.*

Appear—He will not appear personally in this business.—*o dar īn amr khud-rā (poshīda) khwāhad dāsht. (makhfī.)* Or, *o dar īn 'amal rū-posh khwāhad shud.* Or, *o dar īn kār ba zāt-i-khud ẓāhir na khwāhad shud.*

Appears—It appears to me very strange.—*īn kār ba naẓar-i-man bisiyār ('ajīb mī-āyad). (gharīb ast; nādir ast.)* Or, *man az īn kār muta'ajjib-am.* Or, *az īn kār marā ta'ajjub mī-āyad.*

Application—He made an application to the judge.—*o ba ḥākim-i-shara' 'arẓ kard.* (In writing, *'arīẓa.*)

Appraised—His goods will be appraised and sold.—*ba'd az takhmīn asbāb-i-o ba (ḥarrāj) farokhta khwāhad shud. (mazād.)* Or, *ba'd az ta'aiyun-i-ḳīmat sāmān-ash ba farosh khwāhad rasīd.*

Apprehend—I apprehend you have made a mistake.—*man mī-fahmam ki shumā ghalaṭ karda ed.* Or, *(dar fahm-i-man mī-āyad) ki khaṭā khurda ed. (mafhūm-am mī-shavad.)*

Apprehended—He was apprehended and put into prison.

—o giriftār shud, wa maḥbūs gardīd. Or, *eshūn o-rā giriftār karda dar ḳaid-khāna andākhtand.*

Appropriated—He has appropriated all his property to this purpose.—*o az barā,e īn kār hama milkiyat-i-khud-ash (guzāshta) ast. (makhṣūṣ karda.)*

Approve—Do you approve of what I say?—*ānchi mī-goyam (shumā pasand mī-kuned), yā na? (shumā-rā pasand mī-āyad; dar naẓar-i-shumā pasandīda mī-āyad; dar samā'-i-ḳabūl-i-shumā mī-uftād; ba rā,e shumā muwāfiḳat mī-kunad; ba mahall-i-ḳabūl-i-shumā maḳrūn ast.)*

Arabic—He teaches the Persian and Arabic languages.—*o zabānhā,e fārsī wa 'arabī mī-āmozānad.* Or, *o dar 'ajjamī wa 'arabī (ta'līm mī-kunad). (tadrīs mī-kunad; dars mī-dihad.)*

Arches—There are five arches in the veranda.—*dar pesh-khāna panj ṭāḳ ast.* Or, *dar aiwān panj miḥrāb ast.* Or, *ān pesh-gāh panj kamān dārad.*

Arduous—This is an arduous undertaking.—*murtakib shudan-i-īn kār mushkil ast.* Or, *irtikāb-i-īn amr (dushwār ast). (ishkāl dārad.)*

Argue—Let us argue the point together.—*biyā ki mā bāham bar īn nukta (mubāḥasa bi-kunem). (baḥs bi-kunem; burhān bi-namāyem; dalīl bi-dihem; hujjat biy-āwarem.)*

Arguments—He uses very strong arguments.—*o bisiyār ḳawī dalīlhā ba kār mī-āwarad.* Or, *o dalā,il-i-bisiyār ḳawī īrād mī-kunad.* Or, *ṣabūt-i-(mustaḳīm) isti'māl mī-kunad. (ḳā,im; muḥkam; muḳawī; ustuwār.)* Or, *ān kas burhānhā,e ḳāṭi' dārad.*

Arithmetic—I am now learning arithmetic.—*ilḥāl man 'ilm-i-(siyāḳ) mī-khwānam. (ḥisāb.)* Or, *ilḥāl man 'ilm-i-riyāẓī mī-āmozam.* Or, *fi-l-ḥāl dar 'ilm-i-ghāyat ta'līm mī-yābam.*

Army—The king was at the head of his army.—*bādshāh ba sar-i-lashkar)-i-khud būd. (malik·pesh-rau,e 'askar.)*

Arrested—He was arrested for debt by Kāsim.—*ba sabab-*

-i-ḳarẓ (o az dast-i-ḳāsim giriftār shud). (*ḳāsim o-rā giriftār kard.*)

ARRIVAL—Have you heard the news of his arrival?—*āyā shumā khabar-i-(rasīdan)-ash shunīda ed ?* (*wurūd ; rasīdagī ; maḳdam; wārid shudan.*)

ART—I am not acquainted with that art.—*az* (or *bar*) *ān hunar* (*wāḳif nayam*). (*wuḳūf na dāram.*) Or, *dar ān* (*san'at*) *mahārate na dāram.* (*fann,* pl. *funūn.*)

ARTFUL—They are very artful.—*eshān bisiyār* (*ḥīla-bāz*) *and.* (*rūbāh-bāz ; ḥukḳa-bāz ; dū rū ; nīrang-pardāz ; gurpaz.*) Or, *eshān dūm-i-fareb wa daghā mī-gustarand.* Or, *eshān majmī'-i-fasād wa makr wa majmū'a,e zirk wa ghadr and.*

ARTICLES—They deal in various articles.—*eshān dar matā'-i-har nau tijārat mī-kunand.* Or, *eshān pīlawar hastand* (*māl-i-jūzī*) *mī-faroshand.* (*ajnās-i-khurda.*) Or, *eshān tujjār and māl-i-kullī mī-faroshand.*

AS—Has he repaired the carriage as I told him?—*ba mūjib-i-guftan-i-man* (*marammat)-i-kāliska karda ast, yā na ?* (*tajdīd.*)

ASCEND—Let us now ascend the mountain.—*biyā tā il-ḥāl bālā,e koh bi-ravem.*

ASK—Ask him what is his name.—(*az o bi-purs*) *ism-i-shumā chīst !* (*o-rā bi-purs.*)

ASS—To whom does that ass belong?—*ān khar az ān-i-kīst ?* Or, *mālik-i-ān khar kīst ?*

ASSEMBLED—The people of the villages assembled.—*ahl-i-dihāt* (*jam'*) *shudand.* (*majmū' ; mujtami'' ; mujamma'.*) Or, *mardumān-i-bulūkāt* (*firāham*) *āmadand.* (*gird.*) Or, *jamī' muḳīmūn-i-ḳarya* (*ijtimā'*) *namūdand.* (*jam'īyat.*)

ASSEMBLY—I saw a great assembly of people.—*man gurohi-buzurge dīdam.* Or, *izhdihame bisiyār mulāḥaza kardam.* Or, *jam'īyate kaṣīr mushāhida kardam.* Or, (*ṭā,-ifa)e 'aẓīm ba naẓar-i-man āmad.* (*jam' ; jamā'at ; zumra ; kaṣrat-i-khalā,ik ; maḥfil,* pl. *mahāfil ; majma'-i-mardumān.*)

ASSENT—I assent to your proposal.—*man rā,e shumā-rā ḳabūl mī-kunam.* Or, *ba irāda,e shumā muttafiḳ-am.* Or, *man ba khwāhish-i-shumā karār mī-(kunam). (gīram.)* Or, *man muḳirr-i-ārzū,e shumā hastam.*

ASSERTED—He asserted that it is so.—*o (ba yaḳīn guft) ki ham chunīn ast. (iḳrār kard; taḥḳīḳ kard.)*

ASSIST—We ought to assist each other.—*bāyad ki yak dīgar-rā madad bi-dihem.* Or, *marā bāyad ki yak dīgar-rā (mu-'āwin bāshem.) (mu'āwanat; imdād; yāwarī; pushtī; madad bi-kunem.)* Or, *bāyad ki murād-i-yak dīgar-rā bar ārem.*

ASSOCIATE—Why do you associate with evil company?—*ba ṣuḥbat-i-bad chirā (mukhāliṭat) mī-kuned? (ikhtilāṭ; mujālisat; muwāṣilat; ulfat; mubāsharat; mu'āsharat; murāfiḳat; uns.)* Or, *bā bad-raftārān chirā (yār mī-shaved)? (mī-nishīned; mī-paiwanded; dam sāz mī-bāshed; ṣuḥbat dāred.)* Or, *chirā dar ṭawīla,e rindān mī-bāshed?* Or, *chirā ba mardūm-i-sharīr wa fattān ikhtilāṭ mī-warzed?* *Or, *chirā dar silk-i-ṣuḥbat-i-safīhān (ablahān, faromā-yagān, kam-ẓarafān, subuksārān, kamīnagān, bad-ṭīnatān, nāḳiṣān, nā-kasān, bad-sigālān, nafas parwarān, khīra-rūyān, tīra-rāyān, turush-rūyān, bahāna jūyān, bad-khūyān, mu'jibān, nāḳiṣ-'aḳlān, talkh-guftārān, mardum-azārān, gadā-ṭaba'ān; na parhezgān) munsalik mī-shaved?*

ASSURE—I assure you there is no danger in that matter.—*man ba shumā rāst mī-goyam ki dar ān mu'āmala hech khauf wa khaṭar nīst.*

ASSUREDLY—Assuredly this is true.—*(yaḳīn ast ki īn rāst) ast. (be shakk īn ṣādiḳ; al ḥaḳḳ īn ḥaḳḳ; ba khudā īn ṣaḥīḥ; ba sar-i-khudat īn muḥaḳḳaḳ.)*

ASTONISHMENT—He manifested great astonishment on his part.—*o az ṭaraf-i-khud (ta'ajjub)*[1]*-i-bisiyār (ẓāhir)*[2] *kard.* [1]*(taḥaiyur; ḥairat.)* [2]*(āshkār.)* Or, *ma'lūm ast ki ta-*

---

* The meanings of these useful words, here grouped together, should be found from a Dictionary.

ḥaiyur bar o (mustaulī) shud. (girifta.) Or, *az ṭaraf-i-khwesh mutaḥaiyir mānd.* Or, *o angusht-i-taḥaiyur ba dandān girift.*

Astronomy—Are you acquainted with the science of astronomy?—*āyā az 'ilm-i-najūm (wāḳif ed)? (wuḳūf dāred.)* Or, *āyā dar 'ilm-i-astār chīze (mahārat) dāred? (dakhl.)*

Atone—How shall I atone for this conduct?—*ba jihat-i-kaffāra,e īn bad raftārī chi bi-kunam?* Or, *ba chi ṭaur takfīr-i-īn khabāṣat-i-nafas-i-man bi-kunam?*

Attacked—The enemy's cavalry attacked us.—*sawārān-i-dushman bar mā (ḥamla)*[1] *(kardand)*[2]. [1]*(yurish; tākht; hujūm.)* [2]*(burdand; āwardand.)* Or, *sawārān-i-dushman bar mā zadand.*

Attempted—He never attempted to learn.—*o hargiz tan-i-khud ba (ta'līm) na dād. (ta'allum; tadrīs.)* Or, *o bi-l-kull koshish-i-khwāndan na kard.*

Attend—Let us attend to our studies.—*biyā ki mā ba sabaḳ-i-khud (tan bi-dihem). (khayāl bi-dihem; shughl gīrem; mashghūl bāshem; mutawajjih bāshem; tawajjuh bi-kunem; multafit bi-shavem.)*

Attend—I have received notice to attend the court at ten o'clock.—*iḥẓār-nāma ba jihat-i-man āmada ast ki (pesh-i-ḥākim-i-shara') ba sā'at-i-dah ḥāẓir bāsham.* (criminal, *dar maḥkama,e mujrima;* civil, *dar maḥkama,e maḥṣūl;* judicial, *dar maḥkama,e 'adālat.*)

Attendance—Your attendance there is required.—*ḥāẓir shudan-i-shumā dar ān jā ẓarūr ast.* Or, *ḥāẓir būdan-i-shumā dar ān jā az jumla,e ẓarūriyāt ast.*

Attention—She pays attention to learning.—*ān zā,ifa ba 'ilm khwāndan bisiyār (ma,il dārad). (mā,il mī-bāshad; tawajjuh mī-kunad; iltifāt mī-kunad; mutawajjih mī-shavad.)* Or, *ān zan dar taḥṣīl-i-'ilm (tan) mī-dihad. (dil; khayāl.)*

Auction—Do you mean to attend the auction?—*āyā ba harrāj khwāhed raft?* Or, *āyā irāda dāred ki ba mazād bi-raved?*

Authentic—I believe the information is authentic.—*man chunīn mī-fahmam ki īn khabar ṣaḥīḥ ast.* Or, *man bar īn khabar* (*i'timād*) *mī-kunam ki rāst ast.* (*i'tiḳād; i'tibār.*)

Author—Who is the author of this book?—*muṣannif-i-īn kitāb kīst?* (*mu,allif; nawīsanda; naḳlband.*)

Authority—By whose authority do you do this?—*shumā ba ḥukm-i-kudām shakhṣ īn 'amal mī-kuned?*

Avarice—There is no end to his avarice.—(*ṭama'*)[1]-*i-o* (*az ḥadd ziyāda*)[2] *ast.* [1](*ḥirṣ; imsāk; bukhul; bakhīlī.*) [2](*lā intihā; be ghāyat; lā ḥadd; be ḥisāb.*)

Avaricious—He is extremely avaricious.—*o nihāyat* (*bakhīl*) *ast.* (*ḥarīṣ; bākhil; ṭāmi'.*) Or, *o abū-l-ḥirṣ ast.*

Average—What is the average of attendance at your school?—*ba maktab khāna,e shumā* (*sarāsarī*) *ta'adād-i-aṭfāl chi ḳadar ast.* (*takhmīnan.*)

Avoid—I cannot avoid going.—*man az raftan* (*iḥtirāz*) *na mī-tawānam kard.* (*ijtināb; imtinā'; nafrat.*) Or, *man az raftan* (*bāz na mī-tawānam mānd*). (*sar bāz na mī-tawānam zad.*) Or, *man tark-i-raftan-i-ān jā na mī-tawānam girift.*

Awake—Awake me early in the morning.—*ba waḳt-i-pagāh marā bedār bi-kuned.* Or, (*'alạ-ṣ-ṣabāḥ*) *marā iḳāẓ bi-kuned.* (*ṣabūḥ; bām-dād; fajr; tabāshīr-i-ṣabāḥ; ṣubḥ-i-ṣādiḳ; ṣubḥ-i-kāẕib.*)

Aware—I was not aware of this.—*man az īn wāḳif na būdam.* (*khabar na dāshtam; iṭṭilā' na dāshtam; muṭṭali' na būdam; wuḳūf na yāftam.*)

Awful—How inexpressibly awful is the state of those who despise God!—*ḥālat-i-ān ashkhāṣ ki khudā-rā ḥaḳīr mī-dānand chigūna* (*haulnāk*) *ast!* (*sahmgīn; makhūf; haibatwār.*)

Awkward—He is awkward at his work.—*dar kār-i-khud* (*khām*) *ast.* (*nā-ḳābil; muhmil; nā-shinās.*)

Awkward—This is an awkward circumstance.—*wuḳū'-i-īn waḳī'at be waḳt ast.* Or, *īn ḳaziya* (*ghair maḳbūl*) *ast.* (*nā munāsib.*)

AXE—Bring an axe, and chop this wood.—*tabare biyāred wa īn (chūb-rā pāra pāra bi-kuned). (hezum-rā kaṭa' bi-kuned; hema-rā bi-shikaned; ḥaṭab-rā bi-bured; wakaid-rā munkaṭi' bi-kuned.)*

B.

BACHELOR—Is he still a bachelor?—*āyā tā īn roz ān shakhṣ (mujarrad) ast. ('arusī na karda; 'azab; nā kad-khudā.)*

BACK—What has he got on his back?—*ān kas bar pusht-i-khud chi dārad?*

BAG—Put this money in the bag.—*īn pūl-rā dar (kīsa bi-guzār). (kharīṭa bi-nih; jama'dān bi-kun; jīb biyan-dāz.)*

BAGGAGE—The soldiers departed this morning with their baggage.—*imroz ṣubḥ 'askariyān ham rāh-i-asbāb-i-khud rawān shudand.*

BAIL—Are you willing to become bail for him?—*āyā shumā mī-khwāhed ki ẓāman-ash bi-shaved?* Or, *az ṭaraf-i-o (ẓāman) khwāhed shud?* (*kafīl.*) Or, *ẓamānat-i-khud az ṭaraf-i-o kabūl dāred?*

BALANCE—What is the balance of my account?—(*mīzān*)-*i-ḥiṣāb-i-man chīst?* (*tamṣīl; bakāyā,e.*)

BALE—Open the bale of cotton.—*basta,e pumba-rā (wā kun). (bāz kun; bi-kushā.)*

BALLAST—That vessel has come in ballast.—*ān jahāz (dar ṣabra) āmada ast.* (*khālī.*)

BANISH—We may now banish our fears.—*ilḥāl mā dah-shathā,e khud-rā (yak ṭaraf kunem). (bar ṭaraf kunem; yak sū nihem; az dast rihā kunem.)*

BANKERS—They are bankers in Shirāz.—*eshān ṣarrāfān az shīrāz and.* Or, *eshān dar shīrāz ṣarrāfī mī-kunand.*

BANKRUPT—He has lately become a bankrupt.—*o dar īn rozhā (dar) shikasta ast. (war.)* Or, *o dar īn aiyām khisārat-i-hama māl-i-khud girifta ast.* Or, *o-rā khisārat-i-hama milk-i-khud rasīda ast.*

BARE—We sat on the bare ground.—*mā bar (zamīn-i-barahna) nishastem.* (*khāk.*)

BARGAIN—You have made a bad bargain.—*shumā mu'āhadat-i-ḳabīḥ karda ed.*

BARKS—This dog barks at everybody.—*īn sag ba har shakhṣ ('af-'af) mī-kunad.* (*'aw-'aw; nabbāḥ; wak-wak.*)

BARRELS—I have sold my 20 barrels of flour.—*man bīst barmīl-i-ārd-i-khud-rā farokhta am.*

BARREN—This land is entirely barren.—*īn zamīn bi-l-kull (shorabūm) ast.* (*malī'; subrūt; wairān; ḳābil-i-zirā'at na.*)

BASE—Alas! what base conduct am I guilty of!—*afsos! chi 'amal-i-bad az man sādir shuda ast!* Or, *dareghh! murtakib-i-chi 'amal-i-nā-shā,ista shuda am!* Or, *wāe! chi 'amal-i-(ḳabiḥ) az wujūd-i-man sar bar āwarda ast!* (*fāsid; shanī'; karīh; mukkir.*)

BASIN—Bring some water in a basin.—*ḳadre āb dar ṭasht biyāred.*

BASKET—Put these things in a basket.—*andarūn-i-sabad īn chīzhā bi-(guzār).* (*kun; nih.*)

BATHING—I saw numbers of people bathing in the Euphrates.—*jama'īyat-i-khalḳe-rā dīdam ki dar daryā,e farāt (ghuṣl) mī-kunand.* (*ṭahārat.*)

BEARS—He bears this load on his head.—*o bar sar-i-khud īn bār (mī-barad).* (*ḥaml mī-kunad.*) Or, *o bar sar-i-khud īn ḥaml guzāshta, ḥāmil-i-ān mī-bāshad.*

BORE—You bore it very patiently.—*shumā ān-rā ba (ṣabr taḥammul karded).* (*istiḳlāl bar dāsht namūded.*)

BEATEN—I have beaten him twice in learning.—*dar āmokhtan dū bār bar o (ṣabḳat) karda am.* (*burda; girifta.*) Or, *dar dars giriftan (dū martaba az o bar āmada am).* (*dū dafa' az o go,e burda am.*)

BEATEN—The master has thoroughly beaten the slave.—*mālik ghulām-i-khud-rā (khūb kofta) ast.* (*be muḥāba zada; ẓarb be muḥāba zada; be muḥāba faro kofta.*) Or, *khwāja 'abd-i-khud-rā (kūtak-kārī) karda ast.* (*ba ẓarb-i-shalāk khurd khām.*)

BEAUTIFUL—This is a beautiful garden. *īn (bāgh)*[1]*-i-(khūb ṣūrate)*[2] *ast.* [1]([of Eden] *jannat; firdaus; rauẓa*; *'adan*: [flower] *bostān*; *gulistān*; *gulzār*; *gulshan*: [fruit] *daukat*; *bāghcha*; [kitchen] *pāliz.*) [2](*dil-kushā*; *dil-āwez*; *dil-chasp*; *khūsh-namā*; *farḥat-bakhsh*; *rāḥat-angez tafrīḥ-rasān.*)

BECALMED—The ship was becalmed four days.—*jahāz tā chahār roz (sākit) mānd.* (*sākin.*)

BECKON—Beckon to him to come here.—*ishāra bi-kun ki īn jā biyāyad.*

BECOME—He has lately become very proud.—*o dar īn rozhā bisiyār (maghrūr) shuda ast.* (*pur-gharūr*; *mutakabbir*; *mudammigh*; *jibbīr*; *nakhwat-kash*; *khud-pasand.*)

BED—He is ill and confined to his bed.—*o bīmār ast wa bar bistar-i-khud uftāda ast.*

BEE—I have been stung by a bee.—*zambūr-i-'asl marā (nesh zada) ast.* (*gazīda.*)

BEG—I beg your pardon for what I have done.—*az ānchi karda am ('afw ṭalab mī-kunam).* (*istighfār mī-sāzam*; *mustaghfir mī-shavam*; *'uzr mī-sāzam.*) Or, *kalam-i-'afw bar gunāh-am bi-kashed.* Or, *'uzr-i-taḳṣīr-i-mā-salaf-i-khud mī-kunam.*

BEGGAR—There is a beggar at the door.—*ba dar (faḳīre) istāda ast.* (*gadā,e*; *sā,ile*; *darweshe*; *rawān-khwāhe.*)

BEGAN—I have began to speak English.—*dar zabān-i-inglisī sukhan guftan shurū' karda am.* Or, *dar lisān-i-inglisī ḥaraf zadan girifta am.*

BEGINNING—It has neither beginning nor end.—*ān (awwal wa ākhir) na dārad.* (*ibtidā wa intihā*; *aghāz wa anjām*; *shuru' wa khātima*; *muḳaddama wa ākhirat.*)

BELIEVES—He believes whatever people tell him.—*bar ānchi mardumān mī-goyand (i'tiḳād) mī-kunad.* (*i'tibār*; *i'timād*; *bāwar.*) Or, *ba afwāh-i-ām mu'taḳide ast.* (*mu'tamide.*)

BELONG—Does this knife belong to you?—*īn kārd az ān-i-shumā ast?*

BEND—The ears of corn, being ripe, bend to the ground.—*khoshahā,e ghalla az pukhtagī ba sū,e zamīn* (*faro*) *mī-shavand.* (*mā,il; kaj; mutawajjih; multafit.*)

BENEFIT—Has the medicine afforded you benefit?—*īn 'ilāj shumā-rā* (*fā,ida*) *karda ast?* (*tāṣīr; manfa'at.*) Or, *az īn mu'ālaja* (*fā,ida dīda ed*). (*istifāda girifta ed.*) Or, *az khurdan-i-īn dawā shumā-rā ḳadre takhfīf-i-marẓ shuda ast?*

BESEECH—I beseech you to pay attention.—(*iltimās*) *mī-kunam ki shumā badīn kār dil bi-dihed.* (*istid'ā.*) Or, *iltifāt farmūda multafit bi-shaved.* Or, *multafī mī-shavam ki dar īn amr tan bi-dihed.*

BESET—He is beset on all sides with business.—*az har ṭaraf ba kār-i-bisiyār mashghūl ast.* Or, *ba hama aṭrāf dar kār* (*maḥṣūr*) *ast.* (*maṣrūf.*)

BESPEAK—I am going to the shoemaker's to bespeak a pair of shoes.—*ba dukān-i-kafsh-doz mī-ravam tā farmā,ish-i-sākhtan-i-yak juft-i-urusī bi-diham.*

BEST—I think it will be best to do so.—*man chunīn mī-fahmam ki īn chunīn kardan* (*ansab*) *ast.* (*afẓal; aulatar.*) Or, *maṣlaḥat-i-ān mī-bīnam ki īn kār 'ain-i-ṣawāb ast.*

BESTOW—I am a poor man, be pleased to bestow one diram.—*man muḥtāj-am dirame 'aṭā bi-farmāyed.* Or, *man ḥājī-am pashīze ba khairat bi-dihed.* Or, *ḥājatmand-am az rū,e luṭf marā dirame 'ināyat bi-kuned.*

BETTER—Mine is better than yours.—*māl-i-man az māl-i-shumā bihtar ast.*

BEWARE—Beware of idleness and ignorance.—*az ihmāl wa jāhilī iḥtizār bi-sāz.* Or, *az takāsul wa jāhilīyat pur-ḥaẕa bāsh.* Or, *az takāhul wa jahālat* (*ijtināb*) *bi-kun.* (*iḥtirāz.*) Or, (*sustī*) *wa āwāragī-rā bi-guẕar.* (*baṭālat; kāhilī.*)

BEYROUT—I have been three years in Beyrout.—*dar bayrūt tā si sāl būda am.* Or, *ḥālan si sāl guẕashta ast ki man dar bayrūt* (*mu-ṭawaḳḳif būda am*). (*muḳīm būda am;*

sākin shuda am; mutamakkin shuda am; iḳāmat karda am; sukūnat dashta am.)

Bid—Why do you bid me do this?—*chirā marā farmā,ish-i kardan-i-īn kār mī-kuned?*

Big—How big is the book you speak of?—*kitābe ki ẕikr mī-kuned, chi ḳadar hujūm dārad?*

Bill—Give me your bill, I will pay it.—*ḥisāb-i-khud-rā ba-man bi-dihed ān-rā adā khwāham kard.*

Bind—Bind him hand and foot.—*dast wa pāyash bi-band.* Or, *band bar dast wa pāyash bi-nih.*

Bind—Bind him neck and foot.—*silsila dar gardan wa zanjīr bar pāyash bi-(nih). (kun; band.)*

Pinion him.—*dast bar katif-ash bi-band.*

Bound—He has bound up the parcel.—*ān kas (buḳcha)-rā basta ast. (basta.)*

Bitten—He was bitten by a jackal.—*yak shaghāle o-rā (gazīda) ast. (zakhmī karda.)* Or, *o az shaghāle gazīda shuda ast.*

Blameable—Am I blameable in this?—*āyā man dar īn kār (muḳaṣṣar)-am? (taḳṣīrwār.)*

Blame—The blame rests only upon me.—*siwā,e man kase dīgar muḳaṣṣar nīst.* Or, *ilzām-i-īn taḳṣīr khāṣṣ ba ẕimma,e man ast.* Or, *īn jurm maḥẓ az dast-i-man (bar āmada) ast. (ṣādir shuda.)* Or, *siwā,e man kase dīgar (ilzām-i-īn kār na dārad). (malzūm-i-īn kār nīst.)* Or, *ba juz-i-man kase dīgar mujrim na shuda ast.*

Blameless—No, without doubt you are blameless.—*na, be shakk shumā (be ḳuṣūr ed). (ma'ṣūm ed.)*

Bled—After being bled he recovered.—*ba'd az fasd kardan shifā yāft.* Or, *ba'd az rag zadan ifāḳa yāft.* Or, *ba'd az hajāmat kardan andake rāhat yāft.*

Bleeds—I have cut my finger, see how it bleeds.—*angusht-i-khud-rā burīda am, bi-bīned (chigūna khūn az o mī-chakad). (chi ṭaur khūn mī-āyad.)*

Blessing—By the blessing of God I am better.—*ba faẓl-i-allāh ta'ālā ḳadre ārām yāfta am.*

BLIND—He is now quite blind.—*ān shakhṣ bi-l-kull* (*nā-bīnā*) *ast.* (*kūr ; ẓarīr ; a'mā.*)

BLINDFOLD—He led him blindfold through the city.—*o chashm-ash bast wa o-rā gird-i-shahr gardānīd.*

BLOSSOM—Where there is blossom we expect fruit.—*jā,e ki shugūfa ast, ummed-i-mewa ast.*

BLOSSOM—This plant will soon blossom.—*īn nihāl zūd* (*gul khwāhad kard*). (*shugūfa khwāhad dād.*) Or, *īn nihāl zūd bār khwāhad āward.*

BLOTTED—He blotted the whole of his papers.—*o bar hama kāghaz-i-khud dāgh-i-siyāhī andākht.* Or, *o hama kāghaz-i-khud-rā ṭasūm kard.*

BLOW—Blow the dust off your book.—*az kitāb-i-khud-at gard* (*fūt bi-kun*). (*paf bi-dih ; wā pak.*) Or, *kitāb-i-khud-rā bi-takāned.*

BLUNDER—You blunder continually.—*shumā hamesha* (*sahw*) *mī-kuned.* (*khaṭā ; ghalaṭ ; ḳuṣūr.*)

BOLDER—He is bolder than I.—*o az man* (*shujā'tar*) *ast.* (*be bāktar ; shajī'tar ; dilāwartar.*) Or, *o az man ziyāda shujā'at dārad.*

BOLT—Fix a bolt on the window.—*dar darīcha chifte bi-zan.* Or, *dar ghurfa darbande muruttib bi-kun.* Or, *dar rauzan band-kasha,e ḳā,im bi-kun.*

BOND—He wishes to have a bond for this amount.—*barā,e īn mablagh-i-pūl tamassuk mī-khwāhad.*

BONE—The dog has a bone in his mouth.—*sag dar dahan-i-khud 'aẓme dārad.*

BOOKSELLER—I have been to the bookseller's shop.—*ba dukān-i-kitāb-farosh būda am.*

BORN—He was born before you.—*o pesh az shumā* (*paidā*) *shuda būd.* (*maulūd ; zāda ; mutawallad.*)

BORROW—I want some money, from whom can I borrow?—*man ḳadre pūl mī-khwāham az kudām kas* (*ḳarẓ*) *mī-tawānam girift ?* (*wām ; 'āriyat.*)

BOTTLE—Put this oil into a bottle.—*īn raughan-i-talkh-rā dar* (*surāḥī bi-guzār*) (*kūza bi-kun.*)

Bottom—Read to the bottom of the page.—*tā ba (intihā),e ṣafḥa bi-k͟hwāned. (āk͟hir; anjām; k͟hatm; ik͟htitām; muntahā; tā ki tah.)* Or, *ṣaḥīfa-rā tamām bi-k͟hwāned.*

Bow—Having made a bow, he sat.—*o (salām kard) wa nishast. (sar-i-k͟hidmat bar astūn dāsht; zamīn-i-k͟hidmat bosīd; k͟hidmat kard; sharṭ-i-k͟hidmat ba jā āward; rasm-i-adab wa taḥiyat ba jā āward; sar-i-k͟hidmat ba zamīn nihād; alif ḳāmat-i-k͟hud-rā chūn nūn k͟ham sāk͟ht.)*

Bows—Bows and arrows were formerly used in war.—*(dar aiyām-i-guẕashta) tīr wa kamān aṣliḥā,e jang būdand. (sābiḳan; dar aiyām-i-salaf; dar waḳt-i-peshīn; muḳaddaman; pesh az īn; ḳabl az īn.)*

Box—What shall I put in this box?—*dar īn ṣandūḳ chi bi-(guẕāram). (kunam; niham.)*

Bracelets—That lady wears bracelets.—*ān bānū yāra ba dast mī-kunad.* Or, *ān ṣāḥiba mi'ẓad ba dast mī-poshad.* Or, *ān k͟hātūn dast-biranjan dar dast mī-kunad.*

Branches—That tree has many branches.—*ān shajar bisiyār (afanīn) dārad. (furū',* sing. *far'; ag͟hṣā,e,* sing. *g͟huṣu; fājhā; shāk͟hhā.)*

Brass—Don't you know brass from copper?—*āyā birinj-rā az mis na mī-dāned?* Or, *farḳ mā-bain birinj wa mis na mī-kuned?* Or, *farḳ-i-birinj wa mis na mī-dāned?*

Brave—His soldiers are very brave.—*'askariyān-ash k͟hailī (shujā') and. (dilīr; jang-jū; dushman-kush.)*

Bravery—What bravery have they displayed?—*eshān chi (shujā'at namūda) and? (dilāwarī ẓāhir karda; ḥimmat iẓhār sāk͟hta.)*

Braying—The ass is braying.—*ḥimār (nahīk mī-zanad). ('ar-'ar mī-kunad; mī-shorad.)*

Breadth—What is the breadth of that cloth?—*('arẓ)-i-ān pārcha chi ḳadar ast? (pahan; kushādagī.)*

Broken—He has broken it in pieces.—*o ān-rā (k͟hurd-k͟hurd karda) ast. (pāra-pāra shikasta; reza-reza gusek͟hta.)*

BROKEN—He has broken the agreement.—*(khilāf)-i-'ahd karda ast. (nuḳṣ ; faskh.)*

BREATH—I have run to such a degree that I am out of breath.—*man chunīn dawīda am ki (nafs) na mī-tawān-um zad. (tanaffus ; dam.)* Or, *man chunān dawīda am ki majāl-i-nafs kashīdan na (dāram). (āwaram.)*

BREED—These insects breed in the rice.—*īn kirmhā dar birinj paidā mī-shavand.*

BRED—He bred up his children in the best manner.—*o aṭfāl-i-khud-rā ba (ṭarīḳ-i-aḥsan parwarish dād). (afẓalu-l-wajh tarbiyat kard ; bihtarīn-i-ṣūrat nashw o namā dād.)*

BRIBED—He was bribed to commit that wicked deed.—*o rishwat girifta ān kār-i-shanī' kard.* Or, *ba jihat-i-kār-i-shanī' o-rā rishwat dāda shuda ast.*

BRICKS—Bricks are made of this kind of earth.—*az īn ḳism-i-(gil) khishthā sākhta mī-shavand. (khilāb.)*

BRIDEGROOM—I saw both the bridegroom and the bride.—*har dū dāmād wa 'arūṣ dīdam.*

BRIGHT—Do you observe that bright star?—*āyā ān (najm-i-mujallī)-rā mī-bīned? (sitāra,e darafshān; ākhtar-i-darakhshān.)*

BROAD.—How broad shall I make this mat?—*īn (boriyā)*[1] *chi ḳadar ('arīẓ)*[2] *bi-sāzam?* [1]*(zīgh ; ḥūṣir.)* [2]*(pahan ; wāṣi'.)*

BROKER—He is by trade a broker.—*o ba ḥarfat dallāle ast.* Or, *o ba ḳasb baiyā'e ast.* Or, *pesha,e o dallālī ast.*

BRUSH—Here is a brush, where is the paint?—*īn jā kalam-i-mū ast, ammā rang kujā?*

BUD.—These trees are beginning to bud.—*īn darakhthā shuguftan mī-gīrand.* Or, *īn ashjār (dar shuguftan) and. (ba shuguftan dar āmada.)*

BUILD—I am going to build a house.—*man makāme ta'mīr khwāham kard.*

BULL—Are you not afraid of the bull?—*az ān nar-gāw (na mī-tarsed)? (shumā-rā khauf nīst; mukhauwaf na mī-bāshed.)*

BUNDLE—Where shall I put this bundle?—*īn bukcha-rā kujā bi-(guzāram). (niham; kunam; dāram.)*

BURDEN—The whole burden rests upon me.—*tamām bār bar man ast.* Or, *man ḥāmil-i-tamām ḥaml-am.*

BURN—Burn this waste paper.—*īn kāghaz-i-raddī-rā ba ātash bi-dih.* Or, *īn kirtas-i-bekār-rā ba ātash bi-soz.* Or, *īn kāghaz-i-muhra-dār-i-mardūd-rā ba ātash biyandāz.*

BURST—They drank so much that they almost burst.—*ān kadar naushīdand ki (nazdīk būd ki shikam-i-eshān bi-tarkad). (dar tarkīdan-i-shikam-i-eshān chīze na mānda būd.)* Or, *eshān ba ān kadar āshāmīdand ki mi'da,e eshān karīb ba tarkīdan būd.*

BURST—He burst open the door.—*o darwāza-rā shikasta wāz kard.*

BURY—He is gone to bury his father.—*o padar-i-khud-rā dafn kardan rafta ast.* Or, *(o barā,e tajhīz wa takfīn) kardan-i-wālid-i-khud rafta ast. (o barā,e tadfīn.)*

BUSINESS—He is come on business.—*o barā,e (shughl)e āmada ast. (kāre; 'amale; ḥājate.)*

BUSY—He is now very busy, and cannot speak to you.—*ilḥāl (ba kār mashghūl ast) wa ba shumā sukhan guftan na mī-tawānad. (mashghūl-i-khidmat ast; ba kār o bār ishtighāl dārad; ba mu'āmila mushtaghal ast; dar band-i-khwesh ast.)*

BUY—I am going to the bazar to buy paper.—*man ba bāzār az barā,e kharīdan-i-kāghaz mī-ravam.*

C.

CABLE—That ship has lost her anchor and cable.—*langar wa (kals)-i-ān jahāz har dū gum shuda ast. (katāj.)*

CAGE—This cage is to keep birds in.—*īn kafs barā,e nigāh dāshtan-i-paranda ast.*

CAKE—Where did you get that cake?—*ān (kulīcha) az kujā ba dast-i-shumā rasīd. (ka'k; bishmāt; kurs; raghīf, pl. rughūf.)*

CALAMITY—This will be to them a great calamity.—*īn (āfat-i-'azīm)*[1] *bar eshān wāḳi'* (*khwāhad shud*).[2] [1](*ṣadma,e kabīr ; balā,e buzurg ; ḥādiṣa,e kalān.*) [2](*khwāhad uftād.*)

CALUMNIATES—He calumniates a person.—*o dar postīn-i-mardume mī-(uftād).* (*ravad.*) Or, *o ḥarf-i-kase mī-chīnad.* Or, *o ghībat-i-kase mī-kunad.* Or, *o dar 'aib giriftan-i-kase mī-koshad.* Or, *o kase-rā ghaibat mī-kunad.* Or, *o kase-rā ba badī yād mī-kunad.* Or, *o nām-i-kase ba zishtī mī-barad.*

CALCULATION—Have you made a calculation of the cost?—(*ḥisāb*)-*i-kharj jam' karda ed?* (*takhmīna ; muwāzina.*)

CALF—The cow and calf were together.—*māda-gāw wa gūsāla baham yak jā būdand.*

CALM—The sea was quite calm.—*baḥr bi-l-kull (be mauje) būd.* (*bi lā amwāj ; mushauwish na.*)

CANVAS—Where did you buy this canvas?—*īn (palās)-rā az kujā kharīda ed?* (*pārcha,e kanū.*)

CAPACITY—He is a person of great capacity.—*ān shakhṣ bisiyār (ḳābilīyat) dārad.* (*isti'dād ; firāsat ; idrāḳ ; kuwat-i-madriḳa ; dirāyat ; ahliyat ; dānish.*) Or, *ān shakhṣ (dar firāsat kāmil) ast.* (*ṣāḥib-i-fazīlat ; ṣāḥib-i-fazl-i-kamāl.*) Or, *'aḳlmandī,e ān kas ba kamāl rasīda ast.*

CARD—He has sent me a card of invitation.—*ān kas ruḳ'a,e da'wat-rā ba jihat-i-man firistāda ast.*

CARE—I have no care on that account.—*dar ān sukhan (parwā) na dāram.* (*fikr ; andoh ; muẓāyaḳa ; dil-tangī.*) Or, *az ān amr gham na (dāram).* (*khuram.*) Or, *dar dil-i-khud tafakkure-rā rāh na diham.*

CARRYING—I saw him carrying a load on his head.—*man o-rā dīdam ki bār bar sar guzāshta mī-ravad.*

CASE—Have you no case for your razor?—*āyā (ghilāf-i-teg-i-dallākī)-rā na dāred?* (*jild-i-ustura ; miyān-i-mardūda.*)

CASE—This is a very difficult case.—*īn murāfa'a (mushkil ast).* (*ishkāl dārad.*)

CASH—In cash and notes I have 100 dinars.—*dar wajh-i-naḳd wa barāt ṣad dīnar dāram.*

CAST—Cast away this clothing.—*īn libās-rā bar andāz.*

CASTLE—He lives near the castle.—*nazd-i-ḥisār sukūnat dārad.* Or, *ḳarīb-i-(ḳasr) manzil dārad.* (*ḥiṣn.*)

CATALOGUE—Have you seen to-day's catalogue of the sale?—*(fihrist)-i-ḥarrāj-i-imroz-rā dīda ed?* (*fard; fard-i-tafṣīl.*)

CATCH—Catch that bird.—*ān murgh-rā* (*akhẕ bi-kun*). (*bi-gīr.*)

CAUSE—Do you know the cause of this?—*(sabab)-i-īn amr mī-dāned?* (*'illat; wāsiṭa; mūjib.*)

CAUTION—What need of all this caution?—*ḥājat-i-īn chunīn (khabardārī) chīst?* (*dūr-andeshī; 'āḳibat-andeshī; dūr-bīnī; iḥtiyāṭ; ḥaẕar; iḥtirāz; taḥẕīr; ḥazam; ta,ammul; tadbīr.*)

CAUTIOUS—We ought to be cautious, and not to give offence to any.—*marā bāyad ki az zuhmat dādan-i-kase ḥaẕar bi-kunem.* Or, *marā bāyad ki tā tawānem az aẕīyat dādan-i-kase (khabardār sharem).* (*hoshiyār bāshem; ḥaẕūr sharem; ṣāḥib-i-iḥtiyāṭ bāshem; muḥtaẕir bāshem.*)

CEASE—When will you cease talking?—*az sukhan guftan kai (farāghat) khwāhed kard?* (*mauḳūf; farāgh; tawaḳḳuf.*) Or, *kai tark-i-ḥaraf zadan khwāhed (girift)?* (*kard.*)

CELEBRATED—He is a very celebrated poet.—*o shā'ire bisiyār (mashhūr) ast.* (*ma'rūf; mauṣūf; nāmwar; mu'aẕẕam; mamdūḥ.*) Or, *o 'ullūma,e shu'arā ast.*

CENTRE—Place this in the centre.—*īn chīz-rā dar (miyān bi-guẕār).* (*markaz-i-dā,ira bi-nih.*)

CENTURY—This house has been built a century.—*ṣadd sāl guẕashta ast ki īn khāna (ma'mūr shuda ast).* (*-rā ta'mīr karda and.*)

CERTAIN—I am certain of it.—*man īn-rā yaḳīn mī-dānam.*

CERTIFICATE—I have received from him a certificate of my capacity and good conduct.—*man az o ba nisbat-i-ḳābilīyat wa nek-raftārī,e khud (sifārish nāma),e yāfta am.* (*dast aweza; liyāḳat nāma.*)

CHAFF—Here is plenty of chaff, but no wheat.—*īn jā post-*

i-gandum firāwān ast magar gandum na. Or, *īn hama sabos ast (nishān)-i-gandum dar īn nīst.* (*aṣar*.)

CHAIN—Is this chain made of iron?—*āyā īn zanjīr-(i-āhanī) ast?* (*az āhan sākhta shuda*.)

CHALK—He writes only with chalk.—*ān kas faḳat ba gil-i-safaid mī-nawīsad.*

CHANGE—He is gone there for change of climate.—*az barū,e (tabdīl)-i-āb o hawā ān jā rafta ast.* (*taḥwīl*.)

CHANGE—I must change my clothes.—*marā bāyad ki libās-i-khud-rā ('iwaz) bi-kunam.* (*badal; tabdīl; ibdāl*.)

CHANGEABLE—His mind is changeable.—*o mutalauwinu-t-tab' ast.* Or, *o sahilu-l-ḳabūl wa sahilu-l-tark ast.* Or, *o ṣūbitu-l-ḳaul wa ḳā,imu-l-mizāj nīst.* Or, *dil-ash (be ḳarār) ast.* (*nā pāyadār*.) Or, *o talauwun dar tab' dārad.*

CHAPTER—What chapter shall we read?—*kudām bāb bi-khwānam?*

CHARACTER—He bears an excellent character.—*o nām-i-neko dārad.* Or, *o (ṣāḥib-i-'izzat) ast.* (*zū-l-'izzat; mu'azzaz; mukarram*.)

CHARCOAL—She draws pictures with charcoal.—*ān zan taṣwīrhā ba zaghāl mī-kashad.*

CHARGES—He charges very high.—*o girān ḳīmat mī-kunad.* (*khwāhad*.)

CHARITABLE—They are very charitable to the poor.—*eshān ba (gharībūn karīm) and.* (*muflisān raḥīm; maflūkān sakhī; mustamandūn sadḳat-bakhsh*.)

CHARITY—He bestows a great deal in charity.—*o bisiyār (khairāt) mī-dihad.* (*ṣadḳa; taṣadduḳ; zakāt; zakwat*.)

CHARMING—That is a charming song.—*ān naghma,e dil-fareb ast.* Or, *ān sarod-i-ṭarab-angez ast.* Or, *ān samā'-i-dil-āwez ast.* Or, *ān tarannum-i-dil-faroz ast.* Or, *az ān naghma kase-rā shor wa ṭarab dar sar mī-āyad.* Or, *az ān naghma kase dar ḥālat wa ṭarab mī-bāshad.*

CHEAP—These articles, I think, are cheap.—*man mī-pindāram ki īn chīzhā (arzān) and.* (*kam-ḳīmat; subuk-bahā*.)

CHEAT—They cheat whom they can.—*eshān ba har kase ki mī-tawānand fareb mī-dihand.* Or, *eshān ba har kase ba ḳadar-i-maḳdūr-i-k͟hud* (*g͟hadr mī-kunand*). (*g͟habn mī-sāzand; ḥila-bāzī mī-kunand; g͟hābin mī-bāshand.*)

CHEESE—This cheese is not good.—*īn panīr* (*k͟hūb nīst*). (*lih shuda ast.*)

CHICKENS—I saw a hen with ten chickens.—*man mākiyāne-rā ba ma' dah chuza dīdam.*

CHIEF—My chief reason for coming here was to see you.—*man maḥẓ az barā,e dīdan-i-shumā īn jā āmada am.*

CHILDHOOD—I have known him since his childhood.—*man az* (*ḥīn-i-ṭufūliyat-ash*) *o-rā dānista am.* (*aiyām-i-kodakīyash; 'ahd-i-k͟hurdīyash.*) Or, *az waḳte ki o ṭifl būd man o-rā shināk͟hta am.*

CHILDISH—These are but childish employments.—*īn faḳat* (*būzī,e kodakān*) *ast.* (*kār-i-kodakī.*)

CHINA—He has lately come from China.—*dar īn rozhā az chīn wārid shuda ast.*

CHIPS—Why are all these chips here? take them away.—*īn k͟hāshāk chirā īn jā ast? ān-rā bar dār.* Or, *īn* (*tarāshhā*) *chirā īn jā uftāda ast? ān-rā bi-bar.* (*rezahā,e chūb.*)

CHISEL—Cut this stick with a chisel.—*īn chūb-rā ba mabẓa' bi-tarāsh.*

CHOICE—It was his own choice to do so.—*o īn kār ba k͟hwāhish-i-k͟hud kard.* Or, *īn chunīn kār kardan o-rā ik͟htiyār uftād.*

CHOOSE—Choose which of these two you please.—*az īn har dū tā yake-rā* (*bi-guzīn*). (*bi-chīn; ik͟htiyār bi-kun; ḳabūl bi-kun.*)

CINNAMON—Mix some cinnamon with the other spices.—*ham-rāh-i-dīgar maṣāliḥ dār-chīnī* (*biyāmez*). (*mak͟hlūṭ bi-kun; tak͟hlīṭ bi-kun; ik͟htilāṭ bi-kun; bi-k͟hisānīd.*)

CIRCLE—They all sat in a circle.—*eshān* (*dar ṣūrat-i-dā,ira*) *nishastand.* (*halḳa zada.*)

CIRCUIT—He is now judge of circuit.—*ān ilḥāl ḥākim-i-dā,ir ast.*

CIRCULATED—They have circulated notices in all directions. —*eshān ba har ṭaraf ishtihār-rā jārī karda and.* Or, *ba har ṭaraf iṭṭila' nāmajāt-i-eshān ijrā yāfta and.*

CIRCULATION—Has this coin been long in circulation?—*īn ẓarb az bisiyār waḳt murauwaj būda ast.* Or, *āyā bisiyār sāl ast ki īn sikka (rā,ij būda) ast. (rawāj yāfta.)*

CIRCUMSTANCE—This is a curious circumstance—*īn ṣāniḥa,e 'ajīb ast.* Or, *īn kaifiyat-i-bisiyār nādir ast.* Or, *īn aḥwāl-i-khailī ta'ajjub āmez ast.*

CIVIL—He is one of the civil servants of the Government. —*o yake az ṣāḥibān-i-(amūr-i-daulat) ast. ('amāl-i-mamlakat.)*

CIVIL—He is civil to every one.—*o ba har kas (mulā,im) ast. (salīm; halīm; adib; mu,addab; ṣāḥib-i-sulūk; khalīk; ṣāḥib-i-adab; mulāṭif; laṭīf.)* Or, *o ba har kas ta'ẓīm mī-kunad.*

CIVILITY—He received us with great civility.—*o ba bisiyār (tawāẓu') bā mā mulāḳāt kard. (khulḳ; ikhlāḳ; adab; sulūk; mulā,imat; mudārā; mudārāt.)*

CLAIM—Have you any further claim on that gentleman's estate?—*bar imlak-i-ān ṣāḥib iddi'ā,e dīgar dāred?*

CLEVER—She is more clever than he.—*ān zan az ān mard (dānā)-tar ast. (zakī; hoshiyār; kār-guzār; maṣlaḥat-guzār; pukhta.)*

CLIENT—The attorney has written to his client.—*ān wāḳil ba muwakkil-i-khud nawishta ast.*

CLIMATE—The climate of Europe is very fine.—*āb o hawā az mulk-i-maghrib bisiyār khūb ast.*

CLIMBING—He was climbing a tree.—*o (bālā,e darakht bar) mī-raft. (bar darakht bālā.)*

CLINGS—That child clings to its mother.—*ān farzand ba (mādar-i-khud mī-chaspad). (gardan-i-mādar-i-khud mī-awezad.)*

CLOAK—Leave your cloak in the hall.—*(bālā-posh,)-i-khud-rā dar dālān bi-guzār. (farghul; labāda; jawāliḳ.)*

CLOCK—What is the time by the church clock?—*ba sā'at-i-*

('iṣā-kada) chi sā'at ast? (*'ibādat-gāh; khāna,e khudā; ma'bid; sijda-gāh; masjid; jāmi'.*)

It is near two o'clock.—*ḳarīb ba sā'at-i-dū ast.*

CLOTHE—They clothe the naked and feed the hungry. —*(barahnagān)*[1]*-rā mī-poshānand wa (gursinagān)*[2]*-rā khurish mī-dihand.* [1]*('ariyānān; 'ārīyān.)* [2]*(jau'ānān; jā,i'ān; mujī'ān.)*

CLOUDS—There are many clouds, it will rain heavily.—*(abr) bisiyār ast bārān khūb khwāhad bārīd.* (*megh; saḥāb; ghaim.*)

COACHES—Some people ride in coaches, others go on foot. —*ba'ẓe mardumān ba kāliska sawār mī-shavand wa ba'ẓe piyāda mī-ravand.*

COARSE—This cloth is very coarse.—*īn pārcha bisiyār (kuluft) ast.* (*ṣalb; hanguft; jar'ab; nāfij; satīkh; sitabr.*)

COBWEB—Sweep away that cobweb.—*ān parda,e 'ankabūt-rā jārūb bi-kun.* Or, *ān (nasju-l-'ankabūt)-rā az īn jā bi-rūb.* (*malkāṭ.*)

COLD—I feel very cold.—*man burūdat-i-'aẓīm iḥsās mī-kun-am.* Or, *marā (sardī),e bisiyār maḥsūs mī-shavad.* (*bard.*)

COLLECTED—A great crowd was collected.—*majma'-i-buzurg majmū' shud.* Or, *jamā'at-i-kaṣīr (jam') shud.* (*mujtami'; mujamma'.*)

COLLECTOR—He is now collector (revenue-officer) of Shīrāz.—*o ilḥāl (taḥṣīldār)-i-shīrāz mu'aiyan ast.* (*muḥaṣṣil; bāzhgīr; khirāj-i-jam'alīl; jāmi'-i-maḥāṣil.*)

COLLEGE—Have you seen the new college?—*(madrassa,e nau) dīda ed?* (*dāru-l-'ilm-i-jadīd.*)

COLOUR—What colour shall I make it?—*rang-i-ān chi bi-sāzam?*

COMB—Take a comb, and comb your head.—*(shāna)*[1] *bi-gīr wa mūyat-rā (shāna bi-kun)*[2]. [1]*(mashṭ; sarkhāra.)* [2]*(mashṭ bi-kun; shāna bi-zan.)*

COMFORT—This affords me comfort in my trouble.—*īn dar (zaḥmat)-am tasallī mī-bakhshad.* (*taṣdī; ranj; īẕā.*) Or, *īn chīz (marham-i-dil-i-majrūḥ-am) mī-bāshad.* (*tasallī bakhsh-i-dil-hazīn-am.*) Or, *īn chīz marā az takhlīf takhfīf mī-dihad.*

Commanded—He commanded me to go instantly.—*ān shakhṣ ba man ḥukm farmūd ki hamān sā'at ān jā bi-rau.*

Commence—Let us now commence our work.—*biyā tā* (*shurū'-i-kār-i-khud*) *bi-kunem.* (*kār-i-khud-rā shurū'.*)

Commend—I commend your prudence.—*man* (*ta'rīf*)-*i-tamīz-i-shumā mī-kunam.* (*taḥsīn; āfrīn; tauṣīf; sitā,-ish.*) Or, *imtiyāz-i-shumā muwāfiḳu-r-rā,e khud-am mī-āyad.* Or, *ḥazar-i-shumā marā pasand mī-āyad.* Or, *dūr-andeshī,e shumā-rā taṣwīb mī-namāyam.*

Commerce—Baghdad is a first-rate seat of commerce.—*Baghdād 'umda,e jā,e tijārat ast.*

Committed—He was committed to prison.—*o dar maḥbas firistāda shud.* Or, *o dar ḳaid-khāna mursil shud.*

Common—The common people speak thus.—*mardumān-i-'awāmm īn chunīn mī-goyand.* Or, *īn kalām muḥāwara,e 'āmm ast.*

Communicate—Communicate this to him.—*īn sukhan bado* (*baiyān*) *bi-kun.* (*ẓāhir; iẓhār; ashkāra; fāsh; huwaidā.*)

Communicative—He appears to be very communicative.—*ma'lūm mī-shavad ki o* (*zabān-i-darāz dārad*). (*bisiyār go,e ast.*)

Companion—I have no companion.—*man* (*muṣāḥibe*) *na dāram.* (*mūnise; ma,nūse; ham-ṣuḥbate.*)

Company—I am glad to be in his company.—*khāṭir-i-man ba mukhāliṭat-i-o mail dārad.* Or, *ṣuḥbat-ash ghanīmat shumāram wa khidmat-ash yaghmā.* Or, *ba munādimat-ash raghbat mī-*(*dāram*). (*kunam.*) Or, *ba ikhtilāt-i-o bisiyār mail mī-dāram.* Or, *az muṣāḥibat-ash khailī khūshnūd am.* Or, *murāfiḳat-ash marā khūsh mī-āyad.* Or, *sūd-i-sarmāye 'umr-am wiṣāl-i-o-rā mī-shumāram.*

Compare—Let us compare my writing with yours.—*biyā tā khaṭṭ-i-marā ba khaṭṭ-i-shumā* (*dar tashbīh bi-dārem*). (*tashbīh bi-kunem; muḳābil bi-kunem.*) Or, *biyā ki mā har dū khaṭṭ-i-khud-rā dar mīzān-i-taswiyat bi-nihem.*

COMPASS—A ship sails by the compass.—*ba (wāsiṭa),e kutb-numā jahāz rāh mī-ravad. (waṣīla.)*

COMPASSION—Why act thus? have you no compassion?—*chirā chunīn kār mī-kuned? shumā-rā (ruḥmat) na mī-āyad? (raḥm; shafḳat; talaṭṭuf; tarraḥum.)* Or, *chirā ba kase chunīn kār mī-kuned? dil-i-shumā na mī-sozad.*

COMPETENT—Are you competent to the work?—*shumā liyāḳat-i-īn kār dāred?* Or, *shumā ḳābil-i-īn 'amal hasted?* Or, *īn kār az dast-i-shumā bar mī-tawānad āmad?*

COMPLAINED—I have long complained of his conduct.—*bisiyār aiyām (guzashta ast ki az af'āl-ash(shikāyat) karda am. (nālish; gila; faryād; shakwā.)*

COMPLAINTS—He is always coming with complaints.—*o hamesha (daftar-i-shikāyat bāz) mī-kunad. (faryād; nālish.)*

COMPLETE—He is complete master of this language.—*o dar īn zabān kāmil ast.* Or, *o dar īn lisān kāmiliyat dārad.*

COMPLIMENTS—Sir, Mr. —— sends his compliments to you. —*ṣāḥibā ṣāḥib-i-fulān ba shumā (salām mī-rasānad). (taslīm mī-dihad.)*

COMPLY—Unless you comply, what can I do?—*agar shumā rāẓī nīsted chi bi-kunam?*

COMPOSING—He is now composing a grammar.—*o ilḥāl ṣarf wa naḥw (taṣnīf) mī-kunad. (ta,līf.)*

COMPREHEND—I don't exactly comprehend this.—*īn sukhan (-rā khūb na mī-fahmam). (dar 'aḳl-i-man durust na mī-āyad.)*

CONCEAL—I cannot conceal this matter.—*man na mī-tawānam ki īn sukhan-rā (pinhān dāram). (nihufta kunam; mastūr kunam; ikhfā kunam; makhfī dāram; kitman* or *maknūn dāram; bi-posham.)*

CONCEIT—Let us not indulge conceit.—*marā bāyad ki (khud-pasand na bāshem). (az khud na bālem; 'ujb dar sar na dārem; dimagh-i-behūda na pazem; khud-bīn na bāshem.)*

CONCEITED—That man is very conceited.—*ān shakhṣ khailī (mu'jib) ast.* (*maghrūr; khud-pasand; khud-rā,e; khud-bīn; khud namā; mudammagh.*)

CONCEIVE—I conceive you are in the right.—*man mī-dānam ki shumā ba rāh-i-rāstī mī-bāshed.*

CONCERN—This business does not concern you.—*īn kār ba shumā (ta'alluḳ na dārad).* (*'alāḳa na dārad; muta'alliḳ nīst*). Or, *dar īn kār dakhl-i-taṣarruf-i-shumā nīst.* Or, *shumā dar īn kār dakhl-i-taṣarruf na mī-tawāned kard.*

CONCERN—This has caused her much concern.—*az īn kaifiyat ān zan bisiyār mutafakkir gardīd.* Or, *īn amr sabab-i-iẓṭirāb-i-'aẓīm-i-ān nisā shud.*

CONCLUDE—It is time to conclude.—*ilḥāl waḳt-i-(tamām kardan) ast.* (*khatm; khātima.*)

CONCLUSION—This is the conclusion of the chapter.—*īn (ākhir)-i-bāb ast.* (*khatm; ikhtitām.*)

CONDITION—My condition is better than his.—*ḥāl-i-man az aḥwāl-i-o (bihtar) ast.* (*aḥsan.*)

CONDUCT—His conduct is to be commended.—*raftār-ash lā,iḳ-i-ta'rīf wa taḥsīn wa āfrīn ast.*

CONDUCT—Who will conduct us thither?—*ān jā ki marā (rahbarī khwāhad kard)?* (*khwāhad burd; dallālat khwāhad kard.*)

CONFESS—I confess my conduct has been amiss.—*man (i'tirāf) mī-kunam ki kirdar-i-man ma'yūb ast.* (*iḳrār.*) Or, *man khud ḳā,il-am bar ānki dar īn amr chīze taḳṣīr az man ṣādir shuda ast.* Or, *man muḳirr-i-bad raftārī,e khud hastam.*

CONFIDENCE—I place no confidence in what they say.—*bar sukhanhā,e eshān (wuṣūḳ-i-man nīst).* (*i'tibār* or *i'timād na mī-kunam.*) Or, *i'tiḳād-i-ḳaul-i-eshān nazd-i-man bi-l-kull sāḳiṭ shud.*

CONFINED—He is now confined in jail.—*o ilḥāl dar ḳaid-khāna ḳaid karda shuda ast.* Or, *o ilḥāl dar maḥbas maḥbūs ast.* Or, *o aknūn dar (sijn nihāda) shuda ast.* (*zindān basta; ḳaid-khāna muḳaiyid.*)

CONFIRMED—Is the news confirmed or not?—*īn khabar (sābit) shuda ast yā na?* (*taḥḳīḳ; muḳarrar.*)
CONFUSED—You have confused my work.—*kār-i-marā (darham barham) karda ed.* (*pareshān.*)
CONFUSED—He is confused.—*ān kas (sarāsīma) ast.* (*pareshān; mutaraddid; sar-gardān; hairān; muẓṭarib; muẓṭarīr.*)
CONNECTION—There is no connection in these sentences.—*īn jumlahā ba yak dīgar (nisbat na dārand).* (*bā ham munsalik nayand; muntaẓim nayand; 'alāḳa na dārand.*)
CONQUERED—He conquered the whole country.—*o bar tamām mulk (tasalluṭ yāft).* (*musalliṭ shud.*) Or, *zer-i-ḥukm-i-khud tamām diyār-rā dar āward.* Or, *o sulṭanat-rā dar taṣarruf-i-khud dar āward.* Or, *mamālik-i-aṭrāf (o-rā musallam shud).* (*dar ḳabẓ-i-o dar āmad.*) Or, *o tamām mulk-rā (maftūḥ) kard.* (*fatḥ.*) Or, *o mutaṣarrif-i-nāḥiyat shud.*
CONSCIOUS—I am not conscious of having said so.—*man yād na (dāram) ki īn chunīn sukhan gufta am.* (*mī-kunam; mī-gīram.*) Or, (*dar yād-i-man na mī-āyad*) *ki īn chunīn gufta am.* (*ba yād-am na mī-āyad; man ba yād na dāram.*)
CONSENT—Do you consent to my proposal?—*ba rā,e-i-man (rāẓī hasted)?* (*raẓā mī-dihed.*) Or, *tajwīz-i-marā ḳabūl mī-kuned?* Or, *tadbīr-i-man maḳbūl-i-khāṭir-i-shumā ast?*
CONSENT—She went without my consent.—*baghair-i-(ijāzat)-i-man ān ẓa'īfa raft.* (*iẓn; rukhṣat; raẓā,e.*)
CONSEQUENCE—That is of no consequence.—*ān ẓarar na dārad.* Or, *muẓāyaḳa,e īn m'anī nīst.* Or, *dar ān maẓāyaḳa nīst.*
CONSIDER—I will consider it.—*bar ān amr tajwīz khwāham kard.* Or, *dar band-i-ān kār khwāham būd.* Or, *dar īn sukhan taṣauwir khwāham namūd.* Or, *īn sukhan-rā ba mīzān-i-ḳiyās khwāham sanjīd.* Or, *ān-rā ba ḳadam-i-tafakkur khwāham paimūd.*
CONSIGNED—The cargo of the vessel was consigned to him.

—*tamām būr-i-jahāz ba (ḥawāla),e ān kas būd.* (*taḥwīl; sapurd; tafwīẓ.*) Or, *tafwīẓ-i-tamām maḥmūla,e jahāz-rā bado kardand.*

CONSTITUTION—His constitution is very strong.—*ṭabī'at-ash bisiyār (ḳawī) ast.* (*mustaḳīm; maẓbūṭ; mustaḳill.*)

CONSULT—Let us consult upon this subject.—*biyā tā dar īn (maṣlaḥate maṣlaḥat) bi-kunem.* (*amr mashwarat; kār ṣalāḥ.*)

CONTAIN—How much indigo will this box contain?—*dar īn ṣandūḳ chi ḳadar nīl khwāhad gunjīd.* Or, *īn ṣandūḳ chi ḳadar nīl khwāhad girift.*

CONTEMPT—Treat no one with contempt.—*dar kase (naẓar-i-ḥiḳārat) ma kun.* (*ba chashm-i-istiḥḳār naẓar; taḥkīr; karāhat*). Or, *kase-rā ba chashm-i-istikhfāf ma nigar.* Or, *dar kase ba dīda,e istikrāh ma bīn.* Or, *kase-rā* (*khurd*) *ma dān.* (*khwār; ḥaḳīr; taṣghīr; makrūh; karīh.*)

CONTENT—I am content with what I have.—*har chi dāram* (*bar ān ḳāni' mī-bāsham*). (*bā ān dar mī-sāzam; bar ān ḳinā'at mī-kunam; az ān pā,e ḳinā'at dar dāman-i-salā-mat mī-kasham.*)

CONTENTIOUS—They are very contentious.—*eshān bisiyār* (*fitna-angez*) *and.* (*jang-jū; siteza-rū; fasād-āward; mufsid; sharīr; 'arbada-khū; khar-khasha sāz.*) Or, *nizā' bar pā mī-namāyand.* Or, *ba jang-i-har kas mī-*(*khezand*). (*uftand.*) Or, *ba khilāf wa inkār-i-har kas ba dar mī-āyand.* Or, *da'wa,e muḳawamat bar pā mī-kunand.*

CONTINUAL—There is a continual noise in this place.—*dar īn jā* (*shor*) *hamesha mī-mānad.* (*ghaugha; ghol; ghal-ghala; hāw-hū; āshob.*)

CONTRACTED—The Honourable Company contracted for the paper.—*jamā'at-i-bahādur az barā,e īn kāghaz ijāra kard.*

CONTRARY—Contrary winds detained the vessel.—*az bād-i-mukhālif jahāz bāz mānd.* Or, *bād-i-ghair-shurṭa jahāz-rā* (*tauḳīf*) *kard.* (*mutawaḳḳif.*)

CONTRIVANCE—By what contrivance shall we go there?—*ba kudām ḥīla mā ān jā khwāhem raft?*

CONVENIENT—Will your coming to-morrow be convenient? —*fardā āmadan-i-shumā (munāsib) khwāhad būd?* (*muwāfiḳ; shā,ista.*)

CONVERSATION—Are you fond of conversation?—*shauḳ-i-guft-gū dāred?* Or, *shā,iḳ-i-mukālima hasted?*

CONVEY—Will you please to convey this article to him?—*az rū,e (luṭf) īn chīz-rā bado bi-rasāned?* (*alṭāf; talaṭṭuf; mihrbānī.*)

CONVINCED—I am convinced what you say is true.—*man yaḳīn dāram ki ān chi shumā mī-goyed rāst ast.*

COOKS.—Having no cook, he cooks for himself.—*ān shakhṣ ghiẓā,e khud-rā khud (mī-pazad) ki ṭabbākh na dārad.* (*bar sīkh mī-kunad; bar tāba biriyān mī-kunad.*)

COOLER—It is cooler to-day than it was yesterday.—*imroz az dīroz sard-tar ast.*

COPY—Please copy this for me.—*luṭf farmūda barā,e man (naḳl)-i-īn bi-kuned.* (*sawād.*)

CORD—Buy some cord, and tie these things together.—*kadre (rīsman-i-bārīk) bi-khared wa īn chīzhā-rā ba-ham bi-banded.* (*ḥabal.*)

CORK—Is there no cork to this bottle?—*āyā īn kūza,e shīsha (sidād) na dārad?* (*ṣimām.*)

CORN.—There was great plenty of corn last year.—*dar sāl-i-guẕashta (ghalla,e firāwān paidā shud.* (*madākhil-i-ghalla bisiyār būd; ba ifrāṭ ghalla paidā shud.*)

CORRESPONDENCE—Have you any correspondence with him? —*shumā bā o (murāsalat) dāred?* (*nawisht wa khwānd.*) Or, *shumā ṭarīḳa,e rusul wa rasā,il bā o jārī dāred?*

CORRUPT—Society here is extremely corrupt.—*ṣuḥbat-i-majlis-i-mardum-i-īn jā bisiyār (maẕmūm) ast.* (*mashnū'; makhẕūl; maḳbūḥ; fāsid; mukhlaf.*)

COUCH—Move this couch into the other room.—*īn (rakht-i-istirāḥat)-rā ba ūṭāḳ-i-dīgar bi-bared.* (*shaft; shafta; ṣufa; mihād; mahd,* pl. *muhūd.*)

COUNCIL—He is a member of the Supreme Council.—*o yake az ahl-i-majlis-i-('uẓmạ) ast.* (*a'lā ; ūlạ.*) Or, *o mushīr-i-mashwarat-i-a'ẓam ast.* Or, *ān āghā yake az* (*mushāwirān*)*-i-khāṣṣ ast.* (*mudabirān.*)

COUNSEL—Let us regard good counsel.—*mārā bāyad ki* (*maṣlaḥat-i-nek ḳabūl dārem*). (*az naṣīhat-i-'āḳilān rū-kash na shavem.*)

COUNT—Count over the money I gave you.—*pūle ki man ba shumā dādam bi-shumāred.*

COUNTERFEIT—This is a counterfeit coin.—*īn ashrafī ḳalb ast* (gold). Or, *īn zarb-i-sīm daghal ast* (silver).

COTTON—This country produces much cotton.—*dar īn mulk pumba,e bisiyār paidā mī-shavad.* Or, *zirā'at-i-pumba dar īn jā ba ifrāṭ ast.*

COUNTRY—This is my native country.—*īn* (*waṭan*)*-i-man ast.* (*maulid ; waṭan-i-aṣlī ; mauṭin.*)

COUPLE—Buy for me a couple of razors.—*barā,e man juft-i-tegh-i-dallākī bi-khared.*

COURAGE—You possess greater courage than I.—*shumā az man ziyāda* (*shujā'at*) *dārad.* (*himmat ; mardānagī ; dilīrī ; dilāwarī ; jur'at ; tajāsur.*)

CRACK—There is a crack in this basin.—*īn aftāba mū dārad.* Or, *īn lagan shigāf dārad.* Or, *īn ṭasht mū-dar shuda ast.*

CREATED—God created the world.—*allah-ta'ālạ getī-rā afrīd.* Or, (*ḥaḳḳ-ta'ālạ*) *jahān-rā az 'adm ba wujūd āward.* (*ḥaḳḳ-i-jalla wa a'llạ ; bāra ; khudā,e 'azza wa jalla ; īzd ; musabbabu-l-asbāb ; musta'ān.*)

CREATOR—God is the Creator of all creatures.—*khudā khāliḳ-i-hama* (*khalā,iḳ*) *ast.* (*kā,ināt; maujūdāt ; makh-lūḳāt.*) Or, *ṣāni'-i-kull maṣnū'āt khudā ast.*

CREDIT—I agree to give you three months' credit —*shumā-rā tā si māh* (*dain*) *mī-diham.* (*muḳārizat.*)

CREDIT—This action does him great credit.—*az īn kār o-rā bisiyār* (*i'tibār*) *ḥāṣil mī-gardad.* (*'izzat ; sharraf ; āb-rū ; 'azz wa waḳār ; karam ; ikrām ; iḥtirām.*)

CREDITORS—His affairs are in a bad state, therefore he has called together his creditors.—*kār o bār-ash muntashīr shuda ast lihaẕā ḳarẕ-khwāhān-i-khud-rā ṯalabīda ast.*

CREEP—Look how these lizards creep along the wall.—*bi-bīn chigūna īn (karfashān) bar dīwar chaspān mī-ravand. (kalpakān.)*

CREEPER—This is called a creeper.—*īn nihāl-rā (arghaj) mī-nāmand. (buḳlatu-l-bārida.)*

CRIME—What crime has he committed?—*o chi taḳṣīr karda ast?* Or, *chi ḳuṣūr az o sar zada ast?* Or, *chi (khaṯā) az o ṣādir shuda ast? (ẕamb,* pl. *ẕunūb.)*

CRITICISE—He will criticise our composition.—*o (iṣlāḥ-i-taṣnīf)-i-marā khwāhad kard. (taṣḥīḥ-i-musauwada.)*

CROOKED—That line is crooked.—*ān saṯar kaj ast.*

CROSSED—He crossed the river.—*az āb-jū,e guẕasht.* Or, *(bar) rūd 'ubūr kard. (az.)*

CROWS—He rises when the cock crows in the morning,—*o ba (bāng)-i-khurūs bar mī-khezad. (mujarrad-i-āwāz; sharṯ-i-āwāz.)*

CROWD—There was a great crowd of people.—*ān jā kalān (izdihām)-i-khalḳ būd. (jam'īyat; ijtimā'; jamā'at; majma'.)*

CRUELTY—They delight only in cruelty.—*eshān az (be raḥmī) khūshī ḥāṣil mī-namāyand. (sang-dilī; dil-azārī; sab'īyat; ẕulm; sitam.)* Or, *khailī khurramī ẕāhir mī-kunand ki ba dīgarān durushtī ba (kār barand). ('amal āwarand.)*

CRUMBS—The birds will pick up all these crumbs.—*parandagān īn rezhā,e nān khwāhand chīd.*

CRUSHED—He was crushed under the carriage-wheel.—*zer-i-charkh-i-'arāba (mas,ḥūḳ sākhta) shud. (taḳwīb sākhta; raṣīṣ karda.)*

CRY—What is the matter? why do you cry out so?—*chi ḥālat ast? chirā chunīn ghul wa shor mī-kuned?*

*CUBITS—The length of this stick is about four cubits.—(darāzī)¹,e īn chūb ḳarīb ba chahār (gaz)² ast. ¹(ṭūl; ṭawālat.) ²(sā'id; dast; mirfaḳ.)

CULTIVATED—This land is cultivated.—īn zamīn (mazrū') ast. (ma'mūr; ābād; zira'at karda shuda; kishta shuda.)

CUNNING—They are by nature cruel and cunning.—bi-ṭ-ṭab' be raḥm wa ḥarīf and. Or, bi-l-aṣl sang-dil wa g̱haddār and. Or, bi-l-nafs ẓūlim wa na"ār and. Or, bi-ẕ-ẕūt be shafaḳat wa makkār and. Or, ba k̲h̲ū dil azār wa 'aiyār and.

CUPS—They drink tea out of cups and saucers.—eshān chā ba finjān wa nalbakī mī-k̲h̲urand.

CURED—I have been cured by that physician.—man az ān (ṭabīb) shifā yāfta am. (pizishk.)

CURIOUS—This is a curious shell.—īn ṣadaf ('ajīb) ast. (badī'.) Or, īn gosh-i-māhī nādir ast. (g̱harīb.)

CURTAINS—Are there no curtains to this bed?—āyā īn bisṭar pasha-parān na dārad? (parda; sidāfat; sajf.)

CUSTOM—Do you know how this custom arose?—shumā mī-dāned chigūna īn rāh o rasm (uftād)? (paidā shud; sar bār āward; sar bar zad; rū,e namūd.) Or, k̲h̲abar dūred ki īn rasm-rā ki (ījād) kard? (ikhtirā'; waẓa'.)

CUT—You have cut this pen so that it won't write.—īn ḳalam-rā chunān ḳaṭ' karda ed ki az ān nawishtan na mī-shavad.

CYPHER—One and a cypher make ten.—agar ba hindasa,e yak ṣifr dāda shavad hindasa,e dah gardad.

D.

DAMAGE—Has the cargo received any damage?—āyā nuḳṣān ba (mahmūla),e jahāz rasīda ast? (bār.)

DAMP—This house is very damp.—īn k̲h̲āna bisiyār (nam-nāk) ast. (namgīn; marṭūb; marṭab.)

---

* The breadth of one finger = 2 barley corns, end to end.
   „   „   = 7   „   „   side by side.
   „   one hand = 8   „   „   end to end.
   „   six hands = 48 „   „   „   „
   „   „   = one cubit = 18 inches."

DANCING—They spend their time in singing and dancing.—*eshān wakt-i-khud-rā dar (sarā,īdan wa rakṣīdan) mī-guzrānand. (naghma pardākhtan wa rakṣ kardan; tarannum zadan wa rākiṣ shudan.)*

DANGER—Why are you afraid? there is no danger.—*chirā mī-tarsed? hech khauf-i-khatar nīst.*

DARE—I dare not do as you say.—*ān chi shumā mī-goyed jur,at-i-kardan na dāram.*

DARK—The night was very dark.—*shab bisiyār (tārīk) būd. (tār.) Or, lail khailī daijūr būd.*

DARKNESS—They are in gross darkness.—*eshān dar (ẓulmat) and. (ẓulmāt; ẓalāmat.)*

DATE—What is the date of his letter?—*tārīkh-i-taḥrīr-i-khaṭṭ-ash chīst?*

DAWN—They rise at dawn.—*eshān (ba wakt-i-saḥar) bar mī-khezand. (dam-i-subḥ; 'alū-ṣ-ṣabāḥ.)*

DAY—What time of the day is it?—*chi sū'at ast?*

DEAD—I saw a dead snake on the roadside.—*ba kinār-i-rāh (mār-i-murda-rā) dīdam. (afʿa,e-rū lā ḥaiy.)*

DEADLY—Its wound is fatal; its poison deadly.—*zakhm-ash muhlik ast; zahr-ash(kātil). (halāhal.)*

DEAF—He is deaf, and can hear nothing.—*o (kar) ast. hech na mī-tawānad shunīd. (ṣumm; aṣamm; girān-gosh.)*

DEALS—He deals honestly with everybody.—*ba har kase ba (rāst-bāzī) sulūk mī-kunad. (diyānat; īmāndārī; sadākat-kārī; ikhlāṣ.)*

DEAR—The goods you have purchased, I think, are very dear.—*ān asbāb ki shumā kharīda ed, ba rū,e man bisiyār (girān) ast. (girān-bahā; besh-kīmat.)*

DEAR—He is very dear to me.—*ba dil-i-man bisiyār ('azīz) ast. Or, man bā o muḥabbat-i-kāmil dāram. Or, o (munis)-i-dil-am ast. (maḥrum-i-raz.)*

DEBTOR—A debtor is one who owes money.—*karẓdār kase ast ki (karẓ) dārad. (wām; dain; bidih.)*

DECEIT—They only live by deceit.—*eshān fakṭ ba fareb (guzrān mī-kunand). (aukāt ba sar mī-burand; rozgār mī-guzrānand.)* Or, *eshān ba (makr) zindagī mī-kunand. (daghā; talbīs; ghabn; ghadr; kaid; makādat; khad'at; rīw; zark; shaid; 'aiyārī.)*

Deceitful—What is there more deceitful than the human heart?—*az dil-i-insān kudām chīz (daghā-bāz)-tar ast. (ghadīr; ghadār.)*

Deceived—You have been deceived by them.—*shumā badeshān (maghbūn shuda ed). (ghabn khurda ed; mughālata sākhta shuda ed; taghlīt karda shuda ed.)* Or, *shumā az eshān daghā yāfta ed.*

Decide—Let him decide this question.—*bi-guzār ki o (īn mu'āmala-rā faiṣal) bi-kunad. (infisāl-i-īn amr.)*

Declined—I asked him, but he declined.—*man az o pursīdam, magar o (inkār kard). (rāzī na shud; sar bāz zad.)*

Decreases—That article decreases in value daily.—*roz ba roz ḳīmat-i-ān chīz (kam) mī-shavad. (habūṭ; sāḳiṭ; ḳāsid.)*

Decree—A decree was passed for this purpose.—*az barā,e īn ḥukme mukarrar shud.* Or, *ba jihat-i-īn (ḥukm-i-ḳazā mu'aiyan`gardīd). (tauḳī'-i-farmā ijrā yāft.)*

Deduct—I shall deduct so much from his account.—*az ḥisāb-ash īn ḳadar pūl (ḳaṭ) khwāham kard. (wazī'at; waz'.)*

Defect—Do you see any defect in this?—*āyā dar īn hech ('aib) mī-bīned?* (pl. *'ayūb; tawaffun.)*

Defence—He made his defence in court.—*dar 'adālat 'uzr-i-khud-ash kard.* Or, *dar maḥkama ma'zarat-i-khud-rā zāhir kard.* Or, *dar 'adālat (i'tizār)-i-khud-rā ba 'arṣa,e zuhūr āward. (tazkiyat.)*

Defendant—The statements of both defendant and plaintiff were heard.—*kalām-i-mudda'ī-'alaihī wa mudda'ī shunīda shud.* Or, *izhār-i-(āsāmī wa faryādī) istimā' karda shud. (rāfi' wa dā'ī.)*

Deficient—They are not deficient in sense.—*eshān (kam-'aḳl) nayand. (kam-ḥausila.)* Or, *dar tamīz kamī na dārand.*

DEFORMED—She is deformed in person.—*badan-i-ān zan (bad-shakl) ast. (bad-haikal; karīhu-l-mauẓar.)*
DEFRAYS—Who defrays the costs of his learning?—*kharch-i-āmokhtan-ash ki mī-dihad?* Or, *ikhrājat-i-ta'līm-ash ki adā mī-kunad?*
DEJECTED—His mind is much dejected.—*dil-i-o bisiyār (ranjīda) ast. (āzurda; pur-gham; pur-alam.)*
DELAY—There is much delay in this—*dar bāb-i-īn amr (der) bisiyār ast. (tawakkuf; ta,akhīr; dirangī; mihlat; mukūs̤; tahāwun; tasāhul.)*
DELIBERATE—This is my deliberate opinion.—*īn tajwīz-i-man (mustakīm) ast. (mustakill.)*
DELICATE—Her hands and feet are very delicate.—*dast wa pā,e ān ma'shūka bisiyār (nāzuk) ast. (nafīs; latīf; nigārīn; nāzanīn.)*
DELICIOUS—This is a most delicious morsel.—*īn lukma bisiyār lazīz ast.* Or, *maza,e īn lukma khailī nafīs ast.* Or, *lazzat-i-īn lukma marghūb ast.*
DELIGHTED—I was greatly delighted to see him.—*az dīdan-i-o bisiyār khūshnūd shudam.*
DELIRIOUS—The fever is so violent that he is sometimes delirious.—*tab chandān sakht ast ki gāhe (be hosh) mī-shavad. (madhūsh; haẓiyān; hazzār.)* Or, *bukhār chandān maḥrūr ast ki gāhe (o-rā ghash mī-dihad). (ḥawāss-i-o mī-bāzad.)*
DELIVER—Did you deliver to him my message?—*paigham-i-marā bado (dāded)? (rasānīded.)*
DELIVERED—He delivered his brother from much distress.—*o barādar-i-khud-rā az (ḥālat-i-kharābī najāt dād). (bisiyār harānī khalāṣ kard; nā musā'adat-ı-rozgār rihānīd.)*
DEMAND—Have you any demand upon me?—*āyā az man hech (dā'iya) dāred? (da'wā; iddi'ā; bāz khwāst.)* Or, *āyā az man chīze iktizā dāred?*
DEMANDED—He demanded more than his due.—*o az karẓ-i-khud ziyāda (ṭalabīd). (ṭalab kard; da'wā kard; dar khwāst kard; iddi'ā kard.)*

Denies—He denies having said this.—*o az guftan-i-īn sukhan (inkār mī-kunad). (munkir mī-shavad; ibā mī-kunad; tanākur mī-kunad.)*

Depart—When do you intend to depart?—*irāda,e raftan kai dāred?* Or, *kai alwidā' khwāhed shud?* Or, *īn jā-rā kai alwidā' khwāhed guft?* Or, *az īn jā kai (tashrīf khwāhed burd)? (murakhkhaṣ khwāhed shud; ḳadam ranja khwāhed farmūd; 'inān-i-'azīmat mun'aṭif khwāhed sākht; nuhẓat khwāhed farmūd.)*

Depend—I cannot depend upon what he says.—*ān chi o mī-goyad bar ān i'timād na mī-tawānam kard.*

Depends—That depends upon the state of my health.—*ān kār ba tan-durustī,e man (mauḳūf) ast. (muta'alliḳ; munḥaṣir.)* Or, *īn sukhan ba (ṣiḥḥat)-i-man muta'alliḳ ast. (ṣaḥīḥu-l-badan.)*

Depository—This is a depository for books.—*īn kutub-khāna ast.*

Depth—What is the depth of this tank?—*'umuḳ-i-īn ḥauẓ chīst?* Or, *'amīḳ-i-īn (ghadīr) chīst? (āb-gīr; āb-dān; burka; tālāb.)*

Description—What description gave he of the place?—*o waṣf-i-ān jā chi sān kard?* Or, *o ān jā-rā chigūna baiyān kard?* Or, *o (sharḥ)-i-ān jā chigūna dād? (tafṣīl; tafsīr.)*

Deserve—They deserve to be punished.—*eshān (lā,iḳ-i-sazā) and. (mustaḥiḳḳ-i-'aẕāb; ḳābil-i-taubīkh; sazāwār-i-'itāb.)*

Desire—I will desire him to do so.—*man ḥukm khwāham kard ki o ham chunīn bi-kunad.*

Desire—I have a great desire to see him.—*man ba dīdan-i-o (ishtiyāḳ-i-kāmil dāram). (mushtāḳ hastam; shā,iḳ hastam.)* Or, *silsila,e shauḳ-i-dīdan-i-o dar gardān-i-dil-i-khud dāram.* Or, *dar sar-i-dīdār-i-o mī-bāsham.*

Desirous—He is very desirous of seeing you.—*o barā,e dīdan-i-shumā bisiyār (arzūmand) ast. (mushtāḳ.)*

Despairs—He despairs of accomplishing his object.—*o (tawaḳḳu' na dārad) ki kār-i-khud-rā ba sar rasānad.*

(*ma,yūs ast ; nā ummed ast.*) Or, *o-ra* (*ummed-i-ba sar āwardan*)-*i-kār-i-khud nīst.* (*rijā-i-sar anjām dādan ; intizār-i-tamām kardan.*)

DESPAIRED—He despaired of life.—*o dil-i-khud-rā az jān* (*burīd*). (*bar dāsht.*) Or, *o dil-i-khud-rā az jān bar girift wa ba marg nihād.* Or, *o dast-i-khud az jān shust.* Or, *tushna wa be nawā rū,e bar khāk wa dil bar halāk nihād.* Or, *az zindagānī ma,yūs gasht.* Or, *az 'umr ummed bar kand.*

DESPISE—We ought not to despise any one.—*bāyad ki mā kase-rā* (*khwār*) *na dārem.* (*hakīr.*) Or, *bāyad ki mā az kase* (*mutanaffur na bāshem*). (*nafrat* or *karāhiyat* or *tanaffur na kunem.*)

DESTROYED—Your papers have been all destroyed.—*kāghaz-hā,e shumā hama* (*tabāh*) *shuda ast.* (*kharāb ; makhrūb.*)

DETAIN—Do not detain the servant any longer.—*khādim-rā ziyāda az īn* (*muntazir ma guzār*). (*dar intizār ma dār* or *guzār ; mu'attal ma dār.*)

DETERMINED—I am determined to do as you recommend.—(*kasd*) *karda am ki ba hasb-i-nasīhat-i-shumā 'amal bi-kunam.* (*tasmīm ; nīyat ; 'azm ; mukarrar ; irāda.*) Or, *kamar basta am ki &c.*

DICE—He was ruined by playing at dice.—*o ba sabab-i-ka'batain-bāzī tabāh shud.* Or, *o tamām māliyat-i-khud-rā dar kimār-bāzī* (*talaf kard*). (*ba hawā dād ; ba bād-i-fanā dād ; ba hālat-i-tabāh rasānīd.*)

DICTIONARY—See if this word is in the dictionary.—*dar kitāb-i-lughat bi-bīn ki īn lafz ast yā na.*

DIFFERENT—People are of different opinions on the subject.—*az bābat-i-īn amr mardumān* (*mukhtalifu-r-rā,e and*). (*rā,e mukhtalif dārand ; mutafiku-r-rā,e nīstand ; mukhālifu-r-rā,e and.*)

DIFFICULT—Do you think that the English language is difficult?—*āyā tasauwir mī-kuned ki zabān-i-inglisī* (*mushkil*) *ast?* (*mughlak ; ghalik ; dushwār ; muta'azzir ; muta'assir.*)

Dig—Dig up this jungle.—*īn khārbunhā az bekh bar kan.*

Diligence—It requires only diligence.—*faḳaṭ* (*jidd o jihad*) *ẓarūr ast.* (*koshish ; sa'ī ; 'araḳ-rezī.*) Or, *bāyad ki shumā dar īn kār ba sabīl-i-*(*istimrār*) *mashghūl būshed.* (*mudāwamat ; muwāẓabat ; istidāmat.*)

Diligent—They are diligent scholars.—*eshān ṭālibān-i-mujāhid and.* Or, *eshān talmīẕān-i-miḥnat-kash and.*

Dim—Her eyes are become dim through age.—*az sabab-i-pīrī ẓa'f-i-baṣārat ān zan-rā girifta ast.* Or, *az bā'iṡ-i-kuhn-sālī chashm-i-ān fartūta kam-naẓar shuda ast.*

Dinner—I must go now, it is dinner time.—*waḳt-i-shām ast, marā bāyad raft.*

Direct—This is the direct road to Shiraz.—*īn* (*rāh*) *ba Shīrāz rāst mī-ravad.* (*minhāj ; ṭarīḳ ; sabīl.*)

Direct—Please direct me where to find him.—*az rāh-i-mihrbānī ba man nishān bi-dihed ki bado mulāḳāt kujā bi-kunam.*

Directions—I will attend to your directions.—*man ba naṣīḥat-i-shumā mutawajjih khwāham shud.* Or, *man muṭābiḳ-i-dastūru-l-'amal-i-shumā tawajjuh khwāham kard.*

Dirty—This road is very dirty.—*īn rāh bisiyār* (*ghalīẓ*) *ast.* (*pur az khilāb ; pur az wahal ; najis ; palīd.*) Or, *dar īn ṣirāṭ khas wa khashāk ast.*

Disadvantage—If you act thus, it will be to your disadvantage.—*īn ḳism raftār namūdan dar bāb-i-shumā nuḳṣān dārad.* Or, *agar īn chunīn khwāhed kard, nuḳṣān khwāhed yāft.*

Disagree—They disagree with one another.—*eshān ba yak dīgar* (*mukhālif and*). (*mukhtalif and ; ikhtilāf dārand.*)

Disagreeable—On that account it is very disagreeable.—*ba bā'iṡ-i-ān bisiyār* (*nā muwāfiḳu-ṭ-ṭab'*) *ast.* (*nā maṭbū' ; nā marghūb; nā maḳbūl ; maskhūt ; makrūh.*)

Disagreement—They have disagreement.—*darmiyān-i-eshān* (*nā muwāfiḳat*) *ast.* (*ikhtilāf; nifāḳ ; be-ittifāḳī; naḳīẓ.*)

DISAPPOINTED—I was much disappointed.—*man bi-l-kull (maḥrūm) shudam. (be bahra; nā ummed; ma,yūs.)*
DISCHARGE—He is now able to discharge his debts.—*ḥālan ḳarẓhā,e khud-rā adā mī-tawānad kard.*
DISCIPLINE—This army is without discipline.—*īn 'askar ḳawā'id na mī-dānad.* Or, *īn lashkar (be ḳānūn) ast. (lā niẓām; be ā,in.)*
DISCONTINUED—The custom is now discontinued.—*ilḥāl ān rasm (mansūkh) ast. (mardūd; mauḳūf; nā murauwaj.)*
DISCOURAGES—What you say discourages me.—*ḳaul-i-shumā marā (nā ummed) mī-kunad. (be dil; ma,yūs; takhwīf.)*
DISCOURSE—Come, let us hold a discourse.—*biyā tā mā (makālima) bi-kunem. (kīl-kāl; guft o shunīd; guft o gū,e.)*
DISCOVERED—I have not as yet discovered the thief.—*tā īn waḳt duzd-rā (na yāfta am). (paidā na karda am; ba dast nayāwarda am.)*
DISCOVERY—That is an important discovery.—*ān (ījād) bisiyār khūb ast. (ikhtirā'.)*
DISCRETION—He has ability, but wants discretion.—*o (ḳābilīyat)*[1] *dārad wa lekin (imtiyāz)*[2] *na dārad.* [1]*(liyāḳat; 'aḳl.)* [2]*(tamīz; intibāh; iḥtiyāt.)*
DISGUISE—Let us not use disguise.—*mā-rā fareb kardan na bāyad.*
DISGRACE—To do so would be a disgrace to us.—*az chunīn kardan āb rū,e mā rekhta khwāhad shud.* Or, *az chunīn munkire mā dar chāh-i-infi'āl khwāhem uftād.* Or, *īn fi'l ba mā (maẕillat) khwāhad āward. (ẕillat; karāhiyat; be 'izzatī; be ḥurmatī; faẓīḥat; ṭa'nat.)* Or, *īn fi'l marā (makrūh) khwāhad sākht. (mulauwaṣ.)*
DISHONEST—They are very dishonest.—*eshān khailī (khā,in) and. (be-diyānat; khiyānat-kār.)* Or, *khiyānat-i-eshān ma'rūf ast wa fasād-i-afsad ẓāhir.*
DISLIKE—I dislike their company very much.—*murāfiḳat-i-eshān bi-l-kull pasand na dāram.* Or, *az mukhāliṭat-i-eshān (dar dil-i-man nafrat padīd mī-āyad). (karāhiyat*

or *tanaffur* or *ḥaḳūrat dāram.*) Or, *dar silk-i-muwānasat-i-eshān munsalik shudan na mī-khwāham.* Or, *az māndan dar ḥalḳa,e ṣuḥbat-i-eshān dil-am mutanaffir mī-shavad.*

Dismissed—The king dismissed the courtiers.—*pādshāh ahl-i-darbār-rā (murakhkhaṣ) kardand.* (*rukhṣat; barkhāst.*)

Disobey—I cannot disobey his orders.—*man radd-i-farmān-i-o-rā na mī-tawānam kard.* Or, *man ḥukm-ash na mī-tawānam shikast.* Or, *man na mī-tawānam ki (sar-i-khud az ḥalḳa,e inkiyād-ash bar āwaram).* (*'adūl-i-ḥukm-ash bi-kunam; ghāshiya,e muṭāba'at-i-o az dosh-i-khud biyāndāzam.*)

Displays—Herein he displays great talent.—*dar īn maṣlaḥat (isti'dād-i-o ẓāhir mī-shavad).* (*firāsat-ash ba ẓuhūr mī-āyad; idrāk-ash huwaidā mī-āyad* or *gardad; ẓakāwat-ash padīd mī-āyad; majāl-ash rukh mī-namāyad.*)

Displeased—They became much displeased.—*eshān bisiyār (nā khūsh) shudand.* (*mukaddar; ranjīda; āzurda; tīra.*)

Dispose—Can you dispose of these goods for me?—*īn āshiyā barā,e man ba (tijārat) farokhtan mī-tawāned?* (*saudā.*)

Dispute—What is the dispute between you two?—*mā bain-i-shumā har dū chi takrār ast?* Or, *darmiyān-i-shumā wa o chi (baḥs) ast?* (*mubāhaṣa; ibtiḥāṣ; ḳaẓiya; shor wa fasād; nizā'; munāza'at; tanāzu'; khar-khasha; mujādila.*)

Dissatisfied—Why are you dissatisfied?—*chirā (ghair-rāẓī) hasted?* (*az īn amr be rāẓī; nā rāẓ.*)

Dissolves—The sun dissolves the snow.—*āftāb yakh-rā gudāzad.* Or, *partāb-i-shams baraf-i-nishasta-rā āb mī-kunad.* Or, *tāb-i-khurshed yakh basta-rā ḥall mī-kunad.*

Dissuade—Cannot you dissuade him from doing so again.—*shumā o-rā (man' na mī-tawāned kard) ki o īn chunīn kār bāz na kunad?* (*māni' na mī-tawāned shud.*)

DISTANCE—What distance is the city of Baghdād from this place?—*az īn jā shahr-i-baghdād chi mufāṣala dārad?* Or, *mā bain īn jā wa shahr-i-baghdād chi ḳadar* (*tufāwat*) *ast?* (*ba'd; ba'īd; maṣāfat; musāḥat.*)

DISTENDED—Having distended his belly with food, he at last perished.—*shikam-i-khud-rā pur az ṭa'ām karda* (*halāk shud*). (*faut shud; jān-i-zindagīyash lab rez gasht; safr-i-ākhirat kard; intiḳāl kard; riḥlat namūd; ba halāk rasīd; jān ba ḥaḳḳ taslīm kard; jān-ash bar āmad; az dāru-l-fanā ba dāru-l-baḳā shitāft; az jahān-i-fānī rakht bar bast; dā'ī ajal-rā labbaik guft; az jān widā' kard;* nearly, *jān-ash ba lab āmad; ba jān āmad.*)

DISTINCT—His articulation is clear and distinct.—*talaffuẓ-i-o ṣāf wa* (*ṣaḥīḥ*) *ast.* (*makhraj-dār.*)

DISTINGUISH—I cannot distinguish these two letters.—*mā-bain-i-īn ḥaraf har dū* (*tafrīḳ*) *na mī-tawānam kard.* (*farḳ; imtiyāz; tamīz; mumaiyiz.*)

DISTRESS—She is now in great distress.—*aknūn ān bānū dar* (*muṣībat-i-shadīd*) *uftāda ast.* (*sakhtī; iẓṭirāb-i-tamām; tang-dastī.*) Or, *ilḥāl ān sādat* (*dil-āshufta*) *ast.* (*parāganda wa pareshān khāṭir; khasta-khāṭir.*) Or, *bekh-i-jum'īyat-i-khāṭir-ash burīda ast wa gul-i-ārām pazhmūda.*

DIVERSION—This is their diversion.—*īn kār* (*bāzī,*)*e eshān ast.* (*tafarruḥ-i-dil; nuzhat-i-khāṭir; nishāṭ-i-ḳalb; ṭarab-i-dil.*) Or, *az īn kār imbisāṭ-i-ṭab' ḥāṣil mī-namāyand.*

DIVIDEND—A dividend on his estate will be paid the first of next month.—*ba tārīkh-i-ghurra,e māh-i-āyanda* (*ḳisṭ*) *az māl-ash dāda khwāhad shud.* (*maḳsum; ḥiṣṣa; pāra; bakhsh.*)

DOCK—The vessel is now in dock repairing.—*jahāz ilḥāl barā,e* (*marammat dar sunār*) *ast.* (*ta'mīr shudan dar ta'mīr-khāna,e jahāz.*)

DOCTRINE—This is very strange doctrine.—*īn uṣūl-i-bisiyār 'ajīb ast.*

DOSES—He has taken two doses of this medicine.—*o dū*

khurāk az īn dawā khurda ast. Or, *o dū habba,e dārū girifta ast* (pills).

DOUBLE—Double this string, and then it will do.—*īn rassan-i-bārīk dū tā bi-kun ki kifāyat khwāhad kard.* Or, *īn rassan (muẓa'af bi-kun) tā ba kār bi-khurad.* (*dū chand bi-kun; taẓ'īf bi-sāz; aẓ'āf bi-kun.*)

DOUBLE—Is this paper double?—*āyā īn kāghaz dū tā ast?*

DOUBTFUL—It is doubtful if he will come.—*dar bāb-i-āmadan-ash (shakk) ast.* (*shubha.*) Or, *āmadan-ash tashkīk dārad.*

DRAG—How can one horse drag such a load?—*yak asp chigūna īn chunīn bār mī-tawānad kashīd?* Or, *ba chi ṭaur yak asp kifāyat-i-kashīdan-i-īn bār mī-kunad?*

DRAIN—There is a drain under the house.—*zer-i-khāna (badar-rau) ast.* (*āb-guzar; āb-lūla; jūb; āb-rāh; bālū'at.*)

DRAUGHT—Give me one draught of water.—*yak (kaṭrā),e āb ba man bi-dih.* (*jur'a.*)

*DRAW—Make the figures, and draw a line.—*hindasā bi-nawīs wa (khaṭṭ) bi-kash.* (*saṭar.*)

DRAWBACK—Is there any drawback on these goods?—*bar īn asbāb hech (dastūrī) ast? (waẓī'at,* pl. *waẓū,ī'.*)

DREAM—I thought thus in a dream.—*dar khwābe īn chunīn (dīdam).* (*khayāl dāshtam; muḥlim sākhtam.*)

DRESS—He cares nothing about dress.—*o az bābat-i-libās-i-khud fikre na dārad.* Or, *o ba (poshāk) dil-i-khud-ash na mī-dihad.* (*tahzīb kardan; libās kardan.*)

DRESSING—Wait a little, he is now dressing.—*andake ṣabr bi-kun ki o (libās mī-poshad).* (*mulabbis mī-gardad; libās-i-khud-rā dar bar mī-kunad.*)

DRIVES—He always drives very fast.—*o hamesha kūliska zūd mī-rānad.*

DROVE—I drove a nail into the wall.—*man mekhe-rā dar dīwār (zadam).* (*koftam.*)

---

* Parallel line *khaṭṭ-i-mutawāzī*.   Right line *khaṭṭ-i-mustakīm*.
  Circular „   „ *mustadīr*.   Curved „   „ *munḥanī*.

DRUM—The drum is beat in the fort daily.—*roz-marra ṭabl dar ḥiṣṣār nawākhta mī-shavad.* Or, *har roz naubat dar ḳil'a mī-zanand.*

DRY—This house is exceedingly dry.—*īn khāna ba ghāyat (khushk) ast.* (*ṣamīl; ṣāmil.*)

DUE—That note falls due to-morrow.—*mī'ād-i-ān barāt fardā tamām khwāhad shud.* Or, *wa'da,e ān dast-āwez fardā ba itmām mī-rasad.*

DUMB—She is both dumb and deaf.—*ān zan ham (gung) wa ham kar ast.* (*lāl; bukum.*)

DUNCE—He has learned so long, yet he is a dunce. —*muddat-i-madīd khwānda ast wa lekin hanoz ablā,e ast.*

DURABLE—Real and durable happiness is not attainable on earth.—*dar īn dunyā (rāḥat-i-aṣlī wa mustaḳīm) muyassar nīst.* (*'aish-i-'ain wa pā,edār; ṭarab wa nashāṭ-i-bāḳī; 'ishrat-i-aṣlī wa ḳā,im; masarrat-i-ḥaḳīḳī wa ṣābit; imbisāṭ-i-mukhliṣ wa mustamarr.*)

DUTY—Do these articles pay duty?—*āyā īn ajnās maḥṣūl-i-gumruk dārand?* Or, *āyā īn asbāb gumrukī ast?*

DWARF—A dwarf is one who is little in stature.—*shakhṣe-rā (kotāh-ḳadd) mī-goyand ki ḳadd-i-kotāh dārad.* (*ḳaṣīru-l-ḳadd.*)

DWELL—Dwell where he may, he is unhappy.—*jā,e ki o manzil dārad nā khūsh mī-mānad.*

E.

EAGER—He is eager to undertake the business.—*o (mushtāḳ) ba kār kardan ast.* (*shā,iḳ.*) Or, *o ishtiyāḳ ba kār kardan dārad.* Or, *khwāhish dārad ki kār ba ẕimma,e khud gīrad.*

EAGERNESS—He shows great eagerness to learn.—*ba dars khwāndan khwāhish-i-bisiyār (ẓāhir mī-kunad).* (*mī-namāyad.*) Or, *ba tadrīs dil-i-khud-rā mī-dihad*

Ears—You deafen one's ears by your noise.—*ba shor-i-shumā goshhā,e mardum (pāra) mī-sharad. (darīda.)*

Earn—In this way I can earn ten rupees a month.—*badīn ṭaur man dah rūpaiya fī māh ḥāṣil mī-tawānam kard.*

Earnest—You are not in earnest in what you say, you only jest.—*shumā rāst na mī-goyed, shaukhī mī-kuned.* Or, *dar guftār-i-shumā sadāḳat nīst balki (tamaskhur) ma'lūm mī-sharad. (ẓarāfat; mazāḥat; hazal-bāzī; ṭīb-āmezī; muṭāyaba-go,ī; bazla-go,ī; laṭīfa-go,ī; imbisāṭ.)*

Earnest—I gave ten rupees earnest money.—*man dah rūpaiya ba ṭarīḳ-i-(bai'āna) dādam. (ta'rīb; tamsīk.)*

Earthenware—They manufacture earthenware.—*eshān (ẓurūf-i-sifālī) mī-sāzand.*

Earthquake—An earthquake was felt lately in this neighbourhood.—*chand roz guẓashta dar īn nawāhī larza,e zamīn būd.* Or, *ḳabl az īn dar īn maḥalla (jumbish)*[1]*-i-zamīn (āmad)*[2]. [1]*(tazalzul; zulzala.)* [2]*(uftād.)*

East—Do you travel east, west, north, or south?—*āyā ba sū,e mashriḳ, yā maghrib, yā shumāl yā janūb safr mī-kuned?*

Ease—He lives at ease.—*o rozgār-i-khud-rā dar (khūshī) mī-guẓrānad. (rāfāhiyat; ārām; 'aish; farāghat; rāhat; tana'um; asā,ish; fārighu-l-bālīgh; farkhanda-ḥālī; khurramī; amn; imbisāṭ.)*

Easy—I will set you an easy lesson.—*shumā-rā sabaḳ-i-(āsān) khwāham dād. (sahl; ṣalīṣ; as,hal.)*

Eat—[In Persia people eat according to their class, thus:—*ḥakīmān ser khurand; 'ābidān nīm ser khurand; zāhidān tā sadd ramḳ khurand; pīrān khurand tā 'araḳ bar āyad; jawānān khurand tā ṭabaḳ bar gīrand.*]

Ebb—The tide has begun to ebb.—*jazr-i-āb-i-baḥr shurū' shuda ast.* Or, *āb-i-baḥr (jazr shudan girifta) ast. (dar ibtidā,e jazr.)*

Eclipse—There will soon be a solar eclipse.—*ba'd az chand roz (kusūf-i-āftāb wāḳi') khwāhad shud. (āftāb maḥjūb; āftāb giriftā.)*

Edge—I saw him sitting on the edge of the river.—*ba kinār-i-nahr o-rā nishasta dīdam.* Or, *man o-rā dīdam ki ba lab-i-rūd nishasta būd.*

Editor—Who is the editor of this newspaper?—*(muhtamim)-i-īn akhbār-nāma kīst?* *(rāḳim-i-waḳā,i'; muharrir-i-akhbār-nāma; waḳā,i-nigār; muwallif.)*

Education—She has written a book on education.—*īn 'āḳila kitābe dar bāb-i-tarkīb-i-ta'līm (taṣnīf) karda ast. (ta,līf.)*

Effect—I gave him medicine, but it had no effect.—*man o-rā dārū dādam, ammā (aṣar na kard).* *(mu,aṣṣir* or *fā,idamand* or *az o fā,ida na shud.)*

Eggs—I saw a bird's nest with four eggs.—*āshiyāna,e murgh dīdam ki dar ān chahār baiza būd.*

Elegant—Hers is an elegant house.—*khāna,e ān zan pur takalluf wa khūsh-namā ast.*

Eloquent—He is very eloquent.—*o bisiyār (faṣīḥ) ast. (balīgh; zabān-āwar; sukhan-rān; sukhan-guzār; faṣāḥat-pardāz; ṣarīḥu-l-kalām; sarī'u-l-kalām; ṣāḥib-i-balāghat.)* Or, *o bisiyār faṣāḥat dārad.*

Empire—China is a large empire.—*mulk-i-chīn mamlakat-i-(wasī') ast.* *(mabsūṭ; basīṭ; madīd; mamdūd; kushāda.)*

Employ—Who will employ such people?—*ba chunīn ashkhāṣ ki (shughl) khwāhad dād?* *(khidmat; kār o bār.)* Or, *chunīn mardumān-rā ki (mashghūl) khwāhad kard? (mushtaghal.)*

Employer—Who is your employer?—*(munīb)-i-shumā kīst?* *(āghā; āḳā; kār-farmā.)*

Employment—What is your employment?—*(kār)-i-shumā chīst?* *(shughl; ishtighāl; kasb; pesha; ḥirfa; ṣinā'at.)*

Empty—This house is empty, it has no tenant.—*īn khāna khālī ast kirāyadār na dārad.*

Enclose—Enclose my letter in yours.—*andar-i-khaṭṭ-i-khud ruḳ'a,e marā bi-kun.* Or, *khaṭṭ-i-marā dar khaṭṭ-i-khud (malfūf) bi-kun.* *(ṭai; lifāfa.)*

Encourages—Your former kindness encourages me.—

mihrbānī,e sābiḳa,e shumā marā ummed mī-dihad. Or, *talaṯṯuf-i-peshīn-i-shumā marā (jur,at) mī-dihad. (tasallī.)* Or, *alṯāf-i-salf-i-shumā dil-i-marā (istimālat) mī-kunad. (taḥrīṣ ba kāre.)*

Encouragement—This affords me encouragement.—*īn ba man (tasallī) mī-dihad. (istimālat ; taḥrīs ; taḥrīk.)*

End—There is no end to his talking.—*kīl-kāl-i-o intihā na dārad.* Or, *sukhan guftan-i-o-rā andāza nīst.*

Endeavour—I must endeavour to see him to-day.—*marā bāyad ki imroz (ba mulāḳāt-i-o) sā'ī bi-namāyam. (mulāḳāt bā o ; mulāḳāt-i-o-rā.)* Or, *bāyad ki imroz ba (dīdār-ash ḳaṣd bi-kunam). (sharf-i-mulāzim-ash 'azm bi-sāzam.)*

Endorsement—This note wants your endorsement.—*īn tamassuk dast-khaṯṯ-i-shumā mī-khwāhad.* Or, *bar īn barāt ṣaḥīḥ-i-shumā (ẓarūr) ast. (lāzim ; dar-kār.)*

Enemy—The cat is the enemy of the mouse.—*gurba ba mūsh 'adāwat-i-(ẕātī) dārad. (jibillī ; ṯab'ī.)* Or, *gurba wa mūsh bāham az aṣliyat mukhtalif and.* Or, *mā bain-i-gurba wa mūsh az sirisht (ikhtilāf) ast. (khilāf.)*

Energy—He goes to work with great energy.—*o ba sar garmī,e tamām (ba) kār mashghūl mī-sharad. (dar.)* Or, *o ba ḳuwat-i-dil kār mī-kunad.* Or, *az jān wa dil sa'ī,e kār mī-namāyad.*

Engaged—I have engaged him as my servant.—*man o-rā ba ṯaur-i-naukar (guẕāshta) am. (mukarrar karda ; dar kār mu'aiyan karda.)* Or, *man o-rā naukar dāshta am.*

Engagement—I have an engagement this evening, and therefore cannot accept your invitation.—*imshab (shughle) dāram lihaẕā da'wat-i-shumā ijābat na mī-tawānam kard.* (To dinner, *da'wat-i-ẓiyāfat ;* to a dance, *da'wat-i-raḳṣ ;* to a party, fête, *da'wat-i-mihmānī, da'wat-i-ṣuḥbat.)*

England—Have you ever been in England?—*āyā dar mulk-i-inglistān gāhe būda ed?*

Engraver—Send for an engraver.—*(muhrkane)-rā bi-ṯalabed. (ḥakkāke.)*

ENJOY—I enjoy this season of the year.—*az īn mausim-i-sāl rāḥat mī-gīram.* Or, *az ni'mat-i-ḥaẓẓ-i-mausim (mutamatti') mī-shavam.* (*mutalazziz.*)

ENTER—Who will enter this cave?—*dar īn ghār ki dākhil khwāhad shud?* Or, *dar īn maghāra ki (dakhl) khwāhad kard?* (*madkhal; dukhūl; tadakhkhul.*) Or, *dar īn kahf ki dar khwāhad āmad?*

ENTIRELY—That news is entirely false.—*ān khabar bi-l-kull darogh ast.* Or, *ān afwā sar ā sar kāẕib ast.*

EQUAL—Is your writing equal to mine?—*nawishta,e tū barābar-i-dast-khaṭṭ-i-man mī-bāshad?* Or, *dast-khaṭṭ-i-tū lāf-i-barābarī,e dast-khaṭṭ-i-man mī-zanad?* Or, *taḥrīr-at ba taḥrīr-am (masāwī) ast?* (*mutasāwī.*) Or, *raḳam-at ba raḳam-am sawīyat dārad?*

ENVY—Envy is hateful.—*ḥasad makrūh ast.* Or, *rishk karīh ast.* Or, *ḥasrat (kabīḥ) ast.* (*makbūḥ; maẕmūn.*)

ERRAND—He went there, but forgot his errand.—*o ān jā raft, magar paighām(-i-khud-rā farāmosh kard).* (*az yād-ash raft; -i-khud-rā mansī kard.*)

ERRONEOUS—It is incumbent on us to forsake erroneous opinions.—*mā-rā lāzim ast ki khayālāt-i-maḥāl bi-guzārem.* Or, *ẓarūr ast ki mā (taṣauwirāt-i-nā marbūṭ az dast bi-dihem).* (*rū,ehā,e bāṭil az sar badar bi-kunem.*)

ERROR—Do you see any error in this writing?—*āyā dar īn nawishta hech ghalaṭ mī-bīned?*

ESCAPED—They escaped from prison.—*az zindān rū ba firār nihādand.* Or, *az ḥabs gurekhtand.* Or, *az maḥbas mafrūr gashtand.* Or, *az sijn zaḥūf kardand.*

ESPECIAL—This is a matter of especial moment; the rest is by no means essential.—*īn muḳaddama bisiyār ẓarūr ast, bāḳī hech (muẓāyaḳa nīst).* (*iḥtiyāj na dārad; ẓarūrat na dārad.*)

ESTABLISHED—This law has lately been established.—*īn ḳānūn dar īn rozhā (mu'aiyan) shuda ast.* (*muḳarrar; bar ḳarār; mujāwiz; murauwaj.*)

ESTATE—He left all his estate to his eldest son.—*o hama*

māl-i-khud-rā ba pisar-i-a'zam bawaṣīyat dād. Or, *o murd wa waṣīyat kard ki imlāk-i-man ba pisar-i-buzurg-am dāda shavad.*

Eternal—They who fear God will obtain eternal happiness.—*ānān ki az allāh-i-ta'ālą tarsand rāḥat-i-'uḳbą khwāhand yāft.* Or, *ānān ki az khudā khauf mī-dārand 'aish-i-(mudām) ḥāṣil mī-namāyand.* (*jāwīd; abadī; lā fanā; bā baḳā.*)

European—European articles are now plentiful.—*chīzhā,e farangistān ḥālan (farāwān) and.* (*wāfir; ba ifrāṭ; ba kaṣrat; kaṣīr; ba wafūr.*)

Even—Draw two even lines.—*dū khaṭṭ-ī-mutawāzī bi-kash.*

Evident—It is evident you are mistaken.—(*ẓāhir*) *ast ki shumā ghalaṭī khurda ed.* (*wāẓiḥ; huwaidā; paidā; roshan; āshkār; mubaiyin; ba wuẓūḥ.*)

Evening—I expect to see him this evening.—*man imshab mulāḳāt-i-o-rā* (*intiẓār mī-kasham*). (*muntaẓir mī-bāsham.*) Or, *man imshab muntaẓir-i-tashrīf-i-o mī-bāsham.*

Event—This is a melancholy event.—*īn wāḳi'a ghamnāk ast.* Or, *īn sāniḥā maghmūm ast.* Or, *īn ḥādiṣa andoh-āgīn ast.* Or, *īn ittifāḳ ranj-āwar ast.*

Evidence.—By the evidence produced in court, his guilt was proved.—*ba gawāhī ki dar 'adālat āwardand jurmash* (*ṣābit*) *shud.* (*maṣbūt; ṣabūt; iṣbāt; ṣabāt.*)

Evil—His coming caused much evil to many.—*az āmadan-ash ba jam'-i-ḳaṣīr ḳabūḥat rasīd.* Or, *āmadan-ash mūjib-i-(ranj)-i-unās gardīd.* (*malāl; āshob; dāhiyat.*)

Evil—In this world evil and good are found.—*dar īn jahān badī wa neko,ī bāham maujūd ast.* Or, *dar īn dunyā ḳabāḥat wa ṣalāḥiyat yāfta mī-shavand.*

Exalts—He neither exalts nor abases himself.—*o na khweshtan-rā fuzūnī nihad na tan dar zabūnī dihad.* Or, *na khud-rā tarjīḥ dihad wa na zabūn sūzad.*

Example—That lady is an example to all around her.—*ān bānū barā,e dīgar bānūwān* (*miṣale*) *ast.* (*ẓarbu-l-miṣal; namūdār; unmūdaj; unmūz j.*)

EXCEEDS—He exceeds every one in intelligence.—*o dar dānā,ī (bar hama sabkat mī-barad). (az hama go,e sabkat mī-rabayad; az* or *bar hama musābikat mī-kunad* or *barad.)*

EXCEPTIONABLE—What you propose, I think, is exceptionable in one particular.—*ānchi shumā tajwīz mī-kuned, dar ān yak dakīka (kābil-i-i'tirāẓ) ast. (lā,ik-i-ṣaniyat; mustaṣnī.)* Or, *maṣlaḥate ki shumā mī-farmāyed dar yak nukta jā,e (istiṣnā) mī-bāshad. (i'tirāẓ.)*

EXCHANGE—I will give you this in exchange for that.—*man ba 'iwaẓ-i-ān īn chīz ba shumā khwāham dād.* Or, *man īn chīz-rā ba ān chīz ba shumā (tabaddul) khwāham kard. (badal; 'iwaẓ; tabdīl; istibadāl.)*

EXCHANGE—The exchange is a place where merchants meet to transact business.—*bāzār-gāh jā,e ast ki tājirān barā,e ijrā,e kār-i-tijārat jam' mī-sharand.* Or, *(mabdal) jā,e ast ki dar ān saudāgarān ba jihat-i-dād o sitad bāham gird mī-āyand. (maṣrif.)*

EXCHANGE—I have no desire to exchange situations with you.—*man khwāhish na dāram ki jā,e khud-rā ba jā,e shumā badal bi-kunam.*

EXCITE—Let us excite each other to study.—*biyā ki mā yak dīgar-rā (taḥrīṣ ba ta'līm) bi-kunem. (taḥrīṣ-i-ta'līm; targhīb-i-tadrīs.)*

EXCUSE—Pray excuse my not having formerly written to you.—*az 'adam-i-nawishtan-i-man az rū,e luṭf ma'ẕūr bi-dāred.*

EXCUSES—They made many excuses.—*eshān bisiyār 'uẕr (kardand). (āwardand; nihādand.)* Or, *eshān bisiyār ma'ẕarat khwāstand.*

EXECUTOR—Who is the executor to his estate?—*waṣī',e (warṣa),e o kīst? (irṣ; mīrāṣ; maurūṣa.)*

EXECUTED—Three men were executed for murder last Monday.—*dū shamba guẕashta ba sabab-i-khūn-afshānī si mardumān (tanāb andākhta) shudand. (ba dar kashīda; ṣalāba zada.)*

EXPECT—Do you expect to see him shortly?—*muntazir mī-bāshed ki o-rā zūd bi-bīned.* Or, *mutakki' mī-bāshed ki mulākāt-i-o zūd bi-kuned.* Or, (*mutarakkib mī-bāshed*) *ki mulākāt bado zūd bi-kuned.* (*tawakku' dāred ; ummed dāred ; mutawakki'* or *mutarassid mī-bāshed.*)

EXPELLED—The king expelled him from the land.—*bād-shāh farmūd tā o-rā az diyār* (*ikhrāj*) *kardand.* (*khārij ; jila,e watn ; badar ; berūn.*)

EXPENSE—What will be the expense of doing this?—*az kardan-i-īn kharch chī kadar khwāhad būd?*

EXPERIENCE—He has experience in business.—*o dar kār tajriba dārad.* Or, *o dar kār* (*mushākk*) *ast.* (*ahl-i-imtihān.*)

EXPLAIN—If you ask, he will explain any part which you do not understand.—*ānchi shumā na mī-fahmed agar az o khwāhed pursīd o* (*baiyan*)*-i-ān khwāhad kard.* (*sharh : takrīr ; inkishāf ; tafsīr ; izhār ; ta,wīl ; tabyīn ; kashf.*) Or, *agar az o istifsār bi-farmāyed, mushkil-i-shumā hall khwāhad kard.*

EXPORTED—Much indigo was exported last month.—*dar māh-i-guzashta nīl-i-firāwān az diyār* (*rawāna*) *shud.* (*ikhrāj karda ; nakl-i-iskāl karda ; irsāl dāshta.*)

EXPORTATION—These articles are for exportation.—*īn ajnās muntakla ast.* Or, *īn asbāb barā,e* (*nakl-i-iskāl*) *mī-bāshad.* (*ikhrāj shudan az mulk.*)

EXPRESSED—I don't know how this phrase is expressed in English.—*man na mī-dānam ki īn* (*kalām*)*-rā dar lisān-i-inglisī chi sān tarjuma mī-kunand.* (*istilāh ; 'ibārat ; guftār.*)

EXTENT—This is the extent of their learning.—*hadd-i-ta'-līm-i-eshān badīn jā ast.* Or, *īn muntahā,e sawād-i-eshān ast.* Or, *badīn* (*martaba,e*) *'ulūm-i-eshān rasīda ast.* (*māya,e.*)

EXTRACT—I showed you an extract from this letter.—*man az īn khatt* (*intikhābe*) *shumā-rā namūdam.* (*ijmāle ; kat'-i-chīda.*)

EXTRAVAGANT—His children are extravagant.—*farzandān-i-o (musrif) and.* (*fazūl-kharch; mubazzir; bazl-i-māl mī-kun.*)

EYEBROWS—Her eyebrows are arched.—*abrūyān-i-ān zan ba misal-i-mihrāb and.*

EYES—How can you write if you shut your eyes?—*agar shumā chashm-i-khud-rā bi-banded chigūna mī-tawāned nawisht.*

F.

FABLES—This is a book of fables.—*īn kitāb-i-kissa ast.* Or, *īn kitāb (mushtamil) bar afsānaha mī-bāshad.* (*mu-tazammin.*)

FACE—Her face is fair.—*rang-i-rū,e ān bānū (safaid) ast.* (*sapīd.*)

FACTORY—Formerly there was an indigo factory here.—*pesh az īn (kār-khāna,e nīl) īn jā būd.* (*jā,e kār o bār-i-nīl.*)

FAILED—Had it not been for his assistance, I should have failed in my purpose.—*agar o marā (imdād)*[1] *na mī-namūd (dar husūl-i-mudda'ī,e khud mahrūm shudame).* [1](*i'ānat; mu'āwanat; dast-gīrī; pā,e mardī; wasātat; himāyat; madad.*) [2](*kām-i-dil-i-man bar nayāmade; yād-i-man bar murād-i-dil na rasīde; jām-i-arzūyam hamchunān pur mānde.*)

FAINTED—From fatigue and hunger they fainted away.—*az māndagī wa gursinagī dar ghash āmadand.* Or, *az koft-i-safr wa fākih ghash giriftand.* Or, *az* (*be-tākatī*) *wa jū' be-hosh shudand.* (*furo māndagī; dar māndagī.*)

FAIR—It is now fair, you can go.—*ilhāl āsmān be sahāb ast, shumā mī-tawāned raft.*

FAITHFUL—He is an old and faithful servant.—*o naukar-i-kadīm wa īmāndār ast.*

FALL—He was killed by a fall from his horse.—*o az asp-i-khud ba zamīn uftād wa murd.*

FALSE—Be assured that the report is false.—*yakīn kun ki*

īn khabar (darogh ast). (*pāya na dārad; az zewar-i-ṣidḳ mu'arrā ast; bāṭil ast.*)

FAMILY—He has a large family.—*o 'īyāl-i-bisiyār dārad.*

FAMINE*—So scarce was corn in that city, that it was feared there would be a famine.—*dar ān shahr ghalla chandān* (*ba ḳillat*) *būd ki khauf-i-ḳaḥṭ wa khushk-sālī būd.* (*kamī.*)

FAN—It is now cold, what need have you of a fan?—*ilḥāl sard ast, ẓarūratī,e bād-zan chīst?* Or, *ḥālan mausim-i-sarmā ast, iḥtiyāj-i-*(*bād-kash*) *chist?* (*bād-bezan; mirwaha.*)

FASCINATED—She has entirely fascinated my heart.—*ān parī-rū dil-i-marā burda ast.* Or, *ān ma'shūḳa marā farefta karda ast.* Or, *ba muḥabbat-i-ān māh-rū giriftār āmadam.* Or, *ān sarw-sahī dil-am az dast rabūda ast.* Or, *man dil az dast dāda,e ān māhwash hastam.* Or, *ṭā,ir-i-dil-am asīr-i-dām-i-ān mushkīn-bū,e gardīda ast.* Or, *ān dil-fareb marā az sar o pā dar dām-i-'ishḳ-i-khud andākhta ast.* Or, *ān* (*nāznīn*) *dil-i-marā bi-l-kull ba khud kashīda ast.* (*sayād-i-said-i-dil-i-'āshiḳān.*)

FASTENED—Have you fastened the saddle on the horse?—*āyā bar asp zīn nihāda ed?* Or, *ba asp zīn-rā basta ed?* Or, *asp-rā zīn karda ed?*

FAT—Are these sheep fat or lean?—*īn gūsfandhā* (*farbih*)[1] *yā lāghir*)[2] *and?* [1](*samīn.*) [2](*naḥīf; zaft.*)

FATHERLESS—He died there, leaving a widow and five fatherless children.—*o ān jā murd wa bīwā-zan ba ma' panj farzand yatīm guẕāsht.*

FATIGUED—I am very much fatigued with walking.—*az gasht o gard man kofta am.* Or, *az bisiyār raftan marā* (*koftagī*) *girifta ast.* (*māndagī.*) Or, *dar rāh darāz rāndam wa* (*sust*) *māndam.* (*faro; dur.*)

FAULT—Those things are not yet ready, whose fault is it?—*īn chīzhā hanoz taiyār nayand, khaṭā az kīst?*

FAULTLESS—Who is there that is faultless?—*kudām kas* (*be ḳuṣūr*) *ast.* (*ma'ṣūm; be taḳṣīr; be khaṭā; be gunāh.*)

---

* Plenteous year, *sāl-i-farākh.*

FAVOURABLE—The wind on the river is favourable for going up the river.—*barū,e raftan ba bālā,e nahr bād (muwāfiḳ) ast.* (*shurṭa.*)

FAVOUR—Pray favour me with your address.—*az rū,e luṭf nām o nishān-i-khāna,e khud ba man bi-dihed.*

FAVOURITE—This little boy is my favourite.—*īn ṭiflak 'azīz-i-man ast.* Or, *īn kodak (maḥbūb)-i-man ast.* (*maṭlūb.*)

FEAR—We ought to fear God more than man.—*mā-rā bāyad ki mā har ḳadar ki az mardumān mī-tarsem ziyāda az ān khauf-i-khudā dāshta bāshem.*

FEAR—I would have gone there, but I went not. from fear of its being too late ere I arrived.—*man ān jā mī-raftame wa lekin az khauf-i-der āmadan na raftam.*

FEATHER—This feather is very beautiful.—*īn par bisiyār (khūb-ṣūrat) ast.* (*ḥasīn ; jamīl.*)

FEATURES—The features of these two are alike.—*shakl-i-īn dū tā ba yak dīgar (mushtabī ast).* (*mushābahat* or *ishtibāh dārad ; bāham mī-khurad ; mumāṣil* or *mushabīh ast.*)

FEEBLE—He is now very feeble; he is unable to stir from home.—*ḥālan o bisiyār ẓa'īf ast wa az maḳām-i-khud (ḥarakat) na mī-tawānad kard.* (*taḥarruk ; jumbish.*)

FEEDS—The squirrel feeds chiefly upon fruit.—*mūsh-i-paranda bi-l-khaṣṣa bar mewa zindagī mī-kunad.*

FERRY-BOAT—There is a ferry-boat at this place.—*badīn jā (kishtī,e 'ubūr) ast.* (*ma'bar ; kishtī,e guẕāra.*)

FERTILE—The whole soil of that country is fertile.—*tamām zamīn-i-ān diyār (ser-ḥāṣil) ast.* (*zar-khez ; barūmand ; ḳābil-i-ẓirā'at.*)

FETCH—Go, fetch some fruit out of the garden.—*bi-rau ḳadre mewa az bāgh biyār.*

FEW—I know not if many or few were there.—*man na mī-dānam ki dar ān jā kaṣīr būdand yā ḳalīl.*

FIGHT—It is better to sit still than to fight.—*khāmosh nishastan az bar khāstan ba jang bihtar ast.*

FIGURATIVE—This is a figurative mode of speaking.—*īn*

ṭaur-i-guft-gū tamṣīl-āmez ast. Or, *īn ṭarz-i-kalām (musajja') ast. (muraṣṣa'; mukallal; rangīn.)*

FILE—File the screw.—*īn pech-rā (sohan bi-kun). (bi-sā,e.)*

FILE—File these papers.—*īn kāghazhā-rā (rishta bi-kun). (dar miṣal bi-guzār; dākhil-i-daftar bi-kun.)*

FILL—Fill this tub with water.—*īn ḥauẓ-i-chūbīn-rā az āb pur bi-kun.*

FINAL—The final dividend on his estate will be paid to-morrow.—*farda (ḳisṭ-i-ākhirīn) az imlāk-ash adā karda khwāhad shud. (maḳsam-i-mu,akhkhir.)*

FIND—I have lost my pen, see if you can find it.—*man ḳalam-i-khud-rā gum karda am, bi-bīned magar ān-rā paidā bi kuned.*

FOUND—I found it underneath the table.—*ān-rā zer-i-mez (yāftam). (paidā kardam.)*

FINED—If you do so again, you must be fined.—*agar waḳt-i-dīgar īn chunīn kār bi-kuned (az shumā jurmāna girifta) khwāhad shud. (ba shumā muṣādira nihāda.)*

FINISH—Help me to finish this letter.—*dar (tamām kardan)-i-īn khaṭṭ ba man mu'āwanat bi-kun. (itmām.)*

FIRST—What is now the first thing to be done?—*ilḥāl kudām chīz peshtar bāyad kard.*

FISHERMEN.—I saw some fishermen laying their net.—*chand māhī-gīrān-rā dīdam ki (dām)[1]-i-khud-rā mī-(nihādand).[2] [1](shabka; nashbīl.) [2](gustardand; guzāshtand; andākhtand.)*

FIT—He is not at all fit for this work.—*o lā,iḳ-i-īn kār mutlaḳan nīst.*

FIXED—What day have you fixed upon to go there?—*barā,e raftan badān jā kudām roz muḳarrar karda ed?*

FLAG—I have seen a flag at the fort.—*man 'alame-rā dar ḳil'a dīda am.*

FLAT—What is the shape of the earth, round, flat, square, or oval?—*ṣūrat-i-kura,e zamīn chi ṭaur ast? (mudauwir), mustawī, murabba', yā baiẓawī. (mustadīr.)*

FLATTER—Why do you flatter me so?—*chirā īn chunīn*

ṭaur marā (khushāmad) mī-kuned? (*chāplūsī; tamalluk.*)

FLATTERY—We ought not to listen to the words of flattery.—*na shāyad ki (mā ba sukhanān-i-khush-āmad gosh bi-dihem). (mā sukhanān-i-chāplūsī-rā gosh bi-kunem.)*

FLEE—Why should we flee? there is no danger.—*chirā mā bi-gurezem? khauf nīst.*

FLING—What flowers are these? fling them away.—*īn gulhā chi kism and? ānhā-rā biyandāz.*

FLINT—Fire is produced by flint and steel.—*az (chakmāk zadan) ātash paidā mī-shavad. (kaddāḥ wa fūlād.)* [Tinder, *ḥarrāku; sokhta.*]

FLOAT—It is high water, the vessel will now float.—*wakt-i-madd-i-baḥr ast, ilḥūl jahāz bālū,e āb khwāhad raft.*

FLOCK—I saw there a flock of sheep.—*man ān jā (ghalla),e gūsfand dīdam. (rama.)*

FLOOR—The floor of this room wants repairing.—*farrash-i-īn ḥujra marammat (mī-khwāhad). (ṭalab ast.)*

FLOUR—Bread is made of flour.—*nān az ārd sākhta mī-shavad.*

FLOWERS—You must not pluck these flowers.—*shumā-rā na shāyad ki īn gulhā bi-chīned.* Or, *īn gulhā-rā chīdan na bāyad.*

FLUTE—He can play upon the flute.—*o nai,e labak tawānad (damīd). (nawākht; zad.)*

FLIES—There are a number of flies.—*īn jā magasān pur mī-bāshand.*

FLY—He cut the parrot's wing, lest it should fly away.—*o par-i-ṭūṭī-rā (burīd ki o na parad). (kandīd tā o parwāz na kunad; bar kashīd ki o ba parwāz dar nayāyad; chīd ki o dar parwāz nayāyad.)*

FOG—In the morning there is a thick fog here.—*bāmdād īn jā bukhār-i-ghalīẓ mī-bāshad.* Or, *maṭla'e ṣubḥ īn jā nazhm-i-kaṣīf mī-bāshad.*

FOLD—Fold these things in paper.—*īn chīzhā-rā dar*

kāghaz (malfūf bi-kun). (lifāfa bi-kun; dar naward; tai bi-kun; bi-pech.)

FOLLOW—You go before, I will follow.—*pesh bi-rau man pas-i-tū khwāham āmad.* Or, *sābiḳ bāsh man dar ('aḳab)-i-tū khwāham āmad. (pusht; pai.)*

FOND—I am not at all fond of that fruit.—*ān mewa mutlaḳ (pasand na dāram). (marā khūsh na mī-āyad; marā khūsh nīst.)*

FOOD—What sort of food is this?—*īn (khurāk) chi ḳism ast? (khurish; ḳūt; ta'ām; ghizā.)*

FOOL—He is a great fool.—*o (aḥmaḳe) 'aẓīm ast. (abla,e; nā-dāne; sādah-lauḥe; bewuḳūfe; kharife.)*

FOOLISHNESS—To be angry without a cause is foolishness.—*be sabab (dar khashm āmadan)*[1] *(nā-dānī)*[2] *ast.* [1]*(ghuṣṣa shudan; ḳahr giriftan; ghazb namūdan; rū,e darham kashīdan.)* [2]*(kālīw rangī; khayāl-i-bāṭil.)*

FOOT—Look at the horse's foot.—*ba sum-i-asp bi-bīn.* Or, **dar sum-i-asp (nazar) bi-kuned. (nigāh; mulāḥaẓa.)*

FORBID—Why did you forbid him to come?—*chirā az āmadan-i-īn jā o-rā (man' karded)? (mumāna'at* or *nahī karded; mumtani'* or *māni' bāshed.)*

FORCE—The stream now runs with great force.—*jiriyān-i-nahr ilḥāl ba zor mī-ravad.*

FOREHEAD—He fell down and cut his forehead.—*o ba zamīn uftād wa peshāna,e khud-rā (majrūḥ kard). (ḳaṭa'* or *munḳaṭi' kard; burīd.)*

FOREIGN—He is gone to a foreign country.—*o ba mulk-i-ghair rafta ast.*

FORETELL—Who can foretell what will happen on the morrow?—*ki pesh mī-tawānad guft ki farda az parda,e ghaib chi ḥādiṣa (sādir khwāhad shud)? (rū,e khwāhad dād; wāḳi' khwāhad shud; ba ẓuhūr khwāhad paiwast.)*

FORFEIT—For doing this you must forfeit a rupee.—*az chunīn kardan (ba shumā yak rūpaiya jarīmāna dādanī*

---

* *rā*, in its proper place, may be used instead of *dar*.

khwāhad shud). (*az shumā yak rūpaiya jarīma yāfta khwāhad shud.*)

Forget—Don't forget to tell him what I said to you.—*ānchi ba shumā guftam hamān sukhan ba o bi-goyed,* (*farāmosh na kuned.*) (*nāsī ma shaved.*)

Forgiven—If he had acknowledged his fault, I should have forgiven him.—*agar o ba gunāh-i-khud* (*iḳrār karde man o-rā ma'zūr dāshtame*). (*i'tirāf karde man ma'zarat-i-o ḳabūl dāshtame.*) Or, *agar o bar taḳṣīr-i-khud ḳā,il shude man o-rā mu'āf kardame.* Or, *agar o ḳuṣūr-i-khud ẓāhir karde man az gunāh-ash* (*dar guzashtame*). (*mighfarat dādume.*)

Form—The form of the cypress-tree is quite straight.—*shakl-i-sarw bi-l-kull sahī ast.* Or, *ḳāmat-i-sarw bi-l-kull* (*iḳāmat*) *ast.* (*rāst; ḳā.im.*)

Former—Which part of his letter do you think the best, the former or the latter?—*kudām ḥiṣṣa,e khaṭṭ-ash shumā aulą-tar mī-dāned,* (*awwalīn yā ākhirīn*)? (*maḳaddama yā mu,ākhira.*)

Formidable—The objections you make to my plan are indeed formidable.—(*i'tirāẓ*)*-i-shumā bar khilāf-i-rā,e man dar īn sukhan fī-l-wāḳi' sakht ast.* (*i'rāẓ; ta'arruẓ; īrād.*)

Forsake—Let us not forsake our friends in their distress—*dar ḥālat-i-*(*pareshānī*) *dostān-i-khud-rā na shāyad guzāsht.* (*parāgandagī; furo māndagī; dar māndagī; wā māndagī; shikastagī; iẓtirābī; abtarī.*) Or, *dar ḥālat-i-khastagī mā-rā az ashnāyān* (*farāghat na bāyad dāsht*). (*munḳaṭa' na bāyad shud; ḳaṭa' na bāyad kard; inkiṭā' na bāyad kard.*)

Fortune—He has made a large fortune.—*o māl-i-firāwān jam' karda ast.*

Foundation—The foundation of the house was laid.—(*bunyād*)*-i-khāna nihāda shud.* (*binā; pāya; usās; maḳ'udat; ḳā'idat.*)

Fountains—There are fountains of water everywhere.—

har-jā chashmahā,e āb (*jārī and*). (*mujra and; mujrā* or *ijrā dārand.*) Or, *har jā* (*zah-āb*) *hast.* (*chashma,e zāya.*)

FREE—You are free to do as you please.—*kase māni'-i-shumā na mī-shavad har chi mī-khwāhed bi-kuned.* Or, *ānchi dar mizāj-i-janāb bāshad bi-farmāyed.* Or, *ānchi khwāhed be takalluf bi-kuned.*

FREEZE—It is so cold to-day, I think at night it will freeze.—*imroz īn ḳadar sardī ast ki* (*gumān dāram*) *ki ba shab zamīn yakh basta khwāhad shud.* (*iḥtimāl dārad.*)

FREIGHT—I have engaged the whole of this vessel's freight. *ān ḳadar ki maḥmūla dārad īn jahāz-rā ba ujrat girifta am.* Or, *man* (*sharṭ*)-*i-maḥmūla,e tamām jahāz karda am.* (*iḳrār.*)

FRESH—These greens are fresh from the garden.—*īn tara az bāgh tāza and.*

FREQUENT—I have frequent opportunities of seeing it. —*ba dīdan-ash marā* (*mauḳi'*) *bisiyār ast.* (*furṣat; ḳābū.*)

FRIEND—What shall I do? I have no friend.—*chi kunam? man* (*doste*) *na dāram.* (*mukhliṣ; khalīl; mūnis; muhibb; ḥabīb; yār; mushfiḳ; shafiḳ; maḥrum-rāz; ham-nafs.*)

FRIENDLESS—I am now entirely friendless.—*ilḥāl man be dost hastam.*

FRIGHTFUL—I have seen a most frightful figure.—(*shakle haulnāk*) *dīdam.* (*haikale waḥshatnāk; dew-sīmā.*)

FRUGAL—How does he manage his household affairs? is he frugal or extravagant?—*o umūrāt-i-khānagī,e khud-rā chigūna ba saranjām mī-rasānad?* (*ba kifāyat yā ba fazūlī*)? (*ba ḳinā'at yā ba isrāf.*)

FULL—Is this cask empty or full?—*īn* (*barmīl*) *tihī ast yā pur?* (*khambak.*)

FULFILLED—The purpose for which you sent me has been fulfilled.—*kāre ki barā,e ān shumā marā firistāded* (*tamām shuda*) *ast.* (*ba itmām* or *ba sar rasīda.*)

FURNISH—How soon can you furnish these things?—*īn*

chīzhā ba chi 'ujlat (muhaiyā) mī-tawāned kard. (maujūd; muyassar; taiyār.)
FURNITURE—He makes all kinds of furniture.—(rakht-i-khāna) az har kism mī-sāzad. (aṣāṣu-l-bait.)
FUTURITY—We cannot see intô futurity.—mā (khabar-i-mustakbil) na dānem. (aḥwāl-i-āyanda.)

G.

GATHER—Gather up the crumbs.—rezahā,e nān bar chīn.
GAIN—Do you expect much gain from this trade?—az īn pesha tawakku'-i-sūd-i-bisiyār dāred? Or, az īn ḥirfa (mutarakkib)-i-naf'-i-firāwān mī-shaved? (mutaraṣṣid.) Or, rijā dāred ki az īn kasb māl-i-kaṣīr ba dast-i-(shumā khwāhad āmad). (khud khwāhed āward.)
GARDEN—Why have you left the garden gate open?—chirā darwāza,e bāgh wā guẕāshta ed?
GENEROSITY—There are no limits to his generosity.—ḥadd-i-sakhāwat-ash nīst. Or, karm-ash (nā maḥdūd ast). (ḥadd or intihā na dārad.)
GENEROUS—He is very generous and gentle.—o sakhī wa narm-dil ast. Or, o karīm wa raḥīm ast. Or, o faiyāẓ wa ḥalīm ast.
GENTLEMAN—Are you acquainted with that gentleman?—badūn khān-sāḥib (ma'rifat dāred)? (āshnā,ī dāred; rū-shinās mī-bāshed.)
GEOGRAPHY—He has composed a book on geography.—o aar 'ilm-i-(jughrāfiya) kitābe taṣnīf karda ast. ('arẓ.)
GET—Can you get me another book like that?—miṣal-i-ān kitāb dīgare barā,e man (tawāned yāft)? (ba dast tawāned āward; gīr-i-shumā khwāhad āmad.)
GOT—You have got many books—give me one.—shumā kutub-i-bisiyār dāred, yake az ānhā ba man bi-dihed.
GILD—Do you know how to gild paper?—shumā mī-dāned chigūna kāghaẕ-rā zar-afshān mī-kunand? Or, āyā

tarkībe ki ṣaḥḥāffān kitābhā-rā ba zar mulamma' mī-kunand, shumā mī-dāned?

GILT—He showed me a gilt picture-frame.—*ūn shakhṣ ba man khāna,e taṣwīr-i-(mulamma' namūd). (muṭallā nishān dād.)*

GIRLS—He has five children, three boys and two girls.—*o panj tā farzand dārad si pisar wa dū dukhtar.*

GLAD—Are you glad or sorry on this occasion?—*dar bāb-i-īn sukhan khūsh ed yā ghamnāk?*

GLASS—Take care, this will easily break, it is made of glass.—*khabar-dār, īn chīz ba āsānī shikasta mī-shavad az balūr ast.*

GLOVES—I have bought a pair of gloves.—*yak juft-i-(dast posh) kharīda am. (dastāna; dast-tāba.)*

GLUE—Tell the carpenter to glue these two boards together.—*ba darrūdgar bi-go ki īn dū takhta ba sarīsh bāham bi-(paiwand). (chaspān; yak-jā bi-kun; waṣal bi-kun.)*

GOLD—Is this chain made of gold, silver, iron, brass, or copper?—*īn zanjīr az zar, sīm, āhan, birinj yā mis sūkhta shuda ast?*

GOODNESS—Have the goodness to inform me.—*az rū,e luṭf ba man khabar bi-dihed. Or, talaṭṭuf farmūda marā (i'lām) bi-kuned. (iṭṭilā'; muṭṭali'.)*

GOVERN—Every one does not know how to govern.—*har kas ḥukm-rānī kardan na mī-tawānad. Or, ṭāḳat-i-ḥukūmat kardan har kas na dārad.*

GOVERNOR—He is now Governor of Baghdād.—*o ilḥāl (ḥākim)-i-baghdād ast. (ṣūba; wālī,e farmān.)*

GRAIN—In this province much grain is produced.—*dar īn (kishwar) ghalla,e bisiyār paidā mī-shavad. (ṣūba; ẓill'a.)*

GRAND—Whose grand house is that?—*īn khāna,e ('ālī-shān) az ān-i-kīst? (rafī'; wasī'; 'aẓīm.)*

GRANT—Sir, be pleased to grant me this request.—*ṣāḥibā, az rū,e luṭf 'arẓ-i-man ḳabūl bi-kuned. Or, istid'ā,e man ijābat bi-farmāyed.*

GRATEFUL—I am grateful for your kindness.—*man az*

mihrbānī,e shumā mamnūn am. Or, *man shākir-i-iḥsān-i-shumā hastam.* Or, *man az alṭāf-i-shumā (shukr-guẕār) hastam.* (*iḥsānmand ; mashkūr.*) Or, *az madāra,e shumā minnat paẕīr am.*

Gratified—Seeing such a school, I am much gratified.—*man az dīdan-i-chunīn maktab khailī (khūsh) am.* (*masrūr.*)

Grazing—The horses are grazing on the plain.—*aspān dar maidān mī-charand.*

Great—You have done me a very great favour.—*shumā bar man minnat-i-kaṣīr (dāshta) ed.* (*nihāda.*) Or, *shumā ba man iḥsān-i-a'ẓam farmūda ed.*

Grief—He has caused much grief to his father.—*o ba pidar-i-khud (bisiyār ranj) rasānīda ast.* (*shu'la,e āh.*) Or, *o mūjib-i-sar-māya,e gham ba pidar-i-khud būda ast.* Or, *o bā'iṣ-i-malāl-i-kaṣīr ba wālid-ash būda ast.*

Grievous—This is a grievous calamity.—*īn (āfat-i-'aẓīm) ast.* (*muṣībat-i-sangīn ; balā,e sakht.*)

Grind—Grind this wheat in the mill.—*dar āsiyā īn (ghalla-rā biyās).* (*gandum-rā ārd kun.*)

Ground-rent—What is the ground-rent of this house?—*kirāya,e zamīn-i-īn khāna chīst ?*

Grow—Many flowers grow in the Khan's garden.—*gulhā,e bisiyār dar bāgh-i-khān-i-(wālā-shān) mī-ruyand.* (*'ālī-shān ; buland-makān ; rafī'u-d-darjāt ; rafī'u-l-jā,e-gāh ; sulāla,e khāndān ; 'aẓīmu-sh-shān.*)

Grown—You have grown very tall since I saw you last.—*az ān waḳt ki man shumā-rā dīdam (ṭawīlu-l-ḳāmat shuda ed).* (*ḳadd-i-ṭawīl karda ed.*)

Guardian—Who is the guardian of this child?—*murabbī,e īn ṭiflak kīst ?* Or, (*atālīḳ*)-*i-īn ṣāghīr kīst ?* (*ḳaiyim.*)

Guess—Can you guess the meaning of what I say?—*ānchi mī-goyam shumā ba maṭlab-i-ān mī-rased ?*

Guide—I went without a guide, though I had never been that road before.—*agarchi badān rāh gāhe ḳabl az īn na rafta būdam be (rāh-bar) rawāna shudam.* (*rah-namā ; dalīl-i-rāh ; hādī ; badriḳa.*)

H.

HABIT—He is in the habit of walking out early.—*o 'alạ-ṣ-ṣabāḥ 'ādat-i-(gardīdan) dārad.* (*gasht o gard.*) Or, *o bām-dād mu'tād ba gardīdan ast.*

HALL—The house has a hall and three rooms.—*īn khāna yak dālān dārad wa si ḥujra.* Or, *īn maḳām-rā yak aiwān ast wa si kamra.*

HAND—Take hold of his hand.—*dast-ash bi-gīr.*

HANDKERCHIEF—Give me a handkerchief.—(*rū-māle*) *ba man bi-dih.* (*dast-māle.*)

HANDLE—The handle of this drawer is broken.—*dasta,e khāna,e īn mez shikasta shud.*

HANDSOME—In his appearance he is handsome.—*o dar ṣūrat* (*khūb-sūrat*) *ast.* (*laṭīfu-l-i'tidāl ; wajīh ; ḥasīn ; jamīl ; zībā-ṭala't ; zībā-ḥaiyat ; badī'u-l-jamāl.*) Or, *o ba shakl nādiru-l-ḥusn ast.* Or, *o ba shamā,il kamāl bahjat dārad.* Or, *o ba haikal ghāyat-i'tidāl wa nihāyat jamāl dārad.*

HAND-WRITING—Do you know whose hand-writing this is?—*shumā mī-dāned ki īn dast-khaṭṭ az kīst?*

HANG—Hang the keys upon the nail.—*kalīdhā ba mekh biyāwezān.*

HAPPEN—When did that happen?—*īn ḥādiṣa kai ḥādiṣ shud?* Or, *īn wāḳi'a kai wāḳi' shud?* Or, *kudām waḳt īn ittifāḳ* (*shud*)*?* (*uftād.*)

HAPPINESS—In this world no one enjoys perfect happiness. —*dar īn dunyā hech kas* (*rāḥat-i-tamām*) *na dārad. āsā,ish-i-ḥaḳīḳī ; tana'um-i-kāmil.*)

HAPPY—They who fear God here will be happy hereafter. —*ānān ki dar īn jā az khudā mī-tarsand dar 'āḳibat khūsh khwāhand shud.* Or, *ān kasān-rā* (*farḥat*)*-i-'uḳbạ dast khwāhad dād ki dar īn dunyā dar khauf-i-khudā mī-mānand.* (*sa'ādat.*)

HARD—Is the lesson you have given me hard or easy?—

sabake ki marā dāda ed āyā (āsān ast yā mushkil). (yusr ast yā mughlak; sahl ast yā mudakkik.)

HARDSHIP—This is a great hardship.—*īn sakhtī,e 'azīm ast.*

HARE—The hare is a very timid animal.—*khargosh bisiyār (buz-dil) ast. (shutur-dil; khā,if; tarsān; jabī.)*

HARM—Is there any harm in doing this?—*āyā dar īn chunīn kār kardan ('aibe) mī-bāshad? (nuksāne; muzāyaka,e.)*

HASTE—I write in great haste to save the post.—*man mī-khwāham ki khatte ba sabīl-i-chāparī (bi-firistam)*[1] *lihazā ba (sur'at)*[2]*-i-tamām mī-nawīsam.* [1]*(rawāna bi-kunam; mursal dāram; irsāl dāram.)* [2]*(ta'jīl; shitāb.)*

HASTENED—They hastened away as fast as possible.—*eshān tā ba makdūr-i-khud shitāftand.* Or, *ba sur'at harchi tamāmtar shudand.* Or, *ba ta'jīl-i-tamām rāh (girā gar-dīdand). (giriftand.)*

HASTEN—You must try to hasten his coming.—*dar bāb-i-tez rasīdan-ash badīn jā shumā-rā sa'ī bāyad kard.*

HASTY—To act in a hasty manner is not wise.—*dar kār ta'jīl kardan himākat ast.* Or, *dar kār musta'jil shudan az tarīk-i-'akl ba'īd ast.* Or, *dar umūr ta'jīl ba kār burdan az jāda,e danāyat dūr ast.*

HAT—On entering the room he took off his hat.—*ba (mujarrad)-e-dākhil shudan-i-ūtāk kula,e khud-rā az sar bar dāsht. (shart.)*

HATE—Let us hate nothing but sin.—*mā-rā az hech chīz nafrat na bāyad kard magar az gunāh.* Or, *mā-rā ba jūz-i-ma'siyat az chīze kirāhiyat na bāyad kard.*

HAVE—Have you any acquaintance with that gentleman?—*badān āghā (ma'rifate) dāred? (shināsā,ī.)*

HEALED—His wound is now healed.—*zakhm-ash pur shuda ast.* Or, *jarrāhat-i-o (mundamil shuda) ast. (indamāl yāfta.)*

HEALTH—His health is sound.—*sihhat-i-o ba hāl ast.* Or. *o tan-durust ast.* Or, *mizāj-i-o (mustakīm) ast. (ikhtilāl na yāfta.)*

HEAP—Here is a heap of papers, put them away.—*yak āmbār-i-kāghaz dar īn jā jam' shuda ast,* (*berūn bi-bar*). (*ba yak ṭaraf bi-guzār ; bar kinār bi-kun.*)

HEAR—Hear what I say, then give an answer.—*ānchi mī-goyam* (*bi-shinau*), *ba'd az ān jawāb bi-dih.* (*gosh kun* or *dār ; masmū' bi-kun.*)

HEART—The heart of man is inclined to evil.—*dil-i-insān ba gunāh-gārī* (*mā,il mī-bāshad*). (*mail dārad.*)

HEAT—To-day the heat is very great.—*imroz* (*ḥarārat*) *ba shiddat ast.* (*ḥarūr ; garmī.*)

HEAVEN—In heaven is unspeakable happiness, in hell unutterable woe !—*dar bihisht asā,ishe ast ki dar guftan nayāyad wa dar jahannum 'azābe ast az bayān ba'īd.* Or, *dar jannat rāḥat īn ḳadar ast ki dar tafṣīl nayāyad wa dar sakkar alame ast ki sharḥ-i-ān dar ḥiṭa,e taḳrīr na mī-gunjad.*

HEAVY—This box is very heavy, how can I carry it ?—*īn sandūḳ khailī sangīn ast chigūna mī-tawānam ba: dāsht ?*

HEEL—When walking I trod upon his heel with my foot —*ba waḳt-i-raftan pāyam ba ḳa'b-ash khurd.*

HEIGHT—What is the height of this wall ?—(*bulandī,*)*e īn dīwar chi ḳadar ast ?* (*irtifā' ; bālā,ī ; rafa't.*)

HEIR—This large estate is without an heir.—*īn milkīyat-i-'aẕīm lā wāriṣ ast.* Or, *īn mīrāṣ-i-a'ẕam wāriṣ na dārad.*

HELP—Can you afford me any help in this affair of mine ?—*shumā dar īn amr ba man hech* (*madad*) *mī-tawāned dād.* (*mu'āwanat ; i'ānat ; imdād.*)

HERBS—They live only upon herbs.—*eshān faḳaṭ* (*tara mī-khurand*). (*bar sabzahā zindagī mī-kunand.*)

HIDE—The crows steal, and afterwards hide what they can.—*zāghān duzdī mī-kunand wa ba'd az ān ānchi mī-tawānand* (*pinhān*) *mī-kunand.* (*ikhfā ; makhfī ; poshīda.*)

HILLS—There are few hills in Kharazam.—*dar mulk-i-khwarazam kohhā kam and.* (*jabāl.*)

HINT—You can just give him a hint of this affair —*shumā dar bāb-i-īn amr o-rā ishāra mī-tawāned kard.*

HIRE—To go there I must hire a palankeen and boat.—*az barā,e raftan badān jā marā takht-i-rawān wa kishtī kirāya bāyad kard.*

HISTORY—Have you read the history of Persia.—*tārīkh-i-'ajm muṭāla'a karda ed?*

HIT—He hit me a very hard blow on the head.—*o bar sar-am ẓarb-i-shadīd (zad). (rasānīd; koft; dād.)*

HOLDS—He holds his pen in the left hand.—*o dar dast-i-chap ḳalam-i-khud-rā mī-gīrad.*

HOLE—Make a hole in the ground here.—*īn jā dar zamīn maghāke bi-(kun). (kan; kā,o; zan.)*

HOME—It is late, let me now return home.—*(der) shud biguẕār ki man ba maḳām-i-khud-am bi-ravam. (ta,khīr; dirang; tahāwun.)*

HONEY—I ate some honey out of the honey-comb.—*ḳadre shahd az (khāna,e shahd) khurdam.* Or, *ḳadre 'asal az (ma'sal) khurdam. (maḥrān.)*

HONOUR—He has obtained much honour.—*o 'izzat-i-'aẓīm ḥāṣil karda ast.* Or, *o ḥusūl-i-takrīm-i-bisiyār karda ast.* Or, *('izz wa ikrām)-i-madīd ba dast āwarda ast. (rafa'at; ābrū; sharaf; sharāfat; waḳār; iḥtirām.)*

HOPE—I hope to have an interview with you very soon.—*rijā dāram ki zūd (shumā-rā) mulāḳāt khwāham kard. (ba shumā.)* Or, *marā ummed ast ki dar andak roz mulāḳāt-i-man bā shumā khwāhad shud.* Or, *taraṣṣud-i-ān dāram ki man 'an ḳarīb ba shumā mulāḳī khwāham shud.*

HOSPITAL—An hospital is about to be built there.—*yak dāru-sh-shifā ta'mīr shudanī ast.* Or, *yak (baitu-l-marīẓ taiyār) shudanī ast. (shifā-khāna bar pā.)*

HOSPITALITY—They show great hospitality.—*eshān (mihmāndārī),e firāwān mī-kunand. (mihmān-nawāzī; ẓiyāfat-dārī.)*

HOLY—God is holy, just, and pure.—*khudā muḳaddas, 'ādil, wa pāk ast.* Or, *(allah ta'ālā) ḳudūs, rāst-bāz, wa ḥaḳḳ ast.* (*'ālimu-s-sirr; rabbu-l-'ālamain; yazdān-i-dādār; dāwar-i-dādār.*)

HUMANE—He is a man of a very humane disposition, and humble in his own esteem.—*o marde ast salīmu-ṯ-ṯaba' wa* (*khud-rā ḥaḳīr mī-dānad*). (*nā-khud pasand.*)

HUMANITY—He possesses great humanity as well as humility.—*o* (*insānīyat*)[1]*-i-bisiyār dārad wa* (*ḥilmiyat*).[2] [1](*ādmiyat; mardumī; muruwat; ḥiss-i-bashriyat.*) [2](*farotanī; tawāẓu'; maskīnī; khushū'; khuẓū; istikānat.*)

HUNTER—The hunter is gone a-hunting.—(*ṣaiyād ba ṣaid*) *rafta ast.* (*shikārī ba shikār.*)

HURTS—It hurts his mind to see such wickedness.—*az mushāhida,e īn chunīn* (*ḳabāhat*) *dil-ash mī-sozad.* (*badī; shana'at.*)

I.

IDEA—I had no idea that you would come to-day.—*dar khayāl-i-man na būd ki shumā imroz khwāhed āmad.*

IDLENESS—They spend their time in idleness.—*eshān auḳāt-i-khud-rā dar* (*kāhilī ẓā'ī mī-kunand*). (*tasāhilī mī-guẕārand; sustī ba sar mī-burand; lahw o la'b ba bād mī-dihand.*)

IGNORANT—They are ignorant and idle.—*eshān* (*nā-dān wa sust*) *and.* (*jāhil wa kāhil; nā-shinās wa baṯṯāl.*)

ILLIBERAL—Such a sentiment is illiberal.—*īn chunīn khayāl* (*bāṯil*) *ast.* (*bad aṣl; nā karīm.*)

ILLITERATE—It is not good always to associate with illiterate persons.—*ba jāhilān hamesha ṣuḥbat dāshtan munāsib nīst.*

IMAGE—There is an image in that temple.—*dar ān but-khāna but ast.* Or, *dar ān ṣanam-kada ṣanam ast.*

IMAGINATION—Whence arose this imagination?—*az kujā īn khayāl* (*paidā shud*)? (*sar bar zad; sar bar āward.*)

IMAGINE—How do you imagine that I should agree to this?

—chigūna (khayāl mī-kuned) ki man īn sukhan-rā ḳabūl kunam. (ḳiyās mī-gīred; dar sar-i-khud dūred.) Or, *chigūna khayāl mī-banded ki man badīn sukhan (muttafiḳ shavam). (ittifāḳ kunam.)*

IMITATION—This is of wood, in imitation of stone.—*īn chīz ba miṣal-i-sang az chūb sākhta shuda ast.* Or, *īn chīz ki (ishtibāh)-i-sang dārad az chob sākhta shuda ast. (tashbīh; shabīh; mushābahat; mumāṣilat.)*

IMMENSE—The undertaking is likely to be attended with immense expense.—*aghlab ast ki dar īn kār kharch-i-bisiyār khwāhad shud.*

IMMORTAL—The body is mortal, the soul immortal.—*badan fānī ast wa rūḥ (bāḳī). (lā-yamūt.)*

IMMOVABLE—They are immovable in their opinions.—*eshān ba* or *dar tajwīz-i-khud (mustaḳill) and. (ghair-mutaḥarrik.)* Or, *eshān bar rā,e khud mustaḳīm and.*

IMPART—It is our duty to impart knowledge.—*bar mā wājib ast ki faiẓ-i-ta'līm bi-gustarem.*

IMPARTIAL—An upright judge will be impartial.—*ḥākim-i-(rāst-bāz 'ādil) mī-bāshad. (be-riyā be-jānib-dār; ḥaḳḳ-parast be-ṭarafdār.)* Or, *ḥākim-i-munṣif-mizāj ba naẓar-i-taswiyat ṭarafain-rā mī-bīnad.*

IMPASSABLE—These mountains are impassable, having on all sides impenetrable forests.—*ṣu'ūd-i-īn jabāl ghair mumkin ast zīrā ki bar har ṭaraf besha,e (mumtanī'u-d-dukhūl) mī-bāshad. (dushwār-guẓār.)* Or, *īn kohhā be-guẓār and az īn sabab ki bar har aṭrāf besha,e mānī'u-d-dukhūl mī-bāshad.*

IMPERFECT—Everything in this world is imperfect.—*har chīz dar īn dunyā (nāḳiṣ) ast. ('aib-dār; ḳāṣir.)*

IMPERTINENT—His behaviour is impertinent.—*o dar waẓ'-(gustākh) ast. (shaukh; waḳīḥ.)* Or, *akhlāḳ-i-o az adab (ba'īd) ast. (mu'arra.)*

IMPORTANT—It is very important to attend to this.—*bisiyār ẓarūr ast ki mā bā īn 'amal (dil bi-dihem). (mutawajjih bi-shavem.)*

IMPORTS—Have you seen the exports and imports?—*āyā asbāb-i-āmadanī wa raftanī dīda ed?*

IMPOSE—They impose on whomsoever they can.—*ba har kase ki tawānand (ghadr) mī-kunand. (fareb; ghabn; makr.)*

IMPOSITION—They practise every kind of imposition.—*eshān (daghā),e har ṭaur mī-kunand. (makr; shayādī; kaid; ghadr; ghabn.)*

IMPOSSIBILITY—How can I believe an impossibility?—*chigūna bar (muḥāl) bāwar mī-tawānam kard? (ghair-i-imkānī.)* Or, *chīze ki imkān na dārad chigūna bar ān i'timād mī-tawānam kard?*

IMPOSSIBLE—It is impossible for me to comply with what you say.—*(mumkin nīst) ki ānchi shumā mī-goyed ḳabūl bi-kunam. (ghair mumkin ast.)* Or, *imkān na dārad ki ba ḥasb-i-istida'ā,e shumā 'amal namāyam.*

IMPOSTOR—He is a notorious impostor.—*o (makkār)-i-mash-hūr ast. (ghaddār; ghābin; 'aiyār; ṭarār.)* Or, *o (khaddā')-i-ma'rūf ast. (munāfiḳ; ahl-i-nifāḳ; sālūs; murā,i; mulāḥid.)*

IMPRESSION—What he said made an impression on me.—*sukhan-ash dar dil-i-man (aṣar kard). (tāṣīr* or *sirāyat kard; mu'aṣṣar shud; jā,e girift; khurd.)*

IMPROBABLE—What he tells me appears very improbable.—*ānchi marā mī-goyad (khilāf-i-ḳiyās) ma'lūm mī-shavad. (be-iḥtimāl; nā-muḥtamil; dūr az 'aḳl.)*

IMPROPER—To act thus would be highly improper, and therefore imprudent.—*īn chunīn kār kardan bi-l-kull ghair munāsib mī-bāshad wa az īn sabab be tamīzī.*

IMPROVE—Can you improve what he has written?—*ānchi nawishta ast shumā ān-rā (iṣlāḥ) mī-tawāned kard? (bihtar.)*

IMPURE—No impure person will enter heaven.—*shakhṣe (nā-pāk) dar jannat dākhil na khwāhad shud. (khabīs; shanī'.)*

INATTENTION—This has arisen solely from your inattention.

—in fakaṭ az (taghāful)¹-i-shumā (uftāda) 'ast. ¹(ghaflat; ghāfilī; ihmāl.) ²(ittifāk or wākiʿ or hādiṣ shuda.)

INCESSANT—We have lately had incessant rain.—dar īn rozhā dar īn jā bārān (mutawātir) bārīda ast. ('alạ-l-ittiṣāl; muttaṣil.)

INCH—Had this piece of wood been an inch longer, it would have done very well.—agar īn chūb dar ṭūl yak jau darāz-tar mī-būd (kifāyat mī-kard). (ba kār mī-khurd or mī-āmad.)

INCLINATION—He feels no inclination to study.—o mail ba tadrīs dar dil-i-khud na dārad.

INCOME—Do you know what is his income?—ma'lūm-i-shumā ast ki (madkhal)-i-o chand ast? (dukhūl; āmadanī; dakhl; madākhil.)

INCOMPARABLE—This is incomparable writing.—īn khaṭṭ (be naẓīr) ast. (lā-ṣānī.)

INCOMPLETE—Your book is incomplete.—kitāb-i-shumā (nā-tamām) ast. (nāḳiṣ.)

INCONVENIENCE—Will my staying here till the first of next month be any inconvenience to you?—āyā az māndan-i-man dar īn jā tā ba tārīkh-i-ghurra,e māh-i-āyanda (ba shumā taklīf khwāhad rasīd)? (dar kār-i-shumā muzāhimat khwāhad shud.)

INCONVENIENT—It will be inconvenient for me to wait on you to-morrow.—fardā ba jihat-i-mulākāt kardan-i-shumā ba man nā-munāsibat (dast khwāhad dād). (hāṣil khwāhad shud.)

INCORRECT—Is what I say correct or incorrect?—ānchi mī-goyam ṣahīh ast yā ghalaṭ?

INCREASED—My family has lately been increased.—az chand roz 'iyāl-i-man (mazīd) shuda ast. (ziyāda; afzūda; kaṣīr.)

INCREASING—There is a rumour of increasing the army.—afwā,e ziyāda kardan-i-fauj mī-bāshad. Or, afwā ast ki dar ta'adūd-i-fauj afzūnī khwāhad shud.

INDECENT—They speak indecent language.—eshān kalām-i-(fāhish) mī-goyand. (shanī'; tashnī'.)

INDEPENDENT—He is now independent of any one.—*o bi-l-kull ba hech kas (muta'allik̤ nīst).* ('*ilāk̤a* or *istig̲h̲nā na dārad.*) Or, *o az hama kas (mustag̲h̲nī) ast. (be ta'alluk̤; g̲h̲air-muta'allik̤).* Or, *o (be ẓabṯ wa rabṯ) ast. (k̲h̲ud muk̲h̲tār.)*

INDEX—Is there an index to this book?—*īn kitāb-rā fihriste ast.* Or, *īn kitāb (tafṣīl-i-mak̤āla,e) dārad?* (*tāshrīḥ-i-abwāb.*)

INDIFFERENCE—This is not to be treated with indifference.—*īn kār īn chunīn nīst ki (g̲h̲aflat) bi-kuned.* (*musāhilat.*)

INDIGENOUS—Is this an indigenous plant?—*īn nihāl az īn mulk ast?* Or, *paidāyish-i-īn nihāl dar īn jā ast?*

INDIGO—I was formerly employed in Mr. ——'s indigo factory.—*sābik̤an̲ dar kār-k̲h̲āna,e nīl-i-ṣāḥib-i-fulān mash-g̲h̲ūl būda am.*

INDISPOSITION—I heard of your indisposition last week.—*dar hafta,e-guzashta aḥwāl-i-marẓ-i-shumā iṣg̲h̲ā kardam.*

INFANCY—I knew him from his infancy.—*man o-rā az (zamān-i-ṭufūliyat)-ash mī-shināsam.* ('*ahd-i-k̲h̲urdī.*)

INFER—What do you infer from what he said?—*ānchi guft shumā az ān chi (natīja bar āwarda ed)?* (*k̤iyās kashīda ed; istidāl karda ed.*)

INFERIORS—We must show kindness and respect to our inferiors, as well as superiors.—*chunānchi mā ba (mardu-mūn-i-k̲h̲āṣṣ)*[1] *ba adab wa ta'ẓīm sulūk mī-namāyem ba 'āmm nīz bāyad kard.* [1](*k̲h̲wāṣṣ; buzurgān; zabar-dastān; kibār; kabīrān.*) [2](*'awwām; k̲h̲urdān; ṣag̲h̲īrān; zer-dastān; ṣig̲h̲ār.*)

INFINITE—God is infinite in power and wisdom.—*k̤udrat wa ḥikmat-i-k̲h̲udā (be intihā) ast.* (*nā-maḥṣūr; nā-mutanāhī.*)

INFLUENCE—We have no influence over them.—*mā bar eshān k̤udrat na dārem.*

INFORMATION—Is there no one here that can give me information concerning this?—*kase dar īn jā nīst ki marā az īn amr (i'lām tawānad dād)?* (*iṭṭilā' tawānad kard.*)

Or, *kase nīst ki dar īn amr bar man roshan tawānad sakht?*

INGANA—How long have you been in Ingana?—*(chand wakt) ast ki dar ingana būda ed?* *(az chand roz.)*

INGENIOUS—She is very ingenious.—*ān bānū bisiyār (zarīf) ast.* *(ṣāḥib-i-firāsat; zakī; hunar-mand.)*

INGENUITY—He possesses much ingenuity.—*o (kiyāsat)-i-'azīm dārad.* *(firāsat; zarāfat; idrāk; zihn.)*

INHABITANT—The petition was signed by every inhabitant of the village.—*īn 'arīza az har shakhṣ-i-ahl-i-dih dast-khatt karda shuda ast.* Or, *bar īn 'arīza har mukīm-i-kasba dast-khatt kard.*

INHUMAN—Their disposition is inhuman.—*mizāj-i-eshān be (raḥm) ast.* *(insāniyat; marḥamat; muruwat.)*

INIQUITY—They delight in all kinds of iniquity.—*eshān dar kardan-i-har nau'-i-fasād (khūsh and).* *(sarūr mī-kunand.)*

INJURY—I never did him the least injury.—*man hargiz o-rā ziyān na (dāshtam).* *(dādam.)* Or, *man gāhe o-rā (īzā) na rasānīdam.* *(khalal; badī.)* Or, *man hargiz ḥaif bar o na kardam.* Or, *man gāhe bar dil-ash (gazand) na nihādam.* *(mazarrat; zarar.)*

INJURED—His health has been injured by too great exertion.—*az ziyādatī,e miḥnat siḥḥat-i-o (khalal) girifta ast.* *(nukṣān; mazarrat.)*

INJUSTICE—He practises injustice towards all.—*o bar har kas zulm mī-kunad.* *(be-inṣāfī; tajabbur.)*

INNOCENT—They are all innocent.—*eshān az gunāh pāk wa (mu'arrā) and.* *(mubarrā.)*

INOFFENSIVE—These animals are inoffensive.—*īn jānwarān mūzī nayand.*

INQUEST—An inquest was held yesterday on the body of a person who shot himself.—*shakhṣe ki khud-rā ba tufang halāk kard taḥkīkāt-i-ān aḥwāl dīroz shud.*

INSENSIBLE—He is so ill that he is insensible.—*o īn kadar bīmār ast ki be-hosh ast.*

INSERT—You had better insert this in your letter.—*bihtar ast ki dar khaṭṭ-i-khud (īn-rā bi-nawīsed). (īn-rā darj bi-kuned; īn ruḳ'a dākhil bi-kuned.)*

INSIGNIFICANT—How very insignificant is man, compared to the Almighty!—*insān ba nisbat-i-khudā,e 'aẓīm wa jallīl chi ḳadar (nā-chīz) ast! (be ma'nī; be miḳdār.)*

INSINCERE—His words are insincere.—*sukhanān-ash (pur-riyā) and. (nā-mukhliṣ; nā-ṣādiḳ; be-wafā; rang-āmez.)*

INSOLENT—They behaved in an insolent manner.—*eshān be adabāna (sulūk kardand). (pesh āmadand; ḥarakat* or *'amal kardand.)*

INSOLVENT—He has lately become insolvent.—*ḳabl az īn ān shakhṣ (war) shikasta ast. (dar; bar; wā.)*

INSPECT—Call a person to inspect this cloth.—*ṣāḥibe tamīz-rā bi-ṭalab ki ba naẓar-i-tafarrus dar īn pārcha bi-nigarad.*

INSPECTION—The goods are all ready for your inspection.—*ajnās az barā,e (mu'aiyana,e shumā maujūd) and. (mulāḥaẓa,e shumā taiyār.)*

INSTANT—I will be with you in an instant.—*man dar (chashmak zadan) nazd-i-shumā mī-āyam. (ṭurfatu-l-'ain.)*

INSTINCT—Man acts from reason, animals from instinct.—*insān az 'aḳl fi'l mī-kunad wa ḥaiwān az (jibillat). ('aḳl-i-ḥaiwānī.)*

INSTITUTIONS—In Europe are noble institutions for communicating knowledge.—*dar farang az barā,e tadrīs-i-'ilm khūb tarkībāt ḳarār yāfta and.*

INSTRUCT—Can you instruct me in this science?—*dar īn 'ilm ba man ta'līm mī-tawāned dād. (tarbiyat mī-tawāned kard.)*

INSURED—I have insured the vessel for 50,000 tomans, and I have the insurance-policy in my possession.—*ān jahāz-rā ba panjāh hazār tūmān bīma karda am wa kāghaz-i-bīma nazd-i-man ast.*

INTELLECT—She has a wonderful intellect.—*ān bānū idrāk-i-'ajīb dārad.*

INTELLIGENCE—How did you receive this intelligence?—*chigūna īn khabar ba shumā rasīd?*

INTELLIGENT—He is an intelligent man.—*o mard-i-(tez-fahm) ast.* (*zīrak.*)

INTEMPERANCE—Intemperance hurts body and mind.—*'adm-i-i'tidāl badan wa mizāj-rā (ẓarar) mī-dihad.* (*ma-ẓarat; nuḳṣān.*) Or, *bad-parhezī jism wa ṭab'-rā muẓirr ast.*

INTENTION—Have you any intention to go to Europe?—*hech irāda,e raftan ba farang dāred?*

INTERCOURSE—There is no intercourse between us.—*mā bain-i-man wa tū hech ('ilāḳa) nīst.* (*ta'alluḳ; nisbat.*) Or, *man ba tū muta'alliḳ nayām.*

INTEREST.—I have no interest in this matter.—*dar īn amr marā hech (gharaẓ) nīst.* (*maṭlab; 'ilāḳa.*)

INTERFERE—Why should we interfere in that affair?—*chirā dar ān amr (dakhl kunem)?* (*dakhīl shavem; mukhill shavem; dast-andāzī kunem.*)

INTERPRET—You must interpret what he says to me.—*ānchi ba man mī-goyad bāyad ki tarjuma,e ān bi-kuned.*

INTERPRETER—If you know not the language of the country, you must use an interpreter.—*agar zabān-i-mulk na mī-dāned (mutarjim) nazd-i-khud nigāh bāyad dāsht.* (*tar-jamān.*)

INTERRUPT—I hope, sir, I don't interrupt you.—*ṣāḥibā ummedwār-am ki (mukhill-i-shumā na mī-shavam).* (*dar-miyān-i-sukhan-i-shumā na mī-uftam.*)

INTERRUPTION—Your coming here is an interruption to my business.—*āmadan-i-shumā mūjib-i-khalal-i-man ast.* Or, *az āmadan-i-shumā dar kār-i-man khalal mī-uftad.* Or, *āmadan-i-shumā dar kār-i-man khalal mī-andāzad.*

INTRODUCE—Shall I introduce you to that gentleman?—*āyā shumā-rā mulāḳāt-i-ān janāb bi-kunānam?*

INTRUSTED—He was intrusted with the whole business.—*tamām kār bado (mufauwaẓ) shuda būd.* (*sapurda; tafwīẓ karda; ḥawāla-karda.*)

INVALIDS—It is said a house will be built at Isfahan for the benefit of invalids.—*mī-goyand ki dar iṣfahān 'imārate az barā,e (marīẓān) ta'mīr karda khwāhad shud*). (*bīmārān; 'alīlān.*)

INVENTED—Who invented this instrument?—*īn ālat ki (ījād) kard?* (*ikhtirā'.*)

INVINCIBLE—The Amīr imagined his soldiers were invincible.—*dar khayāl-i-amīr āmad ki 'askar-i-mā (ghair-maghlūb) ast. dā,imu-l-muẓaffar; ghair-manfūr; ghair-maḳhūr.*)

INVITATION—He has given me an invitation to dinner, and I have accepted it.—*o marā da'wat-i-ṭa'ām karda ast, wa ijābat-i-ān karda am.*

INVOLVED—His affairs are much involved.—*kār-ash darham barham ast.*

IRREGULAR—These lines are irregular.—*īn saṭūr (rāst) nayand.* (*ba tafāwat rāst.*)

ISLAND—The company have given permission to clear the island of Ceylon.—*jam'īyat-i-saudāgarān barā,e ṣāf kardan-i-jazīra,e sarandīp ijāzat dāda ast.*

J.

JAIL—He is to remain in jail one year.—*tā ba yak sāl dar (ḳaid-khāna) khwāhad mānd.* (*maḥbas; zindān; maḥbūs.*)

JESTER—Is that the king's jester?—*ān kas (muskhara),e pādshāh ast? bazla-bāz; lu'bat-bāz; laṭīfa-go.*)

JEWELS—pearls, diamonds, emeralds, rubies, turquoise, cornelians, &c.—*jawāhir—(durrhā)*[1], *almāshā, zamarrud-hā, (la'lhā)*[2], *pīrūza, 'aḳīḳān, waghaira.* [1](*marwārid.*) [2](*yaḳūthā.*)

JOIN—Join these two boards together.—*īn dū takhta bāham bi-paiwand.* Or, *īn dū takhta ba-yak-dīgar (bi-chaspān).* (*ittiṣāl*, or *muntaẓam*, or *munsalik*, or *muna'ḳid*, or *mutarattib bi-kun.*)

JOKE—What I said was only in joke.—*ānchi guftam faḳat (bazla,e) būd. (muṭāyaba; imbisāṭ; ẓarāfat; mazāḥat mazāḥ; hazal-bāzī.)*

JOURNEY—I am now going to make a long journey.—*ilḥāl marā safar-i-ṭawīl kardunī ast.* Or, *marā ittifaḳ-i-safar-i-darāz kardan uftāda ast.*

JOY—This news affords me great joy.—*īn khabar marā khūshī,e 'aẓīm mī-dihad.* Or, *īn khabar bā,iṣ-i-(ṭarab)-i-kaṣīr-i-man ast. (nishāṭ; tafrīḥ; khurramī, farḥ; farāḥ; masarrat; sarūr; buhjat.)*

JUDGE—How can I judge of his character? I don't know him.—*chigūna dar bāb-i-raftārī,e o sukhan bi-goyam? man o-rā na mī-dānam.*

JURY—The (English) judge summed up the evidence, and the jury gave their verdict.—*ḳāẓī,e inglisī az gawāhān tafāhhus karda khalāṣa,e iẓhārhā,e shawāhid ba rū,e majlis (ẓāhir kard), wa majlis-i-'adālat fatwā dād. (bar khwānd.)*

JUDGE—The (native) judge punished the delinquent.—*ḳāẓī,e bāshanda,e ān mulk (taḳṣīrwār)-rā sazā dād. (mujrim.)*

JUICE—Squeeze some juice out of this lemon.—*az īn līmūn ḳadre 'araḳ hiyafshār.*

JUMP—How far can you jump?—*ba chi ḳadar mī-tawāned (jast)? (khez-zad.)*

JUNIOR—He is the senior, I the junior.—*ān kas bālā-dast ast, wa man zer-dast.* Or, *ān kas az man kalān ast, wa man khurd.*

JUSTIFICATION—He says nothing in justification of it.—*o az kirdār-i-khud ('uẓr) na mī-kunad. (ma'ẓarat.)*

K.

KEEP—Keep this money for me till I want it.—*īn mablagh-i-man nazd-i-khud amānat bi-guẓāred tā waḳte ki dar kār-i-man āyad.* Or, *īn pūl-i-man ba (ẓimma,e) khud bi-kuned tā wakte ki ba kār-i-man bi-khurad.* (*hawala,e.*) Or, *īn pūl-i-man pesh-i-khud* (*bi-nihed*) *tā wakte ki*, &c. (*bi-dāred ; nigāh bi-dāred.*)

KERNEL—Break this cocoa-nut and eat the kernel.—*īn nārjīl-rā bi-shikan, wa maghz-ash bi-khur.*

KILL—It is sinful to kill animals without cause.—*be sabab haiwānat* (*ba katl rasānīdan khatā*) *ast.* (*-rā kushtan harām.*)

KINDLED—They kindled a fire with straw.—*ba kāh ātash dar dādand.* Or, *ba khāshāk ātash* (*zadand*). (*roshan*, or *ishti'āl*, or *mushta'al kardand.*)

KINDNESS—They showed us very great kindness.—*bar* mā* (*lutf*)*-i-'azīm kardand.* (*makramat ; marhamat ; rifk ; 'ināyat ; ihsān ; talattuf ; mulātifat ; ayādī ; tawajjuh ; shafkat.*) Or, *mū-rā ba mahramiyat ikhtisās dādand.* Or, *bar mā* (*rahm āwardand*). (*ghamza,e madāra kardand.*)

KINGDOM—We traversed the kingdom of Persia.—*mā 'ubūr-i-mulk-i-īrān kardem.* Or, *mā az 'ajam 'ubūr kardem.*

KISS—Give me a kiss, then fly your kite.—(*ba man*) *bosa bi-dih, sipas kāghazak-i-khud bi-parān.* (*bar sar wa chashm.*)

KITTENS—This is a beautiful cat; she has two kittens.—*īn ghurba khailī khūb shakīl ast, dū bachcha dārad.*

KNEES—He fell on his knees and asked pardon.—*o bar dū zānū nishast wa 'uzr khwāst.* Or, *o sar-i-'ajz faro* (*kard*) *wa 'uzr-i-taksīr kard.* (*āward.*) Or, *o sar-i-khud ba zamīn-i-niyāz nihād wa 'afw khwāst.* Or, *o zamīn-i-khidmat bosīd wa mu'āfī khwāst.*

KNIFE—Try if you can open this knife.—*bi-bīn ki īn chākū-rā mī-tawāned bāz kardan, yā na.*

KNOT—Here is a knot in this string ; loose it.—*īn jā dar*

---

* *bā* or *ba* may be used.

īn rīsmān gira ast, ān-rā bi-kushā. Or, *īn rassan 'aḳd dārad, ān-rā ḥall bi-kun.*

Knowledge—What is wealth without knowledge!—*be dānish daulat chīst!*

Know—Do you know what people think of him?—*āyā mī-dāned ahl-i-duniyā (o-rā chi ṭaur mī-pindārand? (dar bāb-i-o chi gumān mī-barand.)*

L.

Labour—They labour hard for their living.—*az barā,e guẕrān-i-khud (miḥnat mī-kashand). (miḥnat mī-barand; talkhī,e miḥnat mī-chashand; sakhtī,e miḥnat mī-khurand.)* Or, *eshān ba mushaḳḳat-i-tamān ma'āsh mī-kunand.*

Labourers—Here are fifty labourers employed.—*īn jā badīn kār panjāh mazdūr (mashghūl and). (ishtighāl dārand.)*

Lakh—It will cost a lakh of rupees.—*kharch-i-ān yak ṣad hazār rupaiya khwāhad shud.*

Lame—Being lame he walks with a stick.—*ba sabab-i-langī ba madad-i-'aṣā mī-gardad.*

Land—Will you go by land or by sea?—*az rāh-i-khushkī khwāhed raft yā (ba tarī)? (az rāh-i-baḥr.)*

Land—Where do you mean to land?—*kujā irāda,e (pā,īn shudan) dāred? (farūd āmadan.)*

Landlord—Muhammad Husain is the landlord of this house; I am his tenant.—*Muḥammad ḥussain mālik-i-īn khāna ast; man kirāyadār-ash-am.*

Languor—I am overcome with languor.—*bar man māndagī ghālib ast.* Or, *man maghlūb-i-ẓa'īfī gashta am.*

Large—I caught a large fish yesterday.—*dīroz (ba) dām māhī,e kalān giriftam. (dar.)*

Last—I saw him last Tuesday.—*man ba si-shamba,e guẕashta o-rā dīdam.* Or, *man az si-shamba,e guẕashta o-rā na dīdam.*

LAUGH—Why do you laugh without reason?—*be sabab chirā (mī-khanded)? (khanda shumā-rā mī-gīrad; tabassum mī-kuned; khanda shumā-rā mī-āyad.)*

LAWFUL—Is it lawful to do this?—*āyā īn chunīn kardan (rawā) ast? (jā,iz; mubāḥ; mashrū'.)*

LAID—Having laid by his profits, he became rich.—*o az jam' āwardan-i-manāfa'-i-khud (tawāngar) shud. (daulatmand; khudāwand-i-rozī; ṣāḥib-i-dunyā; ṣāḥib-i-daulat; mustaghnī; ghanī; khudāwand-i-ni'mat.)*

LAY—Let us lay aside everything that is evil.—*mā-rā bāyad ki har sharārat-rā yak ṭaraf bi-nihem.* Or, *mā-rā bāyad ki har khabāṣat-rā bi-guẕārem.* Or, *mā-rā bāyad ki har faḥḥāshī rihā bi-kunem.* Or, *mā-rā bāyad ki az har manāhīyat (bi-pardāzem). (dast bi-kashem; dast bar dārem; tajannub,* or, *ijtināb,* or, *iḥtirāẓ bi-kunem.)*

LEADS.—That poor man is blind, another leads him.—*ān miskīn nā-bīnā ast, dīgare rāh-bar-ash mī-bāshad.* Or, *ān nā-kas a'mạ ast, dīgare 'aṣā-kash-i-o mī-bāshad.*

LEAD—Where does this road lead to?—*īn rāh kujā (mī-ravad)? (sar mī-barad.)*

LEAN—Don't lean upon the table.—*bar mez takiya ma (kun). (zan; sāz.)*

LEAP—I saw a monkey leap over the fence.—*dīdam ki būzina,e bar (sadd) jast zad.* (barrier, *bandrūgh;* thorn-fence, *khār-bandī;* stone-fence, *dīwar-i-sangī;* pale-fence, *dār-bazīn.*)

LEARN—You can learn faster than I.—*shumā az man jaldtar āmokhtan mī-tawāned.*

LEASE—I took a lease of this house for five years.—*īn khāna-rā tā ba muddat-i-panj sāl (kirāya kardam). (ba kirāya giriftam; ba ijāra giriftam.)*

LEAVE—It is late, let us now take leave.—*der shuda ast, bi-guẕār ki murakhkhaṣ bi-shavem.* Or, *tahāwun shuda ast, ijāzat bi-dih ki rukhṣat bi-(gīrem). (shavem.)*

LEAVE—It is said he intends soon to leave this country.—*mī-goyand ki irāda,e raftan az īn mulk jaldī dārad.*

LED—He led so bad a life no one respected him.—*raftār-ash īn chunīn bad būd ki kase o-rā ('izzat) na kard.* (*ikrām; iḥtirām; takrīm; makrimat; ta'ẓīm; ḥurmat.*)

LEFT—He left all his business to his clerk.—*hama kār o bār-i-khud-rā* (*ḥawāla,e muḥarrir kard*). (*dar* or *ba ḥawāla,e kātib dād.*)

LEFT—Being lame of his right hand, he writes with the left.—*chūn ba dast-i-rāst lunj ast ba dast-i-chap mī-nawīsad.*

LEGIBLE—This writing is not legible.—*īn dast-khaṭṭ khwānda shudanī nīst.* Or, *īn dast-khaṭṭ mumkin nīst ki khwānda shavad.*

LEG—He fell off his horse, and broke his leg.—*az asp-i-khud uftād, wa sāḳ-ash shikast.*

LEISURE—Sir, are you now at leisure, can I speak with you?—*ṣāḥibā shumā* (*fārighed*); *marā ijāzat ast ki sukhane bi-goyam?* (*-rā furṣat ast; -rā farāghat ast.*)

LEND—I am very poor, can you lend me a few rupees?—*man khailī* (*muflis*)*-am, shumā mī-tawāned ki ḳadre pūl ba man ḳarẓ bi-dihed?* (*maflūk; maskīn; mustammand; gharīb.*)

LESS—My wages are less than his.—*muwājib-i-man az mushāhira,e o kam ast.*

LET—Why did you let loose the horse?—*chirā asp-rā wā guẕāshted?*

LET—Let us see if we can read this book.—(*dīda shavad*) *ki īn kitāb-rā khwāndan mī-tawānem yā na.* (*bi-bīnem.*)

LEVEL—The ground is quite level.—*zamīn bi-l-kull* (*mu-saṭṭaḥ*) *ast.* (*hamwār; barābar.*)

LIABLE—By doing this you are liable to a penalty.—*az chunīn fi'l ba shumā* (*siyāsat lāzim*) *mī-āyad.* (*jurmāna jā,iz.*)

LIBERAL—He is exceedingly liberal.—*o bisiyār karīm ast.* Or, *o nihāyat* (*sakhī*) *ast.* (*jauwād.*) Or, *o khailī* (*samāḥat*) *dārad.* (*karam; futūwat; jūd o sakhā.*)

LIBERTY—They were in prison, but are set at liberty.—

eshān dar zindān būdand, magar ḥālan (*rihā,ī*) *yāfta and.* (*makhlaṣī ; khalāṣī ; najāt.*)

LICKS—By the deliciousness of the food the dog licks his lips.—*sag ba lazzat-i-gosht dahan-i-khụd khūsh mī-kunad.*

LICKS—The dog licks water with his tongue.—*kalb āb ba zabān mī-khụrad.*

LID—Lift up the lid of this box.—*sar-posh-i-īn ṣandūk bālā bi-gīr.*

LIE—He thinks nothing of telling a lie.—*bar kase darogh bastan pesh-i-o hech muẓāyaḳa nīst.* Or, *darogh guftan-rā hech gunāh na mī-fahmad.*

LIES—He lies down under the shade of a cypress tree.—*o zer-i-sāya,e darakht-i-sarw* (*khụd-rā darāz mī-kashad*). (*istirāḥat mī-kunad.*)

LIFE—Life is short, we ought now to prepare for eternity.—*zindagī kam ast, mā-rā bāyad ki fikr-i-'ūḳibat bi-kunem.* Or, *'umr kotāh ast, mā-rā bāyad ki* (*asbāb-i-ākhirat*) *taiyār bi-kunem.* (*az barā,e ākhirat zād-i-rah.*)

LIFELESS—He fell to the ground lifeless.—*o ba zamīn be jān uftād.* Or, *o ba zamīn be hosh uftād, wa ba khāk yak-sān gasht.*

LIGHT—Is this package light or heavy ?—*īn basta* (*subuk*)[1] *ast yā* (*girān*).[2] [1](*khafīf.*) [2](*ṣaḳīl.*)

LIGHT—Tell him to light a fire.—*o-rā bi-go ki ātash biyāf-rozad.*

LIGHTEN—We must lighten the boat, otherwise it will sink.—*bāyad ki maḥmūla,e kishtī-rā zūd subuk bi-kunem, wa illa darāb* (*faro khwāhad raft*). (*gharḳ*, or *mustagh-riḳ*, or *mugharraḳ*, or *maghrūḳ khwāhad shud.*)

LIGHTENS—It lightens very much.—*barḳ ba ifrāṭ mī-zanad.* Or, *ṣā,iḳa khailī mī-darakhshad.*

LIGHTNING—I was out yesterday in a storm of thunder and lightning.—*man dīroz ba waḳt-i-gharīdan-i-ra'd wa darakhshīdan-i-ṣā,'iḳa berūn būdam.* Or, *man dīroz dar zer-i-ṭūfān wa darakhshīdan-i-barḳ būdam.*

LIKE—My house is very much like yours.—*khāna,e man ba*

khāna,e shumā (mumāṣilat) dārad. (mushābihat.) Or, *khāna,e man (bar miṣāl)-i-khāna,e shumā ast. (ba or bā miṣāl.)*

LIKE—I should like much to visit Europe.—*mara shauk-i-firāwān ast ki sair-i-mulk-i-mughrib bi-kunam.* (*man bisiyār shauk,* or *ishtiyāk dāram.*)

LIMITED—I am limited not to give more than one hundred rupees.—*ziyāda az yak ṣad rūpiya ba man (parwānagī) nīst ki bi-diham.* (*ijāzat.*)

LINING—This cloth must have a lining.—*īn pārcha-rā astar (ẓarūr) ast.* (*lāzim; wājib.*) Or, *īn abra astar mī-khwāhad.*

LINKS—How many links are there in that chain?—*ān zanjīr chand halḳa dārad?* Or, *dar ān silsila chand tā halḳa ast?*

LION—A lion is stronger than a tiger.—*asad az sher (zor-āward)tar ast.* (*ḳawī.*)

LIPS—Her lips are red.—*labhū,e ān zan (surkh) and.* (*la'l; miṣal-i-marjānī.*)

LIQUID—Is the medicine you speak of a liquid?—*dawā,e ki shumā ẓikr-ash mī-kuned rakīk ast.*

LIST—Write a list of the things sent to Tihrān.—*ashyā ki ba ṭehrān mursil shuda ast fihrist-ash bi-nawīs.*

LISTEN—Listen to what I tell you.—*ānchi mī-goyam gosh kun.* Or, *guftār-i-man ba gosh-i-jān bi-shinau.* Or, *ḳaul-i-man andar-i-gosh (bi-gīr).* (*biyāwar.*)

LITERAL—The translation is too literal.—*īn tarjuma ziyā-datar (ḥarf ba ḥarf) ast.* (*lafẓī.*)

LITTLE—Give me a little, I don't ask for much.—*ba man ḳadre bi-dih, bisiyār na mī-khwāham.*

LIVELY—He is of a lively disposition.—*o khūsh ṭab' ast.*

LIVE—I shall respect him as long as I live.—*tā ān ki zinda am (o-rā 'izzat) khwāham kard.* (*ikrām-i-o ; ta'ẓīm-i-o.*)

LOAD—He told me to load the boat with indigo.—*o ba man guft ki man kishtī-rā (az nīl pur) bi-kunam.* (*ba nīl pur bār.*)

LOADED—Is this gun loaded?—*āyā īn tufang pur ast?*

LOADSTONE—Do you know the virtue of the loadstone?—*khāṣṣīyat-i-(sang-i-maḳnāṭīs) mī-dāned?* (*āhan-rubā.*)

LOAN—May I beg the loan of this book?—*az rāh-i-mihrbānī īn kitāb-rā ba man ('āriyat) khwāhed dād.* (*ta'ārrufan; 'āriyatan; amānatan.*)

LOAVES—Tell the baker to give three loaves.—*ba nān-paz ḥukm bi-dih ki o si nān bi-dihad.*

LOCK—There is no lock to your box.—*sandūḳ-i-shumā(-rā ḳufl nīst).* (*ḳufl na dārad; be ḳufl ast.*)

LODGE—Where shall we lodge to-night?—*imshab kujā (manzil bi-dārem)?* (*pā,īn bi-shavem; shab ba sar biyāwarem; bi-guzrānem; mutawaḳḳif bi-shavem; suḳūnat bi-pazīrem; mutamakkin bi-shavem.*)

LOFTY—These rooms are very lofty.—*īn ḥujrahā bisiyār (buland) and.* (*rafī'.*)

LOITER—Why do you thus loiter away your time?—*shumā chirā īn chunīn ṭaur auḳāt-i-khud-rā dar ghaflat ẓā,i' mī-kuned?* Or, *shumā chirā īn chunīn ṭaur aiyām-i-khud-rā (ba bād) mī-dihed?* (*muft az dast.*)

LONG—How long is this piece of cloth?—*īn pārcha,e jāma chi ḳadar (ṭawīl ast).* (*darāz ast; ṭūl* or *ṭawālat dārad.*)

LONG—How long shall you remain there?—*tā ba chand roz ān jā khwāhed mānd?*

LOOK—Let me look through your spying-glass.—*bi-guzār ki man ba dūrbīn-i-shumā bi-bīnam.*

LOOKING-GLASS—When you go to Shīrāz buy me a looking-glass.—*waḳte ki ba shīrāz bi-raved yak (ā,ina) az barā,e man bi-khared.* (*sajanjal.*)

LOOSE—Try if you can loose (untie) this knot.—*koshish bi-kuned ki shumā īn gira-rā (wā) kardan bi-tawāned.* (*ḥall; bāz.*)

LOOSE—The joints of this chair are very loose.—*bandhā,e īn kursī bisiyār (sust) shuda and.* (*hazz; shull.*)

LOSE—Take care you don't lose the knife I gave you.—

kūrde ki man ba shumā dādam khabar-dār ān-rā gum na kuned.

LOSS—He has met with great loss.—*o-rā bisiyār khisārat rasīda ast.* Or, *nuḳṣān-i-firāwān bar o (uftāda) ast.* (*'āriẓ gashta ; 'ā,id gardīda ; wāḳi' shuda ; wārid shuda ; rasīda.*)

LOST—He lost his way in coming from the city.—*waḳte ki az shahr bāz mī-āmad rāh gum kard.*

LOTS—I purchased five lots at to-day's sale.—*ba harrāj-i-imroz panj 'adad-i-ashiyā kharīdam.*

LOTS—They cast lots ; the lot fell on him.—*ḳur'a afgand-and ba nām-ash ḳur'a (uftād).* (*bar āmad.*)

LOTUS—This is the flower of the lotus.—*īn gul-i-nīlūfar ast.*

LOVE—They have no love for each other.—*eshān bāham (muḥabbat) na dārand.* (*muwaddat ; ulfat ; unsiyat ; mu,ānasat ; khullat.*)

LOW—This is a very low room.—*īn ḥujra khailī (past) ast.* (*farūd ; nā-buland.*)

LOW—The price he asks is very low.—*ḳīmat-i-bisiyār kam mī-khwāhad.*

LOWER—Lower this bucket into the well.—*dar chāh īn dalw-rā pā,īn bi-kun.*

LUCRATIVE—Theirs is a lucrative employment.—*kār-i-eshān bisiyār (naf') dārad.* (*manfa'at ; intifā' ; fā,ida.*)

LUGGAGE—Put this luggage in the boat.—*dar zauraḳ īn asbāb-rā bi-guẕār.*

LUSTY—He is now grown very lusty,—*o bisiyār (farbih) gashta ast.* (*chāk.*)

M.

MACHINE—What is the name of this machine?—*ism-i-īn (ṣan'at) chīst?* (*ālat.*)

MAD—He was bit by a mad dog.—*o az sag-i-dīwāna gazīda shud.* Or, *sag-i-dīwāna o-rā gazīd*

MADE—He made me write the letter directly.—*o az man fi-l-faur khaṭṭ nawīsānīd.*

MADE—Having made a pen, he began to write.—*ḳalam tarāshīda nawishtan (girift). (shurū' kard.)*

MAGNIFICENT—These are magnificent apartments.—*īn ḥujrahā khailī ('ālishān) and. (ẕū-l-rafa'at.)*

MAID-SERVANTS—He has two maid-servants.—*o dū (mashāta) dārad. (band-andāz; zan-naukar.)*

MAKE—Make haste and write the letter.—*zūd bāsh wa īn khaṭṭ-rā bi-nawīs.* Or, *īn khaṭṭ fi-l-faur bi-nawīs.*

MANAGES—Who manages his affairs?—*kār-i-o ki (mī-kunad)? (ba sar-anjām mī-rasānad.)* Or, *ki tartīb-i-muhimāt-i-o mī-kunad?* Or, *ādā,e kār-ash ba ẕimma,e kīst?*

MANKIND—We ought to love all mankind.—*mā-rā bāyad ki ba hama insān (dostī) bi-dārem. (ulfat; ikhlāṣ; muḥabbat; uns; istīnās; muwaddat; yagānagiyat.)*

MANNER—He spoke to us in this manner.—*badīn (ṭaur) bā mā sukhan guft. (namaṭ; minwāl; ṭarīḳ; sabīl; wajh; dastūr; nahaj; ṭaraḥ.)*

MANURE—This garden needs some manure.—*īn bostān kūd mī-khwāhad.* Or, *īn bāgh ẓarūrat-i-sargīn dārad.* Or, *īn rauẓa-rā iḥtiyāj-i-sargīn ast.*

MAP—Show me a map of Persia.—*ba man naḳsha,e īrān (bi-namā). (nishān bi-dih.)*

MARBLE—This floor is paved with marble, and inlaid with turquoise.—*farsh-i-īn khāna (rukhām andākhta shuda ast wa khishthā,e fīrūza dar ān sākhta). (az marmar wa khishthā,e fīrūza mī-shavad.)*

MARCH—The regiment will march to-morrow.—*fauj farda kūch khwāhad kard.*

MARK—Put a mark on the paper that is yours.—*kāghaẕe ki az ān-i-shumā ast bar ān nishān bi-kun.*

MARKET—I have been to the market.—*man ba bāzār (būda am). (rafta būdam.)*

MARRIAGE—When will his marriage take place?—*shādī,e o kai khwāhad shud?* Or, *munākaḥat kai khwāhad kard?*

Or, *'akd-i-nikāḥ kai khwāhad bast?* Or, *o zane-rā kai dar 'akd-i-nikāḥ khwāhad āward?* Or, *o kai juftekhwāhad girift?* Or, *o kai zane khwāhad khwāst?*

MASTER—He is a very kind master (meaning, teacher or preceptor).—*o bisiyār mihrbān ustāde ast.*

MASTER—Is your master (meaning a European gentleman) at home?—*āghā,e shumā ba khāna mī-bāshad?*

MATE—Call the carpenter and his mate now.—*najjār wa (rafīk-ash) bi-goyed ki fi-l-faur bi-āyand.* (*shāgird-ash; wa ān ādm ki bā o sar o kār bāshad.*)

MATERIALS—How can they work without materials?—*be sāmān kār chigūna mī-tawānand kard?*

MEANS—By what means can you do this?—*ba chi tadbīr īn-rā mī-tawāned kard?* Or, *shumā dar ādā,e īn kār chi dast ras paidā kardan mī-tawāned?*

MEAN—I mean to go to Baghdād to-morrow.—*farda irāda,e raftan (ba) baghdād dāram.* (*-i-.*)

MEASURE—Measure this cloth.—*īn pārcha-rā (bi-paimā).* (*gaz bi-kun.*)

MEASURE—This is a kind of measure.—*īn yak ḳisme ast az (maḳdār).* (*paimā,ish; andāza.*)

MEET—Meet me at Maulavī Sa'īd's house to-morrow.—*farda ba khāna,e maulawī sa'īd (ba man) mulāḳāt bi-kuned.* (*marā; bā man.*) Or, *az barā,e mulāḳāt (kardan-i-man) farda ba maḳām-i-mullā sa'īd ḥāẓir bāshed.* (*-am.*)

MEMOIRS—I am reading a book of memoirs.—*kitāb-i-tazkirat mī-khwānam.*

MEMORANDUM—Make a memorandum of this.—*yād-dāsht-i-īn bi-nawīs.*

MEMORY—I have a bad memory.—*ḥāfiẓa,e man mukaddar ast.* Or, *man ṭab'-i-ghabī dāram.*

MEND—Tell the carpenter to mend this box.—*ba darrūdgār bi-go ki īn ṣandūk-rā (marammat) bi-kun.* (*ta'mīr.*)

MERCIFUL—We ought ever to be merciful.—*mā-rā bāyad ki hamesha (raḥīm bāshem).* (*mushfiḳ; shafīḳ; muta-raḥḥam.*) Or, *mā-rā bāyad ki ba har kas ba (raḥm wa shafḳat wa marḥamat sulūk bi-namūyem). (muruwat wa futūwat pesh āyem.)*

Merchandise—This is an article of merchandise.—*īn jins-i-(tijārat) ast. (dād o sitad; saudāgarī; bai'-i-farokhtan wa kharīdan.)*

Merchant—He is now a merchant in Teheran.—*o dar ṭahrān (saudāgare) ast. (tājire; bāzargāne.)*

Met—I walked four miles and met no one.—*chahār mīl raftam ba hech kus mulāḳāt na kardam.* Or, *chahār mīl masāfat kardam ba hech kas mulāḳī na shudam.*

Method—What is the best method (mode) of learning a language?—*dar āmokhtan-i-zabān kudām ṭarīḳ bihtar ast?*

Mid-day—I did not arrive there till mid-day.—*tā ba waḳt-i-nīm-roz ān jā na rasīdam.*

Middle—Shall I put it at the top, or in the middle?—*īn-rā bālā bi-guzāram yā darmiyān?*

Middling—This paper is middling.—*īn kāghaz mutawassiṭ ast.*

Mild—She is mild in temper.—*ān ṣāḥiba mizāj-i-(mulā,im) dārad. (ḥalīm.)*

Mind—I have considered this in my own mind.—*man dar bāb-i-īn dar khāṭir-i-khud (andesha) karda am. (fikr; tajwīz; ta,ammal; tafakkur.)*

Minded—Had you minded what he said, then it would be well.—*agar ba ānchi o guft muttafiḳ mī-shuded pas bihtar būde.* Or, *agar sukhan-ash ḳabūl mī-dāshted chi khūsh būde!*

Mines—Lead and copper are dug out of mines.—*surb wa mis az (m'adan) kanda mī-shavad. (kān.)*

Minute—I shall return in one minute.—*dar yak daḳīḳa bāz khwāham āmad.* Or, *dar ṭurfatu-l-'ain murāja'at khwāham kard.*

Mirth—They are full of mirth.—*eshān az khūshī dar jāma na mī-gunjand.*

Mischief—They are always in mischief.—*eshān hamesha mūẕī and.*

MISERABLE—The wicked man is always miserable.—*ādam-i-bad hamesha (dardmand) mī-mānad. (munnaghiṣ; manḥūs; zalīl; shikasta-ḥāl muztarib; muntashirr.)*

MISERS—Misers never think they have enough.—*dīdā,e ahl-i-tama' ba ni'mat-i-dunyā pur na mī-sharad.* Or, *ḥarīsān ba jahāne gursina and.* Or, *dīda,e tang-i-ḥarīṣān ni'mat-i-dunyā pur na mī-kunad.*

MISERY.—They live in great misery.—*eshān dar ḥālat-i-(kharābī) guzrān mī-kunand. (miskīnī; 'usrat; maskanat; zillat; shikasta-ḥālī.)*

MISFORTUNE—He has met with a great misfortune.—*bar o kam bakhtī,e 'azīm uftāda ast.* Or, *bar o āfat-i-buzurg rū,e dāda ast.* Or, *ba anwā'-i-fitnahā mubtala gardīda ast.* Or, *zamāna o-rā hadaf-i-tīr-i-balā sūkhta ast.* Or, *zamāna sang-i-muṣībat az manjanīk-i-balā bar sar-ash zada ast.*

MISLED—I was grievously misled by following your advice.—*az pazīraftan-i-naṣīḥat-i-shumā khaṭūe sakht khurdam.* Or, *az ḳabūl kardan-i-mashwarat-i-shumā khailī fareb khurdam.*

MISMANAGEMENT—This is owing to your mismanagement. —*az be tadbīrī,e shumā īn chunīn kār wāḳi' shud.* Or, *az be intizāmī,e shumā īn ba zuhūr āmada ast.* Or, *az mubāsharat-i-nā-khair-i-shumā īn ittifāḳ uftāda ast.*

MISSPEND—We ought not to misspend our time.—*waḳt-i-khud-rā (zā,i' kardan) munāsib nīst. (be fā,ida az dast dādan.)*

MISRECKONED—I suppose you have misreckoned these rupees; count them again.—*(mazinna dāram ki shumā dar shimurdan-i-īn rūpiyahā ghalaṭ) karda ed; bāz bi-shimāred. (gumān dāram ki dar ta'dād-i-īn mublaghān sahw.)*

MISREPRESENTED—He has much misrepresented the matter.—*o īn muḳaddama-rā bar (khilāf wā) namūda ast. (ghair ḥaḳḳ naḳl munḳalib; nā-rāst; maḥākat; 'aks zāhir.)*

MISSED—They fired several times at a leopard, but missed

it.—*ba palang chand bār tufang* (*khālī kardand*), *ammā khaṭā kardand.* (*sar kardand*; *zadand.*)

Missed—I missed him on the road.—*man dar rāh zāhil shudam, o-rā na dīdam.* Or, *sahwan naẓar-i-man bar o nayuftād.*

Mistake—You mistake my meaning.—*shumā maṭlab-i-marā ghalaṭ mī-dāned.* Or, *ba khāṭir-i-shumā ma'nī,e makṣad-i-man na mī-āyad.* Or, *shumā ba maghẓ-i-mudd'ā,e man na mī-rased.* Or, *ba maṭlab-am ghalaṭ mī-kuned.*

Mistrust—We should not mistrust without cause.—*be sabab az hech kas* (*be 'itibār*) *shudan munāsib nīst.* (*bad-i'tiḳād*; *bad-gumān*; *dar shubha*; *dar shakk.*)

Mix—Mix these together.—*īn har dū-rā bāham* (*biyāmez*). (*makhlūṭ*, or *takhlīṭ*, or *dākhil*, or *jam' bi-kun*; *khīsān.*)

Mock—It is improper to mock any one.—*bar hech kas* (*naḳl*) *kardan munāsib nīst.* (*tamaskhur*; *ṭa'na*; *istihzā*; *mazāḳ*; *maskhara*; *istikhrā*; *maza*; *khanda-rīsh*; *maz-ḥak*; *taghwīt.*)

Modest—He is of a modest disposition.—*o mizāj-i-sharm-āgīn dārad.* Or, *ṭab'-i-ān shakhṣ maḥjūb ast.* Or, *o* (*sharm-rū*) *ast.* (*ṣāḥib-i-ḥaiyā*; *khāshi'.*)

Molest—They molest us very much.—*eshān mārā* (*tash-wīsh-i-'aẓīm mī-dihand.*) (*diḳḳ* or *mushauwash* or *azār mī-kunand*; *taklīf* or *taṣdī' mī-dihand.*) Or, *eshān bar ḥāl-i-mā ta'arruẓ mī-kunand.* Or, *eshān muta'arriẓ-i-ḥāl-i-mā mī-shavand.*

Money—I shall receive the money after one month.—(*ba'd az inḳiẓā,e yak māh*) *pūl ba dast-i-man khwāhad rasīd.* (*waḳte ki yak māh munḳaẓī khwāhad shud.*)

Moon—The moon has not yet risen.—*tā hanoz māhtāb bar na khāsta ast.* [full moon, *badr*; *māh-i-chahār dāh*; new moon, *māh-i-nau*; *hilāl*; *ḳurra,e māh*; *awwal-i-māh.*]

Motion—The motion of this wheel is very quick.—(*ḥara-kat*)[1]*-i-īn* (*charkh*)[2] *bisiyār zūd ast.* [1](*gardish*; *jumbish*; *taḥwīl*; *inḳirāẓ*; *taḥarruk*; *daur.*) [2](*'ujlat.*)

Motive—What is your motive for doing this?—*chi (bā'is ast) ki īn kār mī-kuned?* (*matlab* or *wajh* or *mudd'ā* or *dā'iyat dāred.*)

Mountain—Have you seen the Himālaya mountain?—*āyā koh-i-himālaya mushāhida karda ed?*

Mounted—Having mounted his horse, he rode off.—*bar asp-i-khud sawār shud, wa bar tākht.*

Mourns—The whole country mourns his loss.—*ba mātam-i-marg-ash ahl-i-tamām mulk siyāh mī-poshand.* Or, *az murdan-ash ahl-i-tamām mulk (maghmūm) shuda and.* (*mātam zada.*)

Muddy—Why do you bathe in muddy water?—*chirā dar āb-i-(mukaddar) ghusl mī-kuned?* (*tīra; mutakaddar; mulawwaṣ.*)

Mule—I have bought a mule for 200 rupees.—*kātire (dū ṣad rūpiya-rā) kharīda am.* (*ba dū sad rūpiya.*)

Murdered—He was murdered by robbers.—*o az dast-i-duzdān (kushta shud).* (*ba katl rasīd; munkatl,* or *katīl,* or *maktūl shud.*)

Murmuring—They are always murmuring.—*eshān hamesha (shikāyat) mī-kunand.* (*gila; wa'wa't.*) Or, *eshān dā,imu-l-aukāt marmar mī-zanand.*

Music—Are you fond of music?—*āyā mushtāk ba (sarod) mī-bāshed?* (*tashaiyud; samā'; tarranum; malāhī.*) Or, *āyā (naghma-rā pasand) mī-dāred?* (*'ilm-i-mūsikī-rā dost.*)*

Mute—I spoke several times, but still they continued mute.—*man chand bār guftam, ammā (khāmosh) mānd-and.* (*sākit; sākin.*)

---

* Kettledrum, *nakkāra.*
Bell, *jaras.*
Four-stringed instrument, *rabāb.*
Trumpet, *karnā,e; karnā; sarnā; būk; ṣūr.*
Harp, *chang; barbaṭ.*
Guitar, *sitār.*
Flute, *nai.*

MUTUAL—This will be for our mutual benefit.—*īn (fā,ida,e ṭarafain) khwāhad būd. (mufīd-i-jānibain.)*

N.

NAKED—In parts of Persia little children are accustomed to go naked.—*dar ba'ẓe nawāhī,e fārs ṭiflagān (ba gashtan dar ḥālat-i-barhanagī mu'tād and). ('ādat-i-gashtan dar ḥālat-i-'uryat dārand; 'uryān mī-bāshand.)*

NAME—This vessel's name is the Zuleika.—*ism-i-īn jahāz zulaikhā ast. Or, īn jahāz zulaikhā nām dārad. Or, badīn jahāz zulaikhā nām dāda and. Or, īn jahāz musammạ ba ism-i-zulaikhā ast. Or, īn jahāz ba zulaikhā mausūm gashtā ast.*

NATION—All the people of this nation speak his praise.—*har kaum-i-īn mulk ta'rīf-i-o mī-kunand. Or, sair-i-'awāmmu-n-nās-i-īn balād khuṭba,e taḥsīn ba nām-ash mī-khwānand.*

NATURE—The tiger is fierce by nature.—*sher az (sarisht)¹ (muḥibb)² ast.* ¹*(ẓāt; jibillat.)* ²*(tund-mizāj; shadīd.)*

NAUGHTY—She is a naughty girl.—*ān dukhtarak (sharīr) ast. (shokh-chashm.)*

NAVIGATION—Have you learnt navigation?—*shumā mallāḥī (āmokhta ed)? (yād girifta ed.)*

NECESSARY—It is not anyways necessary that you should go there.—*ba hech wajh (ẓarūr nīst) ki shumā ān jā bi-ravcd. (lāzim or wājib nayāyad.)*

NEED—I have need of your assistance.—*ba madad-i-shumā (muḥtāj) hastam. (ḥājat or iḥtiyāj dāram.) Or, marā imdād-i-shumā ẓarūr ast.*

NEEDFUL—It is absolutely needful that I should go.—*iḥtiyāj maḥẓ ast ki man ān jā bi-ravam. Or, raftan-i-man az jumla,e ẓarūriyāt ast.*

NEGLECT—This is owing to your neglect.—*az ihmāl-i-shumā īn ba ẓuhūr ūmada ast. Or, az taghāful-i-shumā īn wāki' shuda ast. Or, az be-khabarī,e shumā īn ba wukū' rasīda ast. Or, az (tahāwun)-i-shumā īn ba man-*

ṣaba'e shuhūd āmada ast. (*ghaflat; musāhilat; musāmahat; tasāhil.*)

NEGLIGENT—They are idle and negligent.—*eshān* (*sust wa ghāfil*) *and.* (*baṭṭāl wa kāhil; bāṭil wa muhmal; mu'aṭṭal wa musāhil.*) Or, *eshān sustī wa ghaflat mī-*(*warzand*). (*kunand.*)

NEIGHBOUR—He is a neighbour of mine.—*o* (*ham-sāya*),*e man ast.* (*jār; jā,ir; ham-dīwār; ham-jawār.* Or, *o* (*muttaṣil*)*-i-khāna,e man mutawakkif ast.* (*karīb.*)

NEIGHBOURHOOD—He lives in this neighbourhood.—*o dar īn hamsāyagī* (*sukūnat*) *dārad.* (*maskan.*) Or, *o dar īn kurb* (*mukīm*) *ast.* (*sākin; mutawakkif; sukūnat-pazīr.*)

NEXT—We will go there next month.—*mā māh-i-āyanda ān jā khwāham raft.*

NIB—I have broken the nib of my pen.—(*zabān*)*-i-kalam-i-khud shikasta am.* (*nok; sar; fāk; nesh; dam.*)

NIPPED—I nipped my fingers with the pincers.—*angushthā,e khud-rā ba minkāsh afshurdam.*

NOISE—I cannot bear so much noise.—*man tākat-i-īn chunīn ghaughā na mī-tawānam āward.* Or, *man taḥammul-i-chunīn* (*mashghala*) *na mī-tawānam kard.* (*shaghf; ghalghala; shor wa ghul; ghulghul.*) Or, *īn chunīn ghul-ghadar-rā mutaḥammil na mī-tawānam shud.*

NONSENSE—What they say is all nonsense.—*ānchi mī-goyand hama* (*wāhiyāt*) *ast.* (*yāwa-go,ī; behūda-go,ī.*) Or, *eshān sukhan-i-ikhtilāṭ mī-goyand.*

NONSUITED—The plaintiff was nonsuited.—*mukaddama,e mudda'ī* (*khārij*) *shud.* (*nā manẓūr.*)

NOTHING—He asked, but I gave him nothing.—*o khwāst wa lekin pashīze na dīdam.*

NUMB—My fingers are numb with cold.—*az sarmā angushthā,e man* (*khushk*) *shuda and.* (*ghair-i-ḥiss wa jumbish.*)

NUMBER—What number of persons were present?—*chand nafar ḥāẓir būdand?*

NUMEROUS—There are numerous errors in your writing.—*dar nawishta,e shumā bisiyār ghalaṭhā and.*

NURSE—They took with them their little child and its nurse.—*eshān ṭifl-i-kūchak-i-khud bā ma' dāya ham-rāh-i-khud-i-shān burdand.*

NURTURED—He was delicately nurtured.—*o mutana''im būd wa sāya parwarda.* Or, *dar ni'mat wa rāḥat wa āsā,ish auḳāt guẓrānīd.*

O.

OARS—How can the boatmen row without oars?—*baghair az (halīsahā)*[1] *chigūna (halīsa-zanān)*[2] *kashīdan mī-tawānand?* [1]*(khāda; jafdāḳ; majẓāf; miḳẓāf.)* [2]*(mallāḥān.)*

OATH—In a court it is usual for witnesses to take an oath.—*ma'mūl ast ki gawāhān ḥasbu-l-ḳānūn dar 'adālat ḳasam bi-khurand.* Or, *dar 'adālat ḥasbu-l-ma'mūl shāhidān saugand mī-khurand.*

OBEDIENCE—You should pay obedience to his orders.—*munāsib ast ki (muṭāba'at)-i-ḥukm-i-o bi-kuned. (iṭā'at; ṭā'at; muṭāwa'at; inḳiyād.)* Or, *munāsib ast ki shumā (muṭī')-i-ḥukm-i-o bi-bāshed. (farmān-bardār; mutābi'; tābi'.)* Or, *wājib ast ki shumā bar khaṭṭ-i-farmān-ash sar-i-khud bi-nihed.*

OBEDIENT—Good children are obedient to their parents and obliging to every one.—*farzandān-i-arjimand tābi'-i-wālidain-i-khud wa ba hama kas (mutawāẓi') mī-bāshand. (nawāzish-numā; khalīḳ; adab wa azurm-numā.)*

OBEY—I must obey his orders.—*marā bāyad ki ḥukm-ash ba jābiyāram.* Or, *marā bāyad ki ('ubūdiyat)-i-ḥukm-i-o bi-kunam.** *(ṭā'at.)*

OBJECT—What was the object of your going there?—*gharaẓ-i-raftan-i-shumā dar ān jā chi būd?*

---

* *'ubūdiyat* is used to express obedience to God.

OBLIGE—You should try to oblige your master.—*bāyad ki dar (raẓāmandī),e āķā,e khud koshish bi-kuned.* (*khūsh-nūdī.*) Or, *bāyad ki ṣāḥib-i-khud-rā khūsh bi-kuned.* (*masrūr; khūshnūd.*)

OBSCURE—These words are obscure.—*īn alfāẓ* (*mughlaķ*) *and.* (*mu'ammą; ghalķ.*)

OBSOLETE—This term has become obsolete.—*īn iṣṭilāḥ ilḥāl* (*matrūk*) *ast.* (*mansūkh; muhmal; mu'aṭṭal; bilā isti'māl.*)

OBSTACLE—This is an obstacle to my learning.—*īn* (*māni'*)-*i-ta'līm-i-man ast.* (*muta'arriẓ; mawāni'; sadd; mu-zāḥim; mumāni'.*)

OBSTINATE—They are obstinate in their opinions.—*eshān dar rā,e khud bisiyār* (*khud-sar*) *and.* (*sar-kash; muta'-aṣṣab; khud-pasand; mu'ānid; mutamarrid, gardan-kash.*)

OCCASION—There was no occasion for your coming.—*āmadan-i-shumā dar īn jā darkār na būd.*

OCCASIONED—He has occasioned his parents trouble.—*o sabab-i-ranj-i-wālidain-i-khud gardīd.* Or, *o ba pidar o mādar-i-khud* (*taṣdī'*) *dāda ast.* (*zuḥmat; iẓṭirāb; taklīf.*)

OCCUPIED—After another month, I shall have occupied this house twenty years.—*ba'd az itmām-i-māh-i-dīgar bīst sāl kāmil khwāhad shud ki dar īn khāna tawaķķuf warzīda am.*

OCCURRED—I don't remember this ever to have occurred before.—(*dar yād-i-man na mī-āyad*) *ki īn chunīn amr pesh az īn ittifāķ uftād.* (*yād na dāram.*)

OCCURRENCE—This is a very remarkable occurrence.—*īn amre bisiyār* (*'ajīb*) *ast.* (*gharīb; nādir; ta'ajjubnāk; muta'ajjib.*)

ODD—This is a very odd kind of expression.—*īn kalāme-'ajīb ast.*

OFFENCE—What offence have I committed?—*chi jurm az man ba wujūd āmada ast?* Or, *chi taķṣīr az wujūd-i-man sar bar zada ast?* Or, *ba chi ma'ṣī mubtala gardīda am?* Or, *chi khaṭā az man ṣādir shuda ast?*

OFFENDING—I cannot think of thus offending him.—*man na mī-khwāham ki o-rā īn chunīn (nā-khush) sāzam. (ranja-khāṭir; dil-āzurda; taghyīẓ.)* Or, *marā pasand nīst ki mūjib-i-āzār-i-khāṭir-ash shavam.*

OFFERED—Had I known this before, I should have offered you my services.—*agar ḳabl az īn īn amr-rā mī-dānistam barā,e imdād-i-shumā ḥāẓir būdame.*

OFFICE—I am going to Mr. ——'s office.—*ba daftar-khāna,e fulān ṣāḥib mī-ravam.*

OFFICER—He is a European officer.—*o sarhange az ahl-i-farang ast.* [Civil officer, *'uhda-dār; manṣab-dār; 'amal-dār;* military officer, *sipah-sālār; sardār.*]

OLD—Once upon a time an old man and an old woman went to the forest to gather sticks.—*bāre az barā,e jam' kardan-i-hezum pīr-marde wa pīr-zane dar besha raftand.* [Old man, *fartūt; mard-i-kuhn-sāl; mard-i-sāl-khurda;* old woman, *fartūta; 'ajūr; zan-i-kuhn-sāl; zan-i-sāl-khurda.*]

OMISSION—There is some omission in copying.—*dar naḳl kardan-i-īn chīze mānda ast.* Or, *dar sawād kardan-i-īn chīze (faro guzāsht) shuda ast. (tark; imhāl karda.)*

OMITTED—I omitted to mention that.—*man farāmosh kardam ki ān sukhan bi-goyam.*

OMNIPOTENT—God is omnipotent and omnipresent.—*khudā (ḳādir wa har jā ḥāẓir) ast. (kirdagār wa dar hama gāh.)*

OPERATE—How does this medicine operate?—*īn dārū chigūna (asar mī-kunad)? (tāsīr mī-kunad; asar* or *tāsīr dārad.)*

OPINION—What opinion do you form on this subject?—*ba nazdīk-i-shumā dar bāb-i-īn chi maṣlaḥat mī-bāshad?* Or, *dar bāb-i-īn chi (ḳiyās mī-kuned)? (rā,e mī-dāred.)* Or, *dar tarāzū,e 'aḳl-i-shumā īn amr chi wazn dārad?*

OPPOSITE—His house is opposite to mine.—*maḳām-ash (muḳābil)-i-khāna,e man ast. (muhāzī; rū-ba-rū; mu-wāzī; mutaḳābil.)*

OPPOSITION—He has met with much opposition.—*bado mukhālifat-i-bisiyār (rū,e dāda) ast. (rukh namūda;*

'ū,id shuda ; ba ẓuhūr āmada.) Or, *bisiyār mardumān bado (ta'arruẓ) karda and. (ikhtilāf ; ta'ārruẓ ; khilāf.)*

ORANGES—I have brought some oranges.—*man ḳadre narangī (āwarda am). (kharīda āwarda am.)*

ORATOR—He is celebrated as an orator.—*o faṣīḥe-mashhūr ast.* Or, *o sukhan-pardāze-ma'rūf ast.*

ORDER—This is an order for a hundred rupīs.—*īn barūte ast az ṣad rūpiya.* Or, *īn ṣad rūpiya-rā kāghaẓe-zar ast.*

ORDER—This school is without order.—*īn maktab be-(tartīb) ast. (intiẓām ; rabṭ o ẓabṭ.)*

ORDERED—I have ordered the goods to be got ready.—*man dar bāb-i-(amāda) kardan-i-ajnās ḥukm karda am. (muhaiyā ; taiyār ; musta'id.)*

ORIENTAL—He was well versed in oriental literature.—*az 'ilm-i-mashriḳī khūb wāḳif būd.*

ORIGIN—Do you know the origin of this saying?—*(aṣl)-i-īn kalima mī-dāned? (manshā ; bunyād ; mabdā.)*

ORIGINAL—This is not the original writing.—*īn taḥrīr (aṣlī) nīst. (aṣīl ; 'ainī.)* Or, *īn aṣl nīst, sawād ast.*

ORNAMENTS—They wear different kinds of ornaments.—*eshān (zewarhā),e ḳism ba ḳism mī-poshand. (ḥulīhā ; ṭarāzhā.)* Or, *eshān pīrāya,e ṭaraḥ ba ṭaraḥ (dar bar) mī-kunand. (bar badan.)*

ORPHANS—These children are orphans —*īn aṭfāl yatīm and* (fatherless and motherless). Or, *īn farzandān yasīr and* (motherless only).

OVERCOME—We cannot overcome the enemy.—*mā bar dushman (ghālib shudan) na mī-tawānem. (ghālib āmadan ; dastyāftan.)* Or, *mā (bar dushman ghaliba) na mī-tawānem kard. (dushman-rā maghlūb* or *fatḥ.)*

OVERFLOWED—The river has overflowed its banks.—*āb-i-nahr (az kināra bālā) āmada ast. (ba tughyān ; ba sailāb.)* Or, *āb-i-daryā sail-rawān būda ast.*

OVERLOOK—It is better that you overlook his offence.—*īn bihtar ast ki (az khaṭā,e o chashm-poshī bi-farmāyed). (az taḳṣīr-ash dar guẓared ; ẓambash bi-bakhshed ; ḳuṣūr-i-o-rā mu'āf bi-kuned.)*

Overset—A sudden gust of wind overset the boat.—*yak būrgī ṭapāncha,e bād safīna-rā bar gardānīd.* Or, *yak-ā-yak nafḥat-i-bād kishtī-rā* (*wāzh-gūn*) *kard.* (*nigūn; munkalib; wāzh-gūna.*)

Oxen—Whose oxen are these?—*īn muwāshīyān az ān-i-kīst?*

P.

Packet—I have received a packet from Isfahan.—*az iṣfahān ba chāparī khariṭa,e khuṭūṭ* (*ba dast-i-man rasīda ast*). (*yāfta am.*)

Page—In what page of the book does the word occur?—*dar kudām ṣafḥa,e kitāb ān lafẓ* (*mī-āyad*)? (*wāḳi' mī-sharad.*)

Paint—Where did you get this paint?—*āyā az kujā īn rang* (*gīr*)-*i-shumā āmad?* (*ba dast.*)

Painter—In former times, there lived in China a celebrated painter, by name Mānī.—*dar zamān-i-salf naḳḳāshe-mashhūr dar mulk-i-chīn būd ba nām mānī.* Or, *dar zamān-i-sābiḳ* (*musauwire*) *ma'rūf dar diyār-i-chīn sukūnat dāsht ki nām-ash mānī būd.* (*ṣūrat-gare; naḳḳash-pardāze; timṣāl-gare.*)

Pale—He became pale through fear (*literally* yellow).—*o az khauf zard shud.*

Pamphlet—Have you read that pamphlet?—*ān risāla* (*khwānda ed*)? (*muṭā'ala karda ed; mulaḥiẓa karda ed*)

Panes—There are ten panes of glass in this window.—*dar īn ghurfa dah* (*fard*)-*i-shīsha ast.* (*khāna.*)

Parcel—I have forwarded to him the parcel.—*bado* (*buḳcha*) *irsāl karda am.* (*basta; dasta.*)

Pardon—Sir, I beg your pardon.—*ṣāḥibā marā* (*mu'āf bi-farmāyed*). (*ma'ẕūr bi-dāred; 'afw bi-kuned; bi-yāmurzed.**) Or, *ṣāḥibā ṭālib-i-maghfirat-i-shumā hastam.* Or, *ṣāḥibā jā,e ma'ẕarat marā bi-dihed.* Or, *ṣāḥibā az*

---

* *āmurzidan* applies to seeking for forgiveness from God only.

taḳṣīr-i-mā maẓạ dar guẕared. Or, *ai ṣāḥib bar man bi-bakhshed.* Or, *ṣāhibā* (*'uẕram bi-nihed*). (*marā baḥil bi-kuned; marā bihil bi-kuned.*)

PARENTS—He said that his parents had given him leave to do so.—*o guft ki wālidain-i-man ijāzat-i-kardan-i-chunīn kār dāda būdand.*

PARTAKE—I invited him to partake of some fruit, but he would not.—*man o-rā ba tanāwul kardan-i-ḳadre mewa da'wat namūdam, wa lekin o* (*inkār kard*). (*abā* or *istiknāf* or *ḳabūl na kard; sar bāz zad.*) Or, *man o-rā ba sharīk shudan-i-ṭa'ām da'wat dādam, wa lekin o i'rāẓ kard.*

PARTIALITY—We ought not to show partiality in our judgment.—*mārā bāyad ki dar inṣāf* (*ṭarafdārī,e kase na kunem*). (*ṭaraf-i-kase na gīrem.*)

PARTICULAR—I find I am mistaken in this particular.—*ba* (*mafhūm*)-*am mī-rasad ki dar īn nukta ghalaṭ khurda am.* (*fahm.*) Or, *ma'lūm-am mī-shavad ki dar īn daḳīḳa sahw karda am.*

PARTNER—He is a partner in the house of Hājī Hassan and Brothers—*o dar jamā'at-i-ḥājī-ḥassan wa barādarān* (*sharīke*) *ast.* (*mushārik.*)

PARTY—Each of them favours his own party.—*har yak az eshān ṭarafdārī,e farīḳ-i-khud mī-kunad.* Or, *har yak az eshān hawādār-i-*(*farīḳ*)-*i-khud mī-bāshad.* (*ahl-i-tashāwar.*)

PASS—Have you got a pass for these goods?—*az barā,e īn asbāb* (*khaṭṭ-i-rāh-dārī,*)*e dāred?* (*rawāna.*)

PASS—This coin does not pass in Persia.—*īn ẓarb dar īrān* (*murauwaj*) *nīst.* (*rawān, rā,ij.*) Or, *īn sikka-rā dar fārs rawāj nīst.*

PASSED—He passed by him.—*bar o guẕar kard.* Or, *az o guẕasht.*

PASSED—He passed that way.—*o-rā guẕar bar ān rah uftād.*

PASSAGE—A river intercepted their passage.—*nahre a'ẓīm bar guẕar-i-eshān uftād.* Or, *jū,e āb-i-buzurg bar mamarr-i-eshān padīd āmad.*

PASSENGERS—That ship brought many passengers.—*ān*

jahāz bisiyār ma'barān āward. Or, *dar ān jahāz musāfirān-i-kaṡīr āmadand.*

Passion—One ought never to be in a passion.—*bāyad ki kase dar (ghaiẓ) nayāyad.* (*ghuṣṣa; khashm; tashaddud; taghaiyur.*)

Passport—He has obtained a passport to go to Tabrīz.—*az barā,e raftan ba tabrīz (parwāna,e rāhdārī) ḥāṣil karda ast.* (*sunnad-i-rāh-dārī; guẕar-nāma; barāt-i-ẕimmat.*)

Path—This path leads to the village.—*ba dih īn rāh (sar mī-kashad).* (*sar mī-dihad; mī-ravad.*)

Patience—It becomes us to exercise patience in adversity. —*mārā bāyad ki dar muṣībat (ṣabr) ikhtiyār bi-namāyem.* (*burdbārī; ṣabūrī; shikeb.*) Or, *bāyad ki mā dar āfat taḥammul bi-kunem.*

Patient—They are patient and peaceable.—*eshān (ṣābir wa mulā,im) and.* (*salīm wa ḥalīm; muḥtamil wa ṣalāḥ-andesh.*)

Patronizes—He patronizes whatever tends to the welfare of the country.—*dar amre ki mūjib-i-bihbūdī,e mulk būda būshad har chi tamāmtar sā'ī mī-kunad.*

Pattern—You must give me a pattern to work by.—*bāyad ki ba man yak (namūna,e) bi-dihed ki badān kār bi-kunam.* (*inmūdaje.*)

Pause—In reading, you ought to pause where there is a stop. —*bāyad ki dar khwāndan (waḳf)-rā nigāh bi-dāred.* (*jā,e sukūt.*)

Pay—I have had a month's pay beforehand.—*man muwājib-i-yak māh peshgī girifta am.*

Pays—He is a very just man, he pays all his debts.—*o ādam-i bisiyār (diyānat-dār) ast ḳurūẓāt-i-khuḍ-rā adā mī-kunad.* (*munṣif-mizāj; i,mān-dār.*)

Pecuniary—He will have only pecuniary loss.—*nuḳṣān-ash faḳaṭ dar naḳd khwāhad shud.*

Peep—The windows are so small, one can but just peep through them.—*ghurfahā īn ḳadar tang and ki kase faḳaṭ lamaḥ mī-tawānad zad).* (*jamāsh mī-tawānad kard.*)

PEEVISH—These children are peevish and perverse.—*īn aṭfāl* (*ẓajūr wa kajrū*) *and.* (*tez-mizāj wa 'anīd.*)

PENALTY—For doing this you must pay a penalty.—*az kardan-i-īn kār shumā-rā* (*jarimāna*),*e dādanī khwāhad shud.* (*gharm ; gharāmat ; muṣādira.*)

PENKNIFE—Lend me your penknife to cut my pen.—*barā,e tarāshīdan-i-ḳulam-am chākū,e khud 'āriyataṉ bi-dihed.*

PENSIVE—His turn of mind is pensive.—*dil-ash bi-ẕ-ẕāt* (*mutafakkir*) *ast.* (*muta,ammil ; fikrmand.*)

PERCEIVE—I perceive no error in your composition.—*dar taḥrīr-i-shumā hech ghalaṭ* (*paidā na mī-tawānam kard*). *na mī bīnam ; na mī-yābam.*)

PERCEPTIBLE—This blemish is not perceptible.—*īn dāgh* (*ghair-maḥsūs ast*). (*nā-āshkār ast ; ḳābil-i-idrāk nīst.*)

PERFECT—Your work is now perfect.—*ilḥal kār-i-shumā* (*kāmil*) *ast.* (*ba kamāl rasīda ; ba itmām rasīda.*)

PERFECTION—We ought to aim at perfection, though we cannot attain it.—*bāyad ki ba taḥṣīl-i-kamāl koshish bi-kunem agarchi badān na mī-tawānem rasīd.*

PERFORM—He generally promises, but he does not perform.—*o akṣar wa'da mī-kunad, wa lekin* (*ba jā na mī-ārad*). (*tamām na mī-kunad ; ba itmām na mī-rasānad.*)

PERFUME—The whole apartment was filled with perfume. —*tamām ḥujra az* (*khūsh-bo*) *pūr shud.* (*shamīm ; rā,iḥat ; nafḥ ; 'iṭr ; 'abīr.*)

PERFUMED—The house is perfumed by the fragrance of these flowers.—*az shamma.e īn gulhā tamām khāna* (*mu'ambar*) *shud.* (*mu'aṭṭar ; mashmūm ; tashmīm ; muṭīb ; muṭaiyab.*)

PERHAPS—Perhaps this news may be true.—*shāyad ki īn khabar rāst bāshad.*

PERMANENT—Is this regulation to be permanent?—*āyā īn* (*ḳā,ida pā,edār*) *khwāhad mānd?* (*ḳānūn ḳā,im ; ā,in muḥkam ; ẓābṭa-mustaḳīm.*)

PERMISSION—I have permission to go for three months.—*ijāzat-i-raftan tā ba si māh yāfta am.*

PERMIT—Bring a permit for these goods.—*ba jihat-i-bar dāshtan-i-īn asbāb (rawāna), e biyār? (parwāna; ijāzat-nāma.)*

PERMIT—Will you permit me to walk a little in your garden.—*marā izn khwāhed dād ki sā'ate dar bāgh-i-shumā (sair) kunam. (tamāsha; tafarruḥ; siyāḥat.)*

PERPETUAL—There is a perpetual flux and reflux.—*'ala-d-dawām madd o jazr-i-āb-i-baḥr ast.*

PERPLEXED—I am much perplexed in this business.—*dar īn mu'āmala bisiyār (mutaraddid) am. (muẓṭarib; parāganda; mushawwish; hairān.)* Or, *dar īn 'amal man dar maẓīḳ-i-'uḳda hastam.*

PERSUASION—I have done this deed through his persuasion.—*(az targhīb)-ash īn kār karda am. (ba taḥrīṣ; ba taḥrīk.)*

PERTINENT—His answers are pertinent.—*jawābhā,e o (shāyista) and. (sazāwār; muwāfiḳ; mustaujib; munāsib.)*

PETITION—You must make a petition to the merchants.—*bāyad ki saudāgarān-rā ('arẓ-i-ḥāl) bi-kuned. ('arẓdāsht; 'arīẓa; 'arẓī.)*

PHIAL—Have you a phial for the medicine?—*barā,e dārū nigāh dāshtan shīsha'e dāred?*

PHRASE—This phrase is very common.—*īn (kalima) bisiyār 'āmm ast. ('ibārat; muṣṭalaḥ; jumla.)*

PHYSIC—I am not fond of taking physic.—*man dawā giriftan (pasand) na dāram. (dost.)* Or, *man shā,iḳ-i-dawā khurdan nayam.*

PHYSICIAN—Do you know what physician visits him?—*shumā mī-dāned kudām ṭabīb mulāḳāt az barā,e mu'ālaja,e o mī-kunad?*

PIECE—Give me a small piece of paper.—*marā (tikka),e kāghaz bi-dih. (pāra; reza; ḳaṭa'; ruḳ'at.)*

PIETY—He is a person of great piety.—*o ṣāḥib-i-(parsā,ī) ast. (karāmat; ittiḳā; salāḥiyat; taḳwa.)* Or, *o yake az (ṣulḥā) ast. (abrār.)* Or, *ṭarīḳ-i-ān kas zikr wa shukr wa khidmat wa ṭā'at wa iṣār, wa ḳinā'at wa tauḥīd wa tawakkul wa tashīn wa tahammul ast.* Or, *o bisiyār (dīn-dār) ast. (ṣāliḥ; muttaḳī; zāhid; parhezgār; muta'-abbid; parsā; ahl-i-ittiḳā; muwahhid.)* Or, *o yaḳīn dar dil dārad wa wara' dar din wa zuhd dar dunyā wa sharm dar chashm wa bīm dar tan.*

PILGRIM—The pilgrim is gone on pilgrimage.—*ān ḥājī ba ḥajj rafta ast.*

PILLARS—His house is ornamented with pillars.—*khāna-ash ba (sitūn)hā arāsta ast. (rakn,* pl. *arkān; 'amūd,* pl. *'amā,id.)*

PINCERS—I want a pair of pincers from them.—*az eshān yak 'adad-i-minḳāsh mī-khwāham.*

PINNACE—Whose is that pinnace now passing?—*ān dūngī,e ki ilḥāl rāh mī-ravad az ān-i-kīst?*

PIT—I was near falling into a pit.—*nazdīk būd ki man dar maghāk biyuftam.* Or, *dar (ghār) uftādan-am chīze na mānda būd. (ḥufrat.)*

PITY—The afflicted should excite our pity.—*mārā bāyad ki bar (muṣībat-zadagān) rahm biyārem. (ān kasān ki ba dām-i-balā mubtala and.)*

PITY—What a pity you did not tell me this!—*(ḥaif ki ba man khabar) na karded. (afsos ki ba man iṭṭilā,* or *mukhbir.)*

PLACE—What is the place called where he lives?—*maḳāme ki dar ān jā sukūnat dārad nām-ash chīst?*

PLAGUE—The plague of this business is endless.—*(miḥnat wa mushaḳḳat)*[1]*-i-īn kār (intihā na dārad)*[2]. [1]*(zuḥmat; taṣdī'; diḳḳat.)* [2]*(lā-intihā ast.)*

PLAIN—This writing is plain and easy to be read.—*īn raḳam ṣāf ast wa (ba āsānī khwānda mī-shavad). (baghair ma'sūr dar khwāndan mī-āyad; tashīlu-l-muṭāla'a mī-bāshad.)*

PLAINTIFF—Who is the plaintiff in this affair?—*dar īn mu'āmala mudda'ī kīst?*

PLAN—Have you seen the plan of the building?—*naḳsha,e 'imārat dīda ed?* *(mulāḥaẓa karda ed.)*

Plane—Smooth this board with a plane.—*īn takhta,e-rū ba randa (sāf) bi-kun. (musaṭṭaḥ ; tasṭīḥ.)*

Planks—Are these planks for sale?—*āyā īn takhtahā (farokhtanī) and. (māl-i-farokht ; jins-i-baiʿ.)*

Plastered—The inside walls are plastered with lime.—*dīwārān andarūn-i-khāna ba khamīr-i-āhak (astarkārī shuda ast). (kāh-gil shuda ast ; andā,ida and.)*

Play—We have now no time to play.—*mārā ilḥāl fursat-i-bāzī nīst.* Or, *mā aknūn fursat-i-bāzī na dārem.*

Pleased—If he had informed me of this before, I should have been better pleased.—*agar o pesh az īn marā khabar mī-dād man ziyādatar (khūshnūd) būdame. (masrūr ; khurram ; khūrsand ; khūsh-waḳt.)*

Pledge—I pledge my word to act in this manner.—*('ahd o paimūn) mī-kunam ki īn chunīn khwāham kard. (iḳrār.)* Or, *ba adā,e īn kār ḳaul mī-kunam.*

Plentiful—This kind of fruit is plentiful.—*īn ḳism-i-mewa ba kasrat ast.*

Plough—I have an excellent plough and one pair of oxen.—*(ḳulba)¹,e bisiyār khūb (nazd-i-man)² ast wa yak juft-i-gāw. ¹(shiyār ; fadān.) ²(dāram.)*

Plough—When the rains arrive, I shall plough this field.—*waḳte ki bārish khwāhad shud (bar īn zamīn ḳulbarānī) khwāham kard. (zamīn-rā tīmār or falāḥat or ḥars or shiyār.)* Or, *ba mausim-i-bārish īn zamīn khwāham shiyārīd.*

Poet—He is a poet; have you seen his last poem?—*o shā'ire ast shi'r-i-ākhirīn-ash (muṭāla'a karda ed)? (ba muṭāla'a āwarda ed.)*

Point—This needle has no point.—*īn sūzan nok na dārad.* [eye, *sūfār.*]

Point—She has been at the point of death.—*ān ṣāḥiba ḳarību-l-marg būda ast.* Or, *ān bānū dar ḥālat-i-niza' būda ast.* Or, *jān-i-ān khūnam ba lab rasīda būd.* Or, *az nafs-i-ān khātūn ramaḳe mānda būd.*

Pointed—Had you asked, I could have pointed out to you

in what manner to act.—*agar az man istifsār mī-karded man tarkīb-i-īn amr ba shumā namūdame.*

Politeness—He received us with great politeness.—*o ba man ba (luṭf-i-'aẓīm pesh-āmad). (tawāẓu'-i-kaṣīr sulūk kard; akhlāk-i-ḥusna mulāḳī shud.)*

Pony—He rides out every morning on his pony.—*o har ṣubḥ bar (yābū,e khud sawār) mī-shavad. (markab-i-khurd-i-khud rākib.)*

Poor—He is now become poor.—*o ilḥāl bisiyār (muflis) shud. (parāganda,e rozī; maskīn; mustammand; mutaẓa'if; muḥtāj; maflūk; muta'attal; tahī-dast; faḳīr; be-nawā.)* Or, *o aknūn dar ḥālat-i-be-chāragī uftāda ast.* Or, *o aknūn az pāya,e daulat ba iflās uftāda ast.*

Populous—Shīrāz is a very populous city.—*shīrāz shahre ast bisiyār (ma'mūr). (ābād; ābādān.)*

Portrait—I have his portrait in my possession.—*man (taṣwīr-i-rūyash) dāram. (shabīh-ash; taṣwīr-i-ṭala'at-ash.)*

Possessed—Had I studied earlier, by this time I might have possessed much learning.—*agar man ḳabl az īn ta'līm mī-giriftam pas (taraḳḳī dar 'ilm bisiyār namūdame). (mahārat dar 'ilm bisiyār yāftame; dar 'ilm bisiyār māhir shudame; 'ālim shudame.)*

Possibility—There is no possibility of your getting there to-day.—*(mumkin nīst) ki imroz badān jā bi-rased. (imkān na dārad; ṣūrat na bandad; muḥtamal nīst; iḥtimāl na mī-ravad.)*

Post—If the letter goes by to-day's post, you must send it to the post-office now.—*agar mī-khwāhed ki khaṭṭ-i-shumā ba barīd-i-imroza bi-ravad bāyad ki ilḥāl ba barīd-khāna bi-firisted.*

Postage—What will be the postage?—*maḥṣūl-i-khaṭṭ-i-barīd chi ḳadar mī-bāshad?*

Post-master—I have sent word to the post-master.—*ba mukhtār-i-barīd-khāna paighāme firistāda am.*

Postures—The glare of anger was evident in his postures.—

(āṣār)-i-khashm dar ḥarakāt wa sukanāt-ash paidā āmad. (āṭash ; tāb.)

Pot—What is there in this earthen pot?—*dar īn ẓarf-i-sifālīn chīst?* [metallic, *filizzī.*]

Poverty—Though in great poverty she is happy.—*agarchi ān zan dar (falākat)-i-shadīd uftāda ast khūsh mī-bāshad. (muflisī ; iflās ; faḳr ; nā-dārī ; tang-dastī ; tahī-dastī.)*

Power—It is beyond my power to understand this.—*(iḳtidār)-i-fahmīdan-i-īn na dāram. (ḳuwat ; ṭāḳat ; taḳwiyat ; ḳudrat ; maḳdūr ; majāl ; isti'dād.)* Or, *az ḥīṭa,e fahm-am berūn ast ki īn amr-rā bi-fahmam.*

Practicable—What you purpose, I think, is not practicable.—*ānchi irāda dāred ba rā,eyam ghair-mumkin ast.*

Practice—Whence arose this practice?—*az kujā īn ('ādat paidā shud). (rasm bar khāst ; dastūr sar bar āward.)*

Practitioner—He is an effective practitioner, and a competent physician.—*o jarrāḥ-i-kāmil ast wa ṭabīb-i-(ḥāẕiḳ). (ẓarīj.)* Or, *o ba zewūr-i-jarrāḥī arāsta ast wa ba ḥuliya,e ṭabībī pairāsta.*

Praise—We ought not to praise the undeserving.—*na bāyad ki mā (badān-rā madḥ) bi-kunem. (sharīrān-rā taḥsīn wa afrīn wa sitā,ish wa istiḥsān.)* Or, *mārā na bāyad ki bar (shanī'ān) zabān-i-ṡanā bi-kushāyem. (fāhishān ; mufsidān ; fāsidān ; fājirān ; bad-ma'ashān ; mudbirān ; fāsiḳān.)*

Precarious—Her health is very precarious.—*mizāj-i-ūn khānam bisiyār (nā-ḳā,im) ast. (nā-muḳarrar ; nā-mustamir ; nā-mustaḳill ; 'alīl ; be-ḳiyām ; be-ṡabāt ; ghair-i-mutaṡābit.)*

Precepts—In the book which you gave me are many excellent precepts.—*kitābe ki ba man dāded dar ān bisiyār (aḥkām)-i-afẓal and. (naṣīḥat,* pl. *naṣā,iḥ ; pand ; andarz.)*

Predict—We cannot predict what will happen on the morrow.—*mā pesh na mī-tawānem guft ki fardā chi (rū,e khwāhad dād). (khwāhad uftād ; ba ẓuhūr khwāhad āmad.)*

Prediction—Your prediction has been fulfilled—*pesh-go,ī,e*

shumā ba anjām rasīda ast. Or, *khabar-i-ghaib-i-shumā sar anjām yāfta ast.* Or, *ghaib-go,ī,e shumā tamām shuda ast.*

PREFER—I prefer your house to my own.—*man khāna,e shumā az khāna,e khud bihtar mī-dānam.* Or, *man khana,e shumā-rā bar khāna,e khud (tarjīh mī-diham). (ikhtiyār mī-kunam; mī-guzīnam.)* Or, *man khāna,e shumā-rā ba khāna,e khud dar khūbī mukaddam mī-dāram.*

PREFERABLE—Which of these two is preferable?—*az īn har dū tā kudām pasandīda-tar ast?*

PREJUDICE—We ought to get rid of prejudice.—*mārā bāyad ki (ta'aṣṣub-rā bi-guzūrem). (az rā,e be dānish wa tafaḥḥuṣ bi-rahem; az fikr-i-be-khabar wa taftīsh iḥtirāz bi-kunem.)*

PREMIUM—He received a premium of 100 tūman.—*o yak ṣad tūmān ba ṭarīk-i-in'ām yāft.*

PREPARING—They are preparing to go to England.—*eshān barā,e raftan-i-wilāyat (taiyārī) mī-kunand. (tahaiyat; ta'biyat.)*

PREPARED—He prepared his speech.—*o pasīch-i-sukhan-i-khud (kard). (pardūkht.)*

PRESCRIPTION—The doctor wrote this prescription.—*ṭabīb īn nuskha-rā nawisht.*

PRESENCE—He said so in my presence.—*badīn ṭaur (rū-ba-rū,e man) guft. (bā wujūd-i-iḥẓār-i-man; dar muwājihat-i-man.)*

PRESENT—The Amir of Samarcand sent this elephant to the Governor-General as a present.—*amīr-i-samarkand ba ṭaur-i-(tuḥfa) īn pīl barā,e farmān-farmā mursil sākht. (hadīya; saughāt; pesh-kash.)*

PRESERVED—By your kindness my life was preserved.—*ba 'ināyat-i-shumā jān-am (mahfūẓ) mānd. (ba salāmat; mahrūs; maṣūn.)*

PRESERVES—Are you fond of preserves?—*(murabba)hā-rā pasand dāred? (ma'jūn; angubīna.)*

PRESIDENT—Who is the president of that society?—*kudām*

kas dar ān (majlis mīr-i-majlis) ast? (*anjumān sarwar, jamā'at ra,īsu-l-majlis.*)

PRESUME—I presume, sir, you have lately arrived in this country.—*ai āghā maẕinna dāram ki shumā tāza dar īn' diyār wārid shuda ed.*

PREVAIL—I could not prevail upon him to remain here longer.—(*o-rā bar īn na tawānistam dāsht*) *ki dar īn jā ziyāda tawaḳḳuf kunad.* (*o-rā taḥrīk* or *targhib* or *taḥrīṣ na tawānistam kard.*)

PREVALENT—This disorder is at present very prevalent.—*īn marẓ ilḥāl bisiyār* (*ghālib ast*). (*mastulī ast; ghaliba dārad.*)

PREVENTED—I thought you might have prevented their going away.—*gumān dāshtam ki shumā eshān-rā az bar gardīdan man' mī-tawānisted kard.*

PREVIOUS—You went previous to my arrival.—*shumā ḳabl az āmadan-i-man* (*rawāna shuded*). (*rāh girā shuded; rū ba rāh nihāded.*)

PRICE—What is the price of this? Is that really the market-price (or price-current)?—*ḳīmat-i-īn shai chīst? āyā fi-l-wāḳi' nirkh-i-bāzār hamīn ast?*

PRIDE—We ought to shun pride.—*bāyad ki mā az gharūr* (*bi-parhezem*). (*ijtināb* or *tajannub bi-namāyem; iḥtirāz bi-kunem.*) Or, *bāyad ki mā* (*khayāl-i-far'ūnī*) *az sar bi-kashem.* (*kibr; takabbur; nakhwat; 'ujub; pindār; istighnā,i.*)

PRINCIPAL—Who is the principal in the business?—*dar īn mu'āmala kudām kas* (*mukhtār*) *ast?* (*madāru-l-muhām.*)

PRINTED—The book will shortly be printed.—*kitāb 'an-ḳarīb maṭbū' khwāhad shud.*

PRIVATE—They held a private conversation.—*eshān sukhan-i-*(*makhfī*) *kardand.* (*ba tanhā,ī; ikhfā; khufiya; khafī; pinhān.*)

PROBABILITY—Is there a probability of my seeing him?—*āyā* (*iḥtimāl dārad*) *ki man o-rā bi-bīnam.* (*aghlab ast.*)

PROBABLE—That is not at all probable.—*ān bi-l-kull* (*iḥtimāl na dārad*). (*mutaḥammil nīst.*)

PROCURE—Where can I procure a boat?—*āyā kishtī az kujā ba gīr-i-man mī-āyad?*

PRODUCE—Those articles are the produce of this country. —*ān ashiyā dar īn mulk paidā mī-shavand.* Or, *ān ajnās paidā,ish-i-īn diyār ast.*

PRODUCES—This garden produces nothing but weeds.—*dar īn bagh hech paidā na mī-shavad magar (kāh o khas). (kūh-i-nākhāra.)*

PROFANE—They use only profane language.—*eshān fakat kalimāt-i-behūda mī-goyand.* Or, *ba juz az sukhanān-i-(nā-pāk) hech na mī-goyand. (mutanajjis; nā-shā,ista; palīd.)*

PROFLIGATE—He became a profligate.—*o (fājir) gardīd. (fāsik; shakī; zūba'; aubāsh.)* Or, *o dar lahw o la'b mashghūl shud.* Or, *o fisk o fajūr aghāz (kard). (nihād.)*

PROMISED—I promised to call upon him to-day.—*man (wa'da) kardam ki imroz nazd-i-o khwāham raft. ('ahd; ta'ahhud; kaul.)*

PROMOTED—By this our happiness will be promoted.—*az īn khūshī,e mā (ziyāda khwāhad shud). (bartar khwāhad gardīd; khwāhad afzūd; rū ba tarakkī khwāhad nihād 'urūj khwāhad girift; afzūn* or *buland khwāhad shud.)*

PRONE—Man is prone to err.—*ādam mā,il ba khatā ast.* Or, *ādam ma,il ba gunāh dārad.* Or, *insān murakkab az khatā o nisyān ast.*

PRONOUNCE—Let me hear you pronounce this word.—*talaffuz-i-īn lafz (ba man bi-go) ki bi-shinavam. (pesh-i-man zāhir kun.)*

PRONUNCIATION—Is my pronunciation correct?—*āyā talaffuz-i-man sahīh ast?*

PROOF—What proof can you give of this?—*chi dalīl dar bāb-i-subūt-i-īn dāred?* Or, *īn-rā ba chi tarīk ba isbāt mī-rasāned?* Or, *misdāk-i-īn dalīl chi dāred?*

PROP—If you take away this prop, the roof may fall.—*agar īn (sitūn)-rā bar khwāhed dāsht sakf khwāhad uftād. (rukn; 'umūd.)*

PROPAGATED—This doctrine is propagated everywhere.—*īn*

masla dar har jā (murawwaj ast). (rawāj dārad; ifāẓa karda shuda ast; shā,ī' shuda ast.)

PROPER—Do you conceive this to be proper?—*āyā shumā mī-fahmed ki īn (munāsib) ast? (ba jā; ḥalāl; durust.)*

PROPORTION—You will have your proportion of profits.—*shumā az manāfi' (ḥiṣṣa),e tamām khwāhed yāft. (bahra; ḳismat.)*

PROPOSE—I propose that we share the loss between us.—*man mī-goyam ki ānchi nuḳṣān mī-shavad dar ān mā har dū (mushtarik em). (sharīk mī-bāshem; sharākat dārem.)*

PROSECUTE—Will you prosecute him before the judge for his offence?—*barā,e khaṭā,e o shumā bar o ba ḳāẓī nālish khwāhed kard?*

PROSPERITY—He is now in great prosperity.—*o dar īn rozhā (bakhtī-yāwar) dārad. (naṣīb-i-kāmil; tāli'-i-maimūn; bakht-i-himāyūn; chashm-i-daulat bedār.)*

PROSPEROUS—His affairs are now very prosperous.—*ilḥāl umūr-ash rū ba taraḳḳī mī-nihad.* Or, *ilḥāl ba murād-i-khud kām-rān ast.* Or, *aknūn maḥbūb-i-maṭlūb ba o rukh mī-namāyad.* Or, *o ilḥāl (bakhtiyār) ast. (nairūmand; bahramand; bar-khurdār; sa'ādatmand; farkhanda-fāl.)*

PROSPERS—In whatever he undertakes he prospers.—*ānchi ki mī-kunad, dar ān (kām-yāb) mī-shavad. (fīrūzmand; fatḥmand.)*

PROTECT—It is a prince's glory to protect his people.—*fakhr-i-shāh-zāda īn ast ki ra'iyat-i-khud-rā (ba ḥifāẓat dārad). (ḥifāẓat* or *ḥirāsat* or *nigāhdāsht kunad.)* Or, *jāh o jalāl-i-pādshāh-zāda īn ast ki (dar bāb-i-ra'iyat-i-khud ṭarīḳ-i-muḥāfiẓat mar'ī dārad). (ba nigāhbānī,e r'āyā,e khud miyān-i-murāḳibat bi-bandad.)*

PROTECTION—They fled to the king for protection.—*ba nazd-i-shāh barā,e panāh (rū ba firār nihādand). (dar gurekhtand.)*

PROUD—They who are proud have little sense.—*kasāne ki (maghrūr and kam 'aḳl and). (gharūr dar sar dārand 'aḳl kam dārand.)*

PROVE—I can prove this to be true.—*man ṣābit mī-tawānam*

kard ki īn saḥīḥ ast. Or, *man ba is̤bāt mī-tawānam rasānīd ki īn durust ast.*

PROVERB—This is a common proverb.—*īn mas̤ale mashhūr ast.*

PROVIDED—Being in service all the time, have you not provided for your family?—*āyā īn ḳadar-i-'umr dar naukarī guẕrānīded wa lekin ba jihat-i-'aiyāl wa aṭfāl-i-khud chīze jam' na karded?*

PROVIDENCE—Providence directs all things.—*ḥukm-i-rizzāḳ bar hama chīz (jārī) ast.* (*muḥīṭ; dā,ir.*) Or, *parwardigār bar hama makhlūḳāt ḥukm mī-kunad.*

PROVINCE—This disease affects the whole province.—*īn marẓ dar tamām diyār (ishtidād dārad).* (*shiddat dārad; muntashir ast; ghalba dārad.*)

PROVISION—Make provision for your journey.—*barā,e safar-i-khud (tosha,e rāh taiyār) bi-kun.* (*zād-i-rāh āmāda.*)

PROVOKE—He does everything he can to provoke me.—*o har ḳadar ki mī-tawānad marā (ba ghuṣṣa mī-ārad).* (*ba khashm o ba ghaiẓ mī-ārad; ātash-i-khashm mī-afrozad.*)

PRUDENT—She is a wise and prudent woman.—*ān zan dānā wa dūr-andesh ast.* Or, *ān zan (rā,e munīr) wa fikr-i-dūr-andesh dārad.* (*rā,e ṣā,ib; 'aḳl-roshan; rā,e baiẓā wa 'aḳl-i-nūrānī.*)

PULL—We must pull the boat along with a rope.—*bāyad ki mā ba rassane kishtī-rā bi-kashem.*

PULSE—Let me feel your pulse.—*nabẓ-i-khud marā iḥsās kardan bi-dihed.* Or, *bi-guẕāred ki nabẓ-i-shumā-rā iḥsās bi-namāyam.*

PUNISHED—You may expect to be punished for this.—*muntaẓir bāshed ki dar īn amr (ba anwā,e 'aẕāb wa nikāl mu'aẕẕab khwāhed gardīd).* (*sharbat-i-siyāsat khwāhed chashīd.*)

PUPIL—I am reading a dialogue between a pupil and his preceptor.—*su,āl o jawāb ki mā bain-i-ustād wa shāgird ba wuḳū' rasīd mī-khwānam.*

PURCHASED—If I had had sufficient money, I should have purchased the house.—*agar pūl (ba kifāyat mī-dāshtam*) _khāna kharīdame._ (_iktifā mī-kard; kifāyat mī-kard; kāfī mī-shud._)

PURCHASERS—There were few purchasers.—_mushtariyān bisiyār kam būdand._

PURIFIED—Can you inform me how the heart may be purified?—_shumā mī-tawāned guft ki chigūna dil pāk mī-tawānad shud?_

PURPOSE—I purpose to consider this subject.—_dar dil-i-khudam (ḳaṣd)[1] karda am ki (tajwīz)[2]-i-īn muḳaddama bi-kunam._ [1](_'azm; khiyāl; nīyat; 'azīmat._) [2](_taḥḳīḳ; tajassus; taftīsh; tafaḥḥus._)

PURPOSE—For what purpose do you do this?—_az barā,e chi kār īn-rā mī-sāzed?_

PURSE—He found a purse with five ashrafīs in it.—_kīsu,e (panj) ashrafī yāft._ (_bā panj._)

PURSUED—Our soldiers pursued the enemy sixty miles.—_'askariyān-i-mā tā ba shaṣt mīl dar (pai,e)[1] dushman (raftand)[2]._ [1](_'aḳab; ḳafā,e; ta'aḳḳub._) [2](_uftādand._) Or, _lashkariyān-i-mā tā ba shaṣt mīl (ta'aḳḳub)-i-dushman kardand._ (_ta'āḳḳub._)

PURSUIT—Your pursuit of pleasure is fruitless.—_('aish jū,ī)e shumā befū,ida ast._ (_rāḥat-ṭalabī._)

PUT—He put all his savings into the bank.—_hama baḳāyā,e khud-rā dar ṣarrāf-khāna (amānat guẓāsht)._ (_amānat kard; wadī'at nihād; taudī' sākht; īdā' kard._)

Q.

QUALIFICATIONS—He has many good qualifications.—_o (liyāḳat-i-pasandīda) bisiyār dārad._ (_faẓal-i-kamāl; ittiṣāf-i-aḥsān; auṣāf-i-ḥamīda; tauṣīfāt-i-ṭaiyab; shamā,il-i-neko; khiṣālāt-i-khūb; sīrathā,e khūsh._)

QUALIFIED—Are you qualified to do this work?—_shumā (ḳābil)-i-adā,e īn kār hasted?_ (_sazāwār._)

QUALITY—Of what quality is this cloth?—_īn pārcha az kudām ḳism ast? Or, īn kirbās kudām nau' dārud?_

QUANTITY—What quantity do you wish for?—*chi (ḳadar) mī-khwūhed? (miḳdār; andāza.)*

QUARRELS—They appear to be fond of quarrels.—*(ma'lūm mī-shavad) ki mail ba kharkhasha dārand. (ba taṣauwir mī-āyad.)*

QUARREL—Why do you quarrel one with another?—*(nizā' mā bain-i-yak-dīgar chirā bar pā) mī-ḳuned? (munākisha bāham dīgar chirā.)*

QUARTO—Is the work printed in folio, quarto, octavo, or duodecimo?—*kitābe ba barābar andāza,e ṣafḥa maṭbū' shuda ast, yā dū warḳā, yā chahār warḳā, yā si warḳā?*

QUEEN—The king and queen were both present.—*malik wa malika har dū dar ān jā ḥāẓir būdand.*

QUENCH—Take some water to quench your thirst.—*ba jihat-i-(inṭifā,e ātash-i-tushnagī) ḳadre āb bi-khur. (dafa'-i-'aṭsh; minhal-i-'aṭsh.)*

QUICK—That vessel came quick.—*ān jahāz ba ('ujlat)-i-tamām āmad. (sur'at.)*

QUICKEN—We must quicken our pace, if we wish to arrive there this evening.—*agar dar ān jā imshab rasidan mī-khwūhem lāzim ast ki (gām ba shitāb bi-)nihem. (ḳadam ba 'ujlat bi-; ḳadam ba sur'at bi-; ḳadam sust na; pā,e baṭi na; pā,e kund na.)*

QUILL—Give me a quill and a quire of paper.—*yak ḳalam-i-par wa dasta,e kāghaẕ ba man 'ināyat bi-farmāyed.*

QUIT—When do you mean to quit this house?—*irāda,e (khālī kardan-i)-īn khāna kai dāred? (guẕāshtan-i-naḳl az.)*

QUOTATION—This is a quotation from some other book.—*īn muntakhkhibe ast az kitābe dīgar.* Or, *īn intikhāb-i-kitābe dīgar ast.*

R.

RAGS—Paper is made of rags.—*kāghaẕ az (latta)hā sākhta mī-shavad. (pārcha; pīna; khirka; khaẕfarat; pargāla.)*

RAILS—Some of the garden rails are broken.—*ḳadre ḥiṣṣa,e*

bārah)-i-bāgh shikasta shuda ast. (*dar bazīn ; darā bazūn ; ḥulḳus ; jaflaḳ ; ḥadūd-i-chūbīn ; ḥadd-i-chūbīn.*)

Rains—It rains very fast.—*bārān ba ifrāṭ mī-bārad.*

Raisins—Are you fond of raisins ?—*ba kishmish* (*mail dāred*)*?* (*mā,il mī-bāshed.*) Or, *kishmish dost dāred ?*

Rank—What is his rank in the army ?—*dar 'askar kudām 'uhda dārad ?*

Rapid—The stream is very rapid in the rainy season.—*dar aiyām-i-bārish* (*sail*)*-i-nahr tamām sarī' ast.* (*ijrā ; rawānagī,e āb.*)

Rare—This is a very rare plant.—*īn nihāle ast bisiyār* (*shigarf*). (*'ajūba.*)

Rash—He is very rash in his conduct.—*o dar kirdār-i-khud bisiyār* (*ta'jīl mī-kunad*). (*mutahauwir* or *shitābanda mī-bāshad.*)

Rascal—He is a great rascal.—*o yake az ahl-i-fasād-i-'aẓīm ast.* Or, *o* (*fāside buzurg*) *ast.* (*tabāh-kāre buzurg ; khabīṣe rajīm; lawande kabīr ; rinde kharāb ; khafraḳe kalān.*)

Rate—At what rate do you buy this cloth ?—*ba kudām nirkh īn pārcha-rā mī-khared ?*

Raw—It is not good to eat rice raw.—*birinj-i-khām khurdan khūb nīst.*

Reach—I cannot reach so high.—*ba īn ḳadar-i-bulandī na mī-tawānam rasīd.*

Reads—He reads eight or ten hours every day.—*har roz hasht yā dah sā'at mī-khwānad.*

Ready—Sir, the carriage is ready.—*ṣāḥibā kāliska taiyār ast.*

Real—This is all real, not show merely.—*īn hama ḥaḳīḳī na mujāzī ast.* Or, *īn hama ma'nawī na ṣūrī ast.* Or, *īn hama bāṭinī na ẓāhirī ast.* Or, *īn hama az ma'nạ na az ṣūrat ast.*

Reason—What is the reason you cannot be silent ?—*chi sabab ast ki* (*sākit na mī-tawāned shud*)*?* (*sukūt* or *khāmoshī na mī-tawāned warzīd.*)

REASONABLE—What you say is reasonable.—*ānchi ki mī-goyed* (*m'aḳūl*) *ast.* (*pasandīda,e 'aḳl; mustaḥsan; shā,ista; nā-mutajāwiz.*)

REBUILT—That house has been rebuilt.—*ān khāna bāz-pas ta'mīr karda shuda ast.*

RECEIVED—I received your letter, dated 1st March.—*khaṭṭ-i-shumā mu,arrikha ghurra,e māh-i-Mārch ba dast-am rasīd.*

RECEIPT—Give me a receipt for the money.—*īn pūl-rā* (*rasīde*) *ba man marḥammat bi-farmāyed.* (*ḳabẓu-l-wuṣūl.*)

RECENT—Is this intelligence recent?—*īn khabar* (*jadīd*) *ast?* (*nau-khez; nau-paidā; nau-āwarda; nau-rasīda.*)

RECIPE—Tell me the recipe for this medicine.—*nuskha,e īn dawā ba man bi-namā.*

RECKONED—Have you reckoned what these things will come to?—*ḥisāb karda ed ki* (*jam'*)*-i-ḳīmat-i-īn ajnās chi ḳadar khwāhad shud?* (*majmū'a.*)

RECOLLECT—I now recollect what you told me.—*ānchi ki shumā ba man gufted ba yād-am mī-āyad.* Or, *az ānchi gufted* (*marā yād mī-āyad*). (*yād mī-dāram; yād mī-āram; yād-am ast.*)

RECOLLECTION—I have no recollection of his telling me it. —*man yād na dāram ki o īn sukhan ba man guft.*

RECOMMENDATION—Sir, be pleased to give me a letter of recommendation to that gentleman.—*ṣāḥibā sifārish-nāma,e ba nām-i-fulān āghā ba man 'ināyat bi-farmāyed.*

RECOMPENSE—I desire no recompense for serving you.—*az barā,e khidmat-guzārī,e khud* (*ajar*) *na mī-khwāham.* (*pādāsh; ṣilla; 'iwaẓ; jazā; ta'wīẓ; muzd; ujrat.*)

RECONCILED—They two are now reconciled.—*īn har dū muttafiḳ shuda and.* Or, *īn har dū ba muṣāliḥat bāham girā,ida and.* Or, *īn har dū mā bain-i-khud ṣulḥ o ṣalāḥ sākhta and.*

RECOVERING—Have you any expectation of recovering your property?—*ummed dāred ki māl-i-khud bāz khwāhed yāft.*

RECTIFY—If there be any mistakes, rectify them.—*agar*

dar īn sahwe būda bāshad, (*iṣlāḥ bi-farmāyed*). (*bar ān ḳalam-i-iṣlāḥ bi-kashed.*)

Reduced—I have very much reduced my expenses.—*dar ikhrājāt-i-khud khailī* (*takhfīf*) *karda am.* (*tanḳīṣ.*) Or, *kharch-i-khud-rā khailī* (*maḳṣūr*) *karda am.* (*kam; mukhaffif; ḳalīl.*)

Refer—To what do these words refer?—*īn* (*kalimāt*) *dar bāb-i-kudām mī-bāshand?* (*aḳwāl; maḳālāt.*)

Reference—Can you give me a reference to any one?—*shakhse mī-tawāned namūd ki ba shumā* (*ma'rifat dāshta*) *bāshad?* (*wāḳif būda.*)

Reflect—The more I reflect upon this circumstance, the more I regret it.—*chandān ki dar īn muḳaddama ghaur mī-kunam ān ḳadar ba man ranj ziyādatar mī-rasad.* Or, *har ḳadar ki dar īn mu'āmala ta,ammul mī-kunam ān ḳadar* (*ta,assuf-i-beshtar marā dast mī-dihad*). (*ziyādatar nadāmat mī-buram; ziyādatar angusht-i-taḥassur ba dandān mī-gazam.*)

Refreshed—I feel much refreshed by the air.—*az īn hawā ba man* (*khailī tāzagī ḥāṣil ast*). (*ṭarāwat-i-'aẓīm ba ḥuṣūl-i-man mī-anjāmad; istirāḥat-i-wafūr ba man rukh mī-namāyad.*) Or, *az īn bād tāzagī,e tamām iḥsās mī-kunam.*

Refund—He will be obliged to refund this sum.—*bāz dādanī,e īn pūl bar o wājib khwāhad shud.* Or, *īn ḳadar pūl o-rā bāz dādanī khwāhad shud.*

Refused—He has refused what advice I offered.—*naṣīḥate ki bado dādam* (*ḳabūl na kard*). (*na shinuft; radd kard; ba ijābat-ash nayāmad.*)

Regard—I bear him very great regard.—*man o-rā* (*ta'ẓīm*)-*i-wafūr mī-kunam.* (*takrīm; iḥtirām; i'zāz; iḥtishām; ikrām; ḥurmat; martabat.*) Or, *man o-rā* (*mu''azzaz*) *mī-dāram.* (*muḥtarim; muḥtashim; mukarrim; mu'ẓim; mu'aẓẓam.*)

Regarded—You ought to have regarded my advice.—*ba naṣīḥat-i-man* (*iltifāt*) *kardan ba ẕimma,e shumā ẓarūr būd.* (*tawajjuh.*) Or, *mashwarat-i-man mar'ī dāshtan ba shumā lāzim būd.*

REGIMENT—His regiment is gone to Babylonia.—*fauj-ash ba 'irāḳ rafta ast.*

REGRET—I regret I did not follow your advice.—(*pashemānī mī-khḁuram*) *ki ba maṣliḥat-i-shumā iltifāt na kardam.* (*nadāmat* or *ḥasrat mī-buram.*) Or, *ta,assuf mī-kunam ki ba ḥasb-i-mashwarat-i-shumā 'amal na kardam.*

REJOICE—I shall rejoice to see him.—*az dīdan-i-o* (*khūshī marā ḥāṣil khḁāhad āmad*). (*khūshnūd khḁāham shud; khurramī ba man rū khḁāhad dād.*)

REGULATED—These matters need to be regulated.—*ba jihat-i-īn mu'āmalāt* (*intiẓām*) *lāzim āyad.* (*inṣirām; naẓm o naṣaḳ.*)

REGULARITY—The business proceeds with regularity.—*īn kār ba intiẓām-i-tamām* (*mī-shawad*). (*ba 'amal mī-āyad.*)

REMAINING—There is no ready money remaining.—*heck naḳd bāḳī nīst.*

RENEW—I wish to renew the lease of this house.—*kirāya-nāma,e īn khāna jadīd murtasim kardan mī-khḁāham* Or, *raḳam-i-kirāya,e īn khāna tajdīd kardan mī-khḁāham.*

RENT—The monthly rent of this house is fifty rupees.—*kirāya,e īn khāna* (*māhwārī*) *panjāh rūpiya mī-bāshad.* (*az karār-i-māhe.*)

REPAY—Can you lend me two hundred rupees for two days? I will repay you in two days.—*āyā shumā mablagh-i-dū ṣad rūpiya ba* (*muddat*)*-i-dū roz ba man ḳarẓ mī-tawāned dād? ba'd az 'arṣa,e dū roz adū khḁāham kard.* (*wa'da; mau'id; mī'ād; paimān; iḳrār; ta'ahhud.*)

REPEAT—I now repeat what I told you before.—*ānchi ḳabl az īn guftam, ilḥāl* (*mukarrar mī-kunam*). (*i'ādat* or *takrār mī-kunam; bāz* or *ba takrār mī-goyam; ẓikr-i-ān sukhan bāz* or *bāz muẓakira mī-kunam.*)

REPENTANCE—Hereafter our repentance will be useless.—*dar 'uḳbą tauba kardan fā,ida na khḁāhad dād.* Or, *dar ākhirat (tā,ib shudan) sūde na dārad. (nādim shudan; nadāmat kashīdan.)*

REPENTED—Had I acted as they advised me, I should have repented of it very much.—*agar man ba ḥasbu-l-naṣīḥat-i-eshān 'amal mī-kardam nādim mī-shudam.* Or, *agar maṣlihat-i-eshān ba 'amal mī-āwardam, pashemān mī-shudam.* Or, *agar ba mashwirat-i-eshān iḳtidā kardame ḥasrat khurdame.*

REPETITION—This is a repetition of what was said before. —*ānchi ḳabl az īn (tazkara yāfta) ast i'ādat-i-ān īn ast. (gufta shuda.)*

REPLY—What reply do you make to my question?—*ba su'āl-i-man chi jawāb mī-dihed?*

REPORT—I have made a report to Mr. —— on this.—*man ba fulāne ṣāḥib bar īn (i'lām namūda am). (iṭṭilā' or khabar dāda am.)* Or, *man fulāne ṣāḥib-rā dar bāb-i-īn amr (ba 'arẓ rasānīda am). (muṭṭali' karda am.)*

REPORTED—It is so reported.—*īn chunīn dar afwāh uftāda ast.* Or, *chunīn ṭaraḥ īn khabar ishtihār yāfta ast.* Or, *chunīn nau' zabān zad-i-'āmm shuda ast.*

REPRESENT—I will represent the subject to him.—*man badīn kaifīyat o-rā muṭṭali' khwāham sākht.* Or, *man ṣūrat-i-ḥāl pesh-i-o khwāham nihād.*

REPROACHED—His conduct was reproached by many.—*base bar kirdār-ash (malāmat) kardand. (mu'ātibat; ta'n; mazammat; taubīkh; sarzanish; zajr; 'itāb; ta'annut; malām; ṭanz; iftirā; ta'yūb; tashnī'; nikohish; ta'yīb.)* Or, *base bar kirdār-ash ta'na zadand.*

REPROOF—Their conduct deserves reproof.—*af'āl-i-eshān lā,iḳ-i-'itāb ast. (mustaujib; farākhur; shāyār; darkhur; sazāwar.)*

REPROVED—He reproved them very sharply.—*o bar eshān bāng zad.* Or, *o badeshān (ba ṣalābat) guft. (saḳt; ba durushtī.)* Or, *o eshān-rā ba khūbī mu,ākhinat kard.*

REQUEST—What request did they make?—*eshān chi (istida'ā) namūdand? (darkhwāst; iddi'ā; iḳtiẓā; ṭalab.)*

REQUEST—I request of you only this one favour.—*az shumā fakaṭ īn ('ināyat) mī-khwāham.* (*rūfat; talaṭṭuf.*)

RESEMBLE—These two very much resemble each other.—*īn har dū ba yak-dīgar bisiyār mī-mānand.* Or, *īn har dū (mushābih),e yak-dīgar and.* (*mushtabih; imṣāl; miṣal; mumāṣil; mushābih.*) Or, *īn har dū ba yak-dīgar tashbīh dārand.*

RESERVE—You will reserve for me three copies of your book.—*si (nuskha,)¹e kitāb-i-khud barā,e man (nigāh dūred)².* ¹(*muntāsikh.*) ²(*yak-ṭaraf bi-nihed.*)

RESIDENCE—Is that the place of your residence?—*āyā īn (maskīn)-i-shumā ast?* (*jā,e tawakkuf; jā,e sukūnat; jā,e būd o bāsh; jā,e tamakkun; makām; makān.*)

RESIGNED—He has resigned his former office.—*az 'uhda,e peshīn-i-khud (istighfā girifta) ast.* (*dast bardār shuda; tark girifta; tark gufta.*) Or, *manṣab-i-sābika-i-khud-rā (tark) karda ast.* ('*itizāl.*)

RESIST—You cannot resist his claim.—*da'wā,e o-rā radd na mī-tawāned kard.* Or, *shumā-rā bā da'wā,e o imkān-i-mukāwamat na tawānad mānd.* Or, *daf'-i-da'wā,e o na mī-tawāned kard.* Or, *muṭāliba,e o az shumā mundaf' na tawānad shud.* Or, *bar muṭāliba,e o i'tirāẓ na mī-tawānad āward.*

RESISTANCE—The enemy fled without resistance.—*dushman mukābila nā-karda (gurekht).* (*firār kard; mafrūr shud; rū ba firār nihād.*)

RESOLUTE—They are resolute in their purpose.—*eshān bar irāda,e khud (ḳā,im) and.* (*mustaḳīm; mustaḥkam; maḥkum; ṣābit-kadam; muṣbit; mutawassiḳ; rāsikh; mustaḳil.*)

RESOLUTION—To do this requires resolution.—*dar īn kār (istiḳlāl-i-mizāj wājib) ast.* ('*azm-i-muṣammam lāzim; niyat-i-ustuwār ẓarūr; irāda,e mustaḳīm lā-bud.*)

RESOLVED—I am resolved to do so no more.—*ḳaṣd karda am ki īn chunīn bāz na khwāham kard.*

RESPECTED—He is everywhere respected.—*ba har jā ki mī-ravad ('izzat wa ḥurmat mī-bīnad).* (*ba khidmat-ash iḳdām mī-namāyand; ba ikrām-ash pesh mī-āyand; o-rā takrīm wa ta'ẓīm wa ikrām mī-namāyand; o-rā ba 'izzat wa ḥurmat sulūk mī-namāyand.)*

RESPECT—I pay great respect to what he says.—*ānchi mī-goyad man o-rā (waḳār) mī-diham. (waḳ'.)* Or, *man sukhan-i-o-rā (tauḳīr) mī-kunam. (tauḳī'.)*

REST—I had no rest last night.—*dī shab (khwāb-am na girift). (yak laḥẓa na khwābīdam; yak daḳīḳa chashm-am barham na guzārdam; dar chashm-am khwāb na gasht; khwābam na burd.)* See SLEEP.

RESTORED—I have restored more than I took away.—*har ḳadar ki giriftam ziyāda az ān (bāz) dādam. (wāpas; pas.)*

RESULT—What was the result of your deliberation?—*natīja,e mashwarat-i-shumā chi ṭaur (ba wuḳū' āmad)? (ba wuḳū' anjāmīd; ba ẓuhūr āmad; ba ẓuhūr paiwast; sar ba 'arṣa,e shuhūd kashīd.)*

RESULT—From this measure many benefits will result.—*az īn tadbīr manfa'at-i-wafūr (dast khwāhad dād). (taḥṣīl* or *ḥāṣil khwāhad shud; ba ḥuṣūl khwāhad anjāmīd; ba dast khwāhad uftād.)*

RETAIN—Can you retain this in your memory?—*īn-rā ba yād-i-khud mī-tawāned dāsht?* Or, *īn-rā ba madrika,e khud ṡabt mī-tawāned kard.*

RETIRE—At ten o'clock the company began to retire.—*ba sā'at-i-dah maḥfil (barkhwāst). mubā'idat* or *tabā'id kard; bāz gasht.)*

RETURN—When do you propose to return.—*irāda,e (murāja'at) kai dāred? ('audat; mu'āwadat.)* Or, *'inān-i-'azīmat kai mun'aṭif khwāhed kard?*

REVISED—I have revised what I had written.—*ānchi nawishta būdam bar ān naẓar-i-ṡānī karda am.*

REVIVE—Trade is now beginning to revive.—*tijārat ilḥāl bāz raunaḳ giriftan aghāz mī-kunad.* Or, *bāzār-i-tijārat ilḥāl bāz garm mī-shavad.* Or, *saudāgarī aknūn rū ba taraḳḳī mī-nihad.*

REWARDED—The General rewarded the soldiers.—*sipāh-sālār 'askariyūn-rā in'ām bakhshīd.*
RIBAND—Tie this with a riband.—*īn-rā ba (kūr) bi-band.* (*sharbad.*)
RICH—That merchant is very rich.—*ān tājir khailī (tawān-gar) ast. (ghanī; mustaghnī; mun'im.)* Or, *ān saudāgar (ni'mat-i-begirān) dārad. (daulat-i-bekiyās; māl-i-firā-wān.)* Or, *ān bayyi' ṣāḥib-i-dunyā* or *khudāwand-i-ni'mat ast.*)
RICHES—What are riches to him who has no heart to make a right use of them?—*az daulat-ash chi fā,ida ki o īn chunīn himmat na dārad ki ān-rā ba ṣarf-i-jā,iz kharch namāyad.* Or, *shakhṣe-rā ki dil-ash ba kharch-i-jā,iz mā,il na būda būshad, az dunyā chi fā,ida?*
RIDDLE—Can you tell the meaning of this riddle?—(*ma'nī,e īn chīstān ḥall) mī-tawāned kard?* ('*ukda,e mu'ammā ḥall; ma'nī,e īn mu'ammā-rā tashrīḥ.*)
RIDES—He rides on horseback every morning.—*har roz ba waḳt-i-ṣubḥ bar asp sawār mī-shavad.* Or, *roz-murra 'ala-ṣ-ṣabāḥ (rūkib-i-asp) mī-shavad. (markub-i-markub.)*
RIDICULE—They ridicule serious counsel.—*bar ṣalāh-i-nek (tamaskhur) mī-kunand. (taskhur; istihzā.)*
RING—She has lost her diamond ring.—*ān ṣāḥiba angush-tarī ba nagīn-i-almās-i-khud (gum) karda ast. (fiḳdān.)*
RINGS—The bell rings daily at twelve o'clock.—*har roz ba waḳt-i-nof-roz (jaras nawākhta) mī-shavad. (zang zada; darā darā,ida.)*
RIPEN—This fruit is beginning to ripen.—*īn mewa ba pukhtan āmada ast.*
RISE—If you wish to be a good scholar, rise early every day.—*ayar khwāhish-i-fāẓil shudan dāred 'ala-ṣ-ṣabāḥ az (khwāb bedār shaved). (bistar-i-khwāb bar khezed.)*
RISEN—The price of indigo has risen lately.—*az 'arṣa,e ḳalīb ḳīmat-i-nīl rū ba (afzūnī) nihāda ast. (taraḳḳī, izdiyād kasrat; ziyādatī.)*
ROARS—The sea roars loudly.—*baḥr mutamawwij mī-*

sharad. Or, *baḥru-l-muḥīṯ (mutalāṯim mī-sharad.) (mu'talij mī-sharad ; ba ifrāṯ mī-ghurad.)*

Robbed—He has been robbed of all his plate.—*hama ṯasht-i-nuḳra,e o (ba duzdī rafta) ast. (duzd burda ; dast-burd-i-duzd gardīda ; ba sirḳat rafta ; duzdīda shuda.)*

Rock—The ship ran upon a rock, and was lost.—*jahāz ba koh khurd wa (gharḳ) shud. (pāra-pāra ; mughraḳ ; gharīḳ ; mustaghriḳ ; dar āb faro ; shikasta.)*

Roof—The roof of the house fell in.—*(saḳf)-i-khāna ba zamīn uftād. (bām.)*

Roots—Those trees were dug up by the roots.—*ān darakhthā az bekh (bar āwarda) shuda būdand. (kanda.)*

Rope—Make the boat fast with a rope.—*safīna-rā ba (miḳwade) bi-band. (rassan ; ḥabl.)*

Rub—Rub your hands with this leaf.—*dasthā,e khud-rā badīn barg-i-darakht bi-māled.*

Rudder—The vessel ran upon a sand-bank, and lost her rudder.—*jahāz (bar tal-i-reg bar āmad wa sukān-ash shikast.* Or, *jahāz ba tauda,e reg nishast wa (dumbāl)-ash shikast. (khalla ; khalūsha.)*

Ruined—By these deeds he will in the end be ruined.—*o ākhiru-l-amr az īn kārhā (tabāh) khwāhad shud. (talaf o tārāj ; khasta-ḥāl ; shikasta bāl ; be sar o sāmān ; pareshān ; pā,e māl.)*

Rule—What rule do you observe in study?—*dar ta'līm-i-'ilm-i-khud kudām ḳā,ida nigāh dāred?* Or, *dar tadrīs-i-'ilm-i-khud ba kudām dastūr (multafit mī-shaved)? (iltifāt* or *mail* or *tawajjuh mī-kuned ; mā,il mī-shaved.)*

Ruler—God is the ruler of the universe.—*afrīnanda,e jahān ḥākim-i-jahān ast.* Or, *khāliḳ-i-makhlūḳāt dāwar-i-kā,ināt ast.* Or, *ṣāni'-i-maṣnū'āt farmāndih-i-'ālam ast.* Or, *rabbu-l-'ālamain khusrau,e maujūdāt ast.*

Run—Run after him and call him back.—*dar ('aḳab)-ash bi-dawed wa o-rā bāz bi-khwāned. (pai ; ḳafā,e.)*

Rust—This knife is covered with rust—*īn kārd ba zang ālūda ast.* Or, *īn chāḳū-rā morchāna khurda ast.*

S.

Sad—This is indeed a sad misfortune.—*īn fi-l-wāḳi' (muṣībat)-i-'aẓīm ast. (balīyat; ẕillat.)*

Saddle—He is used to ride without a saddle.—*('ādat-ash ast) ki baghair-i-zīn sawār mī-shavad. (o 'ādat dārad.)*

Safe—I heard of his safe arrival in London.—*man shunīdam ki dar shahr-i-landan (ba khair o'āfiyat) wārid shud. (ba aman o āmān; ba ṣiḥḥat; ba salamat; sālāmaṉ o ghārimaṉ.)*

Safety—We may live here in safety.—*dar īn jā ba (salāmat) bi-mānem. (amn; āmān; ārām; 'āfiyat; amniyat; ḥifāẓat.)* Or, *dar īn jā ba pā,e ḳarār jāda,e istiḳāmat bi-paimāyem.*

Sail—This boat has neither mast nor sail.—*īn kishtī tīr na dārad na (bād-bān). (shurā'; kulā'a.)*

Sailors—Sailors visit different parts of the globe.—*mallāḥān sair-i-mulkhā,e (mukhtalif)-i-dunyā mī-kunand. (mutafarriḳ.)*

Salary—His salary is 500 rupees a month.—*muwājib-ash panj ṣad rūpiya ast.* Or, *o mushāhira,e panj ṣad rūpiya dārad.*

Sale—There will be a sale of salt to-morrow.—*fardā ḥarrāj-i-namak khwāhad shud.* Or, *fardā namak ba ḥarrāj farokhta khwāhad shud.*

Saleable.—These articles are not saleable.—*īn ajnās ḳābil-i-farokht nayand.*

Same—Yours and mine are both the same.—*chīze ki az ān-i-man ast wa ān chīz ki az ān-i-shumā ast har dū (yaksān) and. ('alā-s-sawīya; mutasāwī.)* Or, *chīz-i-shumā wa chīz-i-man har dū yak ḳism ast.* Or, *āshiyā,e mā har dū az yak nau' mī-bāshad.*

Sample—Show me a sample of the rice.—*ba man namūna,e birinj bi-namāyed.*

Sand—This rice is full of sand.—*īn birinj az reg pur ast.*

Satisfaction—Your book has afforded me much satisfaction.—*az muṯāla'a,e kitāb-i-shumā bisiyār khūshnūdī ḥāṣil namūda am.*

Satiety—He saw you to satiety.—*o az dīdan-i-tū ser gardīda ast.* Or, *az dīdan-i-tū serī bado rū āwarda ast.*

Save—Save this for to-morrow.—*īn-rā barā,e fardā nigāh bi-dāred.*

Saved—I have saved my friend from a very great danger. —*dost-i-khudam-rā az khaṯra,e muhlik (ba salāmat badar āwarda am). (najāt dādam ; maḥfuẓ dāshta am.)*

Saw—Tell the carpenter to saw this board in two.—*darrūdgar-rā bi-go ki īn takhta-rā ba ārra do pāra bi-(kunad). (kun.)*

Saying—This is an old saying.—*īn (maḳāl)-i-ḳadīm ast. (ḳaul ; guftār ; sukhan.)*

Scarce—These articles are now scarce.—*īn āshiyā (kamyūb) and. (ghair-fā,iẕ ; ghair kaṯīr ; nā-yāb ; nādir ; gharīb.)*

Scatter—Scatter this seed on the ground.—*īn tukhm-rā ba zamīn (biyafshāned). (bi-pāshed ; bi-kāred.)*

Score—I have bought a score of sheep.—*(bīsta,e) gūsfand kharīda am. (bīst 'adad-i.)*

Scorn—He treated my advice with scorn.—*naṣīḥat-i-marā (ḥaḳārat kard). (ḥaḳīr dānist; ba istikrāh shinuft; istikhfāf kard ; kirāhiyat kard.)*

Scrape—Scrape the ink off your pen.—*az ḳalam-i-khud murakkab (pāk kun). (bi-kharāsh ; ḥakk kun.)*

Scratched—I have scratched my finger with a nail.—*angusht-i-khud-rā ba mekhe kharūshīda am.*

Scrawl—Why do you scrawl on my paper?—*chirā bar kāghaẕ-i-man khaṯṯ-i-(khām) mī-kashed? (nā ḥusn.)*

Scream—These children scream all day.—*īn aṯfāl tamām roz ghirew mī-zanand.*

Screws—This lock is fastened on with screws.—*īn ḳufl az pech (band) karda shud. (murattab ; mutarattab.)*

Scribe—This is the village scribe.—*īn kātib-i-ḳarya ast.*

Sea—The ship will go to sea to-morrow.—*fardā jahāz (ba baḥr rawān khwāhad shud). (langar khwāhad bar dāsht.)*

SEAL.—What did you give for that seal?—*az barū,e ān muhr chi dāded?*

SEALED—Have you sealed your letter?—*bar khaṭṭ-i-khud (muhr karda ed)? (khatm or muhr zada ed.)*

SEAMS—There are no seams in this cloth.—*īn libās darz na dārad. Or, dar īn jāma dozishe nīst.*

SEARCH—I had a long search to no purpose.—*man tā ba muddat-i-madīd just o jū,e be-fā,ida kardam.*

SEARCHING—I have been searching for this all day.—*man tumām roz (dar talāsh-i-īn būda am). (tafaḥḥus-i-īn karda am; tajassus-i-īn dāshta am.)*

SEASON—This is a pleasant season of the year.—*īn mausim-i-sāl khūsh ast.*

SEA-SHORE—We walked by the sea-shore.—*mā ba sāhil-i-bahr pā-piyāda (sair) kardem. (tafarruj.)*

SECRET—They keep all things secret.—*hama chīz (nihān) dārand. (pinhān; poshīda; makhfī; ikhfā; mastūr.) Or, sirre ki mī-dārand ba kase darmiyān na mī-(nihand). (ārand goyand.)*

SECTION—You will find this in the fourth chapter, fifth section.— *dar faṣl-i-panjum-i-bāb-i-chahārum īn-rā khwāhed yāft.*

SECURE—You may remain here secure.—*shumā dar īn jā (aiman) bāshed. (ba amān; ba salāmat; ba khairiyat; musallam; sālim; ba'āfiyat.)*

SEE—I see, the trouble I take to teach you is useless.—*man mī-dānam ki miḥnate ki dar ta'līm-i-shumā mī-kunam be-sūd ast.*

SEED—Sow this seed in the garden.—*īn (bazr) dar bāgh bi-kār. (barz; barza; tukhm.)*

SEEK—If we seek for knowledge, we shall find it.—*agar ṭalab-i-'ilm bi-kunem fi-l-wāki' ḥāṣil khwāhem namūd.*

SEIZED—The police officer seized him.—*shaḥna giriftār-ash namūd. Or, 'asas akhz-ash namūd. Or, yake az ahl-i-iḥtisāb (makhūz-ash namūd). (dar wai āwekht; dast dar girebān zad; o-rā girift.)*

SELECT—Select what things you choose.—*ān chizhā,e ki shumā mī-pasanded (bi-guzīned). (ikhtiṣāṣ bi-kuned; bi-chīned; istinbāṭ bi-kuned.)*

SELL—I intend to sell my old books and buy new ones.—*ḳaṣd-i-ān dāram ki kutub-i-kuhn bi-farosham wa kutub-i-nau bi-kharam.*

SEND—I send my servant to Tehran once a week.—*man (khādim)*[1]*-i-khud-rā ba ṭahrān ba hafta yak bār (mī-firistam)*[2]. [1]*(khidmatgār; muta'allik; ḥājib; mulāzim; naukar; chākar; rahī.)* [2]*(rawāna mī-kunam; irsāl* or *mursil dāram.)*

SEND—The king said, Send for the executioner.—*bādshāh farmūd ki jallād-rā bi-ṭalab.* Or, *khusrau ḥukm dād tā ki jallād-rā bi-ṭalaband.*

SENSE—She possesses much sense and judgment.—*ān zan ('aḳl-i-firāwān)*[1] *dārad wa (rā,e durust)*[2]. [1]*(ẓamīr-i-munīr; firāsat-i-mustaḥkam.)* [2]*(tamīz-i-ṣā,ib; dirāyat-i-farākh.)*

SENSES—It behoves us to keep our senses under control.—*mārā bāyad ki ḥawāss-i-khud-rā dar ẓabṭ bi-dārem.*

SENTIMENTS—My sentiments agree with yours.—*dar īn amr rā,e man ba rā,e shumā (muttafiḳ ast). (muwāfiḳ ast; muwāfiḳat* or *ittifāḳ dārad.)*

SEPARATION—How long is it since their separation?—*chand muddat ast ki (judā,ī) darmiyān-i-eshān uftād. (farāḳ; mufāriḳat; mahjūrī; hijrān; farḳat; tafruḳat; hijr; mubā'idat; ḳaṭī'at?)*

SEPARATE—They live in separate houses.—*eshān dar khāna,e (mukhtalif) sukūnat dārand. ('alaḥida; mutafarriḳ; judā.)*

SERENE—The sky is serene and clear.—*āsmān (khūb ṣāf) ast wa nurānī. (be saḥāb; nā tārīk.)*

SERIOUS—Are you serious in what you say?—*ānchi mī-goyed sanjīda ast yā na.*

SERVES—Ivory serves for various purposes.—*'āj dar kārhā,e anwā' mī-āyad.* Or, *('āj) ba kārhā,e anwā' mī-khurad. (dandān-i-pīl.)*

SERVICE—I have been in his service ten years.—*man dar mulāzimat-ash tā ba dah sāl* (*ḥāẓir būda am*). (*miyān-i-k͟hidmat basta am ; mulāzim būda am.*)

SET—I set off to-day for Khaiva.—*man imroz ba samt-i-k͟haiva mī-ravam.* Or, *man rāh-i-k͟haiva imroz* (*ṭai mī-kunam*). (*ḳaṭa' mī-kunam ; mī-paimāyam.*)

SET—I have set the trap in the place you told me.—*jā,e ki ba man nishān dāded dar ān jā dām* (*gustarda am*). (*nihāda am ; naṣb karda am.*)

SETTLE—I will now settle my account.—*man ilḥāl ḥisāb-i-k͟hud-rā* (*be bāḳ*) *k͟hwāham kard.* (*faiṣal ; rafa'.*)

SEVERELY—He was punished severely.—*o 'aẕāb-i-alīm yāft.* Or, *'aḳūbat-i-shadīd bado rasīd.* Or, *ba* (*ta'ẕīb*)[1]*-i-sak͟ht* (*giriftār*)[2] *āmad.* [1](*'iḳāb ; mu'ātabat.*) [2](*giriftār* or *mubtalā* or *māk͟hūẕ* or *asīr* or *muḳaiyad shud.*)

SEW—Sew these two together.—*īn har dū-rā bāham* (*bi-dozed*). (*talfīḳ bi-kuned ; rafū bi-sāzed ; g͟harzat bi-kuned.*)

SHADE—Sit in the shade of this tree.—*dar zer-i-*(*sāya*)*,e īn darak͟ht bi-nishīned.* (*ẓill.*)

SHADED—My house is shaded with trees.—*k͟hāna,e man ba darak͟htān* (*sāyadār*) *ast.* (*muẓallal shuda.*)

SHAKE—Shake the boughs of the tree.—(*shāk͟hhā,*)[1]*e darak͟ht* (*bi-jumbāned*)[2]. [1](*furū' ; afānīn,* sing. *fanan ; ag͟hṣā,e,* sing. *g͟huṣun.*) [2](*mutaḥarrik bi-sāzed ; -rā ḥarakat bi-dihed.*)

SHAKE—Shake off the dust on your clothes.—*jāmahā,e k͟hud-rā az k͟hāk bi-takāned.*

SHAKE—Shake hands.—*biyā ki mā bāham muṣāfiḥa bi-kunem.*

SHAME—What, have you no shame?—*āyā* (*sharm*) *na dāred?* (*k͟hajlat ; ḥaiyā ; nang ; infi'āl.*) Or, *āyā k͟hajālat na mī-*(*kashed*)*?* (*bared.*)

SHAPE—Do you know what shape the earth is?—*mī-dāned ki haikal-i-arẓ chi-sān ast?*

SHARE—He has received his own share out of the property.—*o ḥiṣṣa,e k͟hud az imlāk yāfta ast.* Or, *o ḳismat-i-*

khud az māl huṣūl karda ast. Or, o-rū bahra,e az mil-kiyat ba huṣūl āmada ast.

SHAVE—I am just going to shave.—hālan hajāmat kardan mī-khwāham.

SHED—The sun shed his beams over the earth.—(shu'la,e mihr) ba rū,e arẓ uftād. (shu'ā'-i-shams; lawāmi'-i-khurshed.) Or, āftāb tāb-i-khud-rā ba rū,e zamīn (afgand). (gustard; rekht; pāshīd.)

SHEET—Give me a sheet of paper.—yak (takhta,)e kāghaz ba man bi-dih. (waraḳ; fard.)

SHELL—I have found a beautiful shell.—man (ṣadafe khūsh-numā) yāfta am. (gosh-i-māhī,e ḥasīn.)

SHELTER—It rains fast, let us shelter ourselves.—bārān (sakht) mī-bārad biyā ki panāh bi-gīrem. (ba zūdī; ba ifrāṭ; tund.)

SHINES—The sun shines with great power to-day.—imroz tāb-i-āftāb bisiyār (ḥārr) ast. (maḥrūr; shadīd; sakht; tābandu.)

SHOOT—Do you know how to shoot with arrows?—shumā tīr (andākhtan) mī-dāned? (rihā kardan; zadan; andāzī.)

SHORTEN—Can you shorten this?—shumā (īn-rā khurd) mī-tawāned kard? (In the case of a speech, īn sukhan-rā takāsur.)

SHOULDER—He has an epaulet on his shoulder.—o bar (dosh)-i-khud nishāne dārad. (shāna; kitf.)

SHOW—Please show me the book you spoke of.—kitābe ki shumā zikr-ash karded az rū,e 'ināyat ba man (nishān bi-dihed). (bi-namāyed.)

SICK—He has been sick (or ill) a long time.—az muddat-i-darāz bīmār shuda ast.

SIGH—Why do you sigh?—chirā āh mī-(kuned)? (kashed.) Or, chirā nafs-i-sard az dil bar mī-āred?

SIGN—This is a sign of rainy weather.—īn 'alāmate (bārish) ast. (maṭar.)

SIGN—Please to sign this paper.—az rū,e talaṭṭuf bar īn kāghaz (dast-khaṭṭ) bi-kuned. (ṣaḥīḥ.)

SIGNIFIES—It signifies little what they say.—*ānchi mī-goyand hech* (*muẓāyaḳa*) *na dārad.* (*ẓarar.*)
SILK—This is a silk manufactory.—*īn kār-k͟hāna,e ab-resham ast.*
SILLINESS—What can be greater silliness than to think thus?—*az īn chunīn k͟hayāl bastan kudām* (*ḥimāḳat*) *ziyādatar ast?* (*sādagī; rakākat; fiyālat.*)
SIMILAR—My case is similar to yours.—*ḥāl-i-man* (*ba miṣal*)*-i-ḥālat-i-shumā ast.* (*mushtabih; mushābih.*)
SINCERE—His love towards us is sincere.—*muḥabbat-ash bā mā ba ik͟hlāṣ ast.* Or, *muwaddat-ash bā mā ba ṣadāḳat ast.* Or, *muwālāt-ash bā mā k͟hāliṣ ast.*
SINCERITY—He is a man of sincerity.—*o* (*rāst-bāz*) *ast.* (*pāk-bāz; pāk-rū; muk͟hliṣ; yak-jihat; ik͟hlāṣ-mand; salīmu-l-ḳalb; k͟hāliṣu-l-muk͟hliṣ; ṣadāḳat-gustar; ṣadāḳat pesha; mashkūfu-l-ḳalb.*) Or, *o ṣāḥib-i-*(*rāst bāzī*) *ast.* (*ik͟hlāṣ; ṣadāḳat; ṣidḳ.*)
SINGS—She sings very sweetly.—*ān zan k͟hūb* (*mī-sarāyad*). (*sarod* or *tag͟hannī* or *tarannum* or *zumzuma mī-kunad; sarod* or *tārannum mī-zanad.*)
SINGULAR—Their religious opinions are singular.—*k͟hayā-lāt-i-maẕhab-i-eshān* (*'ajīb*) *ast.* (*'ajab*, pl. *'ajā,ib; g͟harīb; nādir.*)
SINKING—The boat is sinking.—*kishtī dar āb faro mī-ravad.* Or, *kishtī* (*mustag͟hraḳ*) *mī-shavad.* (*g͟harḳ; mag͟hrūḳ; g͟harīḳ.*)
SINS—No man is so just that he sins not.—*kase īn chunīn* (*munṣif-mizāj*) *nīst ki gunāh na kunad.* (*pāk-bāz; k͟hudā-tars; neko-kār.*)
SIT—Sit down, and see if you can understand this or not.—(*bi-nishīned*) *wa bi-bīned ki īn-rā fahmīdan mī-tawāned yā na.* (*tashrīf bi-dāred; taḳā'id bi-kuned; bi-farmāyed.*)
SIZE—What size is the book you speak of?—*kitābe ki ẕikr-ash mī-kuned chi ḳadar* (*ḥujūm dārad*)*?* (*kalān* or *ḳillat ast.*)
SKY—The sky is overcast.—*āsmān ba ẓulmat-i-saḥāb poshīda*

ast. Or, *sipihr ba abr-i-siyāh gashta ast.* Or, *gumbad-i-charkh ba megh tārīk shuda ast.*

Sleep—I had no sleep all last night.—*dīshab khwābam na (girift). (burd.)* Or, *dīshab yak dam khwāb dar chashm-am na (gasht). (āmad.)* Or, *dīshab khwāb marā na rabūd.* *See* Rest.

Smarts—The cut in my hand smarts very much.—*zakhm-i-dast-am ba ifrāṭ dard mī-kunad.*

Smell—Let me smell that flower.—*bi-guẕār ki ān gul-rā (bi-boyam). (istishmām* or *ishtimām bi-kunam; bū,e bi-gīram; bū,e bi-bīnam.)*

Smell—These flowers are without smell.—*īn gulhā (khūsh-bo) na dārand. (rā,iḥa; nashwat; 'iṭr; ṭībat.)*

Smoke—The house is full of smoke.—*khāna az dūd pūr ast.*

Smooth—This is smooth paper.—*īn kāghaẕ-i-muhra-dār ast.*

Snarl—These dogs snarl at one another.—*īn sagān ba yak-dīgar (khur-khur mī-zanand). (gharish* or *harīr mī-kunand.)*

Snatched—He snatched it out of my hand.—*az dast-am īn chīz (rabūd). (ghuṣbīd.)*

Sneeze.—You sneeze, because you have got a cold.—*ba sabab-i-zukām ki dāred (mī-'aṭsed). ('aṭsa mī-zaned; 'aṭsān mī-kuned; mī-safled; shinūsha mī-kuned.)*

Soldier—He is an experienced soldier.—*'askarī,e maṣāff āzmūda, jahān-dīda, safr-karda, kār-dīda, barḳ-i-shamsher-i-jadal ba chashm dīda, ra''d-i-kos-i-dilāwarān ba gosh-i-o rasīda, ast.*

Solicit—May I solicit, sir, this one favour.—*ai ṣāḥib agar ma'ẕūr dāred man ba khidmat ('arẓ kunam). (iltimās kunam; multamis pardāz shavam.)*

Something—I wished to tell you something, but have forgot what.—*man mī-khwāstam ki ba shumā sukhane bi-goyam wa lekin farāmosh kardam.*

Sorrow—This occasions me much sorrow.—*īn ba man khailī alam mī-rasānad.*

SORRY—I am sorry for my offence.—*man ba sabab-i-taķṣīr-i-khud (khailī ranjīda am). (ta,assuf mī-khuram; malūl-am; dil-āzurda am; tang-dil-am; andoh-zada am; maghmūm-am; maḥzūn-am; ba dām-i-gham giriftār-am; dast-i-taghābun bar zānū,e khud mī-zanam.)*

SORT—Sort these papers.—*īn kawāghazāt-rā ('alą-ḥidda bi-namāyed).* [1]*('alą ḥidda bi-chīned; ķism wār bi-dāred; ķismat bi-kuned.)*

SORT—Is this the sort you wanted?—*ķisme ki mī-khwāhed īn ast?*

SOUL—The soul must be happy or miserable.—*ẓarūr ast ki rūḥ ba asā,ish mānad yā ba ranj.*

SOUND—I hear the sound of music.—*(āwāz-i-soz o sāz) mī-shinavam. (shor* or *ghaugha,e musīķī.)*

SOUR—That fruit is sour, don't eat it.—*ān mewa turush ast, ma khur.*

SPACE—Leave more space between the lines.—*dar miyān-i-suṭūr (farķe ziyāda) bi-guẕāred. (tafāwate mazīd; fāsila,e afzūn.)*

SPACE—In the space of three months.—*dar ('arṣa),e si māh. (muddat.)*

SPARE—He besought them to spare his life.—*o az eshān istid'ā,e jān bakhshī,e khud namūd.* Or, *o iltmās kard ki eshān az sar-i-jān-i-o dar guẕarand.*

SPARK—A spark of fire may set in flames a whole village.—*(chūn ātash-i-andak dar ishti'al āyad) tamām dih bi-sozad. yak ẕarra,e sharrar; yak ātash para; yak izhak.)*

SPEAKS—He speaks the Persian language well.—*ba zabān-i-fārsī khūb ḥaraf mī-zanad.* Or, *dar zabān-i-'ajamī khūsh sukhan mī-goyad.*

SPECIMEN—Show me a specimen of your writing.—*namūna,e dast-khaṭṭ-i-khud bi-namā.*

SPECTACLES—They wear spectacles.—*eshān 'ainak ba isti'māl mī-ārand.*

SPENDS—He spends his money as fast as he procures it.—*har ķadar pūl-i-khud zūd mī-yābad ān ķadar zūd (kharch mī-kunad*). (*mī-rezad ; ba bād mī-dihad ; ṣarf* or *iṣrāf* or *talaf* or *taṣarruf* or *itlāf mī-kunad.*)

SPICES—They trade in different kinds of spices.—*eshān* (*asnāf-i*)-*maṣāliḥhā mī-faroshand.* (*ṭaraḥ-ṭaraḥ ; akṣām-i- ; anwā'-i- ; mukhtalif.*)

SPILL—Take care you don't spill the ink.—*khabardār* (*murakkab*)[1] (*na rezed*)[2]. [1](*roshnā,ī ; midād ; siyāhī.*) [2](*insibāb na kuned ; na pāshed.*)

SPITE—He has done this merely out of spite.—*o īn kār ba sabab-i*-(*khuṣūmat*) *karda ast.* (*'adāwat ; dushmanī ; kīn ; ḥaḳad ; bad-khwāhī ; kīnāwarī ; bughẓ ; bad-andeshī.*)

SPLIT—Having split the cocoa-nut, his friend and himself drank the milk.—*jauz-i-hindī-rā* (*shaḳḳ karda*) *o khud wa dost-ash shīr-i-ān jauz khurdand.* (*shigāfta ; tarkīda ; chāk-zada ; munsharij sākhta : shaklīda ; saftīda ; darīda ; ta'ṭīl karda ; mufarrij sākhta.*)

SPOILED—You have spoiled my paper.—*shumā kāghaẓ-i-marā* (*kharāb*) *karda ed.* (*makhrūb ; tabāh.*)

SPOT—There is a spot of ink on your clothes.—*jāmahā,e shumā dāghe siyāh dārad.* Or, *bar kiswat-i-shumā dāghe murakkab ast.*

SPREAD—Spread this mat upon the floor.—*īn ḥaṣīr bar zamīn* (*bi-gustared*). (*farsh bi-kuned ; bi-khwāled.*)

SPREAD—Having spread a net at night, he caught many birds.—*o ba shab* (*shabaka*),*e gustarda parandahā ba kaṣrat ba dām āward.* (*shaṣirat ; ḥibālat.*)

SPRING—The weeds spring up very fast here.—*dar īn jā kāhe nākāra ba zūdī mī-royad.* Or, *dar īn jā sabza,e begāna ba ta'jīl* (*wujūd mī-gīrad*). (*paidā mī-shavad ; mī-damad.*)

STAG—That is a stag of twelve tine.—*ān gawazne ast ki dawāzda shākh dārad.*

STAIRS—He was sitting on the stairs.—*o bar* (*nirdbān*) *nishashta būd.* (*zīna ; sallam ; marḳāt ; mi'raj ; maṣa'd.*)

STAMMERED—Perhaps he stammered.—*magar* (*luknate*) *andar zabān-ash būd.* (*lukūnate.*)

STAND—When you read stand in your proper place.—*wakte ki mī-khwāned dar makām-i-khud* (*kā,im bāshed*). (*biyisted; kiyām bi-kuned; istikāmat warzed.*)

STARED—They all stared to see me.—*eshān hama marā dīda* (*bā chashm-i-kushāda nigrīstand*). (*wā nigrīstand; nigāh zadand; lamak kardand; nazar-i-tez* or *nazar-i-dakīk kardand; latā zadand.*)

STARVING—The people were nearly starving.—*nazdīk būd ki mardumān az* (*gursinagī*) *bi-mīrand.* (*jū'.*)

STATION—He is a person of high station.—*o sāhibe* (*rutba*) *ast.* (*darja; martaba; mansab; sharaf; manzilat; jāh o jallāl; tamkīn; 'izzat; nisāb; makām-i-'ālī.*)

STAY—She intends to make a long stay there.—*ān zan kasd dārad ki dar ān jā tā ba* (*der*) *bi-mānad.* (*muddat-i-madīd.*)

STEADY—He still continues steady to his purpose.—*ilā-hāl ba irāda,e khud* (*kā,im*) *ast.* (*mukirr; musammim; mustakil; ustawār; pāyadār; sābit-kadam.*)

STEALS—The jackal steals what he can lay hold of.—*shaghāl harchi mī-yābad ba duzdī bar dāshta mī-ravad.*

STEEP—The bank of this river is very steep.—*kināra,e īn nahr bisiyār* (*nashīb-dār ast*). (*sarāshīb ast; garīwa dārad.*)

STEER—Can you steer a vessel?—*āyā jahāze* (*rāndan*) *mī-tawāned?* (*sūk kardan; zabt kardan.*)

STICK—He walks with a stick.—*o yak chūb-i-dastī dar dast girifta sair mī-kunad.*

STIFF—This paper is too stiff.—*īn kāghaz nihāyat* (*durusht*) *ast.* (*sakht.*)

STILL—Cannot you be still for one moment?—*āyā yak lahza* (*sākit na mī-tawāned mānd*). (*sukūt na mī-tawāned warzed.*)

STIR—I am now so weak I can scarcely stir.—*ilhāl īn chunīn kamzor-am ki ba dushwārī harakat mī-kunam.* Or, *ilhāl īn chunīn za'īfu-l-badan-am ki ba sakhtī taharruk mī-kunam.*

STORE—He has great store of learning.—*o (khazāna),e 'azīm-i-'ilm dārad. (makhzan; ma'dan.)*

STORY—I did not hear that story.—*man ān (ḳiṣṣa) na shunīdam. (sar-guzasht; dāstān; ḳazīya; ḥadīs; naḳl; afsāna; ḥikāyat.)*

STRAIGHT—Is this ruler straight?—*āyā īn mistar rāst ast?*

STRAIN—Strain this milk through a cloth.—*īn shīr az pārcha (bi-pālū,ed). (biyafshared; bi-fishured; tarwīḳ bi-sāzed; bazl* or *ṣāf bi-kuned.)*

STRANGER—I am a stranger here.—*man dar īn jā (gharībe) am. (ghaire; ajnabī,e; begāna,e; shaṭīre.)*

STRAW—Where can we get straw?—*kāh az kujā ḥāṣil-i-mā mī-āyad?*

STRENGTH—I have but little strength.—*zor dar badan-am kam ast.* Or, *man dar jism taḳwiyat kam dāram.* Or, *ṭāḳat dar ajzā,e badan-i-man rū ba tukāsur nihāda ast.*

STRETCH—Stretch out your hand.—*dast-i-khud-rā darāz bi-kuned.*

STRIKES—I will go as soon as the clock strikes.—*ba mujarrad-i-nawākhtan-i-sā'at man khwāham raft.*

STRUCK—He struck him with a stick on the head.—*o bar sar-ash chūbe zad.*

STRIPPED—They stripped him and took away his clothes.—*eshān jāma az tan-i-o kashīda burdand.* Or, *eshān o-rā (barhna) karda libās-ash burdand. ('uriyān; be poshāk.)*

STRONG—They are strong and healthy.—*eshān (ḳawī) wa tan-durust mī-bāshand. (ḳawī-jussa; mazbūṭu-l-badan; tawānā; nairūmand.)*

STUCK—Getting into the boat, he stuck in the mud.—*o ba waḳt-i-sawār-shudan-i-kishtī dar khilāb dar mānd.* Or, *dar ḥīne ki o dar kishtī bar āmad dar wakhal (faro) shud. (naṣb; mulṣiḳ; 'alaḳ.)*

STUDY—They study all the day long.—*eshān tamām roz (tadrīs) mī-kunand. (taḥṣīl-i-'ulūm; muṭā'ala.)*

STUMBLED—I stumbled in running across the road.—*waḳte ki man az rāh 'ubūr mī-kardam (ṣadma ba man rasīd). (saḳūṭ kardam; saḳṭat yāftam; sāḳiṭ shudam.)*

SUBDUE—We ought to subdue our passions.—*mārā bāyad ki khwāhishhā,e nafsānī,e khud-rā (dar ḳubẓa,e khud dārem). (ẓabṭ bi-kunem.)* Or, *bāyad ki mā nafs-i-khud-rā (taskhīr bi-sāzem). (maghlūb or zer or taghallub or tamalluk or istirḳāḳ or musakhkhar bi-kunem.)*

SUBJECT—What is your advice on this subject?—*dar īn amr (chi maṣlaḥat mī-bīned)? (chi ṣalāḥ dāred; rā,e shumā chīst.)* Or, *dar mashwarat-i-īn maṣāliḥ chi tadbīr mī-(kuned)? (dihed.)*

SUBMITTED—They submitted to the conquerors.—*eshān ba ghālibān muṭī' māndand.* Or, *eshān asīr-i-ḥukm-i-ghālibān āmadand.* Or, *dar taḥt-i-ḥukm-i-ghālibān āmadand.* Or, *(inḳiyād)-i-ḥukm-i-ghālibān kardand. (iṭā'at.)* Or, *khud-rā ba arbāb-i-taghallub (taslīm) kardand. (istilām; istislām.)*

SUBSCRIBE—Will you subscribe to this publication?—*īn taṣnīfa-rā dast-khaṭṭ khwāhed kard?* (i.e. subscribing to the principles of the publication.) Or, *az barā,e kharīd-i-īn taṣnīfa ḳīmat-i-ḥissa ki ba ẓimma,e shumā āyad adā,e khwāhed kard?* (i.e., subscribing for the purchase of the publication.)

SUBSISTENCE—He has a subsistence only.—*o ḳūt lā-yamūt dārad.*

SUBSTITUTE—Some people write on leaves as a substitute for paper.—*ba'ẓe mardumān ba 'iwaẓ-i-kāghaẓ bar barghā mī-nawīsand.*

SUCCEEDED—With your assistance I have succeeded.—*ba mu'āwanat-i-shumā (man kām-yāb shudam). (ba murād-i-khud rasīda am; bahra-mand shuda am; fīroz gashta am.)*

SUCCESS—We have had little success in our work.—*dar īn kār mā kam (fatḥ-yāb) shuda em. (bahra-mand; bakhtiyār.)*

SUCCESSOR?—Who is to be his successor?—*(ḳā,im maḳām)-ash ki khwāhad shud. (jā-nishīn; nā,ib-manāb.)*

SUCK—The squirrels suck this fruit.—*mūsh-i-paranda īn mewa-rā (makk mī-kashad). (tamaṣṣaṣ mī-sāzad; tamazzaz mī-kunad.)*

SUFFER—He did not suffer me to sell the goods.—*ijāzat-i-farokhtan-i-asbāb-am na dād.* Or, *o marā na guzūsht ki man asbāb-rā bi-farosham.*

SUIT—Will this kind suit you?—*īn ḳism (pasand-i-shumā mī-āyad)?* (*ba shumā pasand mī-āyad.*)

SUITABLE—Your advice appears suitable.—*naṣīḥat-i-shumā (munāsib ma'lūm) mī-shavad.* (*shā,ista ẓāhir; lā,iḳ-i-mafhūm; sazāwār huwaida.*)

SUITS—I have but two suits of clothes.—*man faḳaṭ do (dast)-i-jāma dāram.* Or, *ba juz az do rakht-i-poshāk libās-i-dīgar na dāram.*

SUMMER.—It is now the summer season.—*īn mausim-i-(tābistan) ast.* (*tamūz; garmā; ṣaif.*)

SUMMONS—He has received a summons to attend the court to-morrow.—*ḥukm-nāma bado rasīda ast ki fardā dar 'adālat ḥāẓir gardad.* Or, *barā,e iḥẓūr-i-o ahl-i-'adālat i'lām-nāma firistāda ast.*

SUPERINTENDS—Who superintends this work?—(*muhtamim*)-*i-īn kār kīst?* (*muntaẓim; munṣirim; nāẓim; kār-kun; nāẓir; kār-farmā; kār-guzār; munāẓir.*) Or, (*ijra*),*e kār ki mī-kunad?* (*ihtimāl; intiẓām; inṣirām; sar-barāhī.*)

SUPPLICATE—It will then be in vain to supplicate.—*ān waḳt (tazarru') kardan mufīd na khwāhad shud.* (*iltimās; ibtihāl bā rijā; niyāz; lāba; iftiḳār tawajjuh.*)

SUPPLY—Can you supply me with these articles?—*shumā īn chīzhā maujūd karda ba man mī-tawāned dād?*

SUPPORT—He has no means of support.—(*asbāb-i-ma'īshat*) *na dārad.* (*ẓarūriyāt-i-ma'āsh; rakht-i-rozī; idrār-i-rizḳ.*)

SUPPORT—How does he support his family?—*o parwarish-i-(lawāḥiḳān)-i-khud chi ṭaur mī-kunad?* (*muta'alliḳān; 'iyāl wa aṭfāl; ḳabā,il.*)

SUPPOSE—I should suppose you are mistaken.—*man (mī-dānam) ki ghalaṭ karda ed.* (*gumān dāram; mī-fahmam.*)

SURE—I am not sure that it is so.—(*marā yaḳīn nīst*) *ki īn chunīn ast.* (*yaḳīn na dāram; ba yaḳīnam na mī-āyad.*)

SURETY—I am his surety.—*man (zāmin)-ash mī-būsham.* (*kafīl; zamīn; zamndār; z'īm; ṣabīr.*) Or, *zamānat-i-o ba zimma,e khud mī-gīram.*

SURFACE—We saw a dead body floating on the surface of the water.—*mā (lāshe) ba rū,e āb dīdem.* (*na'she; murda,e; jināza,e; maiyate.*)

SURPRISE—I felt great surprise on hearing this.—*ba mujarrad-i-istimā'-i-īn sukhan (muta'ajjib shudam).* ('*ajab-nāk* or *ta'ajjub-nāk* or *ḥairat-āgīn* or *mutahaiyir* or *ḥairān shudam; ta'ajjub* or '*ajab kardam.*)

SURPRISED—He would have been greatly surprised had you told him this.—*agar īn sukhan bado mī-gufted o ta-'ajjub-i-'azīm mī-kard.*

SURROUNDED—I am surrounded with difficulties.—*man ba mushkilāt (giriftār) shuda am.* (*maḥṣūr; mubtalā; asīr; muḥīṭ; mustaḥṣir; maḥāṭ; ḥaṣīr karda.*)

SUSPICION—I have no suspicion that he has done this.—*man (gumān na dāram) ki īn chunīn karda ast.* (*shubha* or *zinn* or *shakk* or *tawahhum na dāram; dar gumān nayam; wahm na mī-buram.*)

SWARM—Look! here is a swarm of bees.—*bi-bīn dar īn jā yak amboh-i-magasān-i-'asl jam' shuda ast.* Or, *bi-bīn dar īn jā magasān-i-'asl pūr shuda ast.*

SWEEP—Sweep away this litter.—*īn khas o khāshāk bi-rūbed.*

SWEET—The sugar-cane is very sweet.—*nai-shakar khūb shīrīn ast.*

SWELLED—My foot swelled greatly.—*pāyam bisiyār (āmās kard).* (*mutawarrim shud; waram kard; āmāsīd; manfukh* or *shāk* or *muzmaghid gasht.*)

SWIM—Can you teach me to swim?—*shumā marā (shināwarī) mī-tawāned āmokht.* (*shinā kardan; shināwish; shinā'.*)

SWINGS—This parrot swings upon a wire.—*īn ṭūṭī bar tāre kafs nishasta khud-rā mī-jumbānad.*

SWORD—I will draw my sword.—*man (shamsher)-i-khud-rā az miyān berūn khwāham kashīd.* (*husām; samṣām.*)

Or, *man tegh-i-khud-rā az ghilāf berūn khwāham bar āward.*

SYSTEM—They teach without any system.—*eshān ta'līm-i-be-ḳā,ida mī-dihand.*

T.

TAKE—Come in, and take off your cloak.—*andarūn biyāyed labūda az badan-i-khud bar kashed.*

TAKES—He takes medicine usually once a month.—*o dar har māh yak bār dawā (ba 'ādat) mī-khurad.* (*ḥasbu-l-mu'tād ; ḥasbu-l-ma'mūl ; ḥasbu-l-dastūr ; ba ḥasbu-l-isti'māl.*)

TAKEN—Having taken the fort, they entered the city.—*eshān ḳila-rā (ba ḳabẓa,e khud āwarda) dar shahr dākhil shudand.* (*taskhīr* or *akhz* or *fatḥ* or *maftūḥ* or *musakh-khar karda ; kushāda.*)

TALK—They talk incessantly.—*eshān ('ala-l-ittiṣāl) sukhan mī-goyand.* (*pai dar pai ; mutawātir ; mutawālī ; muta-rādif.*)

TEACHER—The same teacher that taught you, taught me.—*mu'allime ki ba shumā ta'līm dād man nīz az o ta'līm giriftam.* Or, *mudarrise ki ba shumā dars dād o ba man nīz dars dād.*

TEAR—Mind you don't tear your new book.—*iḥtiyāṭ kun ki kitāb-i-nau-i-khud-rā na darī.*

TELL—Tell me where I may meet with him.—*ba man bi-go ki man bā o kujā (mulāḳī khwāham shud).* (*mulāḳāt khwāham kard ; mī-rasam.*)

TEND—This will tend to increase our knowledge.—*īn ba afzūnī,e taḥṣīl-i-'ilm mārā (mā,il) khwāhad sakht.* (*muta-wajjih ; rāghib.*) Or, *az īn ḳā,ida 'ilm-i-mā rū ba afzūnī khwāhad nihād.*

TERM—It is now term time, the court is open.—*īn wakt-i-darbār ast 'adālat (maftūḥ) ast.* (*makshūf ; wāz ; bāz.*)

TERMINATE—When do you expect this affair will terminate?—*dar khayāl-i-shumā chigūna mī-āyad ki īn muḳaddama kai (anjām khwāhad yāft)? (ba itmām khwāhad rasīd; tamām* or *faiṣal* or *munfaṣil* or *munḳata'* or *munḳaẓī khwāhad shud; infiṣāl* or *inḳiẓā khwāhad yāft.*)

THANKS—Sir, I return you many thanks.—*ṣāḥibā man bisiyār (shukr-guẕār)-i-shumā mī-bāsham. (iḥsānmand; miḥnat-paẕīr; imtinān-paẕīr; marhūn-i-minnat; murtahim-i-iḥsān.)* Or, *ṣāhibā man az 'uhda,e īn 'ināyat berūn na mī-tawānam āmad.* Or, *ṣāḥibā ṭauḳ-i-minnat-i-shumā dar gardan andākhta am.* Or, *bisiyār shukr-i-ni'mat-i-shumā mī-goyam.*

THATCHED—This house must be thatched anew.—*īn khāna-rā az sar-i-nau bā kāhbin bāyad poshīd.* Or, *saḳf-i-īn khāna az sar-i-nau bā ḳashsh durust bāyad kard.*

THICK—Do you wish for thick paper or thin?—*kāghaẕ-i-(durusht)*[1] *mī-khwāhed yā (bārīk)*[2]? [1](*zaft; siṭabr.*) [2](*nizār.*)

THOUGHT—They exercise no thought on the subject.—*dar īn amr (rā,e khud na mī-ārand). ('aḳl-i-khud-rā dakhl na mī-dihand; aḳl-i-khud-rā dakhl-i-taṣarruf na mī-dihand; ḳiyās* or *fikr* or *tafakkur* or *khayāl na mī-kunand.*)

THREATENS—He threatens to punish them.—*o badeshān (tahdīd)-i-sazā mī-dihad. (takhwīf; ī'ād; tahadud; tawaḳḳum; wa'īd.)*

TIDE—The tide has begun to flow.—*ilḥāl madd (dar āghāz) ast. (shurū' shuda.)*

TIGER—There is a tiger in that forest; also a tigress, together with two young ones.—*dar ān besha shere nar ast balki sher-i-māda ba ma do bachcha.*

TILLED—This ground has never been tilled.—*īn zamīn hargiz (shiyār karda) na shuda ast. (zirā'at karda; kāshta.)*

TIMBER—Where shall we procure timber?—*az kujā (shāhtīr) khwāhem yāft. (khashab.)*

TIME—Youth is the time of learning.—*(shabāb) waḳt-i-āmokhtan ast.* (*shabībat ; shabb ; 'unfawān-i-shabāb.*)

TIRED—I am quite tired.—*man bisiyār (dar-mānda) shuda am.* (*ma'tūb ; wā mānda.*) Or, (*takāssul*)*-i-bisiyār dar wujūd-i-man rāhe yāfta ast.* (*māndagī ; takāsur ; tasāhiliyat.*)

TITLE—This is a title only.—*īn faḳaṭ* (*khiṭābe*) *ast.* (*sar-nāma.*)

TOBACCO—They smoke tobacco.—*eshān tambākū mī-kashand.*

TOLERABLE—This is tolerable writing.—*īn khaṭṭ* (*mū-yuḳrū*) *mī-bāshad.* (*muḳārib.*)

TORCHES—We travelled by the light of torches.—*ba roshanī,e mash'alhā 'safr kardem.*

TOSSED—The boat was tossed with the waves.—*ba sabab-i-ṭalātum-i-amwāj kishtī* (*tah o bālā*) *mī-shud.* (*zer o bālā.*)

TOUCH—Touch this with your finger.—*ba angusht-i-khud īn-rā* (*lams*) *bi-kuned.* (*mass ; mumāsat ; imsās ; mujtass.*)

TOYS—There are plenty of toys in the bāzār.—*āshiyā,e bāzīcha dar bāzār bisiyār mī-bāshand.*

TRANSACT—They transact different affairs there.—*eshān dar ān jā kār o bār az har ḳism* (*mī-kunand*). (*ba 'aml mī-ārand.*)

TRANSFERRED—That money has been transferred to me.—*ān pūl ba man* (*sipurda*) *shuda ast.* (*ḥawāla karda ; wad'iyat nihāda.*) Or, *ān pūl dar taḥwīl-i-man āmada ast.*

TRANSGRESSED—We have transgressed God's commands.—*ma az ḥadd-i-ḥukm-i-khudā* (*ḳadam berūn nihāda em*). (*berūn rafta em ; guẕashta em*). Or, *mā az ḥukm-i-īzd* (*tajāwuz*) *karda em.* (*'adūl.*)

TRANSLATE—Translate this into Persian.—*īn-rā dar zabān-i-fārs tarjuma bi-kun.*

TRANSPORTED—He has been transported for life.—*o ḳaid-i-dā,imu-l-ḥabs yāfta jilā-waṭan karda shud.* Or, *o ḥabs-i-da,imu-l-'umr yāfta naḳl-i-waṭan karda shud.*

TRAVELLED—We travelled all the way on foot.—*mā tamām rāh pā piyāda raftem.*

TRAVELLING—He is travelling in Persia.—*o (safr-i-fārs mī-kunad. (dar fārs siyāḥat.)*

TREADS—He treads so softly, I don't hear the sound of his step.—*o īn chunīn ba āhistagī mī-ravad ki (āwāz-i-kadam-ash ba gosh-am) na mī-rasad. (ṣadā,e pāyash ba sama'-i-man.)*

TREACHEROUS—Their conduct is very treacherous.—*eshān dar kirdār-i-khud bisiyār (dagha bāz) and. (khā,in; ghaddār; ghadīr; bā khiyānat; fareb-bāz; ḥamlat; mughaddar; ghadūr; daghal-zan.)*

TREMBLE—I tremble with fear.—*man az khauf mī-larzam.* Or, *az khauf bar man (larza) mustaulī mī-sharad. (ra'sha; irti'āsh; 'arwā; sa'fat.)*

TRIAL—His trial will take place to-day.—*imroz mukad-dama,e o (dā,ir) khwāhad shud. (pesh; rujū'.)*

TRIFLE—Why do you thus trifle away your time?—*shumā chirā ba īn ṭaur aukāt-i khud-rā (rā,egān) az dast mī-dihed. (muft; be fā,ida.)*

TRIVIAL—This is but a trivial affair.—*īn amr-i-(khafīf) ast. (subuk; be-māya; be-wazn; be-mikdār.)*

TROUBLE—He gives them much trouble.—*o badeshān (zaḥmat)-i-firāwān mī-dihad. (dikkat; takhlīf; taṣdī': ṣaklat; miḥnat; takalluf.)*

TRUST—I am not anyways afraid to trust him.—*man hech muẓāyaka na dāram ki (baro i'timād) bi-kunam. (i'tibār-i-o.)*

TRUTH—I am convinced what he says is the whole truth.—*yakīn mī-dānam harchi ki o mī-goyad kullī rāst ast.*

TRYING—It is of no use trying to do this.—*āzmā,ish-i-īn kār ba man be fā,ida ast.*

TUMBLED—They tumbled over one another.—*eshān bar yak dīgar (uftādand). (munhadim shudand; galaṭīd-and; inhidām kardand.)*

Tune—Her voice is a little out of tune.—*āwāz-ash ḳadre (nā sāz) ast.* (*be rang; nā mauzūm.*)

Turn—Turn over this leaf.—*īn waraḳ bi-gardāned.*

Twist—Twist these cords together.—*īn rassanhā bāham (bi-peched).* (*bi-tābed; fatal bi-sāzed; biyāred; charkh bi-kuned.*)

U.

Ugly—This is an ugly shaped letter.—*īn ḥarf (nā zībā) ast.* (*zisht; bad-ṣūrat; bad-shakl; ḳabīḥ; makrūh.*)

Umbrella—I have left behind my umbrella.—*(chatr)-i-khud-rā dar pas guzāshta āmada am.* (*sāyabān; āftāb-gīr; āftāb-gardān; shamsī.*)

Unanimous—They were unanimous in their opinion.—*eshān dar rā,e khud (muttafiḳ) būdand.* (*yak-jihat; yak-dil; hamsāz; yak-ḳaul; yak shaur.*)

Uncertain—It is uncertain whether I shall go or not.—*muḳarrar nīst ki man dar ān jā bi-ravam yā na.*

Unbecoming—To act thus is unbecoming.—*īn chunīn kār kardan (nā munāsib) ast.* (*nā shā,ista; ghair-i-muwāfiḳ; nā lā,iḳ.*)

Unchangeable.—God only is unchangeable.—*maḥz khudā ta'ālā (bar ḳarār) ast.* (*lā yazāl; bilā taghaiyur; dā,im wa ḳā,im.*)

Undergo—Why do you needlessly undergo all this trouble.—*chirā be-ẓarūratan īn hama (taklīf mī-kashed).* (*miḥnat mī-bardāred; zuḥmat mī-bared; taṣdī'* or *diḳḳat mī-kuned.*)

Understand—I do not understand your meaning.—*maṭlab-i-shumā (na mī-fahmam).* (*ba fahm-i-man na mī-āyad; mafhūm-i-man na mī-gardad.*) Or, *mudda'ā-i-shumā dar fahm-am na mī-āyad.* Or, *fahm-i-faḥwā,e shumā na mī-kunam.*

Undertake—Will you undertake to manage this business?—*intiẓām-i-īn kār ba ẓimma,e khud (khwāhed girift)?* (*ḳabūl khwahed ḳard.*)

UNEXPECTEDLY—This letter came unexpectedly.—*īn murāsala (nā gahāna) wārid shud.* (*be-khabar.*)

UNFIT—He is wholly unfit for the task assigned him.—*kāre ki bado ḥawāla shuda ast dar adā,e ān bi-l-kull (nā lā,iḳ ast).* (*'adm-i-liyāḳat dārad; nā ḳābil ast.*)

UNFURNISHED.—The house is unfurnished.—*ān khāna (ārasta nīst).* (*rakht* or *lawāzimāt* or *sāmān na dārad.*)

UNHAPPY—She is quite unhappy on this account.—*az īn jihat ān zan (bisiyār ranjīda-khāṭir) shuda ast.* (*'aish-ash munaghghiṣ; 'ishrat-ash talkh; ān zan dil-tang o maghmūm o andoh-āgīn o ghamnāk.*)

UNHURT—Through God's mercy we escaped unhurt.—*ba fazl-i-khudā mā az (maẓarat maḥfūẓ) māndem.* (*ẓarrar maṣūn; azīyat maḥrūs.*)

UNITED—Our sentiments are united.—*rā,e mā (muttafiḳ) ast.* (*muttaḥid; bā ittifāḳ; bā ittiḥād.*)

UNJUST—Do you conceive this to be unjust?—*āyā shumà khayāl mī-banded ki īn (be inṣāfī) ast?* (*nā ḥaḳḳ; be dādī; khilāf-i-ma'dilat; khilāf-i-shar'.*)

UNKIND—We should not be unkind to each other.—*bāyad ki mā ba yak-dīgar (be raḥm) na shavem.* (*be muruwat; be marḥamat; be shafḳat; ghair-taraḥḥum.*)

UNGRATEFUL—He is ungrateful.—*o (kāfir-i-ni'mat) ast.* (*nā sipās; nā ḥaḳḳ-shinās; nā shukr-guzār.*) Or, *o 'ādat-i-(kufrān-i-ni'mat) dārad.* (*kufr-i-ni'mat; kufrānu-n-na'm.*)

UNLAWFUL—To do so is unlawful.—*īn chunīn kardan (khilāf-i-shar') ast.* (*nā mashrū'; nā ḥaḳḳ.*)

UNLOCK—Unlock the door.—*ḳufl-i-darwāza (wā kun).* (*bi-kushā; az* or *ba kalīd bi-kushā.*)

UNREASONABLE—Their demands are unreasonable.—*da'wā-hā,e eshān (be jā) ast.* (*be i'tidāl; mutajāwiz; nā ma'ḳūl; nā jā,iz.*)

UNSEARCHABLE—The ways of God are unsearchable.—

ḥikmat-i-allāh-ta'ālą az (idrāk-i-mā berūn) mī-bāshad. (fahm-i-mā ba'īd.)

Unspeakable—Our joy is unspeakable.—*khūshī,e mā az ḥadd-i-baiyān berūn ast.*

Unsteady—His mind is very unsteady.—*dil-ash bisiyār (be ḳarār) ast. (nā ḳā,im; be ṣabāt; nā ustuwār; be istiḳlāl.)*

Unwilling—I am altogether unwilling to go there.—*ba raftan-i-ān jā bisiyār (nā rūẓ) hastam. (nā khūshnūd; be dil; nā khwāh.)* Or, *az raftan-i-ān jā daregh (dāram). (mī-kunam; ba man mī-āyad.)*

Unwise—It were unwise not to agree to this.—*az īn kār (inkār kardan) nā dānī ast. (sar bāz zadan; ibā* or *daregh* or *istinkāf* or *nakaf* or *iḳrā' kardan; bāz istādan.)* Or, *īn kār-rā nā ḳabūl kardan be wuḳūfī ast.*

Unworthy—He has proved himself unworthy of your protection.—*az kirdār-ash (ṣābit shuda) ast ki o lā,iḳ-i-ḥimāyat-i-shumā nīst. (ba iṣbāt rasīda; maṣbūt* or *mubaiyin* or *huwaidā* or *wāẓiḥ* or *ẓāhir shuda; ba wuẓūḥ paiwasta.)*

Upper—Are there any upper rooms in this house?—*āyā īn khāna(-rā ṭabake fauḳānī mī-bāshad)? (ṭabake bālā dārad.)*

Upright—They are upright in their dealings.—*dar mu'āmalāt-i-eshān (amānat-guzār) and. (ṣādiḳ; rāst-bāz; ṣadāḳatkār; diyānat-dār.)*

Urged—No one urged him to do so.—*hech kas ba chunīn kār kardan o-rā (taḳāẓą) na kard. (iẓṭirār; āmāda; targhīb; iḳtiẓą; taḥrīs.)*

Urgent—This business is urgent.—*īn kār o bār (ẓarūrī) ast. (mutaḳāẓī; mubram; muhimm; bajjad.)*

Use—Of what use is this?—*īn ba chi kār mī-(āyad)? (khụrad; bandad; paiwandad.)* Or, *īn ba chi sūd mī-bakhshad?* Or, *īn chi sūd dārad?*

Uttered—I never uttered such a word.—*man īn chunīn*

sukhan gāhe bar zabān nayāwardam. Or, *man zikr-i-īn chunīn sukhan bar zabān na rāndam.* Or, *īn chunīn sukhan az dahan-i-man (bar) nayāmad. (berūn.)* Or, *man īn chunīn kalām gāhe takallum na kardam.*

V.

VAIN—He exerts himself in vain.—*o be fā,ida koshish mī-kunad.* Or, *o ranj-i-behūda mī-barad wa sa'ī,e be fā,ida mī-kunad.*

VALUE—I value his friendship greatly.—*man ḳadar-i-dostīyash bisiyār mī-dānam.* Or, *man ulfat-i-o-rā 'azīz dāram.* Or, *muwaddat-i-o-rā sarmāya,e zindagānī mī-shumāram.*

VALUE—What is the value of these precious pearls?—*ḳīmat-i-(durrhā,e yatīm) chīst?* (*marwārīdhā,e shāhwār.*)

VALUABLE—These things are valuable.—*īn chīzhā bisiyār (s̤amīn) and.* (*girāmī; girān-māya; ḳīmatī.*)

VANITY—He is full of vanity.—*o pur az ghurūr ast.* Or, *o dar-sar bisiyār khayāl-i-(khẉud faroshī) dārad.* (*khẉud-bīnī; khẉud-parastī; khẉud-pasandī; takabbur-i-'ujub; kibr; istighnā,ī; za'm; zu'm.*)

VARIOUS—There are various opinions about it.—*dar bāb-i-īn amr (rā,ehā,e mukhtalif) and.* (*ikhtilāf-i-aḳsām; maṣlaḥathā,e mutafarriḳ.*)

VARNISHED—This chair has not been varnished.—*bar īn kursī lak malīda na shuda ast.*

VENTURED—Confiding in his luck, he ventured all his property on this risk.—*bar naṣīb-i-khẉud i'timād karda hama māl-i-khẉud-rā dar maḳām-i-khaṭra* (*afgand*). (*andākht.*)

VERILY—Verily I cannot believe you.—*fi-l-wāḳi' bar shumā i'timād na mī-tawānam kard.*

VEXATION—I meet with nothing but vexation in this business.—*dar īn amr ba juz az taṣdī' hech chīz (ḥāṣil)-i-man na mī-āyad.* (*gīr; ba dast ba ḥāṣil; ba ḥuṣūl.*)

VICE—They make no distinction between vice and virtue.—(mā bain-i-khubş wa fazl fark) na mī-kunand. (ķubḥ az ḥusn tafrīķ; darmiyān-i-shanī'at wa khūbī tafāwut; imtiyāz-i-badī wa neko,ī.) Or, mā bain-i-('aib wa hunar) tamīz na dārand. (ķabūḥat wa ḥusnat; sharr wa khair; ma'ṣiyat wa 'iffat; khubāṣat wa 'iṣmat.)

VIGILANT—We should be vigilant in avoiding evil.—bāyad ki mā dar iḥtirāz kardan az badī (bedār) bāshem. (muntabih; hoshyār; āgāh; mustaikiẓ.)

VINDICATE—He cannot vindicate his conduct.—dar bāb-i-raftār-i-khud hech 'uzr na mī-tawānad āward. Or, ānchi ki dar raftār ast az ān bā 'uzr khud-rā khalāṣ na mī-tawānad kard.

VIOLATE—I must not violate the orders of the government.—bāyad ki man (nā-farmānī,e) ḥukm-i-daulat na kunam. ('adūl-; 'adm-i-iṭā'at; nā-farmā bardārī.) Or, bāyad ki man az farmān-i-riyāsat (mukhālifat) na kunam. (sarkashī; gardan-kashī; ta'āruẓ; i'rāẓ; ta'arruẓ.)

VIOLENT—His temper is very violent.—o mizāj-i-(khashmnāk) dārad. (ghaẓūb; ghaẓab-nāk; arghand; arghada.) Or, o (ātash)-mizāj ast. (tund; tez; sakht.)

VIRTUOUS—Let us always maintain virtuous conduct.—bihtar ast ki mā (raftār-i-nek madām ikhtiyār bi-namāyem). (ba khaṣālāt-i-'afīf dā,imu-l-aukāt 'ādat bi-gīrem.)

VISIT—I am going to visit him.—man (barā,e) mulākāt-i-o mī-ravam. (ba sharaf-i-.)

VOICE—She has a fine voice.—āwāz-i-ān ṣāḥiba (khūsh) ast. (ṭībat-āmez; narm o ḥazīn; ṭaiyibu-l-adā; ṭaiyib-lahjat). Or, ān zan zabān-i-shīrīn dārad.

VOLUMES—Is the book in one or two volumes?—īn kitāb yak jild dārad yā do?

VOYAGE—He is now on a voyage to Bushīr.—o ilḥāl ba bushīr az (rāh-i-tarī) mī-ravad. (ṭarīk-i-baḥr.)

W.

WAFER—Please give me a wafer.—*'ināyat farmūda ba man (kulāje) bi-dihed.* (*chīze az barā,e chaspānīdan.*)

WAGES—What wages do you receive?—*shumā chand ('ujrat) mī-yābed?* (*mazdūrī; muzd; ṭalab;* daily *yaumiya; rozīna; rozāna;* monthly *mushāharat; māhiyāna.*)

WAIT—Tell him to wait in this room.—*ba o bi-goyed ki dar īn kamra (muntaẓir bāshed).* (*intiẓār bi-kuned; chande tawaḳḳuf bi-kuned; andake bi-māned; mutawaḳḳif bāshed.*)

WAITING—I have been waiting for you two hours.—*tū ba dū sā'at (intiẓār-i-shumā kashīda am).* (*barā,e shumā muntaẓir būda am; do chashm ba rāh-i-shumā dāshta am; chashm-i-khud-rā nargiswār ba shāh-rāh-i-shumā nigrān dāshta am; barā,e shumā mutawaḳḳif būda am; ba jihat-i-shumā tawaḳḳuf karda am.*)

WAKE—You must endeavour to wake early.—*shumā-rā 'alạ-ṣ-ṣubāḥ az bistar bar khāstan bāyad.*

WALK—Do you mean to walk or ride?—*shumā pā piyāda rāh raftan mī-khwāhed yā (sawār)?* (*ba sawārī.*)

WALL—The garden wall has fallen.—*dīwār-i-bāgh (uftāda) ast.* (*manhadim shuda; inhidām yāfta; az pā dar āmada.*)

WANDERED—I have wandered in all directions over the country.—*ba hama ṭaraf-i-mulk (sair karda am).* (*siyāḥat* or *tafarruj karda am; gashta am; gardīda am.*) Or, *man jawānib-i-diyār ba ḳadam paimūda am.*

WANT—I want much to see him.—*man o-rā dīdan bisiyār mī-khwāham.*

WAREHOUSE—This is his warehouse.—*īn (khāna,e ajnās)-i-o ast.* (*asbāb-khāna; ambār-khāna; karbaj.*)

WARPED—This table is warped.—*īn mez (kaj) shuda ast.* (*khamīda; mu'awwij; kozh; munḥanī.*)

WARRANTED—The horse is warranted without blemish.—(*wa'da karda*) *shuda ast ki īn asp 'aibe na dārad.* (*ḳarār dāda; iḳrār karda; ẓamānat-i-īn ma'nī girifta.*)

WASTE—Why do you waste your paper?—*chirā kāghaz-i-khud-rā* (*tazyī'*) *mī-kuned?* (*zā,ī'*; *kharāb*; *makhrūb.*)

WATCH—I watch an opportunity of going there.—*man ba jihat-i-raftan-i-ān jā* (*mauka',e mī-bīnam*). (*kābū mī-jūyam*; *muntazir-i-furṣat mī-bāsham*; *mutaraṣṣid-i-wakt-i-shā,ista mī-bāsham.*)

WATCH—Your watch goes remarkably well.—*sā'at-i-shumā ba ṭaraḥ-i-khūb mī-ravad.*

WAX—These candles are of wax.—*īn sham'hā az mom sākhta shuda ast.*

WEAR—I wear a suit of clean clothes every day.—*har roz daste jāma'e ṣāf* (*mī-posham*). (*dar bar mī-kunam.*)

WEAVES—He weaves the kind of cloth we wear.—*ḳisme pārcha ki mā mī-poshem ān shakhṣ mī-bāfad.*

WEEK—He will return in a week.—*dar 'arsa,e yak hafta* (*murāja'at*) *khwāhad kard.* (*mu'āwadat*; *'ūdat.*)

WEEPS—He weeps because of the death of his son.—*ba sabab-i-riḥlat-i-pisar-ash* (*mī-nālad*). (*nāla o āh* or *giriya o zārī* or *shor o fighān* or *ashkbārī mī-kunad.*)

WEIGHED—Has this sugar been weighed?—*īn shakar* (*sanjīda*) *shuda ast.* (*wazn* or *tarṭīl karda.*)

WEIGHT—What is the weight of this stone?—*īn sang chi* (*wazn*) *dārad?* (*sangīnī*; *sanj*; *bār*; *ṣaḳlat.*)

WELCOME—You are welcome.—*shumā* (*khūsh*) *āmada ed!* (*ba-khair.*) Or, *marḥabā!* Or, *marḥaban o sahlan!*

WELL—Tell them to dig a well here.—*badeshān bi-goyed ki dar īn jā chāhe bi-kanand.*

WELL—I understand well what you say.—*ānchi ki shumā mī-goyed* (*dar fahm-i-man khūb mī-āyad*). (*man ba khūbī mī-fahmam.*)

WET—This paper is very wet.—*īn kāghaz bisiyār* (*nam*) *ast.* (*tar*; *namgīn*; *marṭūb*; *nam-nāk.*)

WHISPERED—I whispered that to him.—*man ān sukhan dār gosh-ash* (*āhista*) *guftam.* (*ba āhistagī*; *ba khafiya*; *ba nihuftagī.*)

WHISTLING—I heard somebody whistling.—*shakhṣe-rā shunīdam ki* (*ṣafīr mī-zanad*). (*safār mī-kunad.*)

WHOLE—You are welcome to the whole.—*agar khwāhish-i-shumā bāshad hama bi-gīred.*

WIDER—I want some cloth wider than this.—*man ḳadre pārcha az īn 'arīẓtar mī-khwāham.*

WINDOW—The bird flew out at the window.—*paranda az darīcha (parwāz kard). (parwāz kunān raft; parīd.)*

WINTER—I like the winter season.—*marā (mausim-i-sarmā) pasand mī-āyad. (shitā; zamistān.)*

WISDOM—She possesses much wisdom.—*ān zan ('aḳl)-i-kāmil dārad. (firāsat; fiṭrat; dirāyat; kiyāsat.)*

WISE—They only are wise who fear God.—*maḥz ān kasān ('aḳlmand) mī-bāshand ki tars-i-khudā dārand. ('āḳil; dānā; ẕū-l-'aḳūl; ṣāḥib-i-idrāk; muḥaḳḳaḳ.)*

WISH—What is your wish?—*khwāhish-i-shumā chīst?*

WISH—They wish to remain here.—*eshān (mī-khwāhand) ki dar īn jā bi-mānand. (tamannā* or *ārzū* or *irāda* or *shauḳ dārand.)*

WITNESSES.—Has he any witnesses?—*o (gawāhe) dārad? (shāhide.)*

WORLD—This world was created by the power of God.—*ba ḳudrat-i-ilāhī īn dunyā (ba wujūd āmad). (paidā* or *āfrīda shud.)*

WONDER—Nobody can evince wonder at this.—*hech kas dar īn ('ajab) na mī-tawānad kard. (shigufṭ; ta'ajjub.)*

WORKS—She works to support herself and family.—*ān zan ba jihat-i-parwarish-i-khud-ash wa aṭfāl-i-khud miḥnat mī-kunad.*

WORSHIP—We worship one God only.—*mā (parastish)-i-khudā,e wāḥid mī-kunem. ('ibādat; ṭā'ut; bandagī; namāz.)* Or, *mā mu'takif-i-tauḥīd mī-bāshem.*

WORTHY—I am not worthy of so much kindness.—*man lā,iḳ-i-īn ḳadar-i-mihrbānī nīstam.*

WOUND—Deadly venom was extracted from the wound.—*az zakhm (zahr-i-ḳātil) bar āwarda shud. (samm-i-halhal; masāmm-i-halāhal.)*

WOUNDED—Some of our sepoys were wounded.—*ba'ze az lashkiriyān-i-mā (majrūḥ gashtand). (-rā jarrāḥat rasīd.)*

WRECKED—That ship was wrecked.—*ān jahāz (tabāh) shud. (takhrīb; inhidām; zer-i-āb faro zada; shikasta; ghark; gharīk; mustaghrik.)*

WRITE—Let me see if I can write as well as you.—*bibīnam ki man ba misal-i-shumā khūsh khatt nawishtan mī-tawānam yā na.*

WRONG—You have bought the wrong kind of seed.—*shumā bazr az kism-i-dīgar kharīda ed.*

Y.

YARD—This stick is a yard long.—*īn chūb' yak gaz darāz ast.*

YEARS—He is ten years old.—*o ba 'umr dah sāla mībāshad.* Or, *'umr-ash dah sāl ast.* Or, *o dah sāl 'umr dārad.*

YELLOW—That appears yellow.—*ān zard (ma'lūm mīshavad). (mī-namāyad.)*

YESTERDAY—Yesterday it rained much.—*dī roz bārān ba (shiddat) bārid. (ifrāt.)*

YOUNG—She is quite young.—*ān zan (nau-jawān) ast. (barnā.)* Or, *mewa,e 'unfawān-i-shabāb-ash nau rasīda ast.*

YOUTH—In the season of youth.—*dar (aiyām)-i-jawānī. ('ahd; daur; mausim-i-bahār; zamān.)*

Z.

ZEAL—He showed great zeal.—*o (sar-garmī),e firāwān zāhir kard. (ghabt; ghabta; ghairat; 'asabiyat; hamīyat.)*

ZEALOUS—They are very zealous.—*eshān bisiyār (sar-garm) and. (ghā,ir; ghayūr; shā,ih; mudāwin; mudmin; mutahauwir.)*

ZEPHYR—The breath of the zephyr feels pleasant to us.—*bād-i-ṣabā ba mā k͟hūsh mī-āyad.* Or, *rīḥ-i-janūbī ba mā k͟hūsh maḥsūs mī-shavad.*

The book is finished, by the aid of the Merciful King, in the year 1877.

tammatu-l-kitāb ba 'aunu-l-maliku-l-wahhāb fī sannat ۱۸۷۷.

EXAMINATIONS.

In India there are the following examinations in Persian and Arabic, at which persons other than members of the Indian Civil Service (*see* note, page 160) may present themselves:—

1.—*The* Second *or* Higher *Standard* * *in Persian, or Arabic.*

(*a*) The books which have to be read are—

PERSIAN.	ARABIC.
'Iḳd-i-gul. (Selection of the Gulistan.)	*'Ajabu-l-'ajā,ib.*
'Iḳd-i-manẕūm. (Selection of the Bostan.)	*Nafḥatu-l-yaman* (1st part).

(*b*) Half of an ordinary octavo page of plain English has to be rendered into:—

Persian *or* Arabic.

(*c*) Manuscripts in Persian *or* Arabic have to be read fairly and translated readily.

The reward for passing is, in

PERSIAN.	ARABIC.
Rs. 500	Rs. 800

(*d*) Conversation with fluency, and with such correctness of pronunciation, grammar and idiom as to be at once intelligible, has to be carried on with a native.†

* So called because it corresponds with the examination styled the Second, or Higher, Standard in Hindustani; there is no examination in Persian or Arabic by the First or Lower Standard.

† Except in Bombay, this portion of the test is, in Arabic, omitted.

2.—*Standard of High Proficiency.*

(*a*) The books which have to be read are :—

PERSIAN.	ARABIC.
Gulistān.	*Ikhwānu-ṣ-ṣafā.*
Bostān.	*Nafḥatu-l-yaman.*
Anwār-i-Suhaili.	

(*b*) A passage of moderate difficulty, half of an octavo page in length, not taken from a text-book, has to be rendered into English.

(*c*) An English paper of moderate difficulty has to be translated accurately and idiomatically.

(*d*) Similarly, a paper of English sentences has to be rendered.

Reward for passing in

PERSIAN.	ARABIC.
Rs. 1500	Rs. 2000

3.—*Examination for a Degree of Honour.*

(*a*) The books which have to be read are :—

PERSIAN.	ARABIC.
Akhlāķ-i-jalālī.	*Ḥammāsah.*
Inshā,e Abū-l-fazl.	*Jaimur-nāmah.*
Sikandar nāmah.	*Maķāmāt-i-Ḥarīrī.*
Dīwān-i-Ḥāfiẓ.	

(*b*) Two octavo pages, one in prose, the other in verse, selected from some difficult work, not a text-book,—have to be translated with accuracy into English.

(*c*) A difficult passage from English has to be rendered with accuracy, elegance and neatness of expression, and with perfect correctness of spelling and grammar.

(*d*) Conversation has to be carried on with idiomatic accuracy and fluency.*

Reward for passing in

PERSIAN.	ARABIC.
Rs. (4000)	Rs. (5000)

* Except in Bombay, this portion of the test is, in Arabic, omitted.

4.—*In the Province of Sind, there is a Special Examination in Persian.*

The books which have to be read are:—

(*a*) Gulistān.
First Four Chapters of the Anwār-i-Suhailī.

(*b*) A passage, in an easy narrative style, not taken from the text-books has to be translated into English.

(*c*) An English paper of easy narrative style has to be rendered, intelligibly and with accuracy of grammar, into Persian.

(*d*) A paper of English sentences has, similarly, to be rendered.

(*e*) Conversation, with accuracy and fluency, has to be carried on with a native of Persia.

Reward for passing —(1000) Rs.

Remarks.

Examinations 1, 2 and 3, are regulated by G. G. O. Military Department, No. 734 of 9th September, 1864; and No. 294 of 24th March, 1866. These orders of Government relate to the following languages:—

Hindustani, Sanskrit, Bengālī, Burmese, Assamese, Panjābī, Pushtū, Uriyā, Guzerāthī, Mahrathī, Canarese, Tamil, Telugū, Malayālam, Sindī.

As well as to Persian and Arabic.

In respect to Pushtū the following Government order specially applies:—

G. G. O. Military Department, No. 733 of 15th July, 1873.

The Special Examination (4) *in Persian for the Province of Sind is based on:—*

General Department, Bombay Castle, No. 2741 of 22nd September, 1874; and No. 1122 of 14th April, 1875.

A person, who intends to serve in India, would do well to apply to an Indian Agent, in London, for copies of these orders.

The Government of India and the Governments of Madras and Bombay may, in addition to the pecuniary rewards already noted, award a gold medal to any officer, who is reported to have passed an examination, in any language, with extra-ordinary merit.

No officer will obtain rewards for passing the tests of the Second Standard, or High Proficiency, whose period of actual residence in India, exceeds 10 years; nor will any officer receive any reward for passing the test for the Degree of Honour, whose period of actual residence in India exceeds 15 years.

Examinations for Degrees of Honour, Certificates of High Proficiency and for the Second or Higher Standard, will take place at Presidency Towns.

The special examination in Persian for the Province of Sind, will take place at Bombay; travelling allowance for the journey from Sind to Bombay and return will be given. Length of service is no bar to any one's appearing.

Rules for the examination, at Fort William, of Candidates other than Her Majesty's Indian Civil Servants.

1.—A general examination is held by the Board of Examiners monthly, usually the 1st Monday (not being the 1st or 2nd) of the month, to which military officers and all gentlemen,* authorized by Government to be examined by the Board, are admitted.

2.—Applications for examination from Military Officers are to be made to the Adjutant-General of the Army, or the officer in charge of his office at the Presidency; and, from all other gentlemen in the public service to the Head of the Department, in which they may be serving at the Presidency.

Candidates, in their applications, are invariably to state their addresses.

---

* Officers in the Public Works and Education Departments and officers of the Bengal Police Battalions. Other gentlemen by order of the Government of India, in the Home Department.

3.—All applications are to be forwarded, in sufficient time to reach the Secretary to the Board, on or before the 25th, or [if for the High Proficiency Examination, or for a Degree of Honour] on, or before the 20th of the month preceding that in which the examination is held.

4.—Examinations commence at 11 a.m.; and all papers are to be delivered to the Secretary by 4·0 p.m. Candidates arriving after 11·15 a.m. are excluded from the examination.

5.—Candidates are to sign their names legibly on each of their exercises.

6.—No Candidate can present himself for examination by the same standard at two consecutive monthly examinations; or, by the High Proficiency test, or for a Degree of Honour, until three monthly examinations, or four months, have intervened from the date of the examination at which such Candidates may have been examined and failed to pass.

7.—Special examinations are not granted except by the order of Government.

8.—Candidates are not to call on the Secretary to the Board, or any of the Examiners, for the purpose of ascertaining the result of their examinations.

A copy of the Board's report, embodying the remarks of the Examiners on his oral and written exercises is sent to each Candidate as soon after the examination as is practicable.

Extract from the Proceedings of the Government of India in the Foreign Department.

No. 1470 P, dated Fort William, 13th August, 1874.

Observations.—In the dispatch above quoted, Her Majesty's Secretary of State dwelt on the necessity for encouraging officers employed in the Political Department to study Persian and Arabic languages.

Probably such encouragement could most effectually be afforded by holding out some reasonable prospect of employment to officers who devote themselves to the study of these languages. In the opinion of the Honourable the President in Council, however, it is impossible to give any definite promise of employment in the Political Department as a reward to officers who pass examinations or even high examinations in Arabic and Persian.

Other qualifications must necessarily be regarded as of even greater importance than linguistic attainments. At the same time a thorough knowledge of these languages should be allowed much weight in the selection of Candidates Civil or Military for employment in the Political Department.

2. The President in Council deems it necessary that officers who are hereafter appointed to the Political Service without having passed the High Proficiency or Honour tests in Persian or Arabic should, after their appointment pass a linguistic test of a higher standard than that now demanded.

Under Foreign Department Resolution No. 541 P, dated 17th March, 1871, officers in the Political Department are at present required to translate a passage of Persian into English and a passage of English into Persian. They are also required to hold with moderate fluency a conversation in Persian, and to read with fair facility a Persian manuscript.

In order both to raise the present standard of qualification and to bring it into accordance with the standards recognised under the Civil and Military Examination Rules, the President in Council considers it necessary to prescribe that in future officers appointed to the Political Department in and below the grade of 1st Class Political Assistant shall be required to pass either in Arabic, or in Persian, by the High Proficiency test; further that such officers if employed in Turkish Arabia, the Persian Gulf and Muscat shall be required to pass a colloquial examination in Arabic; and if employed at Zanzibar, a colloquial examination in Arabic or Swaheli, even though they may have already passed in Persian; and if employed in the Continent of India, a colloquial examination either in Hindī, or the local vernacular of the place where they are serving. If such officers be appointed to Burma, they will be required to pass the High Proficiency test in Burmese, but will not be required to pass in Arabic or Persian.

3. When the exigencies of the public service require the employ-

ment of an officer in any of the higher posts of the Political Department, Government reserves to itself the right of appointing any officer whom it considers to possess the best general qualifications even though he may not have passed in these languages.

But for the retention of appointments in and below the grade of 1st Class Political Assistant, it will be essential that officers hereafter appointed shall have passed or shall within three years from date of appointment pass the tests above prescribed, besides qualifying in the other subjects laid down for examination in the Political Department.

To officers above the grade of 1st Class Political Assistant neither these rules, nor the rules contained in the Resolution No. 541 P, dated 17th March, 1871, are applicable.

In August, 1874, the number of officers belonging to the Indian Service who had passed the tests for the Degree of Honour and High Proficiency was as set forth in the following Table :—

Designation of Officer.	Nature of Examination,				REMARKS.
	Degree of Honor.		High Proficiency.		
	Persian	Arabic	Persian	Arabic	
Indian Civil Service Men	nil	nil	14	2*	*These two officers also passed the test for High Proficiency in Persian.
Military Officer	6	nil	19	3†	†Two of these officers passed the test for High Proficiency in Persian.
Total in India .	6	nil	33	5	

Under Notification of the 24th March, 1870, by the Government of India, the rules for the examination of ***members of the Civil Service of India*** are as follows :—

A Civil Servant, attached to the Upper Provinces, may present himself for the High Proficiency Examination in Persian or Hindūstānī: if attached to the Lower Provinces, he must pass in Bangālī or Uryah before he can compete in Persian or Arabic.

Until he shall have obtained the certificate for High Proficiency in Persian or Hindūstānī (or Bangālī or Uryah, as the case may be) he is not permitted to present himself for distinction in other languages. He may compete for a Degree of Honour without obtaining a certificate of High Proficiency.

He is not allowed to present himself more than twice at any examination; but, if specially recommended by the Examiners, he may appear a third time.

He is not allowed to present himself for the High Proficiency Examination after the lapse of 7 years, nor for the Degree of Honour Examination after 10 years, from the date of his first arrival in India.

No exception will be made on account of leave of absence, &c.

Examinations will be held on the first Monday in

January	July
April	October

of each year, at the Presidency towns.

Application to be examined must be made 3 months before the date of the examination.

A Civil Servant desirous of attending examinations for prizes for the study of the Oriental languages, is allowed leave of absence on full pay for one month before the examination; if he passes the examination, he is allowed another month. This leave of 2 months counts as service and residence. The amount of leave is not to exceed 2 months at one time, nor 12 months in the aggregate.

The tests for High Proficiency and the Degree of Honour examinations are the same as those for Military Officers, or persons not belonging to the Indian Civil Service, but the rewards are different.

The reward for passing—

		Persian.		Arabic.
(*a*) The High Proficiency Examination is	Rs.	2,000	—	2,000
(*b*) The Degree of Honour	„	4,000	—	4,000

There is no examination by the Second or Higher Standard for a member of the Indian Civil Service.

These rules affect particularly the members of the Civil Service of Bengal; in the Presidencies of Madras and Bombay they are modified by local regulations.

A member of the Indian Civil Service should obtain:—

Resolution, Financial Department, No. 2,749 of 24th September, 1864, by the Government of India; Letter, Home Department, No. 4,127, of 10th September, 1870, from the Government of India; Notification of 24th March, 1870, by the Government of India; Notification No. 49, of 4th September, 1874, by the Government of India.

TABLES OF PERSIAN MONEY, MEASURES, AND WEIGHTS.

(The English Equivalents for the French Measures are taken from Professor Rankine's Useful Rules and Tables, page 110.)

TABLE I.

PERSIAN MONEY.		French Equivalent.	English Equivalent.	
		Francs.	Pence.	Shillings.
1 *Dīnār* . =	=	0·001 =	0·009516	
10 *dīnār* † . =	1 *ghāz* † . =	0·01 =	0·095162	
2½ *ghāz* . . =	1 *pūl* ‡ . =	0·025 =	0·237906	
2 *pūl* . . =	1 *shāhī* † . =	0·05 =	0·475812	
4 *shāhī* . =	1 *'abāsī* † . =	0·2 =	1·90324 =	0·158604
2½ *'abāsī* . =	1 *panā bād* § =	0·5 =	4·75812 =	0·39651
2 *panā-bād* =	1 *ḳarān* ‖ . =	1·0 =	9·51624 =	0·79302
1¼ *ḳarān* . =	1 *riyāl* † . =	1·25 =	11·8953 =	0·991275
10 *ḳarān* . =	1 *tūmān* * . =	10·00 =	95·1624 =	7·9302

† Not coined.
‡ Often called *pūl-i-siyāh*.
§ " " *nīm ḳarān* or *dah-shāhī*.
‖ " " *yak hazār dīnār*.
* " " *ashrafī*; it is not often met with in the bāzārs.

Only five coins are in circulation:
COPPER—*nīm-pūl* and *pūl*.
SILVER—*nīm ḳarān* and *ḳarān*.
GOLD—*Tūmān*.

In accounts, the following coins are used:—
By Persians, *dīnār*, *ḳarān* and *tūmān*.
By Arabs, *ghāz*, *ḳarān* and *tūmān*.

TABLE II.

PERSIAN MEASURES.—Distance.					French Equivalents.	English Equivalents.
					Metres.	Feet.
1 *bahr*				=	0·0325	0·106628
2 *bahr*	=	1 *gira*		=	0·065	0·213256
4 *gira*	=	1 *chārak*		=	0·26	0·853026
4 *charaḳ*	=	1 *zar'*		=	1·04	3·412104
6000 *zar'*	=	1 *farsakh*		=	6240·0	20472·624432

These measures are general throughout the country of Persia; but the values differ according to locality. Thus at Yazd and Kirmān, the *zar'* is one *gira* less than that given in the table.

The Persians have no square measure.

TABLE III.

Table of Persian WEIGHTS current in Shiraz and the surrounding country.		French Equivalent.	English Equivalent.	
		Grammes.	Grains.	Pounds Avoirdupois.
gandum =	=	0·048 =	0·7407528	
4 *gandum* =	1 *nakhud* =	0·192 =	2·9630112	
24 *nakhud* =	1 *miṣḳāl* =	4·608 =	71·1122688	
11¼ *miṣḳāl* =	1 *sīnāh-mīzār* =	51·84 =	800·013024 =	0·1142875748
2 *sīnāh-mīzār* =	1 *nīm mih* =	103·68 =	1600·026048 =	0·228575149
4 *nīm mih* =	1 *waḳī'* =	414·72 =	6400·104192 =	0·914300599
2 *waḳī'* =	1 *chārak* =	829·44 =	12800·208384 =	1·828601197
4 *chārak* =	1 *man-i-shīrāz* = 720 *miṣḳāl* =	3317·76 =	51200·833536 =	7·314404791

TABLE IV.

TABLE OF GOLDSMITHS' & JEWELLERS' WEIGHTS current in Shiraz, Persia.		French Equivalent.	English Equivalent.	
		Grammes.	Grains.	Pounds Avoirdupois
1 *ūnā*	=	0·013090909 =	0·20202349	
16 *ūnā* =	1 *ḳīrāṭ* =	0·209454545 =	3·2323758	
22 *ḳīrāṭ* =	1 *miṣḳāl* =	4·608 =	71·1122688	
720 *miṣḳāl* =	1 *man-i-shīrāz* =	3317·76 =	51200·833536 =	7·314404791

TABLE V.

TABLE OF PIECE-GOODS' WEIGHTS current in Shiraz, Persia.		French Equivalent	English Equivalent.	
		Grammes.	Grains.	Pounds Avoirdupois
4½ *dartang* =	1 *miṣḳāl* =	4·608 =	71·1122688	
18 *miṣḳāl* =	1 *sīr* =	82·944 =	1280·0208384 =	0·1828601197
40 *sīr* =	1 *man-i-shīrāz* =	3317·76 =	51200·833536 =	7·314404791

TABLE VI.

TABLE OF PERSIAN WEIGHTS current in Bûshahr and the surrounding country.		French Equivalent. Grammes.	English Equivalent. Grains.	English Equivalent. Pounds Avoirdupois,
1 *gandum*	=	0·048 =	0·7407528	
4 *gandum* =	1 *nakhhud* =	0·192 =	2·9630112	
24 *nakhhud* =	1 *miṣḳāl* =	4·608 =	71·1122688	
48 *miṣḳāl* =	1 *giyā* =	221·184 =	3413·3889024	
4 *giyā* =	1 *chārak* =	884·736 =	13653·5556096 =	1·9505079442
4 *chārak* =	1 *man-i-būshahr* = 768 *miṣḳāl* =	3538·944 =	54614·2224384 =	7·8020317769
16 *man-i-būshahr* =	1 *man-i-ḥasham* =	56623·104 =	873827·5590144 =	124·8325084306
100 *man-i-ḥasham* =	1 *ḳara* =	5662310·4 =	87382755·90144 =	12483·25084306

TABLE VII.

TABLE OF PERSIAN WEIGHTS current in Isfahân and the surrounding country.		French Equivalent.	English Equivalent.	
		Grammes.	Grains.	Pounds Avoirdupois.
1 *gandum*	=	0·048 =	0·7407528	
4 *gandum* =	1 *nakhud* =	0·192 =	2·9630112	
24 *nakhud* =	1 *miṣkāl* =	4·608 =	71·1122688	
20 *miṣkāl* =	1 *pinār* =	92·16 =	1422·245376	
2 *pinār* =	1 *danār* =	184·32 =	2844·490752 =	0·406355821
8 *danār* =	1 *ṣad dirham* =	1474·56 =	22755·926016 =	3·250846573
4 *ṣad dirham* =	1 *man-i-shāh*= 1280 *miṣkāl* =	5898·24 =	91023·704064 =	13·003386295

TABLE VIII.

TABLE OF PERSIAN WEIGHTS current in Tahran and the surrounding country.		French Equivalent.	English Equivalent.	
		Grammes.	Grains.	Pounds Avoirdupois.
1 *gandum*	=	0·048=	0·7407528	
4 *gandum* =	1 *nakhụd* =	0·192=	2·9630112	
24 *nakhụd* =	1 *miṣḳāl* =	4·608=	71·1122688	
16 *miṣḳāl* =	1 *sīr* =	73·728=	1137·7963008	0·1625423286
40 *sīr* =	1 *man-i-tabrīz* =640 *miṣḳāl*=	2949·12 =	45511·852032	6·5016931474
100 *man-i-tabrīz* =	1 *kharwār* =	294912·0 =	4551185·2032	650·16931474

TABLE IX.

TABLE OF PERSIAN WEIGHTS current in Yazd and the surrounding country.				French Equivalent.		English Equivalent.		
				Grammes.		Grains.		Pounds Avoirdupois.
1 *gandum*			=	0·048	=	0·7407528		
4 *gandum*	=	1 *nakhud*	=	0 192	=	2·9630112		
24 *nakhud*	=	1 *miṣḳāl*	=	4·608	=	71·1122688		
$3\frac{1}{5}$ *miṣḳāl*	=	1 *diram*	=	14·7456	=	227·55926016		
100 *diram*	=	1 *ṣad diram*	=	1474·56	=	22755·926016	=	3·250846573
4 *ṣad diram*	=	1 *man-i-shāh* = 1280 *miṣḳāl*	=	5898·24	=	91023·704064	=	13·003386295

Forbes's Smaller Dictionary, Hindustani and English, in the English Character. 12s.

Forbes's Bagh o Bahar, with Vocabulary. English Character. 5s.

Singhasan Battisi. Translated into Hindi from the Sanscrit. A New Edition. Revised, Corrected, and Accompanied with Copious Notes. By Syed Abdoolah. Royal 8vo. 12s. 6d.

Eastwick's Prem Sagur. 4to. 30s.

Akhlaki Hindi, translated into Urdu, with an Introduction and Notes. By Syed Abdoolah. Royal 8vo. 12s. 6d.

Sakuntala. Translated into Hindi from the Sanskrit, by Frederic Pincott. 4to. 12s. 6d.

SANSCRIT.

Haughton's Sanscrit and Bengali Dictionary in the Bengali Character, with Index, serving as a reversed dictionary. 4to. 30s.

Williams's English and Sanscrit Dictionary. 4to., cloth. £3 3s.

Williams's Sanscrit and English Dictionary. 4to., cloth. £4 14s. 6d.

Williams's (Monier) Sanscrit Grammar. 8vo. 15s.

Williams's (Monier) Sanscrit Manual; to which is added, a Vocabulary, by A. E. Gough. 18mo. 7s. 6d.

Gough's (A. E.) Key to the Exercises in Williams's Sanscrit Manual. 18mo. 4s.

Haughton's Menu, with English Translation. 2 vols. 4to. 24s.

Johnson's Hitopadesa, with Vocabulary. 15s.

Williams's (Monier) Sakuntala, with Literal English Translation of all the Metrical Passages, Schemes of the Metres, and copious Critical and Explanatory Notes. Royal 8vo. 21s.

Williams's (Monier) Sakuntula. Translated into English Prose and Verse. Fourth Edition. 8s.

Williams's (Monier) Vikramorvasi. The Text. 8vo. 5s.

Cowell's (E. B.) Translation of the Vikramorvasi. 8vo. 3s. 6d.

Thompson's (J. C.) Bhagavat Gita. Sanscrit Text. 5s.

PERSIAN.

Richardson's Persian, Arabic, and English Dictionary. Edition of 1852. By F. Johnson. 4to. £4.

Forbes's Persian Grammar, Reading Lessons, and Vocabulary. Royal 8vo. 12s. 6d.

Ibraheem's Persian Grammar, Dialogues, &c. Royal 8vo. 12s. 6d.

Gulistan. Carefully collated with the original MS., with a full Vocabulary. By JOHN PLATTS, late Inspector of Schools, Central Provinces, India. Royal 8vo. 12s. 6d.

Gulistan. Translated from a revised Text, with Copious Notes. By JOHN PLATTS. 8vo. 12s. 6d.

Ouseley's Anwari Soheili. 4to. 42s.

Wollaston's (Arthur N.) Translation of the Anvari Soheli. Royal 8vo. 42s. Or with illuminated borders. £3 13s. 6d.

Keene's (Rev. H. G.) First Book of the Anwari Soheili. Persian Text. 8vo. 5s.

Ouseley's (Col.) Akhlaki Mushini. Persian Text. 8vo. 5s.

Keene's (Rev. H. G.) Akhlaki Mushini. Translated into English. 8vo. 3s. 6d.

BENGALI.

Haughton's Bengali, Sanscrit, and English Dictionary, adapted for Students in either language; to which is added an Index, serving as a rexersed dictionary. 4to. 30s.

Forbes's Bengali Grammar, with Phrases and Dialogues. Royal 8vo. 12s. 6d.

Forbes's Bengali Reader, with a Translation and Vocabulary. Royal 8vo. 12s. 6d.

ARABIC.

Richardson's Arabic, Persian and English Dictionary. Edition of 1852. By F. JOHNSON. 4to., cloth. £4.

Forbes's Arabic Grammar, intended more especially for the use of young men preparing for the East India Civil Service, and also for the use of self-instructing students in general. Royal 8vo. 18s.

Palmer's Arabic Grammar. 8vo. 18s.

Forbes's Arabic Reading Lessons, consisting of Easy Extracts from the best Authors, with Vocabulary. Royal 8vo., cloth. 15s.

Beresford's Arabic Syntax. Royal 8vo. 6s.

www.ingramcontent.com/pod-product-compliance
Lightning Source LLC
Chambersburg PA
CBHW031958300426
44117CB00008B/810
* 9 7 8 3 3 3 7 2 8 6 9 5 8 *